ics

Explorations into Constitutional Economics

NUMBER NINE
Texas A & M University Economics Series

Explorations into Constitutional Economics

James M. Buchanan

COMPILED AND WITH A PREFACE BY

ROBERT D. TOLLISON AND VIKTOR J. VANBERG

Texas A&M University Press
College Station

"The Achievement and Limits of Public Choice in Diagnosing Government Failure
and in Offering Bases for Constructive Reform," in *Anatomy of Government Deficiencies*,
ed. Horst Hanusch. Copyright © 1983 by Springer-Verlag. Reprinted by permission.
"Predictability: The Criterion of Monetary Constitutions," in *In Search of a Monetary
Constitution*, ed. Leland B. Yeager. Copyright © 1962 by the University of Virginia.
Reprinted by permission of Harvard University Press. "An Outside Economist's
Defense of Pesek and Saving," *Journal of Economic Literature* 17 (September, 1969):
812–14. Copyright © 1969 by the American Economic Association. "A Note on Public
Goods Supply," *American Economic Review* 53 (June, 1963): 403–14. Copyright © 1963
by the American Economic Association. "Public Goods in Theory and Practice,"
Journal of Law and Economics 10 (1967): 193–97. Copyright © 1967 by the University of
Chicago. "The Evaluation of Public Services," *Journal of Political Economy* 69 (April,
1961): 107–21. Copyright © 1961 by the University of Chicago. "Entrepreneurship
and Internalization of Externality," *Journal of Law and Economics* 24, no. 1 (April, 1981):
95–111. Copyright © 1981 by the University of Chicago.

The paper used in this book meets the minimum requirements
of the American National Standard for Permanence
of Paper for Printed Library Materials, Z39.48-1984.
Binding materials have been chosen for durability.

Library of Congress Cataloging-in-Publication Data
Buchanan, James M.
    Explorations into constitutional economics/by James M. Buchanan;
    compiled and with a preface by Robert D. Tollison and Viktor J.
    Vanberg.—1st ed.
      p. cm.—(Texas A&M University economics series; no. 9)
    ISBN 0-89096-325-8:
    1. Social choice. I. Title. II. Series.
HB846.8.B79 1989
302'.13—dc19   88-16082
                                      CIP

Contents

Preface

Explorations into Constitutional Economics is a companion volume to *Economics: Between Predictive Science and Moral Philosophy*, published by Texas A&M University Press in 1987. The latter volume contains a selection of James M. Buchanan's major essays, ranging from his earlier contributions on public finance in the 1950s to his more recent publications on contractarian social philosophy. As we stated in our preface to that volume, the essays collected there can be viewed as unfolding the distinct research program which Buchanan was able to establish, a program for which the name Constitutional Political Economy or Constitutional Economics has been widely adopted. The essays collected in the present volume fall under the same rubric. They also represent important examples of Buchanan's pioneering contributions to the foundation and formation of Constitutional Economics as a distinct approach in modern economics. What distinguishes the present collection from its predecessor is that many of the essays collected here were originally published in less accessible sources, less accessible even to the specialized reader (indeed, some of them have not been previously published). Because of this, and without being in any way less "major," the essays collected here circulated less widely, and, consequently, have received less attention than those that we included in the first volume, less attention anyhow than we think they deserve. The purpose of this volume is to provide easier access to these essays which have been written over a thirty-year period, and thus to give a wider exposure to a set of arguments and ideas which mark important steps in Buchanan's building of the Constitutional Economics paradigm.

As was the case with the first volume, we have again been the selectors and organizers of this collection. Arrows of criticism in this regard should be directed at us, not at Buchanan. We are confident, however, that we both know the author and his work well enough to make an appropriate selection of papers for this volume and to organize them effectively.

In our preface to *Economics: Between Predictive Science and Moral Philosophy*, we traced the lineage of Buchanan's work to the concerns of classical political economists that went beyond the normal economist's enterprise of understanding how a given economy or economic process works. The modern Constitutional Economics of James Buchanan, like the classical political economics of Adam Smith, urges the economist to inquire how the rules of the political order and other institutional constraints under which the economy operates affect economic processes. At the heart of Buchanan's constitutional political economy is the constant reminder that we ought to distinguish carefully in our analyses between the *level of rules* and the level of actions *within those rules*, and between the kinds of choices that are related to these different levels.

This rules-based paradigm has attracted wide attention in the economics profession, and it has been of considerable influence within the interrelated set of interests known as the New Institutional Economics. The magnitude of Buchanan's contributions to the emergence of this field is reflected in his 1986 Nobel Prize in Economic Science. And it is reflected in a no less significant way in the fact that an increasing number of young scholars from law, philosophy, economics, political science, sociology, and other fields have begun the process of building upon the roots that Buchanan has established. As this volume illustrates, these roots are deep and manifold. They go beyond the trivial in economics to the fundamental issues of our political economy. The issue is not what the growth rate of M_1 should be; it is rather what the contours of a monetary constitution should be. The issue is not what level of deficit shall be run, but what constitutional rules ought to constrain government's fiscal behavior. The issue is not whether the president should veto a protectionist bill, but whether the rules of the political decision-making process ought to be changed so as to limit the potential for tariff-seekers to petition the legislature. By shifting our attention from the *operational* to the *constitutional* level of economic and political decision-making Constitutional Economics offers hope for a rational discourse about our political economy and our future as a prosperous and free society.

A number of the essays in this volume have previously appeared in print, and the original publishers have generously given us permission to include them here. "Predictive Power and Choice among Regimes" (with G. Brennan), from *Economic Journal* 93 (March, 1983): 89–105, is reprinted with permission from Basil Blackwell. "The Achievements and Limits of Public Choice in Diagnosing Government Failure and in Offering Bases for Constructive Reform," was originally published in *Anatomy of Government Deficiencies*, ed. Horst Hanusch (Berlin: Springer-Verlag, 1983), pp. 15–26. "Constitutional Economics" is reprinted from *Palgrave* (London: Macmillan and Co., 1987). "Toward a Theory of Yes-No Voting" (with Roger Faith) was originally printed in *Public Choice* 37, no. 2 (1981): 231–46, and "What If There Is No Majority Motion?" in *Toward a Science of Politics: Papers in Honor of Duncan Black*, ed. Gordon Tullock (Blacksburg, Va.: Center for Study of Public Choice, 1981), pp. 79–90. "Voter Choice: Evaluating Political Alternatives" (with G. Brennan) is from *American Behavioral Scientist* 28, no. 2 (November–December, 1984): 185–201, and "Vote Buying in a Stylized Setting" (with D. Lee), from *Public Choice* 49 (1986): 3–16.

"Predictability: The Criterion of Monetary Constitutions," pp. 155–83 in *In Search of a Monetary Constitution*, ed. Leland B. Yeager (Cambridge, Mass.: Harvard University Press, 1962), is reprinted by permission. The American Economic Association gave permission for us to use "An Outside Economist's Defense of Pesek and Saving," which appeared in *Journal of Economic Literature* 7 (September 1969): 812–14. "Can Policy Activism Succeed?" was published in *The Monetary versus Fiscal Policy Debate*, ed. R. W. Hafer (Totowa, N.J.: Rowman and Allanheld, 1986), and "Ideas, Institutions, and Political Economy: A Plea for Disestablishment" in *Carnegie-Rochester Conference Series on Public Policy* 25 (1986): 245–58.

The University of Chicago Press gave permission for us to reprint "The Evaluation of Public Services" (with F. Forte), from *Journal of Political Economy* 69 (April, 1961): 107–21, and "A Note on Public Goods Supply" (with Milton Kafoglis), *American Economic Review* 53 (June, 1963): 403–14, appears courtesy the American Economic Association. "Breton and Weldon on Public Goods" appeared in the *Canadian Journal of Economics and Political Science* 33 (February, 1967): 111–15, and "Public Goods in Theory and Practice" in *Journal of Law and Economics* 10 (1967): 193–97, courtesy the University of Chicago Press. "Convexity Constraints in Public Goods Theory" (with A. Pinto Barbosa) appeared in *Kyklos* 33 (Fasc. 1, 1980): 63–75.

"Fiscal Choice through Time: A Case for Indirect Taxation" (with F. Forte), originally published in *National Tax Journal* 17 (June, 1964): 144–57, appears here courtesy the National Tax Association–Tax Institute of America. Elsevier Science Publishers gave us permission to use "Efficiency Limits of Fiscal Mobility" (with Charles Goetz), *Journal of Public Economics* 1 (1972): 25–43, as well as "Tax Instruments as Constraints on the Disposition of Public Revenues" (with Geoffrey Brennan), *Journal of Public Economics* 9 (June, 1978): 301–18, and "Dialogues Concerning Fiscal Religion" (with Richard Wagner), *Journal of Monetary Economics* 4 (July, 1978): 627–36. "Proportional and Progressive Income Taxation with Utility-maximizing Governments" (with R. Congleton) originally appeared in *Public Choice* 34 (1979): 217–30, and "Organization Theory and Fiscal Economics: Society, State, and Public Debt" (with V. Vanberg), in *Journal of Law, Economics, and Organization* 2 (1986): 35–47.

"Private Ownership and Common Usage" is reprinted, with permission, from *Southern Economic Journal* 22 (January, 1956): 305–16.

"Notes on Irrelevant Externalities, Enforcement Costs and the Atrophy of Property Rights" appeared in *Explorations in the Theory of Anarchy*, ed. Gordon Tullock (Blacksburg, Va.: Center for Study of Public Choice, 1972), pp. 78–86, and "The Institutional Structure of Externality," in *Public Choice* 14 (Spring, 1973): 69–82. "The Coase Theorem and the Theory of the State," first appeared in *Natural Resources Journal* 13 (October, 1973): 579–94, and "Entrepreneurship and the Internalization of Externality" (with Roger Faith), *Journal of Law and Economics* 24, no. 1 (April, 1981): 95–111, appears with permission from the University of Chicago Press. Finally, we acknowledge the permission granted to use "Market Failure and Political Failure," originally pages 41–52 in *Individual Liberty and Democratic Decision-Making*, ed. Peter Koslowski (Tübingen: J. C. B. Mohr [Paul Siebeck], 1987).

ROBERT D. TOLLISON
VIKTOR J. VANBERG

Center for Study of Public Choice
George Mason University
Fairfax, Virginia

Part I.
THEORETICAL FOUNDATIONS: THE CONSTITUTIONAL PARADIGM

1.

Predictive Power
and the Choice Among Regimes

WITH GEOFFREY BRENNAN

*In constraining any system of government, and fixing the several
checks and controls of the constitution, every man ought to be
supposed a knave, and to have no other end, in all his actions,
than private interest.*

David Hume

*The very principle of constitutional government requires it to be
assumed that political power will be abused to promote the particular purposes of the holder; not because it always is so, but
because such is the natural tendency of things to guard against
which is the especial use of free institutions.*

J. S. Mill

A basic analytic instrument in the economist's kit bag is the model of
human behavior used—a model that, in fact, takes its name from the
dismal science. In its most general (if empty) formulation, the *Homo
economicus* model presumes nothing beyond the proposition that each
individual acts purposefully in pursuit of his own particular ends; for
some purposes at least, the ends can remain unspecified. However, if
the behavioral model is to be used to generate predictions as to the
effect of changes in the underlying state of the world, or explanations
as to why the world is as it is, further specification of the model becomes necessary. Standard professional practice in this regard is to
formulate *Homo economicus* as a wealth-maximizer, and to justify the
use of such simplification on the basis of its elegance and power.

This behavioral model in its market setting is so familiar as to be hardly worthy of comment. Its use in less traditional settings, such as in modern "public choice" theory where the methods and analytic techniques of economics are applied to the study of *political* processes, remains controversial. Most economists seem to be more comfortable with a "benevolent despot" model of government in which those who hold political power exercise it in the "public interest" (appropriately construed). Policy advice is offered on such a basis, and policy recommendations typically presuppose that this is the way in which political agents will operate. To suggest, as public choice scholars do, that those who possess discretionary power under some prevailing political order can be usefully modeled as simple wealth-maximizers apparently strikes many commentators as, at best, naive and, at worst, biased ideologically. Such critics will typically claim that "politics is simply not like that," and call forth examples of apparently public-interested behavior on the part of government agents. They will insist that internal moral considerations *are relevant* in constraining the behavior of those who act in political agency roles. It is difficult to respond to such critics in a manner that is fully convincing because, descriptively, there seems to be some substance in their rejection of the *Homo economicus* model in application to political behavior.

As the opening citations indicate, however, modern public choice scholars are in excellent company. The classical political economists insisted that political agents should be modeled on the basis of private interest—not, as Mill concedes, because such agents always behave in this way, but rather because of the nature of the particular exercise that classical political economy embodied. Our argument, in this essay and elsewhere, is that if public choice theory is interpreted to incorporate essentially the same *purposes* as classical political economy, its method is entirely appropriate and that the criticisms are fundamentally misconceived.

Classical political economy was, from its eighteenth-century origins on, largely concerned with the comparison of alternative social or institutional orders. Its main purpose was not the predicting of economic behavior for its own sake; its purpose was, instead, that of developing appropriate models of the working of alternative institutions in order that the choice between those institutions might be better informed. Modern economics, with its orientation toward empiricism and prediction, toward positivism generally defined, seems to have moved some distance from, and in the process obscured, this classical focus. The prevailing methodology is strongly oriented toward predictive analysis of choice *within* a well-defined institutional structure (or system of constraints) rather than a choice *between* alternative social institutions.

This shift in focus has important implications for the way in which analysis is conducted. One of these implications relates to the choice of models, and it does so because the model that is appropriate depends critically on the purpose for which the analysis is to be used.

Specifically, in the argument that follows, we attempt to demonstrate the following propositions:

(i) that the model of behavior which provides the best *predictions* of market price and output levels is *not* the best model of behavior, in general, for the purposes of comparative institutional analysis;

(ii) that the *Homo economicus* model of human behavior may be superior in comparative institutional analysis to a more "accurate" model of human behavior in the conventional predictive sense; and

(iii) that an attack on the use of *Homo economicus* in any institutional setting based solely on direct appeal to observation cannot be decisive, and is largely misconceived.

We shall illustrate these propositions by appeal to the simplest and most familiar institutional comparison within economics—that between monopoly and other forms of market organization. This illustration is of some interest in its own right because it has important implications for the measurement of welfare losses from aggregated data. But our overall purpose here is much more general. We wish to argue that the monopoly illustration can be generalized to virtually all institutional forms, including, specifically, the political institutions that are the subject matter of public choice.

The central observation on which the analysis rests is that the welfare loss relevant for any institutional comparison is a convex function of the magnitude of the quantity (or price) distortion. In other words, the addition to welfare loss caused by a movement away from the efficiency ideal is *larger*, the further equilibrium happens to be from that ideal. Or, equivalently, large departures from the ideal cause more than proportionately large harm. For this reason, measuring welfare losses on the basis of average or "expected" behavior will always lead to underestimation: an adequate measure of expected welfare loss from a single behavioral model will necessarily require a model that generates outcomes somewhat further from the ideal than ordinary observation would seem to justify.

Throughout, our discussion is cast in the simplest possible diagrammatic terms. In Section I, we offer a simple monopoly example. In Section II, we provide a more general statement of the central result. In Section III, the analogy between the monopoly example and other institutional comparisons is drawn generally, and in the specific context of some simple models of political process in Section IV. Section V offers the relevant conclusions.

I. A Simple Example

The proposition to be demonstrated here is that the theory of monopoly behavior that gives the best empirical "fit" is, in general, *not* the theory of monopoly behavior that gives the best estimate of the costs of the monopoly institution for purposes of comparison with alternative regimes.

We introduce a highly simplified hypothetical example, designed for the purpose of demonstrating our results, rather than for any suggestion as to applicability. Consider a single municipality, recently created. The citizens, directly or through elected representatives, are trying to decide on an appropriate institutional arrangement for the provision of a particular service, say garbage disposal.[1] There are two basic options: the municipality can grant a monopoly franchise to some private firm (the owners of which firm are resident citizens of the municipality in question); or, the municipality can establish a local government instrumentality, charged with pricing the service at cost and subject to the regulatory scrutiny of a local government agency. Both sorts of arrangements are observed to be operative in neighboring municipalities. The citizens of the new government unit would like to know which regime works "better": they need to estimate the predicted costs and benefits of each of the two arrangements in order to make an intelligent institutional choice.

In order to assist in this calculation, let us assume a professional economist (Dr. H) is hired as a consultant. H gathers together a sample of two hundred municipalities—one hundred that use the monopoly franchise, one hundred that use the regulated instrumentality. The municipalities used in the sample are essentially identical (or can be normalized to be so) in all externally observable relevant respects (size, income, tastes, etc.). For each municipality, H collects information on the demand and cost conditions relating to garbage disposal, along with estimates of the current price and output policies in each case.

For the regulated instrumentalities, the outcome emerges simply for him. The consultant finds that these bodies do indeed price at marginal cost and produce the optimal output—almost without exception. However, the monitoring undertaken by the regulatory agencies is not costless—it absorbs a quantity of resources of value A, per municipality, on average. This is a fixed cost that does not bear on the optimality of pricing and output decisions for garbage disposal, but that must be reckoned with in comparing the regulated arrangement with the private franchise alternative.[2]

For the private franchised monopolists, the outcome is more complicated. The consultant is able to obtain a "best fit" on the demand and cost curves for garbage disposal, which exhibit, let us say, the properties shown in Fig. 1-1, namely linearity of the demand curve, and constant costs. Armed with these initial results, he could, of course, exploit the elementary textbook construction for the monopoly firm and derive the corresponding profit-maximizing price and output.

However, H has been charged with the task of obtaining the "best

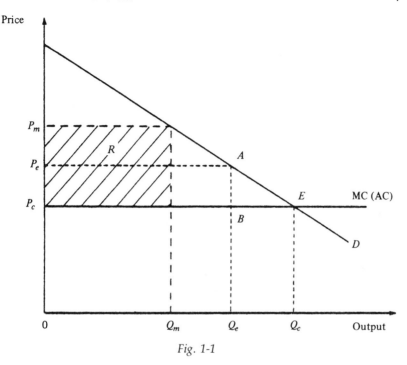

Fig. 1-1

fit" monopoly behavior model. The textbook model of monopoly cannot simply be *assumed*: it must be justified empirically. As H pursues his investigations, he finds that by no means do all of the monopoly firms maximize profits. Some are sales maximizers; some are "satisficers"; some—perhaps from altruistic motives, or perhaps because they fear regulation—seem to be charging a price close to marginal cost. The best *predictive* model of monopoly behavior—the model that gives the best "fit" in the conventional sense that it minimizes the variance of the observations—is one that generates an expected price-output equilibrium (P_e, Q_e) as shown in Fig. 1-1. For expositional convenience, suppose that this equilibrium lies halfway between that predicted by the textbook monopoly analysis and the perfectly competitive outcome (the outcome under the purely "public interest" model of monopoly behavior).

It should perhaps be emphasized that, in any explanatory sense, the model of monopoly that yields this outcome is superior to the simple textbook model. It will systematically outpredict the conventional profit-maximizing model: the latter will yield predictions of price and output that are just plain wrong.

Dr. H now submits his conclusions to the community residents, collects his fee, and hurries off to write up a short note for some learned journal showing how the textbook monopoly model is empirically flawed. The community residents, in turn, take the "best" monopoly model—now empirically validated—and calculate the expected net cost of monopoly organization, as measured by area of the triangle ABE which, in the linear case, is equal to $\frac{1}{8}R$, where R is the maximum profit that can be derived from the franchise (the shaded area in Fig. 1-1). Since, by assumption the franchise holders are also citizens of the municipalities where the franchise is exercised, their own profits are not, of course, part of "social costs" of monopoly.[3]

This cost is to be compared with that which would be expected under the regulated municipal agency, already estimated to $A. Let us suppose that A is $\frac{1}{6}R$, as defined above. Since the costs of the private franchised monopoly arrangement are smaller, this is the arrangement that the community provisionally accepts.

Suppose now, however, that there are certain consumer-oriented groups in the community who do not readily acquiesce in the provisional decision. They proceed to hire a second consultant and charge him with the task of somehow demonstrating that the decision based on the report of the first consultant is in error.

Upon careful review, the second consultant finds no errors in the empirical estimates. Nonetheless, he can report that the inferences from these estimates are totally in error, and that the proper use of cost-benefit computation suggests that the municipal agency, subject to regulation, should be installed. He does this by showing that the behavioral model derived by the first consultant will generate incorrect *estimates of welfare losses* if used directly. The second consultant uses a different procedure for determining the expected welfare loss from monopoly. He considers the price-output equilibrium in *each* case, determines on that basis the welfare loss, and then simply adds up the welfare loss over all cases. He does not assume, as the community did in computing losses from the predicted behavioral model, that all monopolists operate precisely at the average (best estimate) price-output equilibrium. The second consultant derives a different and larger "expected" welfare loss for monopoly—the arithmetic mean of the welfare losses taken separately.

The expected welfare loss measure derived by the second consultant will be unambiguously larger than the first. We can illustrate this fact by a simple example. For analytic convenience assume that the behavior of the firms remains constant over time periods; this assumption allows us to look only at a single period for the distribution of positions among the separate firms. Suppose that we find a very simple distribution. One-half of the firms do, indeed, operate at roughly the predicted price-output combination, at (P_e, Q_e). For the remaining fifty monopolists, however, we note that twenty-five of these operate as profit-maximizing monopolists, at (P_m, Q_m). The other half, the remaining twenty-five franchisees, however, operate as if they are in fully competitive settings, at (P_c, Q_c).

Given this distribution, what is the proper measure of average welfare loss over the set for the period?

For the fifty firms operating at (P_e, Q_e), the total welfare loss is $50R/8$. For the twenty-five firms operating at (P_m, Q_m), the welfare loss is $25R/2$; for the twenty-five firms operating at the competitive equilibrium, there is no net welfare loss. The total welfare loss for the hundred monopoly arrangements is, therefore,

$$50R/8 + 25R/2 = 150R/8.$$

The average, or expected, welfare loss for the private franchise solution is therefore $\frac{3}{2}(R/8)$. Clearly, this exceeds $R/8$, the measure of excess burden calculated by the first consultant. More to the point, it also exceeds the cost of enforcing the regulatory regime, $R/6$. Consequently, the conclusion that seems to flow naturally from the first consultant's report should be reversed: the municipality should adopt the arrangement using a regulated municipal agency.

Why is there this divergence in measures of expected welfare loss? The answer is simple. As price increases from P_c, total welfare losses increase at an increasing rate. That is, marginal welfare losses increase with price increases above P_c, given our linear demand and cost constructions. From this it follows that there is an asymmetry between losses and gains as actual positions lie above and below the single best prediction of the expected position for monopoly operation (which must, of course, lie somewhere above P_c in the price dimension). That is to say, an increase in price above P_e, with the accompanying reduction in quantity, adds more to total welfare losses than an equal decrease in price below P_e subtracts from total welfare losses.[4]

II. A General Statement

The monopoly example set out in the previous section is an application of a much more general result in economics—namely that welfare losses (or "excess burdens" as they are more commonly called in public finance circles) are a convex function of the distortion that generates them. Generally, these welfare losses are measured by reference to Harberger triangles (or their general equilibrium equivalents[5]) and a typical measure would be:

(1) $W = \dfrac{1}{2} Sd^2$

where W is the welfare loss, S is the slope of the demand curve, dp/dq, and d is the quantity distortion, $d = (q - q^*)$.

In fact, this formulation implicity assumes linearity of the demand curve, and the analogous measure of welfare losses involving elasticity rather than slope assumes loglinearity. But it is entirely general that, if welfare loss is measured by the area over the relevant range under the income-compensated demand curve, then:

(2) $W = F(d)$

where $f'' > 0$, that is, welfare loss is such that it increases at a faster rate as d increases. This depends only on the requirement that the compensated demand curve is downward sloping (see Appendix).

In any case, we can follow professional practice and treat (1) as a totally satisfactory approximation. On this basis, the propositions that underlie the monopoly example can be conveniently depicted diagrammatically in Fig. 1-2. In this diagram the quantity distortion is depicted along the horizontal axis, and the welfare loss along the vertical. Consider first the proposition that the average value of W exceeds the welfare loss derived from the average distortion, that is:

(3) $\overline{W} > W(\overline{d})$.

A simple example suffices. Let d_1 and d_2 be two values of d, and $\overline{d}$ the average of the two. In Fig. 1-2, the horizontal distances $d_1\overline{d}$ and $\overline{d}d_2$ are equal. The welfare losses associated with d_1 and d_2 are W_1 and W_2, and $\overline{W}$ is the average of the welfare losses, that is $W_1\overline{W}$ equals $\overline{W}W_2$. It can be seen by inspection that $W(\overline{d})$ is less than $\overline{W}$ (as claimed in Equation (3)).

Furthermore, it is clear that there does exist a value of the distortion, d_M, which is such that $W(d_M) = \overline{W}$. This value of d is the value that would have to emerge from a single model of the institution if that single model were accurately to reflect the true expected welfare cost of that institution. Clearly, d_M exceeds $\overline{d}$, and this must always be true if the W curve is convex.

Note that the single model of monopolist's behavior that is best for predicting price and output equilibrium is one that generates $\overline{d}$ as the predicted outcome. The single model of monopolist's behavior that is best for predicting welfare losses—the model relevant for evaluation of monopoly as an institutional form—is one that "predicts" d_M, an outcome that is systematically worse than the average or best-predicted outcome.

Of course, this discussion does not validate the use of the textbook model of the profit-maximizing monopolist, either as a means of predicting equilibrium price-output decisions or as a model for measuring welfare losses. What it does clearly suggest, however, is that, for

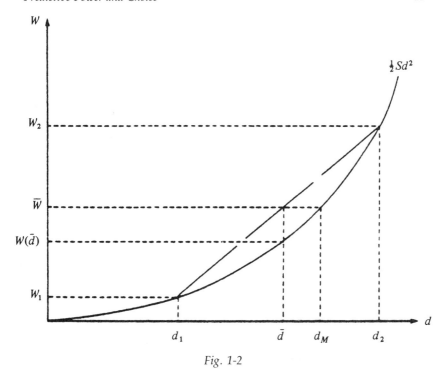

Fig. 1-2

the purposes of institutional comparison, the "best fit" or "most realistic" model does not suffice, and that a bias *toward* the profit-maximizing model is required.[6]

In presenting the simple monopoly example here, we have implicitly assumed that the observing economist has available to him the complete set of disaggregated data from which an accurate measure of monopoly welfare costs can be derived. If, indeed, such data exist, there might seem little reason for the ordinary economist to resort to any single "best predictor" model in his estimation of welfare costs. He can measure welfare losses in each case, and derive the average of them directly. The problem emerges necessarily, however, when the economist is confronted with data that are already in aggregated form. If he has no knowledge about the distribution of observations around the expected values, there is no way in which accurate measures of welfare cost can be derived. At least in such cases, the bias toward underestimation inherent in the use of expected values can be acknowledged. A superior procedure would presumably be to "guess at" some underlying distribution of outcomes and recalculate the welfare losses on this basis. But one cannot rule out, equally, the explicit use of a model of monopoly behavior rather closer to the profit-maximizing model than the empirical evidence indicates. In other words, the use of the *Homo economicus* caricature in the monopoly context *may* be justified, even though its price/output predictions are less good than some alternative model of monopolist behavior.

III. *Homo economicus* and Public Choice

The monopoly issue is, of course, of considerable interest to economists in its own right. It would be possible to leave the discussion at this point with a warning against careless empiricism in industrial organization, and perhaps with a catalog of empirical studies in which the procedures for measuring welfare losses seem to have been most imappropriate. Nothing in all this would strike the economist as particularly controversial or alarming.

But our claim here is much more general: the monopoly case is offered as an *example* of a broader proposition relating to the use of the *Homo economicus* construction in comparative institutional analysis of all types. In particular, the assumption that political agents will use any discretionary power that they possess to further their particular private interests can, we believe, be justified even where there seems to be ample empirical evidence to the contrary, on grounds essentially analogous to those for using *Homo economicus* in the monopoly context.

We begin with the proposition, probably unexceptionable to most economists and other social scientists in the classical tradition, that political institutions can be normatively justified only to the extent that they provide citizens with goods and services that those citizens value. Such goods and services may be conventional commodities, much like marketed goods and services (such as statistical data, weather reports, electricity, recreational parks, etc.) and may or may not have the properties of Samuelsonian public goods. Equally, the services provided may be rather more abstract things, such as the rule of law (without which Hobbesian anarchy would prevail) or "justice" (somehow defined). In all such cases, however, the services or goods in question are valued in essentially the same sort of way as the goods with which economists more typically deal in market settings. For all these services or goods, it is possible to conceptualize having more or less of them, and of additional units being valued more highly or less. Within this broad conceptualization, it is possible to hypothesize a demand curve for the good or service in question, and it is reasonable to conjecture that the demand curve will exhibit conventional properties, specifically that it should reflect the principle of diminishing relative marginal utility.

Furthermore, given the general state of the world, and specifically a sense of what is and is not feasible, it is possible to conceive of some output level of these politically provided goods that is "optimal," or that in some other sense represents the "public interest" outcome. If departures from this "optimal" output level occur, it is necessary only to assume that demand curves "slope downward" in order to sustain the claim that the marginal loss imposed is larger the further the output level is from optimality, and hence that greater losses will be imposed on a society over any period of history than would be suggested by the evaluation of the "average" outcome over that period.

As we see it, the assumptions required to justify this claim are extremely weak. Yet they do establish a case *against* too ready a rejection of the *Homo economicus* assumption in analyzing the workings of political institutions. The common grounds for such rejection rely on an "argument of general realism." The critic observes that many public officials seem to act to promote their versions of the "public interest," that moral considerations do seem to constrain political agents, in at least some cases and perhaps much of the time. He concludes on this basis that the *Homo economicus* model is unrealistic, and therefore inapplicable. Our central point in response to this is that the model may well be unrealistic, but remain applicable for the comparative analysis of political institutions.

In this sense, the monopoly construct and the public choice analysis of political institutions are analogous. However, the study of market institutions differs from that of political institutions in one major respect: whereas in market contexts, one may often have access to data that permit the direct calculation of demand curves, price markups, elasticities, and the like, the analogous information in respect of politically provided goods is rarely available, at least directly. In the monopoly example, therefore, an obvious solution to the problem is simply to calculate welfare losses in each case separately and determine the expected welfare loss accordingly. There is simply no need to try to allow for aggregation bias by an appropriately caricatured single model of monopoly behavior. Consequently, the basic moral to be derived from the monopoly example might be construed as being that one should measure aggregated excess burdens properly. But in the analysis of political processes, the measurement of welfare losses directly is rarely possible. Rather, the analyst is thrown back on less refined sources of information—the broad historical record, general experience and casual observation, extrapolation from similar cases, and so on. Here we cannot really "measure" excess burdens in a whole range of cases and thereby obtain some notion of the normative character of alternative political institutions. What we *can* do is to use our general understandings of the way in which excess burdens respond to deviations from "optimal" output to inform the choice of behavioral model. This is, as we see it, precisely what the classical political economists did: their choice of a *Homo economicus* model for political agents, deliberately fashioned to abstract from public interested behavior, involved a proper procedure for the task of constitutional design in which they were involved.

IV. Some Political Examples

In order to point out the direct relevance of the monopoly example, it may be useful to examine briefly some simple models of political process in which the market analogy is most conspicuous. In each of the particular cases examined below, we consider a governmental bureau charged with providing a single good or service to citizens of the community.

Standard Bureaucratic Inefficiency: Public Services at High Cost

Consider, first, bureaus that make no attempt to control their budgetary allocations. They provide the required service but do so (or may do so) at a cost higher than that which is "necessary" in the opportunity cost sense. Bureaucrats may succeed in using their position to secure net rents, whether those be in the form of pecuniary or nonpecuniary benefits.

In this model, the analysis developed from the monopoly example above may be applied without substantial change. Suppose, for illustrative purposes, that one out of three such bureaus should operate at a level such that the cost presented to the community is as high as P_m in Fig. 1-1; a second bureau operates with cost at P_e, while a third operates at genuine opportunity cost. The best predictive model of bureaucratic behavior involves cost, P_e, and output, Q_e. But, as the example of monopoly shows, this model is not appropriate for measuring the welfare costs of bureaucratic inefficiency.

The Niskanen Bureaucracy Model

As a second case, consider a setting in which bureaucratic agents exercise more discretionary decision-making power. They can, by appropriate behavior vis-à-vis the legislature of the community, manipulate the size of the bureau's budgetary allocation. We suppose that, half of the time (or in half the cases), these agents are constrained by internal moral considerations to pursue the "public interest," and (more heroically) that their calculation of the "public interest" outcome corresponds exactly with that which is optimal in the familiar Paretian sense. Suppose, further, that in the remaining percentage of cases, bureaucrats operate like Niskanen bureaucrats, that is, they act to maximize the size of the bureaus' budgets.[7] This "Niskanen" output level corresponds to that at which total net consumer surplus is zero. Expected output for a bureau will then lie exactly halfway between "optimal output" and "Niskanen output." Will the measure of expected welfare loss correspond to the welfare loss at expected output? Clearly not, in general—and for precisely the same reasons analyzed above.

The diagrams in this case are essentially analogous to those in Fig. 1-1. In Fig. 1-3, the curve D depicts the community demand for some publicly provided good, G. This consists, let us say, of the vertical sum of n exactly identical consumers, facing a common income tax, and is drawn to be linear for convenience. The optimal level of G for the community is given by q^*, the output level at E where D cuts the horizontal average (and marginal) cost schedule. This output level prevails when bureaucrats act in the public interest, which, by assumption, they do half the time.[8]

The remainder of the time, however, the bureaucrats select output at the level q_N, which is such as to obliterate the net surplus generated by G. This output level will, in the linear case, be exactly twice the output level q^*. Accordingly, expected output is $\bar{q}$, halfway between q^* and q_N. If we were to base our normative calculus on this "expected" behavior pattern, however, we would be systematically wrong. For the welfare loss associated with $\bar{q}$ (the triangle ELM, shaded in Fig. 1-3) is less than the expected welfare loss, which is half the area EST. In the linear case, EST is *four* times the area ELM. The single behavioral model which yields the appropriate measure of expected welfare loss is one which yields output q', where the ratio of q^*q_N to q^*q' is $\sqrt{2}$ (*not* 2).

As in the monopoly case, therefore, the behavioral model which yields the best estimate of *output* will not yield the best estimate of welfare loss. If our interest in modeling bureaucracy therefore issues from the normative concerns of institutional comparison, the appeal to "observed" bureaucratic behavior is misplaced. For example, suppose we are to choose whether the government "should" intervene in market processes in some case where the market is believed to fail to generate optimality. Suppose further that the allocative losses attributable to this market failure happen to be equal to one-third of the area EST. To make the relevant comparison of market and political institutions on the basis of average or "best predicted" bureaucratic behavior would lead to the conclusion that intervention is justified (since ⅓ EST > ¼ EST); to calculate welfare losses attributable to bureaucratic behavior properly, however, leads to precisely the opposite conclusion (since ½ EST > ⅓ EST). If a single model of bureaucratic behav-

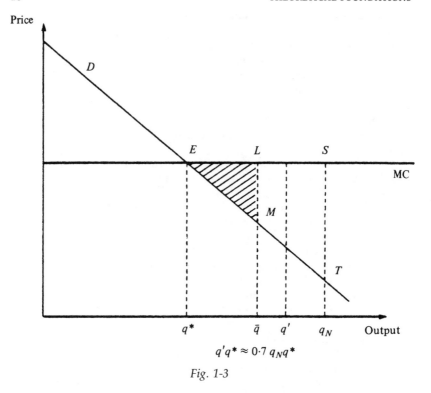

$$q'q^* \approx 0.7 \, q_N q^*$$

Fig. 1-3

ior is required for such purposes, therefore, it will be closer to the "cynical" Niskanen model than casual observation would indicate.

The Generalized "Political Failure" Model

It may be objected (and has been by some critics)[9] that both the bureaucratic inefficiency model and the Niskanen model of bureau budgetary maximization are extreme and that professional opinion is divided (not necessarily evenly) on the question of whether the political mechanism leads either to grossly higher costs or to overexpanded budgets,[10] and that any conclusion drawn from these models is tainted with a certain ideological "bias."

We should, therefore, emphasize that the force of the general argument does not depend in any way on the particular models, but merely on the inherent convexity of the situation. Suppose, for example, one were to take the view that, over the whole range of public outputs supplied through particular bureaus, the likelihood of overexpansion is about as great as the likelihood of underexpansion in any

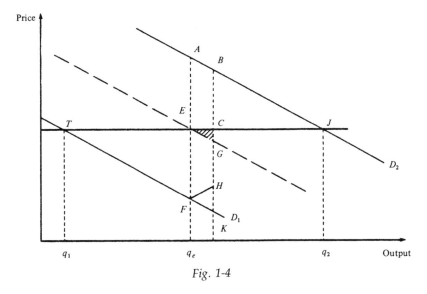

Fig. 1-4

given case. Ideologically, this is surely an evenhanded position, and seems consistent with an acknowledgment of the theoretical arguments on both sides. To be more specific, suppose, as depicted in Fig. 1-4, that q_e is the observed output of the publicly provided good, G, and that there is an equal chance that the true demand curve for G is either D_1 or D_2, that is, an equal chance that q_1 or q_2 is the "optimal" output. Can we now conclude that the best estimate of public sector outcomes is that they are optimal?

For certain purposes, the answer is clearly "yes." If, for example, we wish to calculate the efficiency effects of changes in output, the appropriate assumption is precisely that q_e is optimal. That is, in our linear demand case, the expected welfare loss of an expansion (or contraction) of output is equal to the welfare loss when q_e is known to be optimal.[11] The expected welfare loss of an expansion of output from q_e to q'_e is

$E(W) = \frac{1}{2}$(welfare gain when D_2 applies)

$\qquad - \frac{1}{2}$(welfare loss when D_1 applies)

$\qquad = \frac{1}{2}ABCE - \frac{1}{2}ECFK.$

Let point H be such that $BC = CH$. Since EF equals EA, then $ABCE$ equals $EFHC$. So $E(W) = \frac{1}{2}FHK = ECG$.

But for comparative institutional analysis, the assumption that the public sector will generate optimal outcomes is totally unacceptable.

The expected welfare loss associated with the institution is not that generated by some sort of general "best predicted" bureaucratic behavior. For we know that the expected welfare loss from bureaucratic provision is the area EAJ (or equally TEF) and not *zero*. In this particular case, it does not matter which of the under- or overexpansion models we use to estimate welfare loss. Either will do. But the procedure of making institutional comparisons on the basis of the "best fit" model of the political mechanism will yield a measure of welfare losses of zero; the procedure therefore generates systematically wrong results, just as in the other models.

V. Conclusions

Modern public choice theorists have followed classical political economists in modeling individuals in their political roles in terms of the same "private interest" models of human behavior that are commonly used in market settings. This procedure is frequently criticized on the grounds that it pays no attention to the obvious relevance of moral considerations in constraining the behavior of individuals in political contexts.

But even if the empirical claim is valid, this line of criticism is not by any means decisive *provided that* the purpose of public choice analysis is seen as being the comparative evaluation of alternative institutions rather than the development of purely predictive theories of political behavior. Our claim here is that the model of human behavior appropriate for comparative institutional analysis will generally be one that generates worse outcomes (i.e., outcomes further from some conceptual optimum) than the empirical record would justify. For this reason, it may be appropriate to use the *Homo economicus* construction precisely *because* it indicates worse outcomes (in both political and market settings) than would seem likely on average. We have attempted to indicate the *nature* of our general reasoning first by appeal to an extremely simple and familiar case—the question of the choice between nonregulated monopoly and regulated monopoly. Our argument in this context suggests that there may be a case for retaining something like the textbook profit-maximizing model, even where the empirical evidence in favor of satisficing and sales maximization seems strong, *if the purpose of the analysis is to assist in the evaluation of monopoly as an institutional form.* Even though the profit-maximizing model is an abstraction that does much violence to "predictive" reality, it may still produce better results in measuring welfare losses than the genuinely "realistic" model of positive predictive science. We have extended the results drawn from the simple monopoly example to several cases of bureaucratic supply of public goods.

Our more general argument, one that we believe would be entirely congenial to classical "political economists," is that the general characteristics of the monopoly example apply commonly in the whole range of political/social contexts, and specifically that there *is* a generalized analogue to the downward sloping demand curve embedded in political and social institutions. To deny this seems to deny the notion that politicians or bureaucrats serve as suppliers of services that are valued by the citizenry. The evaluation of these public services, even if they are not directly priced, is not essentially different from the evaluation of services purchased in markets. If, therefore, we take any defined "public interest" model of behavior as an idealized benchmark, and conceptualize the output of services generated by such behavior, it becomes apparent that restrictions (or expansions) of valued output from that idealized benchmark will involve increasing marginal welfare losses to the citizens.

Once this view of things is accepted, it follows that, for purposes of constitutional dialogue, the model which embodies self-serving behavior on the part of *all* politicians may be superior to that which accurately predicts behavior in the conventional probabilistic sense.

There is one final observation to be made. *Homo economicus* by no means represents the worst imaginable character for the social drama. The natural monopolist whose predilection toward the "small is beautiful" philosophy leads him to produce *less* output than would be profit-maximizing, inflicts even larger marginal losses on the community than would his rapacious wealth-maximizing counterpart. The political zealot who works with self-sacrificing conscientiousness to pursue some ideological goal—such as the purification of the race, or securing the world for Islam—can cause much greater harm than the mere budget-maximizer. It may be that this budget-maximizer is somewhat "worse" than the average or representative politico-economic agent; but, as we have tried to show, this may be a *virtue* of our disciplinary method, not a weakness.

Appendix

The reader should be alerted to the fact that this condition is sufficient to ensure that f in Equation (2) is convex (i.e., $f'' > 0$) only in the case where welfare loss is expressed as a function of *quantity* distortion. If instead we express welfare loss as a function of *price* distortion, then the assumption that the compensated demand curve is negatively sloped is *not* sufficient to ensure that welfare loss increases at a faster rate the larger the distortion.

To see this, consider without loss of generality the case in which quantity distortion is positive. Then $d^+ = q - q^* > 0$ and

(i) $\dfrac{dd^+}{dq} = 1.$

Then $W = f(d)$ will be convex in d if $W = f(q)$ is convex in q. Note that

(ii) $W = -\left[\displaystyle\int_{q^*}^q g(q) - \int_{q^*}^q c'(q) \right] dq$

where $g(q)$ is the compensated demand curve and $c(q)$ is the cost function, and for convenience is assumed linear.

(iii) $\dfrac{dW}{dq} = [g(q^*) - c'(q^*)] - [g(q) - c'(q)].$

Since q^* defines optimality, the first bracketed term on the right-hand side is zero, and $c'(q)$ is a constant. Hence:

$$\dfrac{d^2W}{dq^2} = -g'(q) > 0 \quad \text{iff} \quad g'(q) < 0 \quad \text{and q.e.d.}$$

Suppose instead that we define welfare loss as a function of *price* distortion, that is,

(iv) $W = h(v)$

where   (v) $v = p - p^*.$

Is the fact that $W = f(d)$ is convex sufficient to ensure that h is convex? Clearly not, for:

(vi) $W = h(v) = f[k(v)]$

where $d = k(v)$

and   (vii) $h' = f'[k(v)]\, k'$

and   (viii) $h'' = f''[k(v)](k')^2 + k''f'[k(v)].$

Now, in (viii), we know that f'', $(k')^2$, $f' > 0$. But the sign of k' is indeterminate. Note that k' is $-dq/dp$ and k'' is $-d^2q/dp^2$. So if d^2q/dp^2 is positive and sufficiently large, (viii) *may* conceivably be negative.

One might conjecture that the cases in which the demand curve is sufficiently concave (from above) to ensure that h'' is negative are so rare as to be ignorable: that is, there is a strong *presumption* that doubling the price distortion will more than double the welfare loss. And this conclusion seems reasonable. But a presumption is not a certainty, and plausible formulations of the demand curve exist for which the presumption is violated. (We are grateful to David Austen-Smith for bringing some examples to our attention.)

To avoid such caveats in the text, we have defined distortion exclusively in *quantity* terms. Then pure logic generates the conclusions from standard demand theory.

Of course, in the empirical literature on the estimation of welfare losses, some form of linearity is assumed, in which case, k'' is zero and h'' positive. Linearity is also assumed whenever one uses average price and average quantity data to determine bench-marks for welfare loss estimation: in general, $(\bar{p}, \bar{q})$ will not lie on the demand curve. To assume that it does implies linearity.

Notes

We are indebted to James Heins, Dennis Mueller, Jonathan Pincus, and Robert Tollison and anonymous referees for helpful comments.

1. This choice of example is arbitrary. There is in fact some evidence that private monopoly franchises outperform municipal government in garbage disposal, but that evidence is somewhat beside the point. In fact, much of that evidence is susceptible to the argument made here, because it focuses on a comparison of average prices under the two institutional forms.

2. Our assumption that the municipal agencies operate efficiently and that the full costs of the regime arise from monitoring outlays independent of output is made here for expositional simplicity only. The same conclusions emerge if we allow some inefficiency in operation, but the presentation becomes messy.

3. We shall ignore those costs that may go into securing the franchises, the rent-seeking costs. We do so, not because we think these irrelevant, but because our purpose here is not the relevance of the simple construction, but rather the methodological one of suggesting the limits of empirical estimates in institutional comparisons. For relevant papers in rent-seeking, see J. Buchanan, R. Tollison, and G. Tullock, *Toward a Theory of the Rent-Seeking Society* (College Station: Texas A&M University Press, 1980).

4. In the extensive literature on the empirical measurement of monopoly welfare losses, the general point here seems either to have been widely overlooked or left unarticulated. Dean Worcester ("New Estimates of the Welfare Losses Due to Monopoly," *Southern Economic Journal* 40 [October, 1973]: 234–45) mentions that "aggregation" problems will arise in moving from

finer to grosser industry definitions and that such moves will tend to bias welfare loss estimates downward, but he does not explain how he gets this conclusion, and, in any case, he believes such changes to be relatively insignificant. Keith Cowling and Dennis Mueller ("The Social Costs of Monopoly Power," *Economic Journal* 88 [December, 1978]: 727–48) are immune from aggregation difficulties because they *assume* profit maximization and calculate welfare losses directly as one-half of profit (appropriate for the linear case). However, in his seminal paper, Arnold Harberger ("Monopoly and Resource Allocation," *American Economic Review* 44 [May, 1954]: 77–87), in averaging profit rates over firms in the industry to obtain an "average" price distortion, d, for each industry, is clearly guilty of aggregation bias. We have no way of determining how significant empirically such bias is, a matter that clearly depends on the variance of profit rates across firms in the industry. We should emphasize, however, that our concern in this essay is *not* that of making a contribution to the debate-discussion over the proper measure of welfare loss from monopoly. Our usage of this discussion is illustrative of the more general point of our emphasis.

There may, of course, be many choice situations to which the "best prediction" model is entirely appropriate. In terms of an example, suppose that, instead of some institutional comparison between regulated and unregulated monopoly, the choice is that which would face, say, a supplier of garbage bags to the municipality that had chosen to establish an unregulated monopoly in garbage disposal. The supplier may well, in this case, use the price-output prediction that best "fits" the data drawn from comparable operations. He will do so if the potential losses emergent from erroneous prediction are symmetrically related to the extent of error. The central thrust of our argument is that such symmetry in the cost of "errors" does not obtain generally in comparisons among institutions.

5. See A. Harberger, "Three Basic Postulates for Applied Welfare Economics: An Interpretive Essay," *Journal of Economic Literature* 9, no. 3 (September, 1971): 785–97.

6. Note that we have implicitly assumed that the individual faced with the institutional choice in the example is strictly risk-neutral in the sense that he would pay at most x dollars for a 50 percent chance of winning $2x$ dollars. The introduction of risk-averseness will, of course, imply that the proper welfare-loss estimates will diverge even more from those derived from the best-fit empirical model of monopoly equilibrium.

7. See William Niskanen, *Bureaucracy and Representative Government* (Chicago: Aldine Press, 1971), part III, for a full exposition of the basic model.

8. This choice of probabilities is for analytic convenience only. Precisely the same general point holds for other distribution of behavior, provided only that the variance is non-zero.

9. Most notably Richard Musgrave ("Leviathan Cometh—or Does He?" in H. Ladd and N. Tideman, *Tax and Expenditure Limitations* [Washington, D.C.: Urban Institute Press, 1981], pp. 77–117).

10. As a counterpoise to the overexpansion result in the Niskanen model, or the same result reached by the different model outlined by Buchanan and Tullock (*The Calculus of Consent* [Ann Arbor: University of Michigan Press, 1962]), see Anthony Downs's "Why the Government Is Too Small in a Democracy," *World Politics* 13 (1960): 541–63, or the more journalistic claims of John

Galbraith. Ryan Amacher, R. Tollison, and T. Willett provide a survey of the relevant literature in "Budget Size in a Democracy: A Review of the Arguments," *Public Finance Quarterly* 3 (1975): 99–120.

11. This point is made in another context by G. Brennan and Tom McGuire ("Optimal Policy Choice under Uncertainty," *Journal of Public Economics* 4 [February, 1975]: 205–209).

2.

The Achievement and Limits of Public Choice in Diagnosing Government Failure and in Offering Bases for Constructive Reform

I. Introduction

I was asked to present a paper on the public choice approach to government deficiencies, and I want to use this occasion to go beyond orthodox analysis and to discuss some issues that have been at least partially neglected in the public choice approach.

It is useful to review the orthodoxy at the outset; this is attempted in Section II. Section III summarizes the implications that may be drawn from the standard discussion. In Sections IV, V, and VI I explore methodological issues in the discussion from a perspective that is "beyond public choice" in one sense. In Section VII I challenge the domain of *Homo economicus* with respect to individual behavior both in markets and in politics. In Section VIII I discuss the minimax principle for the design of institutional reform, and in Section IX I relate this to public choice analysis. Conclusions are contained in Section X.

II. Public Choice as a Theory of Government Failure

Theoretical welfare economics is properly labeled as a "theory of market failure." Analytical developments of the 1930s, 1940s, and 1950s, when the essential elements of theoretical welfare economics were articulated, first took the form of rigorous statements of the necessary and sufficient conditions required for efficiency in the allocation of resources in an economy, and, secondly, of definitions of relationships among economic variables that failed to satisfy such required conditions. There was relatively little institutional content, as such, in this welfare economics, but, by common acknowledgment, observed relationships in the capitalist economy were deemed such as to indicate "failure" in achieving allocative efficiency.

By implication almost universally, and by explicit statement in many instances, these "market failure" demonstrations of theoretical welfare economics were held to offer a prima facie case for corrective measures implemented through political-governmental means. There was no consideration given to the institutional structure within which such idealized corrective measures were to take place. To the theoretical welfare economists, markets "failed" in the allocative process; "ideal" government was assumed to be the alternative.

On several occasions I have referred to public choice, inclusively defined and as developed largely in the 1960s and 1970s, as a "theory of government failure" that offsets the "theory of market failure" that emerged from theoretical welfare economics. Just as the latter contains demonstrations that observed market processes fail to produce results that satisfy the conditions for allocative efficiency, public choice theory (once labeled "welfare politics" by Paul Samuelson) contains demonstrations that observed political-governmental processes fail to satisfy the requirements for efficiency in the implementation of corrective measures.

At an elementary level of analysis, public choice theory does little more than puncture the "benevolent despot" image or model of government and politics that theoretical welfare economics had incorporated as its standard of institutional comparison. At a more sophisticated level, public choice theory includes its own models of the processes of political decision-making, building in this respect on the economists' postulate of methodological individualism, with utility-maximizing actors in varying public choice roles.

Almost out of necessity, public choice theory has been somewhat more positive, or at least somewhat less normative, in content than theoretical welfare economics. As I have suggested, the thrust of the latter was to demonstrate that a particular institutional form, markets, fail. Against what? By comparison with what? Once this flaw in the normative implication of theoretical welfare economics was exposed, basically through an elementary but positive analysis of the alternative institutional structure, there is less emphasis on "failure." That is to say, public choice theorists have not duplicated the error or oversight of the theoretical welfare economists; they have not compared an actuality with an ideal. "Governments fail" against an ideal conception, but who might have expected any contrary finding? And public choice theorists have not held out some idealized market as the effective institutional alternative to politics.

III. Institutional Comparison

With some legitimacy, public choice theorists can claim to have advanced the discussion of comparative institutional alternatives. If we acknowledge that *both* markets and governments fail against idealized standards for operation, whether the objective be allocative efficiency, maintenance of individual liberty, distributive justice, or other desiderata, what is to be said about organizational structure? How should the interdependencies among persons in a society be institutionalized?

At the level of comparison between alternative organizational form for specifically designated sectors or "industries," the implication is that such a comparison can best be, and indeed must be made on a case-by-case basis. For some "industries," the comparison may yield rather straightforward results. The efficiency-generating properties of a free and open market in the production-distribution of a partitionable good or service, say, shoes or plumbing, may outweigh any arguments for politicization, with the latter's inherent inability to embody incentives efficaciously. At the other extreme, the "publicness" or "commonality" properties of, say, national defense effort, may be such that the politicized institutional structure, despite its incentive-efficiency defects, may dominate serious consideration of market-like "privatization."

It is to be expected that, in any such case-by-case comparison, there will be numerous "industries" that fall somewhere near the margin of indifference, with the advantages and disadvantages of market-like and political organization roughly balancing each other. For this set of "industries," which may be called the "public utilities," we might expect to observe different organizational structures in different societies.

Public choice theory, in its redress of the imbalance in the institutional comparisons informed by and inspired by welfare economics, has shifted the pendulum "right-ward," so to speak. A comparison of market and governmental alternatives, both examined "warts and all" and without the "benevolent despot" blinders on, will necessarily produce a private sector–public sector mix less dominated by the public sector than that mix that might have been generated on the basis of prevailing ideas in, say, 1950 or 1960. Such a change in comparative results has nothing to do with any shift in the underlying ideology or nonideology of public choice, or of anything else. The change in question emerges strictly from a better-informed comparison of relevant alternatives.

Exclusive reliance on a pragmatic or case-by-case comparison of organizational structures, and without attention paid to the extension in the margins, however, is not acceptable procedure. Spillover or external effects may occur within the total organizational structure, effects that will tend to be obscured in any case-by-case, industry-by-industry comparison. The overall ratio of the value generated through the market sector, where individuals do adjust to private prices, to the value generated through the governmental sector, where private prices do not motivate behavioral adjustments on the part of individuals, may be of critical importance as an input into a properly conceived comparative evaluation for any single "industry." The differential weights assigned to allocative efficiency, to economic growth, to individual liberty, to political participation, and to distributive justice may affect the preferred degree or margin of politicization of the social order. At this level of comparison, normative principles enter the discussion, and public choice theory, as such, has nothing to offer beyond the clarification of the relevant trade-offs that are faced.

IV. Utility Maximization as a Logic of Choice

In remaining parts of this essay I want to discuss some developing concerns that may, in one sense, seem to be "anti–public choice," at least in some of their implications. I want to look not at "government failure" or even at "market failure," but rather at that which we might call analytical-methodological failure on the part of economists, and particularly public choice economists.

By "market failure" or "government failure," we refer to institutional-organizational structure. We analyze the predicted working properties of institutions, or rules, of constraints, and by adducing "failure" we imply that, if the rules could be changed, "better" results would be forthcoming. This institutional focus ignores or bypasses the characteristics of the persons who operate within the rules, who behave in accordance with the constraints that the rules define. The whole analysis, as I have noted, commences with utility-maximizing individuals.

There is no problem created by the utility-maximization postulate if we remain at the level of a strict logic of choice. That is to say, if we leave the arguments in individual utility functions unspecified and undefined, we can then use the utility-maximizing construction in analyzing processes of interaction. We cannot, however, operationalize the analysis so as to generate testable hypotheses or implications, even conceptually. In order to be able to generate such testable implications, the arguments in individual utility functions must be defined. And it is with this step of definition that major difficulties emerge.

V. *Homo economicus* and Market Failure

In their analyses of market relationships, economists have long relied on *Homo economicus*, old-fashioned economic man, who does have well-defined arguments in his utility function. In its least restrictive formulation, the *Homo economicus* construction requires only that objectively measurable economic value, designated in monetary units, enter as *one* argument in the representative person's utility function. In this version, the construction does not require that economic value be the only argument in the preference function or even that this argument be dominant in influencing behavior. But armed with this minimal, and widely accepted, model of behavior, economists are able to generate operational predictions. Quantities demanded increase as prices fall; quantities supplied increase as prices rise. Properly qualified, these predictions have been amply corroborated by empirical evidence.

It will be useful, however, to see precisely how this minimal formulation of the *Homo economicus* operationalization of economic theory bears on the market failure hypotheses that emerged from theoretical welfare economics. Consider one of the standard examples where markets are alleged to fail to generate efficient results, that in which externalities (spillover or neighborhood effects) exist. Take the classic example of the factory's smoking chimney that dirties the next-door laundry of the housewife. The Pigovian line of reasoning is familiar. The "true social costs" of the production that involves smoke generation should include the damages to the laundry. The factory owner does not incorporate these spillover damages as a part of his private costs which enter into his production decisions. The market fails; idealized efficiency norms would require an adjustment toward somewhat less smoke emission.

For purpose of discussion here I want to ignore the Coase-related possibilities that bargains may well be struck between the factory owner and the housewife to eliminate any inefficiency.[1] Even within the strict Pigovian setting, the conclusion that some corrective action is required to achieve efficiency depends critically on the assumption, and one that is rarely stated, that the factory owner disregards costs that he imposes on the housewife, that he acts solely and exclusively in his own narrowly defined economic interest, in this case, that he maximizes monetary profits. But note that this assumption embodies a much more restricted and circumscribed version of the *Homo economicus* construction than that which I outlined in the preceding discussion about the operationalization of market relationships generally. To assess market failure in the externality setting, we require the assumption that economic value is either the only argument in the utility function or that this argument dominates all others in influencing behavior. Unless we make such a restrictive assumption, we cannot determine that the factory owner does not take into account the costs of the damages imposed in his own decision calculus, in which case there may be no basis for the claim that markets fail in generating efficient results. And there is no means empirically of determining whether or to what extent these external costs may be taken into account in the actual decision processes of persons in market relation-ships generally. The market-failure diagnosis is without clear empirical support.[2]

Note that I am not suggesting that there is no empirical content in the economic setting offered by the interaction between the factory owner and the housewife. We could predict, for example, that a tax imposed on smoke emission would reduce such emission. This prediction requires only that economic value be *one* argument in the factory owner's preference function, and it is a prediction that may be tested. What cannot be tested is whether or not the imposition of a tax (even one that ideally measures the costs imposed on the housewife) improves or decreases the efficiency of resource allocation in the economy that contains the factory and the housewife.

VI. *Homo economicus* and Government Failure

I do not make the points above to suggest or to imply that markets do not fail in the sense sketched out in welfare economics. And I am not suggesting that persons take into account the full effects of their own actions on third parties who are not directly involved with them in economic interchanges. I make the points of the preceding section only as a way station or bridge toward further discussion of the public choice diagnosis of "government failure."

As we know, the central methodological thrust of public choice is the extension of straightforward utility maximization to explain the behavior of persons who act in public choice roles. Voters, bureaucrats, judges, legislators—these roles are filled by persons much like all others who seek to maximize their own utilities, subject to the constraints (rules) within which they operate. But let us examine some of the problems that emerge when we try to put operational content into the formal logical models. Let us try to employ our old friend, *Homo economicus*, and suppose that persons who act in public choice roles proceed as if they are predominantly influenced by economic value. That is to say, let us adopt the *Homo economicus* model in its strong form, that which allows us to diagnose market failure from the presence of externalities.

Our effort runs aground immediately when we look at the behavior of individual voters. In large-number groups, there is a very small probability that any single vote will affect the majority-determined outcome. Hence, if the act of voting involves any cost at all, *economically* rational persons will not vote. This widely discussed paradox may, of course, be resolved by dropping the restrictive form of *Homo economicus* and by introducing other than net wealth arguments in the utility functions of voters, but the observed fact that persons do vote suggests that *Homo economicus* in the strict sense is not properly descriptive of behavior.

If this much is acknowledged, it is also necessary to acknowledge that the same problems arise with the "information failure" hypothesis that is subsidiary to the voter paradox and which is often cited as one of the basic sources of "government failure." The latter hypothesis states that, even for those persons in a large electorate who do vote, there is no economic incentive for them to invest resources in becoming informed about the choice alternatives that the group confronts. Since they do not individually bear the costs or reap the benefits, they have no privatized responsibility for making the choice. But, again, this hypothesis presumes that the strict *Homo economicus* model describes behavior. If this presumption is dropped, and if arguments other than net wealth are introduced in the individual's utility function, how can we conclude that there will be "information failure"? Just as in the case with "market failure" in the smoking chimney example, there is no direct empirical support for the hypothesis.

Again it must be noted that I am not suggesting that the analysis is drained of all empirical content. So long as a *Homo economicus* construction in its more limited, and surely more acceptable, sense is retained, we may still predict that more persons will vote if the costs of voting are reduced, that persons are more likely to become informed about the choice alternatives if the costs of information acquisition are reduced, and other like propositions. These offer empirically testable hypotheses, but they do not depend on the assignment of exclusive domain to *Homo economicus*.

We may extend analysis to the behavior of persons who act in other public choice roles. Consider the ordinary bureaucrat employed by government with an assigned set of duties to perform. It is plausible to model his behavior in the same way that we model the behavior of an employee in a private firm. In both settings, strict adherence to the more restricted *Homo economicus* construction suggests that the employee will seek to minimize work effort that is unpleasant to the extent that it is possible within the constraints that he faces. For the private-sector employee, however, these constraints may be more restrictive because behavior is more likely to be monitored carefully by the residual claimants to the firm's profits. In the governmental hierarchy, by contrast, supervisors of bureaucratic employees have no direct economic incentive for close monitoring of employee efforts, except in so far as such efforts impinge negatively on the rewards of the supervisors. There are no residual claimants in monitoring roles. Further, if bureaucratic rewards generally depend on size of agency, which in turn depends on the size of agency budgets, supervisors of bureaus will seek to maximize budget sizes, quite independently of any "demand" for the services actually provided. Unlike the owners of a private firm, bureaucrats are unable to capture rents or profits directly. They, therefore, seek to expand agency size beyond meaningful efficiency limits.

There are differing incentive structures in market and in governmental organization; these different structures allow us to predict differences in behavior, and these hypotheses may be empirically tested. But corroboration of these hypotheses does not legitimize the *Homo economicus* model for bureaucratic behavior, defined in the restricted sense that assigns the dominant role to net wealth maximization. There is no "proof" that bureaucracies "fail" in the sense that individual bureaucrats try to maximize budget size, that employees seek only private interest and shun their more traditionally conceived roles as promoters of "public interest."

When we extend the analysis to the behavior of elected politicians, to legislators, these are modeled as seeking almost single-mindedly to maintain the perquisites of office. Each legislator tries to "buy" the favor of voters by spending on the provision of services and transfers that cater directly to the particular coalition of voters selected exclusively on electoral grounds. It is not surprising that the strong version of *Homo economicus*, which incorporates net wealth maximization on the part of voters, bureaucrats, and legislators should produce demonstrations of "government failure." Indeed, if we accept this model, we may wonder that government works at all. There are self-evident paradoxes in the observations that some of the goods and services desired by citizens do get supplied by governments and that taxes are not at their strict revenue-maximizing limits.

VII. The Relevant Domain of *Homo economicus*

I suggest that we cease and desist in any attempts to model man, *either* in his market *or* in his public choice behavior, as seeking exclusively or even predominantly to maximize the value of his net wealth. I suggest that we restrict ourselves methodologically to the more limited model of *Homo economicus*, one that allows the argument for economic value to enter into the individual utility function, in market or in public choice behavior, but to enter as only one among several arguments, and not necessarily as the critical influencing factor in many cases. There is, without doubt, an element of old-fashioned economic man in every one of us, and on the average this may be important for a lot of our ordinary behavior, but there are always other elements that operate alongside "old Adam." There are several "noneconomic" men that live with *Homo economicus,* and it is folly to ignore their existence and their tempering influence because they are difficult to quantify.

As noted, it is indeed easy to diagnose "government failure" if we adopt *Homo economicus* as the all-encompassing explanatory model. In such a model, however, voters do not vote; those that do are ill-informed; bureaucrats shirk their duties and use their discretionary powers to manipulate budget sizes and budget compositions to their own advantage; elected politicians seek to retain the perks of office and pander to the demands of minimally sized constituencies necessary for reelection; judges enjoy the quiet life and spend little time and effort in their duties. Considerations of "public interest" simply do not enter into the analysis at all.

It is hardly surprising that this model seems a caricature of what "politics" and "government" is all about from the perspective of the orthodox political scientist. It is, nonetheless, equivalent to that model for market behavior that the same orthodox political scientist is quite willing to adopt when he accepts the "market failure" diagnosis from the theoretical welfare economist, and uses this diagnosis to justify the extension of political controls over markets.

What I am suggesting here is that *neither* markets *nor* politics can be appropriately modeled in the strict formulation of the *Homo economicus* construction. We must reckon on *other-than-economic* arguments in individual utility functions, both in market dealings and in political dealings. But we must also keep in mind that the *economic* argument always remains in utility functions as an important and relevant argument, in individual behavior, in markets, and in politics. In a somewhat modest, but surely defensible sense, I think we can say that the methodological lesson to be drawn from public choice is nothing more than this admonition.

VIII. The Minimax Principle of Institutional Design

There are important implications for institutional design, however, that are contained in the ecumenical utility-function approach that I think we must adopt to make meaningful progress, both in diagnosing the performance of institutions and in organizing improvements. It was the genius of the eighteenth-century philosophers, and of Mandeville, Hume, and Smith in particular, to recognize that man's behavior in market institutions, even if wholly directed by the narrow pursuit of private interest, may, at the same time, indirectly and unintentionally promote what may be called the "public interest." These philosophers did not model man as being so narrowly focused, however; their interest lay in the design of institutions, and they sought to show that, even if narrow economic interest should dominate behavior, desired results might follow. By implication, therefore, market-like rather than government-like organization was to be preferred where possible, by a genuine minimax principle of choice. In politics, by sharp contrast with markets, there seemed to be no inherent structural linkage that could generate a correspondence between individual economic interest and the "public interest." We may, with Adam Smith, feel better if we know that our butcher is allowed to seek his own profits, because only in this way can we be sure that he will provide us with meat for supper. But we may, in sharp contrast with this, be quite displeased when we think that our bureaucrat may be also seeking his own economic interest, because we sense that he can do so only at our expense, rather than at our own improvement.

It is easy, for me at least, to understand the genuine intellectual excitement generated in the discoveries of classical political economy, discoveries of the efficacy of market coordination. The total and critical dependency of man upon the moral and ethical precepts of his fellows seemed to be at least partially mitigated. To the extent that markets were well designed and allowed to function in a constitutional-legal order, that men were allowed to follow the system of natural liberty in free and open competition one with another, there was less need to be concerned by man's failure to live up to the behavioral standards dictated by his bishop.

Many social scientists and philosophers of this century do not seem to understand and to appreciate the setting within which classical political economy was developed. Adam Smith did not construct his system of market order on any presumption that *Homo economicus* dominated all aspects of human behavior. Persons behaved in accordance with law and within the constraints of custom; perhaps exhibited "moral sentiments" one for another, which included sympathy and fellow-feeling. A legal order was a necessary part of the environment of a workable market economy. But to Smith the market did offer a unique setting within which men, acting in their own private interest, did not run squarely afoul of the like interests of their fellows. There seemed to be no political-governmental counterpart; to the extent that our affairs are subject to the decisions of persons in political office, be they bureaucrats, legislators, or judges, we necessarily depend on their willingness and proclivity to sublimate their own private interest to more "general interest" at least to some degree. It is little wonder that classical political economy came to be understood as a defense of the market and the market process, or by its critics as an apology for capitalistic institutions.

IX. Public Choice and Institutional Reform

Why did the normative principles of classical political economy come to be forgotten in the late nineteenth and early twentieth centuries? In what respects is it accurate to state that public choice amounts to an indirect "rediscovery" of these principles? A bit of history is helpful here, and in particular it is useful to recall that the late nineteenth and early twentieth centuries were also described by the practical realization of the "democratic ideal" and specifically by the rapid expansion of the voting franchise. There was the new romance of electoral participation and the accompanying implicit faith that electoral controls were in themselves sufficient to keep the behavior of governments and governmental officeholders in bounds. These offered a fertile atmosphere for the promulgation and propagation of political-governmental nostrums for almost all conceivable social "ills," an atmosphere in which the motivational structure required for implementation was more or less totally neglected.

Public choice has essentially brought this motivational structure to the light of day, after almost a full century of delusion. But, as I have emphasized, public choice economists reduce the normative impact of their own efforts if they advance their explanatory models as "strictly positive" theories of behavior of persons in public choice roles. Public choice economists should take lessons also from the classical political economists; they should present the models that embody public choosers as maximizers of economic interest in the same sense that Adam Smith presented his models of man's behavior in markets. There need be no implication that such models fully or even primarily describe actual behavior. The models should, instead, be used normatively as bases for institutional design on the minimax principle noted. The objective should be that of designing institutions such that, if participants do seek economic interest above all else, the damages to the social fabric are minimized.

Within the structure of political-governmental organization, much can be done toward generating at least some rough correspondence between individual self-interest and the general interest. Dramatic changes can be made in the incentive structure within politics and government. Constitutional constraints can be imposed that will keep extreme patterns of behavior in limits.

The incentive structure of the political-governmental sector cannot, of course, become analogous to that of the market sector. As I have already noted, there is an argument for allowing the market order, which does channel individual self-interest in directions that correspond with the general interest, to organize as large a part of our interdependencies as is possible. And it is surely the case that, in 1980, there can be considerable "privatization" in most western economies. This result will emerge straightforwardly from a careful industry-by-industry comparative evaluation of the sort previously discussed. The movement toward deregulation in the United States reflects at least something of the flavor of this avenue for constructive reform.

The potential for improvement in the moral-ethical standards of conduct on the part of persons who act in positions of decision-making authority should never be neglected. Sir Dennis Robertson said we should always try to economize on love and try to find ways to do so institutionally. But this is not the same thing as saying that greed is better than love in those settings where dependence on the "good offices" of others is necessary. The balance here can, of course, be overdrawn. The moral zealot in positions of political power may well be less desirable than the private self-seeker who is on the take more or less openly. But within broad tolerance limits, it is better to have the career bureaucrat who is dedicated to his own conception of "the public interest" than it is to have the time-serving drone who minimizes effort. Economists in particular are likely to neglect the importance of ethical content in quite ordinary behavior, whether this be in market or nonmarket settings. There is a role for the moral teacher, "the preacher," that can be socially productive.

X. Conclusions

But can we unscramble the eggs? Can we get Humpty-Dumpty back together? This offers the challenge to our age. There are no lacunae in the normative theory, model, or conception of a social order in which persons can remain free, prosperous, and tolerant in a regime of law that constrains citizen and state alike. This ideal order has not, of course, ever been realized, but in the eighteenth and early nineteenth centuries, there seemed to be legitimacy in the hope that realization was on the way. Progress was visible and rapid, and persons believed in the possibility of progress. But western man lost his way; he lost the wisdom of his forebears, and he unwittingly allowed the fruits of progress toward the ideal order to be dissipated. The advances in material well-being clouded retrogression in public philosophy and in the general understanding of the limits of social engineering. The healthy skepticism of the eighteenth century changed slowly but surely into the perfectionist naiveté of the early twentieth century.

How can "public good" be produced by "private man"? This eighteenth-century question is with us still. But "public good" in the 1980s is surely to be defined in part by dismantling of the institutional apparatus that seems now to thwart our efforts and our liberties at every turn. But how was "public good" ever produced? How did the nineteenth-century world emerge from the mercantilist epoch? The historians have not told us a fully convincing story. Those among our colleagues who insist that ideas of "public good" and of the "good society" cannot have consequences and, that the course of history is set by the determinate play of the forces of private self-interest, offer only despair at the fate that awaits us. As Professor Hayek has said, however, nothing is inevitable but thinking makes it so. For myself, I want "public choice" to merge with and to develop into "public philosophy," as a set of integrated ideas about the foundations of social order that will set us back on the high road.

Notes

I am indebted to my colleague, Geoffrey Brennan, for helpful comments.

1. Cf. R. H. Coase, "The Problem of Social Cost," *Journal of Law and Economics* 3 (1960): 1–44.

2. I have elaborated the argument of this paragraph in my *Cost and Choice: An Inquiry in Economic Theory* (Chicago: Markham Publishing, 1969).

3.

Rational Choice Models in the Social Sciences

I. Introduction

By profession and discipline I am an economist, and some of my work has involved the extension of the economists' model of rational choice behavior to areas of human interaction other than the market, broadly defined. I shall first discuss several elements of this basic model: (1) methodological individualism, (2) utility maximization, (3) the structure of constraints, and (4) the levels of choice. These elements are, of course, interrelated, but they can provide a useful scheme for organizing the essay. Following the treatment of these elements, I shall, in Section VI, examine the purpose of the whole analytical enterprise. Finally, in Section VII, I shall isolate one glaring omission in my discussion of rational choice and suggest some of the implications of this omission.

II. Methodological Individualism

The central presupposition of any and all rational choice models, including those of the economist, must be the definition of the choosing-acting agent as the individual human being, the unit equipped with some presumed capacity to evaluate options or alternatives and to choose among them. Many of the sophisticated analyses of rationality in choice simply take this presupposition as given, but its central importance should be emphasized. Only individuals choose; only individuals act. An understanding of any social interaction process must be based on an analysis of the choice behavior of persons who participate in that process. Results that are predicted or that may be observed in social interaction must be factored down into the separate choices made by individuals. In ordinary discourse, confusion abounds from failure to take this step. For example, a corporation does not "choose" among alternatives; the choices of individuals, acting as agents for the corporation, are the relevant subjects for meaningful inquiry.

Several qualifications must be placed on this elementary presupposition. First of all, methodological individualism does not imply or require that individual choice behavior is invariant over changes in the institutional setting, that persons choose always "as if" they exist in social isolation, one from another. Acceptance of the classic Aristotelian proposition that man is a social animal reflects, in no way, a criticism of the individualistic presupposition. Persons behave differently in differing social interactions, and these differences are important (see Section V below). The individualistic postulate suggests only that, regardless of the social setting, all choice behavior is finally individualistic.

A second caveat is that methodological individualism, as a framework for conducting social science, does not imply anything at all about the objectives sought by those who choose. To say that only individuals choose among alternatives suggests nothing whatsoever about what these alternatives are or how the individual arrays or orders these. There is no implicit inference that these choices are or are not "narrowly self-interested." The rational altruist and the rational egoist can fit equally in the model's structure. The individualistic postulate identifies the unit to whose choices rationality precepts are applied; it remains silent on the objects of these choices.

A third inference that must be clarified concerns the differentiation between the set of alternatives for choice faced by the individual participants and the results of the choice process in which many persons participate. This relationship is perhaps the most difficult "principle" for noneconomists to understand, and, indeed, we may suggest that a thorough understanding of this "principle" is the most distinguishing feature of the economist, as such. The discovery and elaboration of this principle were the crowning achievements of the eighteenth-century moral philosophers, from whose work economics, as a discipline, emerged. The idea is often summarized in the phrase "unintended consequences." The network of economic exchanges, in which many persons participate in various capacities, generates results that may be described in terms of "allocations" and/or "distributions." These results may be evaluated by observers, while at the same time it is recognized that these results are "chosen" by no one. There is no "allocative choice," as such, in a functioning market economy; individuals choose, not among resource allocations or distributions, but among the alternatives that each person, separately, confronts. Personally, I chose to present this lecture, a choice that affects the allocation of economic resources today only in a very small way.

An important methodological principle surfaces at this point. Because allocative-distributive "choices" are not made, the aggregative results do not lend themselves to evaluation in terms of the criteria developed in rational choice models which are, as noted, applicable only to the individual's selection among options. While it may be legitimate to use the terms "efficient" and "optimal" in evaluating the results of an individual's choosing process (see Section III below), the more familiar usage of these terms in regard to aggregative results that emerge from the simultaneous choices of many persons must be recognized to be categorically different. In this second usage, "efficiency" and "optimality" are potential properties that are related to individual choices only through an indirect nexus that cannot be adequately treated here.

A fourth inference to the individualistic presupposition is closely related to that just discussed. Because choice behavior is limited to individual choosing agents, the precepts for rationality that may be used to evaluate individual choice cannot be extended to nonindividual entities in any direct sense. The familiar extension is to the collective, as such. There may arise settings in which only the collective seems to confront a selection among alternatives. The decision process must generate a single result from among several options available. The political unit, the state, must (1) go to war, or (2) maintain the peace. It is natural linguistic usage to refer to the state as "choosing" among the options, and from this to infer directly that the decision process of the state should exhibit the rationality properties of the individual.

Careful attention to the basic individualistic presupposition would prevent such an extension. Even if the collective entity, as such, confronts the alternatives, the only genuine choices made are those of the individuals who participate in the decision process. Given a decision rule, individuals "choose," and such choices may be evaluated in accordance with rationality precepts. From this participation by separate persons, the decision rule or institution generates an outcome which may be one from those that the collective confronts. No one "chooses" this outcome, however, and it is an error of major proportion to attribute to the choosing process, as such, any rationality precepts.

Failure to appreciate the illegitimacy of such an attribution made the economists' mid-century search for social welfare functions seem initially to be an appropriate exercise. And, even in 1985, economists remain who act as if such functions are meaningful constructions. In this context, Kenneth Arrow's impossibility theorem appeared surprising only to those who failed to understand the restrictive limits imposed by the individualistic presupposition.[1]

III. Utility Maximization

The second element in the economist's model of rational choice behavior is summarized under the rubric "utility maximization." In its most general sense, this rubric refers only to the "as if" maximand for individual choice behavior, with the content of this maximand left totally open ended. Terms such as "happiness," "satisfaction," or, simply, "X," might be substituted for utility. At this level of generality, there is no suggestion that the maximand contain the same specific arguments for different persons, or that the same person's maximand contains the same arguments over extended time. In the limit, there is not even the notion that there exists a single common denominator such as utility, in which all arguments may be expressed. In a purely formal construction, operationality of the utility-maximization hypothesis is limited to criteria for consistency in observed choice behavior. With no specification of the arguments, there is no means of predicting directions of behavioral response to changes in constraints. Utility maximization implies only that persons "choose what they choose" in a noncontradictory fashion.

A less empty but still quite general formulation involves the specification of arguments in the utility function, along with the signing of these arguments as positively or negatively valued. There need be no presumption that the chooser maximizes some common denominator of evaluation such as "utility." All that is required is that, so long as an argument is classified as a "good," the chooser will seek more rather than less of it.[2] For example, so long as measurable net wealth is defined to be positively valued by the individual, regardless of how insignificant this argument might be relative to other "goods" (prestige, status, friendship, peace, privacy, tranquility, etc.), hypotheses about changes in the individual's choices under changes in constraints may be advanced, hypotheses that can be tested empirically.

The standard economist's textbook model is more specified. The individual is presumed able to evaluate "goods" and "bads" in terms of a unidimensional denominator, "utility," and is presumed also to seek to attain a maximum achievement level, given the constraints faced. Further, the chooser is presumed able to internally trade off "goods" and "bads," one against another. This model allows for the derivation of testable hypotheses, over and beyond those derivable from the less specified model.

More ambitious effort involves some specification of the trade-offs among the arguments in the utility function, a specification sufficient to allow the derivation of refutable hypotheses that amount to predictions about patterns of behavior defined in some absolute rather than in a relative sense. The most familiar example here is the hypothesis that individuals seek to maximize net wealth, or that this argument dominates choice behavior. This construction really substitutes the wealth maximization hypothesis for the more general utility maximization one.

Critics of the economists' general model of utility maximization have tended to interpret the whole framework for analyzing individual behavior in terms of the most restrictive hypotheses rather than the more flexible, and more general, formulations. And critics often consider themselves to have destroyed the efficacy of utility maximization, as an hypothesis of rational choice, when they point to empirical refutations of the wealth-maximization hypothesis. Economists themselves have been partly responsible for this biased interpretation of their models of choice behavior. In their sometimes overly zealous attempt to introduce empirical content into their research inquiries, modern economists may have been led to incorporate too readily the wealth-maximization hypothesis. Wealth is objectively measurable; other possible arguments are less amenable to the observer's calculus.

IV. The Structure of Constraints

The third element in the economists' model of choice behavior involves the relationships between precepts for rationality and the structure of the constraints that are faced by persons in varying choosing roles or positions. "Individuals maximize utility subject to constraints"—the central, and simple, principle here is that the choice which qualifies as rational under one set of constraints is not that which qualifies under another set. That is to say, the utility-maximizing choice behavior of an individual depends on the constraints that define and describe the set of alternatives that are available. (Failure to recognize this simple principle has led sophisticated intellectuals to mouth absurdities about public policies in the modern welfare state setting.)

The dependence of choice on constraints is straightforward in the elementary economics textbook exercise in which the individual, as consumer-buyer, is constrained by his income-wealth, along with the set of prices for the market alternatives. In the more general setting, the constraints may not be reducible to a single numeraire value. The individual making the choice may be subject to a whole set of conditions, only some of which may be binding.

Another familiar emphasis of the elementary economics textbooks must be carefully qualified before acceptance. We find frequent reference to the resource and technology constraints that limit the feasibility space for "the economy," considered as a functioning organization. This reference is misleading in that neither "the economy," nor its political agent, "the state," chooses. Only persons choose, and the single person is affected in his behavior by economy-wide resource scarcities, only in so far as these are translated into effects on his own endowments or choice options. Within an individual's private calculus, there is a resource constraint, which becomes almost equivalent to the income-wealth constraint, and, of course, the whole set of individual constraints must be consistent with the total resource availability in the economy. Similarly, the individual can choose only among alternatives that he actually confronts, which implies technical possibility.

The emphasis on economy-wide rather than on individual constraints has been partly responsible for a serious omission in analysis. If we adopt the methodological imperative that all choice analysis be reduced to inquiry into individual behavior, the importance of *institutional* constraints becomes evident. The feasible choice options open to the individual are, in part, determined by the institutional setting. I shall defer, until Section V, the analysis of rational choice *among* constraints, as contrasted with the economists' model, which concentrates attention on choice *within* exogenously given constraints. In the standard framework, recognition of the importance of introducing institutional constraints has led to developments within economic analysis that have extended the explanatory power of the rational choice model, horizontally as it were, by examination of the incentive structures of alternative institutions.

Several areas of research inquiry embody developments worthy of notice here. "Property rights economics," much of it based on the seminal work of Armen Alchian, had been influential both in the emergence of "law and economics" as a subdiscipline in its own right, and in the construction of what is sometimes called the "new institutional economics."[3] A second major extension of the explanatory power of the economists' basic model of rational choice, again in the horizontal sense noted, originates at the University of Chicago with the work of Gary Becker and his colleagues. Becker uses the basic model to develop a general theory of social interaction, but his central contribution has been to our understanding of individual behavior within households and families.[4] Also deserving of notice in this respect is much of the analysis in public choice, inclusively defined. The choice behavior of persons located in bureaucratic positions, analyzed by Tullock, Niskanen, and others, is now acknowledged to yield refutable predictions that are helpful in understanding how bureaucratic institutions operate.[5]

The choice behavior of the individual in a large-number electorate has also been subjected to exhaustive analysis. This behavior is worth discussing in some detail since it can illustrate well the effects of the choice setting on rational behavior. The first choice faced by the person in a large-number electorate is that involving the act of voting itself. Even if the individual places a relatively high value on the differential effects of the alternatives that the collective faces, rationality precepts may dictate abstention.[6] If, for any reason, this choice threshold is passed and the individual plans to vote, the individual may not find it rational to acquire more than cursory information about the alternatives. Beyond this, even if the individual decides to vote and does acquire some information about the alternatives, he may rationally use participation to express whim and prejudice rather than valued interests.[7]

The large-number electoral setting, in particular, illustrates the point made earlier that the results generated from the collective-decision rule, say, majority voting, are "chosen" by no one. In an election between Candidate A and Candidate B, these alternative collective results are *not* the alternatives for choice as faced by any individual, as voter. The voter faces starkly different alternatives—the "lever marked A" and the "lever marked B." There is only a probabilistically very small correspondence between the individual's act in the voting booth and the collective results generated from the choice behavior of the many persons along with the decision rule in being.

For purposes of discussion here, the relevant point of emphasis is that rational choice precepts dictate totally different behavior in divergent institutional settings. Consider and compare an individual's choice among alternatives in the market and his choice among alternatives in a large-number election. The same person, with the same rational norms, will act differently in the two cases, even when the differentials in value placed on the alternative results are identical. In the market, confronted with a choice between a restaurant dinner and a book purchase, there is a direct one-to-one correspondence between choice and consequence. If the market prices of the two options are the same, and the individual places a differential value of ten dollars, in utility, on the dinner, the person knows that, having made his choice, he will enjoy the consequences. Before making the choice, he has an incentive to invest effort in information about the alternatives. If he chooses wrongly, if he makes an error, he alone will suffer the consequences. In the voting booth, by sharp contrast, the linkage between an individual choice and the consequence is almost totally absent.[8] The individual will remain "rationally ignorant," since there is little or no return from additional information. Even if the individual values one alternative more than the other, and by the same ten dollars as before, he is unlikely to participate at all, and, if he does so, there is no assured prospect that he will even vote for the alternative that he most highly values.

Note that the difference in choice behavior here stems exclusively from the differences in the institutional-incentive structure within which the individuals confront choices and not from any differences in the specification of arguments in the utility function or from any differences in the precepts for rational choice behavior. The person who sincerely acts exclusively from what he thinks to be the "public interest" has precisely the same incentive for remaining rationally ignorant in the voting booth relative to the marketplace as does the person who acts exclusively in his own interest, narrowly defined. Recognition of the effects of the institutional setting on rational choice behavior, and on observed results of choices made in different settings, would do much to eliminate the proclivity of many social scientists to introduce one model of behavior for market interaction and another for politics.

V. The Choice within Constraints and the Choice among Constraints

An important extension of the economists' basic model of rational choice has been a shift of attention, *vertically*, to the choice among constraints themselves, as opposed to the standard presumption that constraints faced by choosers are exogenously determined. Clearly, such presumption seems legitimate when reference is to the overall resource or technological limits of "the economy." But, as previously noted, "the economy" does not choose. Once we recognize that institutional structures, as well as the individualized endowment constraints, define the potential boundaries of choice, the prospect of deliberative selection among these structures emerges. If persons can choose among the constraints that are imposed on their own within-constraint choice behavior, surely we should be able to analyze the first set of choices in some fashion analogous to that employed for analyzing the second- or lower-level choices. This shift in the level of choice extends the model of rational choice vertically as contrasted with the horizontal extensions embodied in the nonmarket applications mentioned earlier.

A generalization of the evolutionist paradigm may suggest that, although institutions of social interaction do change through time, these changes can only emerge through the long process of cultural evolution. According to this perception, it is not legitimate to infer that basic institutions of social order, basic rules for the socio-economic-legal-political "game," can be deliberately "chosen" in any manner analogous to the choices among options that are available to persons, in a collective decision process, within an existing set of institutional rules.

Such a stance would seem, however, to close off the most constructive avenue for social reform or improvement. If the institutional constraints are assumed to be beyond the range of choice and control, and, further, if, within the constraints that exist, individuals choose in predictable patterns, there remains little or no scope for "reform," as such, apart from moral preaching. The whole exercise of political economy is eliminated. This exercise is the demonstration that, within certain sets of constraints, individual utility-maximizing behavior, even if narrowly self-interested, can generate overall results that may be "better," under agreed-on criteria of evaluation, then those results predicted to emerge under alternative sets of constraints. Normative evaluation of institutional arrangements implies that a potential modification of such arrangements is possible, that the rules of social interaction are subject to directed change.

Economists do not find such vertical extension of rational choice models amenable to analysis with their familiar tools, and it is not, therefore, surprising that relatively few of them have made efforts in this direction. Choice, as such, requires the limitations of alternatives, and the very notion of utility maximization implies that, if subject to control, the set of alternatives should be as inclusive as possible. Why should anyone choose deliberately to restrict the available choice set, to reduce the range of options?

Economists' prejudgments on such a question stem from their analytical models rather than from any empirical observation of behavior. Persons do impose constraints on their own behavior, both as individuals and as members of socially interacting groups. They deliberately adopt rules that restrict situational responses. It is useful, however, to distinguish between the choice of individualized constraints and the selection of general constraining rules or laws.

The "economics of self-control" is now emerging as an important area of inquiry. Work by Schelling, Elster, and Shefrin and Thaler may be noted here.[9] The relatively more important area is, however, the one that involves constraints that are imposed *generally* on the choice behavior of all persons in a community. These constraints emerge, or may emerge, from a radically different calculus on the part of the individual, and from a calculus that is much more readily brought within the rational choice calculus emphasized by economists. Once it is acknowledged that institutions enter as constraints on individual choice behavior, and once we allow institutions to be treated as variables subject to reform or change, the potential for selection from among alternative sets of institutions seems to follow. In expressing a preference for a *general rule*, one that will equally constrain the behavior of *all* persons in a community, the individual is, effectively, trading off the possible negative value of losing his own freedom of action (of having his choice set constrained) in exchange for the positive value that he expects to secure from the constraints imposed on the behavior of others, behavior that he anticipates may impact on his own well-being in a negative fashion. Ideally, the individual may prefer that his own behavior be exempted from the application of a constraining rule. There may be no explicit desire for self-control with respect to the activity that is constrained. Practically, no such individualized exemption from a general rule is feasible. The individual supports the introduction and enforcement of a general rule because the benefits from "control of others" are valued more highly than the costs, measured by loss of self-liberty.

The area of inquiry into the choices among alternative sets of general rules which has been called the "theory of constitutions," "constitutional political economy" or, even, the "theory of law," involves both positive and normative elements. The individual, in determining what is, for himself, the most preferred set of general rules, applicable to his own as well as to others' behavior, must call on his analytical skills in modeling the expected working properties of alternative sets of rules, or changes in such rules. Only after this essentially positive analysis is complete can the individual make an informed judgment as to the preferred set.

This extension of rational choice modeling to the "constitutional choices" of an individual seems straightforward enough until the necessarily collective action of the whole rule-making exercise is recalled. As in the within-rule settings for collective decision discussed earlier, where the mutually exclusive alternatives are, somehow, emergent from a process involving the participation of many persons, no individual effectively faces the final choice options in any sense analogous to that treated in orthodox rational choice models. This severe limitation on any simple application of such models in either within-constraints or among-constraints large-number settings must be acknowledged. The predictive-explanatory power of rational choice models is reduced, not because the participants depart from rationality norms for behavior, but because these norms themselves are not related so closely to identified arguments in individual utility functions as is the case in strictly private choice settings.

VI. The Purpose of the "Scientific" Enterprise

The economists' model of rational choice behavior was initially developed for application in market interaction, the whole set of voluntary exchange relationships in which persons participate as buyers and/or sellers of final products and/or resource inputs. What I have called horizontal extensions of this model involve attempts to analyze behavior in other than ordinary market settings, behavior of persons in family interactions, of persons as potential criminals, as managers of nonproprietary organizations, as legal contractors, as adjudicators, as charitable contributors, as rent seekers, as public choosers, as team members. By contrast, what I have called vertical extensions of the economists' model involve attempts to analyze behavior where the objects of choice are shifted upward to the constraints or rules that will limit or restrict subsequent within-constraint choices. These attempts may apply to the individual's effort at self control or to the participation of many individuals in constitutional evaluation, with a view toward possible changes in the generalized institutional setting within which the choices of all persons in the community are made.

It is these extensions, both horizontal and vertical, of the economists' model of rational choice that raise most of the hackles of noneconomist critics, who accuse economists of disciplinary imperialism and who admonish us to "stick to our lasts." The most familiar of these criticisms may be discussed in terms of the separate elements of the model examined. There would seem to be relatively little basis for serious concern about the individualistic postulate. Those who prefer to conduct inquiry into the relationships among classes, states, and other organizations as such, and without attempts to reduce analysis to the individuals who participate, do not, in my view, pass muster as social scientists in any useful sense of the term. Or, to put it more charitably, let me say that there seems little prospect of constructive dialogue between the methodological individualists and those whose work commences with nonindividualistic organic units as building blocks.

We can engage in more constructive discussion with those research scholars who accept the individualistic postulate, but who criticize utility-maximizing models. As I have noted earlier, there is little objection to be raised as long as the arguments in the utility functions remain nonspecified. Objections are raised primarily to the predominant place economists tend to assign to private net wealth as a motive force in choice behavior, and particularly in nonmarket interactions. These objections warrant discussion here, and they allow me to call attention to the purposes of the whole scientific enterprise.

To what end do we construct and use the rational choice models of individual behavior? Do we seek only to be able to predict patterns of behavioral response to changes in constraints? Is our objective wholly descriptive? Or do we seek to use our models to assist in the same ultimate reform in the constraint structure? The central point to be made here is that the methodological legitimacy of the wealth-maximizing model may depend on the purpose to be served. If the purpose is restricted to that of empirical prediction, we seek corroboration (or nonrefutation) of the hypotheses that the model implies. On this count, the wealth-maximizing model may fall short of economists' expectations, in nonmarket settings in particular, and its critics may appropriately point to the descriptive limits of *Homo economicus*, and especially as extended beyond markets.

On the other hand, if the purpose of the wealth-maximizing model is that of offering a basis for institutional-constitutional evaluation and reform, the descriptive limits of the model may not be critically destructive to its introduction and use. "Best fit" models in the strictly predictive sense may not offer the appropriate base for making institutional judgments. A deliberately chosen bias toward the "worst case" behavioral model may insure against disproportionate losses emergent under potentially realizable worst cases.[10]

The point here was clearly understood by both David Hume and John Stuart Mill. Citations seem warranted.

> Political writers have established it as a maxim, that, in contriving any system of government, and fixing several checks and controuls of the constitution, every man ought to be supposed a *knave*, and to have no other end, in all his actions, than private interest.[11]

> The very principle of constitutional government requires it to be assumed that political power will be abused to promote the particular purpose of the holder; not because it is always so, but because such is the natural tendency of things, to guard against which is the especial use of free institutions.[12]

Let me not be misunderstood here. The argument does not defend the use of the narrowly restricted economic model of behavior independently of its descriptive qualities. The predictive model is relevant for the selection of the presumptive model of behavior that can serve as the basis for making institutional comparisons. The positivist attributes of the model of choice interact with the normative usage. My emphasis on this point here is largely to warn against the somewhat naive criticism to the effect that because politicians and bureaucrats are not really observed to behave like the economists' models, then these models provide no basis for evaluating alternative constitutional structures.

If the raison d'être of social science is to advance discussion of potential institutional-constitutional reform, we must acknowledge both the dependence of individual choice alternatives on the institutional-constitutional constraints and the possible variability of such constraints. Rational choice models, as such, remain sterile exercises until and unless the ultimate end objective for analysis is specified.

Personally, I remain unconcerned about the inclusion or exclusion of the vertical extensions of analysis, discussed above, in the domain of rational choice modeling in some taxonomic sense. I fail to see how "social science," as such, can establish a claim to legitimacy unless it can claim some contribution toward understanding human behavior and, further, that this enhanced understanding can offer assistance in institutional-constitutional change.

VII. Choice, Ignorance, and Uncertainty

One glaring omission will have seemed obvious from my treatment of rational choice models to this point. Nowhere have I introduced the critically important distinction between rational choice behavior under conditions of full knowledge and choice behavior under ignorance and/or uncertainty, a distinction that has commanded the attention of many modern choice theorists, and which affects the potential linkage between the analytical models of interaction and the predictive usefulness of these models, along with the implications for normative policy change. In a very real sense, choice, as such, assumes meaning only under conditions of ignorance/uncertainty, as Shackle has repeatedly emphasized, and the individual necessarily chooses among "alternative futures," none of which can be known before choice and only one of which can be experienced after choice. This central fact ensures that the whole utility-maximizing apparatus assumes meaning only in some reconstructive and explanatory sense. In its most general formulation, "to choose" reduces to "doing the best one can," under the particular circumstances faced, circumstances that are described by time, place, and setting.

Because of my own sympathies for the Shacklean position, which carries quasi-nihilistic methodological implications for much of social science, including economics, I may conclude by calling into question the initial wisdom of those who invited me to write this paper. I am a long way from being the most ardent advocate for rational choice models in the social sciences. On the other hand, and in partial justification for my acceptance of the challenge, I fail to see how inquiry can proceed at all unless we reduce analysis to the choice behavior of individuals. From such a base, the social sciences, broadly defined, have added and can add to our understanding and explanation of the social-interaction processes that we observe and in which we participate.

Care must be taken lest we claim too much for our "science," however, and especially lest we slip into the arrogant presumption that any "science" of behavior offers direction to some persons who seek control over the choices of others. Let us not think of the "science of economics" or of anything else as providing the basis for proffering advice to some benevolent despot. Ultimately, our "science" becomes constructively useful only if it can serve as an input into the never-ending discussion among all persons, ourselves included, on ways and means to modify the existing set of general rules so as to achieve higher levels of commonly shared values.

Notes

I am indebted to Peter Bernholz, Frank Forman, David Levy, Robert Tollison, and Viktor Vanberg for helpful comments.
   1. K. Arrow, *Social Choice and Individual Values* (New York: Wiley, 1951).
   2. See G. Becker, "Irrational Behavior and Economic Theory," *Journal of Po-*

litical Economy 70 (February, 1962): 1–13; I. Kirzner, "Rational Action and Economic Theory," *Journal of Political Economy* 70 (August, 1962): 380–85; and J. Buchanan, *What Should Economists Do?* (Indianapolis: Liberty Press, 1979).

3. A. Alchian, *Economic Forces at Work* (Indianapolis: Liberty Press, 1977).

4. G. Becker, *The Economic Approach to Human Behavior* (Chicago: University of Chicago Press, 1976).

5. G. Tullock, *The Politics of Bureaucracy* (Washington, D.C.: Public Affairs Press, 1965); W. Niskanen, *Bureaucracy and Representative Government* (Chicago: Aldine, 1971).

6. A. Downs, *An Economic Theory of Democracy* (New York: Harper, 1957); G. Tullock, *Towards a Mathematics of Politics* (Ann Arbor: University of Michigan Press, 1967).

7. G. Brennan and J. Buchanan, "Voter Choice," *American Behavioral Scientist* 28, no. 2 (November–December, 1984): 185–201.

8. J. Buchanan, "Individual Choice in Voting and the Market," *Journal of Political Economy* 62 (1954): 334–43.

9. T. Schelling, "Self-Command in Practice, in Policy, and in a Theory of Rational Choice," *American Economic Review* 74, no. 2 (May, 1984): 1–11; J. Elster, *Ulysses and the Sirens* (Cambridge: Cambridge University Press, 1979); A. M. Shefrin and R. Thaler, "An Economic Theory of Self Control," Working Paper No. 208, Center for Economic Analysis of Human Behavior and Social Institutions (Stanford, Calif.: National Bureau of Economic Research, 1977).

10. For extended treatment of this point, see G. Brennan and J. Buchanan, "The Normative Purpose of Economic Science," *International Journal of Law and Economics* 1 (1981): 155–66.

11. David Hume, "On the Independency of Parliament," *Essays, Moral, Political, and Literary* (Indianapolis: Liberty Classics, 1985), p. 42.

12. J. S. Mill, *Considerations on Representative Government*, vol. 19 of *Essays on Politics and Society, Collected Works* (Toronto: University of Toronto Press, 1977), p. 505.

4.

Man and the State

Thirty-one years ago this month (September, 1955), I arrived in Italy for a year's research on the classic Italian tradition in public finance ("scienza delle finanze"). That year had an immense influence on my intellectual development in ways that I could never have anticipated. In particular, my exposure to the classical Italian thought affected my approach to the subject matter conveyed in my title "Man and the State." I think that it is appropriate that I discuss this subject as my Mt. Pelerin Presidential Address since the ultimate sources of our liberties are to be found in our relations with, and control over the state.

Professionally, economists have dominated the membership of the Mt. Pelerin Society from its founding, but the whole thrust of the society, as initially expressed in its founding documents, has been toward elaborating the philosophical ideas without which a free society cannot exist. That is to say, political philosophy is what this society has been, is, and ought to be all about. And, as Max Hartwell indicates in another paper, in the very founding of the society, Hayek referred explicitly to his aim to set up an international academy of political philosophy.

Among our members, there are some who are able to imagine a viable society without a state. These libertarian anarchists, or anarcho-capitalists, have made major contributions in demonstrating how many of the modern state's activities might be better carried out through the spontaneous processes of the market. And these arguments are exerting an effect now in the cross-national movements toward privatization. I do not want to underestimate the importance of the challenge that the libertarian anarchists have posed for all of us who defend state action.

For most of our members, however, social order without a state is not readily imagined, or at least in any normatively preferred sense. We find it difficult to model the working properties of such a social arrangement, especially as we look at the behavior of persons in the world about us. We fall back on Thomas Hobbes to provide the description of what the genuinely stateless or lawless society might be like. The normative rejection of this model forces us to raise a whole set of issues that the libertarian anarchist need not concern himself with at all.

Of necessity, we must look at our relations with the state from several windows, to use the familiar Nietschzean metaphor. To consider two extremes, we can, with Herbert Spencer and the libertarians, consider the state as an adversary, and convert my title into "Man versus the State." At the same time, however, we must also recognize that "man is the state" in the basic sense that it describes the set of institutions through which we organize ourselves politically and collectively for the achievement of purposes that simply cannot be otherwise secured at all efficiently.

It was precisely in this dual modeling of our relations with the state that I found the Italians so helpful to my own thinking, which had already commenced to develop along the dual lines indicated. The Italians were explicit in their emphasis that some understanding of the operation of the state is required before any discussion about the assignment of this or that function to the state or about policy options in carrying out this or that function. This very simple principle was simply overlooked by most economists until the middle of this century, and with tragic consequences.

Descriptively, we know that the state fits no single model, and that the two general models mentioned do not nearly exhaust the set of the possible. The state is not a monolithic entity empowered with a monopoly of coercion and equipped with a will of its own. It is not voluntaristic in the Wicksellian sense where all collective decisions reflect unanimous agreement among all persons in the polity. It is not the embodiment of the will of the possibly shifting median voter in majoritarian processes. It is not the instrument through which a ruling coalition, temporarily in office, enriches itself at the expense of others in the polity. It is not a freely floating bureaucracy constrained only by its inner organizational logic. It is not the mere agent for a ruling class or establishment.

There are elements of each of these models, and possibly others, in the state as it variously exists in different nations. How we choose to model the state depends on the purpose to be served, on the questions to be asked, and answered.

Rather than concentrate attention on what the state is, however, it may be best to examine the position of the individual in relation to the state. In this context it may be helpful to think of the state as an organization that possesses the peculiar feature of *compulsory* membership, thereby contrasting it with other organizations in which membership is *voluntary*. As with most models, this is a limiting case. We know that states vary widely in the compulsiveness of membership and further that the costs of exit vary widely among persons. Nonetheless, the absence of a cost-effective exit option does distinguish the state from almost all other organizations. For most purposes, the individual is a member of the organization that is the state, and a member he must remain.

What does it mean to say that the individual is a member of an organization? Membership implies adherence to the rules of the organization, whatever these may be, and, in application to the state, this approach calls attention immediately to the importance of the rules, the constitution of the polity. There are two dimensions of the rules that define the organization of the state, dimensions that can vary independently. One dimension involves the extent to which the individual is subject to the state's authority, or, conversely, the extent of his private sphere protected from state intervention. The second dimension of rules concerns the structure of the decision-making process through which the state's authority is exercised. In particular, this dimension defines the participation or nonparticipation of the individual in political choice.

In a totalitarian society, there are no rule-protected spheres within which the individual is guaranteed exercise of liberty. The individual is a slave to the state-as-master, quite independently of the ways in which state decisions are made and also of the benevolence or malevolence reflected in the patterns of state choices. The answer to the question posed by Robert Nozick in his clever "Tale of the Slave" is clear.[1] Even in the final stage, where the individual is subject to the will of the majority, he remains a slave.

In nontotalitarian societies, however, there remain rule-protected spheres within which the individual has liberty of choice and action. But it is worth emphasizing that in all areas of action within which the state may act, the individual is necessarily subject to the state's authority. The well-being of the individual, however this may be measured, *depends* on the state. The individual's position in the polity is fully analogous to that of the resource owner in an economic relationship embodying *rent*. The sign, as well as the magnitude, of the rent finally assigned to the individual is beyond his own powers of control through choice. There is no *exit* option. This relationship is not affected, in its fundamental aspect, by the possible participation of the individual in collective-political decision processes, save in the limiting case where the operative voting rule is unanimity.

Recognition of the necessary vulnerability of the individual to state action does not imply that "voice" is an unimportant attribute of membership in the compulsory organization that is the state. Most persons may prefer a participatory democracy to government by an elite, even if both are bound by the constitutional-legal order to the same range of authority.

My emphasis, however, is on the critical importance of the rules that limit the exercise of the state's authority, rules that are independent of the way collective choices are made within such rules. The participatory exercise of voice in an unrestricted parliamentary democracy may be valued, but limits on the range and extent of state action may be substantively of much more significance. Possible participation in the shaping of the polity's constitution, the set of rules that constrain the potential exercise of state authority, is categorically of greater import than any guarantee of voting franchise within a given constitutional structure.[2]

In a very real sense, the set of rules that defines the respective spheres for state and private action locate the individual along the freedom-slavery spectrum. Once these rules are settled, and independently of how they may have been derived, and/or how much or how little voice the individual is allowed to exercise in shaping state action, the individual remains a *subject* within the domain of the state's constituted authority. Within the authorized sphere of collective action, the individual remains dependent on the state. Dependence need not, of course, imply impoverishment; the individual may fare well or poorly under the dependence umbrella. But it is self-evident that recognition of dependency status invokes a behavioral pattern quite different from that which genuine independence affords.

My argument may seem fully consistent with that of the libertarian anarchists who see individuals as subjects of the state on the one hand and as adversaries of the state along the boundary lines of state power. I part company with the libertarian anarchists, however, as noted above, when I accept, with Hobbes, that individuals would, if given genuine constitutional choice, grant some authority to the state, even in the full recognition that such a grant of authority comes with the certain sacrifice of individual autonomy.

We should never be trapped in the delusion that the enhancement of the state's authority to "do good things for us collectively" involves no cost to use as free individuals. But recognizing that this cost exists is not the same as saying that it is a cost we shall never pay. The cost in liberty will, over some ranges of state action, be lower than the expected benefit from the exercise of state authority within the defined limits. We are able to satisfy our preferences, to achieve a higher level of utility, where some of our liberties have been sacrificed and where there does exist a well-defined but limited domain for the exercise of the coercive power of the state.

But we must recognize full well that, within the limits of the authority so assigned to the state, we are necessarily subjects, or, more dramatically, slaves, to the state, as master. The slave may, indeed, enjoy a higher standard of living than the free man, but he is a fool if he neglects for a moment the elementary fact that he remains a slave. In a very real sense, the constitutional contract that sets the limits of state authority over individuals is a slave contract, and we sell ourselves into slavery with each and every extension of the state's power.

Why is a slavery contract, as such, different from any contract? Why do all of us (except possibly for a few extreme libertarians) think that the slavery contract is not normally an ethically legitimate embodiment of voluntary exchange? We reject such an "exchange" because it does not allow for a post-contract viable exit option; the person who finds himself in a slave relationship does not have effective alternatives. Membership in a state embodies this attribute of the slave contract to the extent that the state, as such, possesses the authority to direct the activities of the individual, including the authority to extract a share of the resource or product that is nominally under the individual's "private" possession. We are dependents, slaves, rent recipients (these are equivalent terms for purposes of my argument here) to the extent that we are unable to escape the extractions demanded by the state. (Bruno Leoni recognized this point all along; it took me two decades to shuck the normative trappings of orthodox economics and to write in defense of tax loopholes.)

Confusion arises here because there seems to be no identifiable master in the democratic polity. As an individual, a person may well acknowledge his dependence on the state, but he may also recognize that there seems to be no single person or group that can be identified as master. In the idealized model of majoritarian democracy, the individual's fate depends on a process, and, in the limit, no one person has more than minimal influence in determining the result. We are, in such a setting, all "slaves without masters."

We are, however, slaves or subjects only to the extent that the state is authorized to act, quite independently of the decision rules through which it operates (again, save in the limiting case of an unanimity rule). We are free within those spheres of our activity that are protected from state intrusion by effective constitutional order.

The monumental folly of the past two centuries has been the presumption that, so long as the state operates in accordance with democratic procedures (free and periodic elections, open franchise, open entry for parties, candidates, and interests, majority or plurality voting rules) the individual does, indeed, have insurance against exploitation, quite apart from any viable exit option. Modern states have been allowed to invade increasing areas of "private space" under the pretense of democratic process. (In saying this, I do not want to imply that the legal form of state expansion is unimportant. States that broadly adhere to the rule of law are, of course, more protective of individual liberty than states which discriminate among persons arbitrarily, even with the same level of total activity.)

Few members of this society would disagree with the primary thrust of my argument here. Almost all of you come down squarely behind the classically liberal notion that markets work and governments fail, at least at the level of general presuppositions. But I hope that my argument here has shifted the emphasis somewhat. Failure or success has too often been measured in terms of the standard economists' criterion of efficiency, the ability to get goods and services produced and distributed, to add to the wealth of nations. This emphasis has, I think, been mistaken, at least in part. Markets may fail against the efficiency standard, even in some relative sense. But even in failure markets allow persons to retain exit options without which liberty cannot be secured. The state may succeed against the efficiency standard, even in some relative sense. But even in success, the state necessarily closes off (or narrowly restricts) the exit option for its members, implying necessarily that while liberty may be allowed, it cannot be guaranteed. In retrospect, it seems singularly unfortunate that Adam Smith chose to entitle his great work *The Wealth of Nations* rather than *The System of Natural Liberty*.

Finally, let me express the main point of these remarks by reference to Hayek's notable (and notorious) *The Road to Serfdom* (1944). In my view, the thesis should not be that an initiation of state intrusion must lead, ultimately, to man's serfdom to the state. The thesis should be interpreted to suggest that *any intrusion* by the state ensures man's serfdom, *within the limits defined by the intrusion*. Man is, and must remain, a slave to the state. But it is critically and vitally important to recognize that 10 percent slavery is different from 50 percent.

Notes

This paper was presented as the Presidential Address at the 1986 Mt. Pelerin Society General Meeting. I am indebted to Viktor Vanberg and Hartmut Kliemt for helpful suggestions.

1. "Tale of the Slave," in *Anarchy, State, and Utopia* (New York: Basic Books, 1974), pp. 290–92.

2. See F. A. Hayek, *The Constitution of Liberty* (Chicago: University of Chicago Press, 1960), p. 103.

5.

Constitutional Economics

"Constitutional economics" (constitutional political economy) was introduced as a term to define and to classify a distinct strand of research inquiry and related policy discourse in the 1970s and beyond. The subject matter is not new or novel, and it may be argued that "constitutional economics" is more closely related to the work of Adam Smith and the classical economists than its modern "nonconstitutional" counterpart. Both areas of inquiry involve positive analysis that is ultimately aimed at contributing to the discussion of policy questions. The difference lies in the level of or the setting for analysis, which in turn implies communication with different audiences.

Orthodox economic analysis, whether this be interpreted in Marshallian or Walrasian terms, attempts to explain the choices of economic agents, their interactions one with another, and the results of these interactions, within the existing legal-institutional-constitutional structure of the polity. Normative considerations enter through the efficiency criteria of theoretical welfare economics, and policy options are evaluated in terms of these criteria. The policy analyst, building on the analysis, presents his results, whether explicitly or implicitly, to the political decision-makers, who then make some ultimate determination from among the available set. In this role the policy analyst directly, and the theorist, indirectly, are necessarily advising governmental decision-makers, whoever these may be.

By both contrast and comparison, constitutional economic analysis attempts to explain the working properties of alternative sets of legal-institutional-constitutional rules that constrain the choices and activities of economic and political agents, the rules that define the framework within which the ordinary choices of economic and political agents are made. In this sense, constitutional economics involves a "higher" level of inquiry than orthodox economics; it must incorporate the results of the latter along with many less-sophisticated subdisciplines. Normative considerations enter the analysis in a much more complex manner than through the artificially straightforward efficiency criteria. Alternative sets of rules must be evaluated in some sense analogously to the ranking of policy options within a specified institutional structure, but the epistemological content of the "efficiency" criteria becomes more exposed.

The constitutional economist, precisely because the subject matter is the analysis of alternate sets of rules, has nothing to offer by way of policy advice to political agents who act within defined rules. In this sense, constitutional economics is not appropriately included within "policy science" at all. At another level, however, the whole exercise is aimed at offering guidance to those who participate in the discussion of constitutional change. In other words, constitutional economics offers a potential for normative advice to the member of the continuing constitutional convention, whereas orthodox economics offers a potential for advice to the practicing politician. In a real sense, constitutional economics examines the *choice of constraints* as opposed to the *choice within constraints,* and as this terminology suggests, the disciplinary attention of economists has almost exclusively been placed on the second of these two problems.

A preliminary illustration of the distinction may be drawn from the economics of monetary policy. The constitutional economist is not directly concerned with determining whether monetary ease or monetary restrictiveness is required for furthering stabilization objectives in a particular setting. On the other hand, he is directly concerned with evaluating the properties of alternative monetary regimes (e.g., rule-directed versus discretionary, fiat versus commodity standards). The ultimate objective of analysis is the choice among the institutions within which political agents act. The predicted behavior of these agents is incorporated in the analysis of alternative sets of constraints.

I. Constitutional Economics and Classical Political Economy

As suggested, constitutional economics is related to classical political economy and it may be considered to be an important component of a more general revival of the classical emphasis, and particularly as represented in the works of Adam Smith. (The closely related complementary components are discussed briefly in Section III.) One obvious aim of the classical political economists was to offer an explanation and an understanding of how markets operate without detailed political direction. In this respect, orthodox neoclassical economics follows directly in the classical tradition. But the basic classical analysis of the working of markets was only a necessary step toward the more comprehensive purpose of the whole exercise, which was that of demonstrating that, precisely because markets function with tolerable efficiency independently of political direction, a powerful normative argument for constitutional structure exists. That is to say, Adam Smith was engaged directly in comparing alternative institutional structures, alternative sets of constraints within which economic agents make choices. In this comparative analysis, he found it essential to model the working properties of a nonpoliticized economy, which did not exist in reality, as well as the working properties of a highly politicized mercantilist economy, which could be directly observed.

There is no need here to enter the lists on either side of the "ideas have consequences" debate. We know that the economy of Great Britain was effectively depoliticized in the late eighteenth and early nineteenth centuries, and from the analysis of Smith and his classical fellow travelers there emerged both positive understanding of economic process and philosophical argument for a particular regime. The normative argument for laissez faire was, perhaps inevitably, intermingled with the positive analysis of interaction within a particular structure of constraints, essentially those that describe the minimal, protective, or night-watchman state. Economics, as a social science, emerged, but, in the process, attention was diverted from the institutional structure. Even the predicted normative reaction against the overly zealous extension of the laissez faire argument was couched in "market failure" terms, rather than in the Smithian context of institutional comparison. The early socialist critique of market order, both in its Marxist and non-Marxist variants, was almost exclusively negative in that it elaborated putative failures of markets within an unexamined set of legal-political rules while it neglected analysis of the alternative rules that any correction of the alleged failures might require. Only with the debates on socialist calculation in the decades prior to World War II did the issues of comparative structure come to be examined.

It was only in the half century after these debates that political economy, inclusively defined, returned, in fits and starts, to its classical tradition. Given the legal order of the protective state (the protection of property and the enforcement of contracts), we now know that under some conditions "markets fail" when evaluated against idealized criteria, whether these be "efficiency," "justice," or other abstract norms. We also know that "politics fails" when evaluated by the same criteria. Any positive analysis that purports to be of use in an ultimate normative judgment must reflect an informed comparison of the working properties of alternative sets of rules or constraints. This analysis is the domain of Constitutional Economics.

II. Constitutional Economics and Social Philosophy

Classical political economy emerged from moral philosophy, and its propounders considered their efforts to fall naturally within the limits of philosophical discourse. As a modern embodiment, constitutional economics is similarly located, regardless of disciplinary fragmentation. How can persons live together in liberty, peace, and prosperity? This central question of social philosophy requires continuing contributions from many specialists in inquiry, surely including those of the constitutional economists. By their focus directly on the ultimate selection of a set of constraining rules within which ordinary social interaction takes place, constitutional economists remove themselves at least one stage further from the false position of "social engineer" than their counterparts in orthodox economics. Precisely because there is no apparently simple evaluative criterion analogous to "allocative efficiency" at hand, the constitutional economist is less tempted to array alternatives as if an unexamined criterion commands universal assent. The artificial abstraction of "social utility" is likely to be less appealing to those who concentrate on choices among constraints than to those who examine choices within constraints.

If, however, there is no maximand, how can ultimate normative consequence emerge? In this respect, one contribution lies at the level of positive analysis rather than in a too-hasty leap into normative evaluation. Classical political economy contains the important principle of spontaneous coordination, the great discovery of the eighteenth century. This principle states that, within the legal umbrella of the minimal state and given certain conditions, the market "works." Even if in the principle's modern embellishment we must add "warts and all," we still have come a long way toward a more comprehensive understanding of the alternatives for social order. To the extent that his efforts expand the public understanding of this principle, in application to all institutional settings, the constitutional economist remains under less apparent compulsion to advance his own privately preferred "solutions" to the ultimate choice among regimes.

III. The New Political Economy

Care should be taken not to claim too much for constitutional economics, especially if a narrow definition is used. As noted earlier, this research program, by designation, emerged in the 1970s to describe efforts at analyzing the effects of alternative sets of rules, as opposed to analyzing choices made within existing and unexamined structures. In a more comprehensive overview of developments after World War II, constitutional economics takes its place among an intersecting set of several research programs, all of which have roots in classical political economy. Critical emphases differ among the separate programs, but each reflects efforts to move beyond the relatively narrow confines of orthodox neoclassical economics.

In continental Europe, the whole set of subdisciplines is included under the rubric of the "New Political Economy." Within this set we can place (1) public choice, from which constitutional economics emerged, (2) economics of property rights, (3) law and economics or economic analysis of law, (4) political economy of regulation, (5) the new institutional economics, and (6) the new economic history. Defined imperialistically, constitutional economics would parallel the inclusive term and embrace all of these programs, since some attention is drawn in each case of the legal-political constraints within which economic and political agents choose. Differences can be identified, however, and it may be useful to summarize some of these here. Public choice, in its nonconstitutional aspects of inquiry, concentrates attention on analyses of alternative political choice structures and on behavior within those structures. Its focus is on predictive models of political interaction, and is a preliminary but necessary stage in the more general constitutional inquiry. The economics of property rights, law and economics, and the political economy of regulation remain somewhat closer to orthodox economic theory than constitutional economics or public choice. The standard efficiency norm remains central to these subdisciplines, both as an explanatory benchmark and as a normative ideal. The new institutional economics is directed more toward the interactions within particular institutional forms rather than toward the comprehensive structure of political rules.[1] Some elements of the new economic history closely parallel constitutional economics, with, of course, a historical rather than a comparative emphasis.[2]

IV. Presuppositions

Constitutional economics, along with the related research programs mentioned above, shares a central methodological presupposition with both its precursor, classical political economy, and its counterpart in modern neoclassical microeconomics. Only individuals choose and act. Collectivities as such neither choose nor act, and analysis that proceeds as if they do is not within the accepted scientific canon. Social aggregates are considered only as the results of choices made and actions taken by individuals. The emphasis on explaining nonintended aggregative results of interaction has carried through since the early insights of the Scottish moral philosophers. An aggregative result that is observed but which cannot, somehow, be factored down and explained by the choices of individuals stands as a challenge to the scholar rather than as some demonstration of nonindividualistic organic unity.

Methodological individualism, as summarized above, is almost universally accepted by economists who work within mainstream, or non-Marxist, traditions. A philosophical complement of this position that assumes a central role in constitutional economics is much less widely accepted and is often explicitly rejected. A distinction must be drawn between the methodological individualism that builds on individual choice as the basic unit of analysis and a second presupposition that locates the ultimate sources of value exclusively in individuals.

The first of these presuppositions without the second leaves relatively little scope for the derivation of constitutional structures from individual preferences. There is no conceptual normative bridge between those interests and values that individuals might want to promote and those nonindividualistic values that are presumed to serve as ultimate normative criteria. The whole constitutional exercise loses most if not all of its raison d'être in such a setting. If the ultimate values which are to be called upon to inform the choices among institutions are nonindividualistic, then there is, at best, only an instrumental argument for using individually expressed preferences in the process of discovering those values.

On the other hand, if the second presupposition concerning the location of the ultimate sources of value is accepted, there is no *other* means of deriving a "logic of rules" than that of utilizing individually expressed interests. At base, the second presupposition implies democracy in governance, along with the accompanying precept that this structure of decision-making only takes on normative legitimacy with the prefix "constitutional" appended to it.

V. Wicksell as Precursor

The single most important precursor to constitutional economics in its modern variant is Knut Wicksell, who was individualist in both of the senses discussed above. In his basic work on fiscal theory (*Finanztheoretische Untersuchungen*, 1896), Wicksell called attention to the significance of the rules within which choices are made by political agents, and he recognized that efforts at reform must be directed toward changes in the rules for making decisions rather than toward modifying expected results through influence on the behavior of the actors.[3]

In order to take these steps, Wicksell needed some criterion by which the possible efficacy of a proposed change in rules could be judged. He introduced the now-familiar unanimity or consensus test, which is carried over into constitutional economics and also allows the whole research program to be related closely to the contractarian tradition in political philosophy. The relationship between the Wicksellian and the Paretian criteria is also worthy of note. If only individual evaluations are to count, and if the only source of information about such evaluations is the revealed choice behavior of individuals themselves, then no change could be considered "efficient" until and unless some means could be worked out to bring all persons (and groups) into agreement. If no such scheme can be arranged, the observing political economist remains silent. The Wicksellian contribution allowed the modern economist to bring the comparative analysis of rules or institutions within a methodological framework that utilizes and builds on the efficiency criterion, which, when interpreted as indicated, does not require departure from either of the individualistic presuppositions previously discussed.

VI. *Homo economicus* in Constitutional Choice

Constitutional economics, as distinct from the complementary research programs on political constitutions that are within the boundaries of law, political science, sociology, and other disciplines, goes beyond the logical presuppositions of individualism to incorporate nontautological models of individual utility maximization. *Homo economicus* takes a central role in comparative institutional inquiry. Individuals are assumed to seek their own interests, which are defined so as to retain operational content.

Two quite different arguments can be made in support of this postulate in constitutional economics. The first is based simply on methodological consistency. To the extent that individuals are modeled as utility maximizers as they participate in market relationships, there would seem to be no basis for postulating a shift in motivation as they behave within nonmarket constraints. There is at least a strong presumption that individuals do not undergo character transformation when they shift from roles as buyers or sellers in the marketplace to roles as voters, taxpayers, beneficiaries, politicians, or bureaucrats in the political process. A more sophisticated reason for postulating consistency in behavior lies in the usefulness of the model for the whole exercise of institutional comparison. If the purpose is to compare the effects of alternative sets of constraints, some presumption of behavioral consistency over the alternatives is necessary in order to identify those differences in results that are attributable to the differences in constraints.

A second argument for introducing *Homo economicus* in constitutional economics is both more complex and more important. It is also the source of confusion because it is necessary to distinguish carefully between the use of *Homo economicus* in predictive social science, specifically in positive public choice and in neoclassical economics, and in constitutional economics. There is an argument for using the construction in the latter, even if there are demonstrated empirical limits on the explanatory power of the model in the former.

The argument is implicit in the work of the classical economists. It was stated as a methodological principle by both David Hume and J. S. Mill.

> Political writers have established it as a maxim, that, in contriving any system of government, and fixing several checks and controuls of the constitution, every man ought to be supposed a *knave*, and to have no other end, in all his actions, than private interest.[4]

> The very principle of constitutional government requires it to be assumed that political power will be abused to promote the particular purpose of the holder; not because it is always so, but because such is the natural tendency of things, to guard against which is the especial use of free institutions.[5]

The ultimate purpose of analyzing alternative sets of rules is to inform the choice among these sets. The predicted operating properties of each alternative must be examined, and these properties will reflect the embodied models of individual behavior within the defined constraints. Behavioral departures from the presumptive models used in deriving the operating properties will, of course, be expected. But the costs of errors may not be symmetrically distributed around the single best predictive model. The predicted differential loss from behavioral departures from a model that involves "optimistic" motivational assumptions may be much larger than the predicted differential gain if the model is shown to be an accurate predictor. Hence, comparative evaluation of an institution based on an altruistic model of behavior should take into account the possible nonlinearity in the loss function that describes departures from the best estimates. (In legal practice, formal contracts include protections against worst-case behavior patterns.) In constitutional choice, therefore, there is an argument for incorporating models of individual behavior that presume more narrowly defined self-interest than any empirical record may warrant.[6]

VII. Applications

Applications of constitutional economics, as a research program, have emerged in several settings. First, consider taxation. Post-Marshallian economic theory, either in its partial or general equilibrium model, was often applied to tax incidence. Analysis was directed toward predicting the effects of an exogenously imposed tax on the private economizing behavior of persons in their varying capacities as demanders and suppliers of goods and services in the marketplace. Building on this base of positive analysis, normative welfare economics allows a ranking among alternative equi-revenue tax instruments in terms of the Paretian standard. In both the positive and normative aspects, neoclassical tax theory embodies the presumption that taxes, as such, are exogenous to the choice process.

The major contribution of modern public choice, as a subdiscipline in its own right, has been that of endogenizing political decision-making. In its direct emphasis, public choice theory examines the political decision rules that exist with a view toward making some predictions about just what sort of tax institutions or tax instruments will emerge. Constitutional economics, as an extended research program that emerges from public choice, goes a step further and uses the inputs from both neoclassical economics and public choice theory to analyze how alternative political rules might generate differing tax rules.

The relevant constitutional choice may be that of granting government authority to levy taxes on Tax Base A or Tax Base B. Suppose that under the neoclassical equi-revenue assumption, analysis demonstrates that the taxing of A generates a lower excess burden than the taxing of B. Analysis of the political choice process may demonstrate, however, that government, if given the authority to tax A, will tend to levy a tax that will generate *more* revenue than would be forthcoming under an authority to tax B. The equi-revenue alternatives may not be effective political alternatives under any plausibly acceptable modeling of the behavior of political agents. Once this simple point is recognized, the normative significance of the neoclassical ranking of tax instruments is reduced. Discussion shifts necessarily to the level of interaction between political decision structures and fiscal institutions.

A second application of constitutional economics is found in the post-Keynesian discussion of budgetary policy. The Keynesian advocacy of the use of governmental budgets to accomplish macroeconomic objectives was based on a neglect of the political decision structure. The proclivity of democratic governments to prefer spending over taxing, and hence to bias budgets toward deficit, is readily explained in elementary public choice theory.[7] This essential step in public choice reasoning leads naturally to inquiry into the relationships between the constraints that may be placed on political choice and predicted patterns of budgetary outcomes. Out of this intensely practical, and important, application of constitutional economics emerged the intellectual bases for the normative argument that, in the post-Keynesian era when moral constraints on political agents have lost much of their previous effectiveness, formal rules limiting deficit financing may be required to ensure responsible fiscal decisions. In the modern setting, such rules would limit spending rates. But it is perhaps worth noting that, in the political environment of Sweden in the 1890s, Wicksell advanced analytically similar proposals for reform in the expectation that, if the suggested reforms should be implemented, public sector outlay would increase.

The analysis of alternative rules for the "transfer constitution" represents a third application of constitutional economics. With the 1971 publication of John Rawls's, *A Theory of Justice*, renewed attention came to be placed on principles of distributive justice.[8] Although explicitly preconstitutional, Rawls's work has a close relationship with the efforts to develop criteria for political and economic rules of social interaction. Economists, as well as other social scientists and social philosophers, have increasingly come to recognize that the untrammeled interplay of interest-group politics is unlikely to promote objectives for distributive justice. Analysis of how this politics operates in the making of fiscal transfers suggests that principled adjustments in the post-tax, post-transfer distribution of values is likely to be achieved only if the institutional rules severely restrict the profitability of investment in attempts to subvert the transfer process.

Further applications include the regulatory constitution, along with the organization of public enterprises. In its inclusive definition, constitutional economics becomes the analytical route through which institutional relevance is reintroduced into a sometimes sterile social science. In its less inclusive definition, constitutional economics, along with its related and complementary research programs, restores "political" to "economy," thereby bringing a coherence that was absent during the long hiatus during which "economics" made putative claims to independent status.

Notes

1. E. G. Furubotn, and R. Richter, eds., "The New Institutional Economics—A Symposium," *Zeitschrift für die gesamte Staatswissenschaft* 140 (1980); Bruno Frey, "A New View of Economics: Comparative Analysis of Institutions," *Scelte Pubbliche* 1 (1984): 17–28.

2. Douglass C. North and Robert P. Thomas, *The Rise of the Western World: A New Economic History* (Cambridge: Cambridge University Press, 1973).

3. Knut Wicksell, *Finanztheoretische Untersuchungen* (Jena: Gustav Fischer, 1896). Central portions of this work are published in English as "A New Principle of Just Taxation," in *Classics in the Theory of Public Finance*, ed. R. A. Musgrave and A. T. Peacock (London: Macmillan and Co., 1959).

4. David Hume, "On the Independency of Parliament," *Essays, Moral, Political, and Literary* (Indianapolis: Liberty Classics, 1985), p. 42.

5. J. S. Mill, *Considerations on Representative Government*, vol. 19 of *Essays on Politics and Society, Collected Works* (Toronto: University of Toronto Press, 1977), p. 505.

6. Geoffrey Brennan and James Buchanan, *The Power to Tax: Analytical Foundations of the Fiscal Constitution* (Cambridge: Cambridge University Press, 1980).

7. James M. Buchanan and Richard E. Wagner, *Democracy in Deficit: The Political Legacy of Lord Keynes* (New York: Academic Press, 1977).

8. John Rawls, *A Theory of Justice* (Cambridge, Mass.: Harvard University Press, 1971).

Part II.
APPLICATIONS

6.

Toward a Theory of Yes-No Voting

WITH ROGER L. FAITH

The formal theory of majority-rule voting has dealt almost entirely with the unique selection of a single candidate(s) or motion(s) from a set of alternatives greater than two. The analysis presumes that there is only a single group or collective decision to be made, a single "election," or a single "proposition."[1] This orthodox conceptual setting for collective choice is necessary to generate the possibility of the cyclically rotating, and hence disequilibrium, set of outcomes on the one hand and for the median-voter dominated equilibrium outcome on the other. If the number of alternatives in the choice set is limited to two, simple majority rule voting yields unambiguous results provided only that we assume an odd number of voters, with each voter assumed to have strictly ordered preferences. In the orthodox voting-model setting, few problems of analytical interest seem to arise in the single pairwise choice between two alternatives, for example, between approval and disapproval of a proposition.

When the voting population is presented with a whole set of independent propositions, however, each one of which is to be resolved by simple "yes-no," "up-down," or "approve-disapprove" majority voting, questions of considerable analytical interest do arise. To our knowledge no one has discussed or investigated the analogues and contrasts between yes-no voting and the conventional, multi-alternative, majority-rule voting. The relative neglect of the properties of yes-no voting under majority rule is itself puzzling since many real-world collective choice institutions formally operate in this way. Examples that come to mind include zoning boards, referenda and initiatives; in several states judges are reelected on a yes-no basis.

I. The Basic Model

The institutional setting we wish to analyze is one in which there are several propositions to be settled by simple majority rule. The propositions are characterized by dichotomous choice—yes or no—and counterproposals are not permitted.[2] The propositions are independent in the sense that none, some, or all may be approved as a result of the voting process. There is no technological or consumptive complementarity or mutual exclusivity among propositions. With respect to voters, we assume they vote without strategic considerations. Vote trading or other mechanisms by which differences in preference intensities are resolved are precluded here. Each voter makes his or her own subjective evaluation of each proposition being voted upon. Note that this assumption does not preclude representation, where an individual voter acts as an agent or "representative" of some constituency or even for some special interest group.

For purposes of exposition let us initially consider a board of zoning appeals made up of three members. Their job is to vote, yes or no, on separate requests for zoning variances. Several requests are allowed to accumulate before any voting occurs, say, before the regular monthly meeting of the board. Suppose that six different, and independent, requests for zoning variances are placed on the agenda facing the three-person board.

As a first step, assume that the individual evaluations (or subjective benefit-cost computations) of the different requests for variance are such that all board members ordinally rank the six requests in the same way. This does not mean that evaluations for all six proposals are identical over all three members in some cardinal sense—the precise benefit-cost ratios need not be equal. If such a level of "objectivity" could be reached, no decision problem would arise and all members would agree unanimously on the number and identity of proposals to be approved. Equivalence of ordinal rankings means only that if each member were asked to rank or array the six proposals according to his/her subjective estimates of benefits and costs, the three rankings would be the same. This assumption of equivalent ordinal ranking does not tell us anything about how many proposals are looked upon favorably or unfavorably by the individual voters. Two voters could have the same ranking with one voter approving all proposals while the other voter approves none.

A hypothetical set of ordinal rankings is illustrated in Table 6-1, where the rows represent the six requests, numbered 1 through 6, and the columns represent the three voters, i, j, and k. The vote of each member is either "yes" (Y) or "no" (N) on each request as it comes under consideration.

Table 6-1. Yes/no voting on a set of proposals

	i	j	k
1	Y	Y	Y
2	Y	Y	Y
3	Y	Y	N
4	Y	N	N
5	N	N	N
6	N	N	N

II. Analogues and Contrasts to Conventional Majority-Rule Voting Models

The three board members of Table 6-1 differ in the number of requests approved. Member *i* votes "yes" on two-thirds of the requests, *j* votes "yes" on one-half of the requests, and *k* votes "yes" on only one-third of the requests. Stated alternatively, the three voters or board members differ along what we might term the "proclivity to affirm" or "yea-saying" dimension.[3] If the six proposals are generically equivalent, for example, all requests for zoning variances are to allow the development of separate and unrelated entrepreneurial projects, the underlying dimension might be classified on some scale of optimism-pessimism about the potential productivity of the projects. For other kinds of proposals, the underlying dimension might fall along ideological lines such as "liberal-conservative." Member *i* tends to evaluate benefits highly and costs minimally, while member *k* estimates costs highly and benefits minimally. Member *j* falls somewhere in between.

Under majority rule voting, requests 1, 2, and 3 will be approved while requests 4 through 6 will fail to secure the requisite majority of "yes" votes. This set of outcomes, not coincidentally, is precisely that set of outcomes desired by member *j*. In a very real sense, *j*'s decision-making status is the same as that of the median voter in conventional voting models where a single alternative is to be selected from a set of mutually exclusive alternatives and where individual preferences are single-peaked. In yes-no voting the analogue to the single-peakedness is the equivalence of the ordinal rankings of the separate propositions across all voters. The board member whose position is median on the "proclivity to affirm" dimension tends to dominate the results. The difference between this "median voter" and the conventional one is that here "median" is not defined with reference to the evaluation of a set of separate mutually exclusive alternatives from which one is to be selected. Rather "median" is defined with respect to the relative frequency of favorable votes cast in a set of independent proposals.

The relationship between the "median voter" construction in conventional models and that introduced here can be illustrated by a modification of our example. Consider a school board facing separate proposals for spending on six new schools, each costing $1 million. Voter i, in our construction, will approve four such proposals, voter j three, and voter k two. But note that this example might be translated into a single-election, conventional model by introducing the total budget dimension, in which case voter j, who prefers the $3 million outlay, will dominate the result.

It is, however, highly restrictive to assume that the ordinal rankings of the separate projects are identical over all board members, perhaps even more restrictive than to assume single-peakedness in preferences for all voters in the conventional majority-rule voting models. Since the benefit-cost calculus must in any case be highly subjective, it seems apparent that the ordinal rankings would probably differ across voters or board members. How would this affect our "median voter" result? As we shall see shortly, interpersonal differences in ordinal rankings need not make our "proclivity to affirm" dimension lose all of its descriptive or predictive value.

Under nonidentical ordinal rankings, the comparisons of our model of yes-no voting with the model of majority-rule voting in the absence of single-peakedness are both interesting and complex. A characteristic feature of the latter voting model is the absence of any stable equilibrium. In contrast, our model of yes-no voting always yields a stable and unique voting outcome. Despite variation in the ordinal rankings across voters, one need only count up the number of "yes" votes cast on each proposal to see if a proposition is or is not approved. There will always be a definitive number of proposals approved; the voting process terminates. But will the median voter, the person who approves the median number of proposals, still dominate the proceedings? In general, the answer is negative. That is, there is an analogue between our model of yes-no voting on several issues and the cyclical-majority model in terms of the loss of direct correspondence between the preferences of the median voter and the actual set of emergent outcomes.

Despite the fact that there will be a unique set of outcomes given *any* set of individual evaluations, one cannot predict, in advance, that these outcomes will correspond to those desired by the board member who is median in terms of our "proclivity to affirm" scale. However, the median voter does not lose all correspondence with the voting outcome, at least for a variety of different distributions of "proclivities for yea-saying" among voters. In the conventional model with a majority-rule cycle, by contrast, the voter with "median preferences" is no more likely to have his preferences satisfied than any other voter within the range of cyclical results. Median preferences are, of course, hard to define in the cyclical or rotating majority case, but for the sake of comparison we may say that along some dimension measured independently of the voting process, the "median voter" is defined as the one whose *first preference* is median with respect to the first preference of other voters. As the voting outcomes rotate among the possible outcomes, no voter is more successful than others in the relevant set of achieving his/her most preferred outcome.

III. Yes-No Voting Power Indices

Having claimed that in yes-no voting the person with median proclivities to affirm has, in most cases, a greater likelihood of having his/her preferences satisfied than his/her counterparts, the question of interest is under what conditions is our claim valid? How likely is the median voter to have his/her preferences satisfied vis-à-vis other nonmedian voters?[4]

As mentioned above, given any pattern of ordinal rankings of propositions by the members of the voting group, a definitive set of outcomes results. And by association, some members' own preferences over the defined set of propositions correspond more closely with the set of outcomes than do others'. There is, of course, no reason to assume that the voter with the greater number of issues resolved in his/her favor is more "satisfied" in some utility sense. Such an implication would, of course, require an assumption about the intensities and interpersonal comparabilities of individual preferences.

We can, however, in some expected sense identify that voter who will have the greatest number of issues resolved in accord with his/her own preferences. (We shall, largely for purposes of expositional economy, refer to the relative positions of voters along such an "ability to have preferences satisfied" scale as "power," but the restricted meaning of this term should be kept in mind.) Consider again the example in Table 6-1. In order to ascertain voter i's chance of having his/her way on each of the six issues, we assume, without loss of generality, that the six issues are numbered in accordance with i's subjective benefit-cost ratios with issues 1 through 4 having benefit-cost ratios greater than one and issues 5 and 6 ratios less than one. We do not specify the ordinal rankings for voters j and k, but we retain the "proclivity to affirm" parameters for these two voters at one-half and one-third. Given any conceivable evaluation of the propositions by voters j and k, the probability of any given proposal securing majority approval *given that* i *votes "yes"* is .67. The probability of a given issue not passing *given that* i *votes "no"* is .83.[5] The *power index* for voter i can now be defined as the number of times i votes "yes" multiplied by the probability of majority approval plus the number of times i votes "no" multiplied by the probability of majority disapproval. Hence, in the current example the *power index* for i is $(4 \times .67) + (2 \times .83) = 4.34$. Similar calculations for voters j and k yield power indices of 4.67 and 4.34, respectively. Note that, as claimed earlier, voter j, the person with the median proclivity to approve propositions, has the highest power index.[6]

The most straightforward interpretation of the power index is that it measures the expected number of propositions to be resolved in a particular voter's favor. That is, over repeated votes taken on the same set of six propositions by the same three voters with fixed preferences, voters i, j, and k can expect to have 4.34, 4.67, and 4.34 propositions, respectively, resolved in accord with their preferences. In order to compare and contrast indices when the number of proposals vary, we can "normalize" by dividing the power indices by the number of propositions yielding power indices of .72, .78, and .72 respectively. These numbers are interpreted as the expected fraction of group decisions resolved in the three voters' respective favors.

To see how the power index changes and the effect on the median voter's influence when the parameters of the model change we shall initially hold the number of voters fixed at three. Let N equal the number of propositions under consideration, and V_i, V_j, and V_k equal the number of "yes" votes that voters i, j, and k, respectively, are expected to cast when presented with N independent propositions. Thus, V_i/N equals the probability of voter i voting "yes" on a given proposal. Further, assume that $V_i > V_j > V_k$. Generalizing the formulation presented above for the simple case, the power indices (PI) of the three voters can be written:

$$PI(i) = \frac{1}{N} [V_iV_j + V_iV_k - V_jV_k + N(N - V_i)]$$

$$(1) \quad PI(j) = \frac{1}{N} [V_iV_j + V_jV_k - V_iV_k + N(N - V_j)]$$

$$PI(k) = \frac{1}{N} [V_iV_k + V_jV_k - V_iV_j + N(N - V_k)]$$

It follows that:

$$(2) \quad PI(j) - PI(k) = (2V_i - N)(V_j - V_k)/N.$$

and that given $V_i > V_j > V_k$,

(3) $PI(j) - PI(k)\{\leqq\}0$ if $V_i\{\leqq\}N/2$.

Further, it follows that:

(4) $PI(j) - PI(i)\{\leqq\}0$ if $V_k\{\geqq\}N/2$.

From conditions (3) and (4) we see that the median voter has the highest power index if

(5) $\dfrac{V_i}{N} > \dfrac{1}{2} > \dfrac{V_k}{N}$. [7]

Thus, in the three-voter case, the power of the median voter depends solely on the "proclivities to affirm" of the two extreme voters. The example in Table 6-1 where $V_i/N = .67$ and $V_k/N = .33$ satisfies the above condition, and, as we saw, voter j has the highest power index. It also follows from (3) and (4) that if either of the inequalities in (5) is an equality, the median voter shares the highest power index with that voter whose proclivity to affirm is not equal to one-half. For example, if $V_i = 3$, $V_j = 2$, and $V_k = 1$, implying that $V_i/N = \frac{1}{2}$, the power indices of i, j, and k are 4.16, 4.83, and 4.83, respectively; while if $V_i = 5$, $V_j = 4$, and $V_k = 3$, implying that $V_k/N = \frac{1}{2}$, the power indices are 4.83, 4.83, and 4.16, respectively. Finally, it follows from (3) and (4) that if all voters have proclivities to affirm greater (less) than $\frac{1}{2}$, the voter with the highest (lowest) proclivity has the highest power index. These relationships hold regardless of the absolute difference between any two voters' proclivity to "yea-say."

Before illustrating the effect of adding more voters, some simple comparative statics can be derived for voter i from the conditions of (1).[8] For greater generality we make no assumptions regarding the relative magnitudes of V_i, V_j, and V_k.

(6) $\dfrac{\Delta PI(i)}{\Delta V_i} = \dfrac{V_j}{N} + \dfrac{V_k}{N} - 1$

(7) $\dfrac{\Delta PI(i)}{\Delta V_j} = \dfrac{V_i}{N} - \dfrac{V_k}{N}$

(8) $\dfrac{\Delta PI(i)}{\Delta N} = \dfrac{V_j V_k - V_i(V_j + V_k)}{N^2 + N} + 1$

Equation (6) states an increase in one's own proclivity to affirm will increase one's power index if the sum of the affirming proclivities of the remaining voters is greater than one and vice versa. If the sum of the other two voters' proclivities to affirm is greater than one, then, on average, these voters prefer that a proposal will pass. Thus, an increase in i's desire to see more propositions passed will be reinforced with an expectation of favorable votes from the remaining voters, increasing i's power index. On the other hand if the other voters on average tend to disapprove propositions, an increase in voter i's approval proclivity is a move away from the majority position and hence will reduce his power index. Equation (7) states that an increase in the "proclivity to affirm" of another voter increases (decreases) i's power index if the remaining voter is less (more) likely to vote affirmatively than voter i. If voter i is more prone to voting "yes" than voter k, then i's power index will rise with an increase in j's proclivity to affirm, which reinforces i's preferences relative to k's. If $V_k > V_i$ then an increase in V_j reinforces voter k's preferences relative to i's, and i's power index will fall. Finally, Equation (8) states that an increase in the number of propositions increases or decreases one's power index depending upon the distribution of proclivities among the three voters.

Consider now an increase in the number of voters from three to five. The power index for each of the five voters is calculated in a similar manner as for three voters. In this expanded case, how does the median voter's power index compare to that of the remaining four voters?

For the sake of brevity, let us compare the median voter, voter k in the five-voter model, with the two voters who tend to be less prone to vote "yes" than k, voters l and m. In Table 6-2, we illustrate a hypothetical case of five voters voting on ten propositions, their respective voting proclivities, and the resulting power indices. Note that once again the median voter is, in one sense, more "powerful," and because of the symmetric distribution of probabilities, the pairwise extreme voters on either side of the median voter have identical indices. Letting V_i, V_j, V_k, V_l, and V_m represent the expected number of "yes" votes to be cast on a set of N propositions for voters i, j, k, l, and m, respectively, it follows that:

$$(9) \quad PI(k)\{\geqq\}PI(l) \text{ if } 2N(V_iV_j + V_iV_m + V_jV_m)\{\geqq\}N^3 + 4V_iV_jV_m,$$

and

$$(10) \quad PI(k)\{\geqq\}PI(m) \text{ if } 2N(V_iV_j + V_iV_l + V_jV_l)\{\geqq\}N^3 + 4V_iV_jV_m.$$

A little arithmetic reveals some interesting properties. Suppose that voter m approves no proposition so that $V_m = 0$. Conditions (9) and (10) reduce to:

Table 6-2. Power indices—five voters and
ten propositions

Voter	Proclivity to vote "yes"	Power index
i	.7	6.59
j	.6	6.89
k	.5	7.01
l	.4	6.89
m	.3	6.59

$$(11) \quad PI(k)\{\geq\}PI(l) \text{ if } \frac{V_i V_j}{N^2} \{\geq\} \frac{1}{2},$$

and

$$(12) \quad PI(k)\{\geq\}PI(m) \text{ if } \frac{V_i V_j}{N^2} \{\geq\} \frac{1}{2} - \frac{V_l(V_i + V_j)}{N^2} + \frac{2V_i V_j V_l}{N^3}.$$

Assuming $V_i > V_j > V_k > V_l > V_m$, condition (11) says that the median voter's power index is greater than that of the relative negativist (voter l, as opposed to extreme negativist, voter m) if and only if the *product* of the relative and extreme affirmist's proclivities to affirm is greater than ½. Consider the maximum value V_i can undertake, 10 (as there are only ten propositions). Then V_j must equal 6 or greater to give voter k, the median, a greater power index than l. This also implies via condition (12) that if $V_l = 0$, voter k dominates voter m. This result follows from our previous analysis of the three-voter case. If $V_i = 10$ and $V_m = 0$, then i and m cancel each other out leaving only three voters to determine the outcome.[9] In this case, voter j becomes the extreme affirmist and by our earlier result for three voters, the now-median voter dominates if V_j is greater than $N/2$, which is true when $V_j = 6$. Now suppose that $V_l = 1$ while $V_m = 0$. Condition (12) says if V_i assumes its maximum value, 10, V_j need only be equal to 5 for voter k to dominate voter m. Again, we can interpret this as saying voters i and m pair off. However, now that voter l is slightly more prone to vote yes, his affirming counterpart, voter j, need not be as affirmative in order for the median to have the highest power index. Hence, whether the median will have the highest power index depends on the *aggregate* proclivity to vote "yes" of the pairs of voters on either side of the median voter. For example, in the case where $V_m = 0$ and $V_l = 0$ any sum of expected "yes" votes equal to or greater than 16 will give voter k the most power. When $V_l = 1$, this sum drops to 15. Finally, as in the case of three voters, if all voters have a probability of voting "yes" ("no") less than 0.5, then the absolute negativist (affirm-

Table 6-3. Recalculated power indices—five voters and
ten propositions

Distribution of expected number of "yes" votes for voters i, j, k, l, m					i	j	k	l	m
10	4	2	1	0	1.24	4.89	8.59	8.78*	8.76
10	5	2	1	0	1.49	4.89	8.69*	8.69*	8.49
10	5	3	1	0	1.99	6.69	8.29*	8.29*	7.99
10	6	2	1	0	1.76	4.89	8.79*	8.59*	8.24
9	7	2	1	0	2.80	4.72	8.82*	8.56	8.16
8	8	2	1	0	3.79	3.79	8.83*	8.55	8.14
4	3	2	1	0	6.36	7.32	8.24	8.97	9.57*
5	4	3	2	1	6.07	6.88	7.58	8.08	8.38*
7	6	5	4	3	6.29	6.90	7.01*	6.90	6.29
9	7	5	3	1	5.71	6.91	7.56*	6.91	5.71

*Indicates highest power index for a given distribution.

ist) dominates. These properties are illustrated in Table 6-3 where power indices for various distributions of voting proclivities are displayed. It should be obvious that if the orders of the distributions are reversed, the power indices will be in reverse order.

IV. Generalized Information

Suppose that there is no information about individual proclivities to vote "yes" but there is general information about the whole group of voters. That is, only the proclivity of the *population* of voters to vote "yes" on a given proposition, is known. Obviously, the notion of a particular voter with the median proclivity to vote "yes" vanishes. Some properties of the voting outcomes may, however, still be examined under these assumptions. For example, let there be a committee of seven voters casting "yes" or "no" votes on five independent proposals. Further, assume that the population proclivity to affirm is known, historically perhaps, to be .6 for the group. The probability of any proposal passing is the sum of the probabilities of getting exactly four "yes" votes, exactly five "yes" votes, exactly six "yes" votes, and exactly seven "yes" votes.[10] In the current example, this totals .727. Notice the difference obtained here. The proportion of "yes" votes in the population over *all* issues in the set is .6. These votes, for lack of sufficient reason, can be thought of as randomly distributed across the five voters and the five issues. The probability that any *given issue* will obtain a majority exceeds the population probability that a *given vote* will be "yes."

Table 6-4. Probability of a given proposition passing
for various numbers of voters and propositions
and a group proclivity to vote yes of .67

Number of propositions	Number of voters			
	3	5	7	9
3	.773	.831	.871	.900
6	.755	.808	.847	.876
9	.748	.800	.838	.866
12	.747	.798	.836	.865

Table 6-4 shows probabilities of passage of a single proposition for alternative values of numbers of propositions to be voted on and numbers of voters when the general proclivity to vote "yes" is two-thirds. Fixing the number of propositions and the *proportion* of "yes" votes, an increase in the number of voters increases the probability of a proposal passing. On the other hand, increasing the number of propositions reduces (and apparently more slowly) the probability of any one proposition passing. Intuitively, as the number of voters becomes large, given the number of propositions to be considered and the group proclivity to affirm, the probability of any given proposal securing majority approval approaches 1(0) if the general proclivity to affirm is greater (less) than .5. This is because the random sample of votes drawn from the population approaches the population size and hence the expected number of "yes" votes in the sample will be close to the fraction of "yes" votes in the population. If this fraction is greater than one-half, a proposal will have majority approval.[11] On the other hand, as the number of propositions becomes large, given the number of voters and the average proclivity to affirm, the probability of any given proposal passing approaches the average proclivity to affirm since one is drawing a sample of fixed size from an ever-increasing population.

An extension of this model is "casting lots" where there is a fixed number of "yes" votes in the group. There is no specific information on the number of "yes" votes held by each voter (cf. note 6). Assuming the "yes" votes are distributed randomly across voters and issues, the probability of any single issue passing remains the same as before. However, the probability of passage for subsequent proposals, contingent on the passage of prior propositions falls as "yes" votes, or lots, are used up in passing the prior propositions. For example in our seven voter–five proposition case where there was a .6 group proclivity to affirm, let there be a total of twenty-one "yes" votes randomly distributed through the population of votes. In this case, the probability of any one proposal passing is .727, as before. The probability of any second proposal passing, given that one proposition has

Table 6-5. Probability of a proposition passing
when all prior propositions have passed—seven
voters and a group proclivity to affirm of .6

Proposition	Probability of passage
1st	.727
2nd	.687
3rd	.454
4th	.359
5th	.181

Table 6-6. Expected fraction of propositions
passed when there is a .6 group proclivity
to affirm

Voters	Propositions
3	.355
5	.429
7	.482
9	.491

Table 6-7. Expected fraction of propositions
passed under various group proclivities to
affirm, given five voters and five propositions

Number (percentage) of "yes" votes in total votes cast on all propositions	Expected fraction of propositions passed
10 (40%)	.091
15 (60%)	.429
20 (80%)	.922

already passed, is .687, and the probability of any third proposal passing, given that two have passed, is .454. Table 6-5 lists the conditional probability of passage for all five propositions. The average probability for the set of five propositions is .482, which can be interpreted as the expected fraction of propositions under consideration that will pass, given the voting scheme outlined above. Table 6-6 reports the expected fraction of propositions passed under the "casting lots" model for some selected voter-proposition combinations when 60 percent of the votes are "yes" votes. Table 6-7 reports the expected fraction of propositions passed for the five voter–five proposition case given various percentages of "yes" votes in the total number of votes cast on all propositions.

As we saw earlier, the expected fraction of proposals passing, for a given percentage of "yes" votes in the population, rises with the number of voters and falls with the number of propositions. Not surprisingly, the expected passage rate increases with the percentage of "yes" votes in the population and appears to do so at an increasing rate.

V. Concluding Remarks

In conventional majority-rule voting models, a weakening of the information concerning individual voter preference orderings effectively rules out any analysis of the voting outcomes. In the model of yes-no voting presented here, information assumptions can be progressively weakened without removing all of the model's predictive content.

We saw that when the rank ordering of the separate proposals is known and identical across voters, a unique outcome results and that this outcome exactly matches the median voter's preferred outcome. When ordinal rankings are assumed to differ among voters, majority-rule voting still yields unique and stable results while the equivalence between the outcome and the median voter's preferences is weakened but not lost. That is, when the only information available is each voter's probability of voting "yes," the voting outcome, under many circumstances, more closely corresponds to the preferences of the median voter than for any other voter. Finally, we considered the case where the only information is the voting group's aggregate likelihood to vote "yes." Here, the median voter has no meaning and all that can be said is that the expected number of propositions passed by the group depends on the number considered, the number of voters, and the group proclivity to vote "yes."

It should be pointed out that the results reported in this paper are preliminary. Our arguments have been made by reference to specific examples rather than by formal theorems and proofs. One possible way of generalizing our model is to construct a large-scale computer simulation of the model under various information assumptions in order to discover the properties of the model when there are large numbers of voters and issues.[12]

In the past we have argued that the allocation of resources and the potential for economic growth will be affected differently when disputes over property are resolved privately or collectively by majority rule.[13] When such disputes are resolved by yes-no voting such as deciding upon zoning variances, our analysis of yes-no voting outcomes becomes both relevant and important. It is interesting to speculate on the reasons for the relative analytical neglect of the voting institutions discussed in this paper, which, as we have noted, are descriptive of frequently observed collective choice situations. Attention may have been concentrated on the single-election setting primarily because of the underlying motivation to answer questions concerning the "rationality" or "irrationality" of collective choice, questions that have been presumed to have normative or evaluative content. In straightforward yes-no majority-rule voting on a proposition, there is a unique result. The question of "collective rationality" that has preoccupied public choice and social choice theorists simply does not arise. But the absence of this particular "rationality" question does not make the positive analysis of yes-no voting either uninteresting or unimportant, perhaps even for normative questions of institutional-constitutional design.

Notes

We should like to thank our colleagues Geoffrey Brennan and Joseph Reid for helpful suggestions on earlier drafts of this paper, and Janet Faith, Richard Carter, and David Laband for their research assistance. Finally, we thank Akira Yokoyama of Josai University for saving us from some mathematical errors.

1. We use the term "proposition" here rather than "issue" in order to avoid confusion with the treatment of multi-issue space in public choice analysis. In the latter, candidates, party platforms, and voters' ideal positions are described by vectors that employ several issue dimensions. But the analysis is directed toward the selection of a single candidate (a list), or platform, in a single election. Our analysis, by contrast, explicitly examines a bundle of "elections," or "group choices," each one of which is presented as a single yes-no proposition.

2. One might interpret this as a setting of an agenda by an exogenous actor. The voters themselves do not offer new proposals for consideration. Some of the recent work on agenda manipulation where voters are presented with only two options may readily be brought within our framework of analysis. See, for example, T. Romer and H. Rosenthal, "Political Resource Allocations, Controlled Agenda, and the Status Quo," *Public Choice* 33 (Winter, 1978): 27–43; or R. J. Mackay and C. L. Weaver, "Monopoly Bureaus and Fiscal Outcomes: Deductive Models and Implications for Reform," in G. Tullock and R. Wagner, eds., *Policy Analysis and Deductive Reasoning* (Lexington, Mass.: D. C. Heath, 1978), pp. 141–65; and A. T. Denzau, R. J. Mackay, and C. L. Weaver, "On the Initiative-Referendum Option and the Control of Monopoly Government," *Papers of the Committee on Urban Public Economics*, vol. 5.

An alternative interpretation is that the costs of communicating and enforcing compromise proposals are prohibitively high. This may particularly be the case when the issue is largely an emotional one such as the legalization of marijuana, the development of nuclear power, or the adoption of capital punishment. In other cases, the amount of wealth at stake simply may be insufficient to induce the affected party (or parties) to make expensive counterproposals.

3. This requires that propositions are defined such that "yes" has a consistent meaning. For example, a "yes" vote "to grant a zoning variance" is

equivalent to a "no" vote "to not grant a zoning variance." We shall assume henceforth that propositions are worded so that affirmation is always denoted by a "yes" vote.

4. From both an empirical and practical viewpoint this question of correspondence of preferences with outcomes is interesting. Consider an individual board member. If every voting member had an established history or known frequency of voting "yes" or "no" on single issues drawn from a certain broadly defined set, then one might be able to predict the probable outcome of each vote. For a hypothetical board member, such information would be important particularly if he were new to the board and were trying to figure out on which proposals his vote would be most highly weighted in the outcome (cf. W. W. Badger, "Political Individualism, Positional Preferences, and Optimal Decision-Rules," in R. Niemi and H. Weisberg, eds., *Probability Models of Collective Choice* [Columbus, Ohio: Charles Merrill, 1972]). By extension, a set of citizens searching for a person to represent them in some governmental body would want to know which of the candidates would have the most "power" to deliver legislation preferred by the constituency. In a rough sense, one might scan the voting proclivities of the current members of the legislative body and the proclivities of the candidates so as to decide upon the most effective candidate. The same may hold true within legislative bodies, like Congress, where newly elected representatives must be assigned to existing committees and subcommittees. In this case, the impact of one representative's purely random voting (a reasonable assumption if there is no prior information on the new representative) on the committee outcomes would be taken into account by the party leader in assigning legislators to committees.

5. If voter i votes "yes" on a proposition, then to secure majority approval it is required that either j or k or both vote "yes." The probability that j will vote "yes" on any given proposition, that is for a randomly selected ordering of j's preferences, is .5. For voter k this same probability is .33. As there are three pairs of votes from j and k which in conjunction with i's "yes" vote will result in a majority—yes-yes, yes-no, no-yes—the probability of approval is $(\frac{1}{2} \cdot \frac{1}{3}) + (\frac{1}{2} \cdot \frac{2}{3}) + (\frac{1}{2} \cdot \frac{1}{3}) = .67$. To obtain a majority "no," the necessary possibilities are yes-no, no-yes, and no-no; and the probability of majority disapproval given i votes "no" is $(\frac{1}{2} \cdot \frac{2}{3}) + (\frac{1}{2} \cdot \frac{1}{3}) + \frac{1}{2} \cdot \frac{2}{3}) = .83$.

6. An alternative voting model is to allocate each voter a fixed number of "yes" votes to cast over all propositions in the set. The probability of a subsequent proposal passing given a prior proposal has passed will then decrease since some "yes" votes are "used up" in passing the earlier one. Calculating probabilities in such an analytical setting is extremely time-consuming. For example, if there are five voters and six propositions, to calculate the probability of the sixth proposal passing given the first five have passed for just one voter requires over ten hours of computer execution time! Thus as a model with any empirical content along the lines suggested in note 4, this alternative formulation would be inappropriate. On the other hand, the probabilities discussed in the essay can be easily calculated.

7. This result is analogous to the "pairing off" condition for majority-rule equilibrium with the median preference dominating. See C. R. Plott, "A Notion of Equilibrium and Its Possibility under Majority Rule," *American Economic Review* 57 (September, 1967): 788–806. However, as expression (5) shows, in our model median dominance also requires that the extreme voters do not both have proclivities greater than one-half.

8. Since we are dealing with discrete changes in the parameters, differential calculus is inappropriate for determining sensitivities. Thus, average rates of change are used where all changes in the independent variables are unit changes.

9. See note 7 above.

10. Letting L = total votes cast (voters times propositions), R = number of "yes" votes in L, D = number of voters, and k = number of "yes" votes in a random sample of D votes, the probability of getting exactly K "yes" votes on a given proposal is given by the hypergeometric probability:

$$k = \frac{\binom{D}{K}\binom{L-D}{R-k}}{\binom{L}{R}}$$

See W. Feller, *An Introduction to Probability Theory and Its Applications*, vol. 1, 2nd ed. (New York: Wiley, 1957), p. 42.

11. This result, in a somewhat different context, has been obtained by R. G. Kazmann ("Democratic Organization: A Preliminary Mathematical Model," *Public Choice* 16 [Fall, 1973]: 17–26) and B. Grofman ("A Comment on 'Democratic Theory': A Preliminary Mathematical Model," *Public Choice* 21 [Spring, 1975]: 99–103).

12. In a sense our efforts are at a stage analogous to that of G. Tullock and C. D. Campbell's ("Computer Simulation of a Small Voting System," *Economic Journal* 80 [March, 1970]: 97–104). They used simulation techniques to determine the probability of the occurrence of majority-rule cycles as the number of voters and number of candidates change.

7.

What If There Is No Majority Motion?

I. The Pure Majority Voting Cycle

The theory of majority voting should occupy a central place in any effort to celebrate the achievements of Duncan Black. In this essay, I propose to examine the results of majority voting rules when the preferences of committee members are such as to produce the familiar cycle. Many investigators, from Duncan Black onward, upon discovering the logical possibility of the cycle, have turned their efforts toward narrowing the range for cyclical prospects on the one hand, and/or toward complementary or alternative rules on the other, rules that will make a unique selection from among the several potentially co-equal majority-vote outcomes. Duncan Black's discovery of the single-peaked preference theorem is an example of the first line of inquiry; the Borda method is perhaps the most familiar of the alternative rules designed to get around the majority-voting cycle.[1]

In order to eliminate all concern with these sorts of issues, I shall discuss the operation of simple majority voting rules in an abstract model that is highly idealized to produce a pure cycle. By "pure" I mean that neither simple majority voting nor any conceivable alternative procedure will make a definitive selection from among a finite set of specifically defined states or objects of choice. This idealization requires much more than the ordinal rankings minimally necessary to generate a cyclical result in a sequence of pairwise majority votes. The distribution of all voters over all of the preference rankings must be fully symmetrical. In addition, within the preferences of each voter, all differences among the choice options must be equal. If these additional restrictions are not imposed, we should have an "impure" cycle, which could be removed by resort to some alternative selection procedure.

Faced with such pure cycles, investigators have concluded that the group or committee cannot act consistently or coherently in selecting among the alternatives, that any outcome must be arbitrary. Such a conclusion is unwarranted in a general sense, and it depends on certain implicit assumptions or presuppositions about the "motions" that should at least be clearly enunciated. Precise characteristics of the choice set must be specified; in particular the temporal sequence of the pairwise votes among the separate choice options must be postulated. As I shall demonstrate, the attributes of the majority voting cycle are quite different under different settings.

Predictability in the Cyclical Sequence

For purposes of expositional simplicity, we may work with a three-element choice set: A, B, and C. The elements may represent motions, candidates, or options. No elements outside this restricted set are considered to be possible. For additional simplicity, we may work with a three-person group. The three voters are labeled as: i, j, and k. The evelutions of the three alternatives are such as to generate the pure majority voting cycle, as defined above.

The first of several straightforward logical points to be made concerns the directional form of the cycles that may exist among the separate elements of the choice set. Among the three elements, A, B, and C, there are only two directional forms of cycle that are possible, which I shall call the *clockwise* and the *counterclockwise*. These two forms are represented in Fig. 7-1, with the arrows indicating the direction of movement in successive rounds of votes in the cycle.

It is clear from the figure that, once the form of the pure cycle is identified, the precise pattern of the sequence of results is fully predictable. Any one of the motions can be majority-dominated by only one other motion just as the initial motion, in its turn, dominates only one other motion of element in the choice set. Hence, if any element of the set is defined over any two of the three motions, the sequence of results in successive rounds of voting is fully predictable. From this regularity of pattern there follows the conclusion that the precise outcome is predictable if the number of votes is specified. The predictability that stems from the regularity of the cyclical sequence tends to have been obscured in the literature perhaps because such words as "inconsistency" and "incoherence" were applied to the majority cycle. But, as suggested, there is nothing that is inconsistent or incoherent in the operation of majority voting through a series of rounds, so long as the starting point is specified and the series is finite, given the implicit assumptions of unchanged preferences and the stability of the choice set.

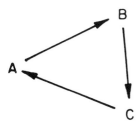

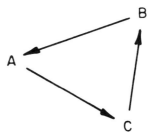

Clockwise   Counterclockwise

Fig. 7-1

Where Does the Cycle Start?

There are two distinct settings within which the majority cycle, even
in its pure variety, may arise. If one of the elements in the choice set is
the status quo, or, to use Black's term, "things as they are," the starting point is defined. The first vote in any sequence must be that between the status quo and one of the other options in the choice set. If
the status quo wins in the initial pairwise comparison, there is no
"start" to the cycle. If the status quo is defeated by majority vote, it
must be paired against the single option that majority dominates it.
We may call the vote that shifts the outcome to be an effective stage of
the cycle. If A, among the three options in our example, is the status
quo, the first effective vote in the cyclical sequence is that between A
and B in the clockwise form of the cycle depicted in Fig. 7-1, or between A and C in the counterclockwise form.

As Black indicated, however, the choice set may be made up entirely of elements that are nonexistent at the time of the initial vote.
The group choice is to be made *de novo*, from among the several options that remain as prospects. With candidates, this is the setting
where there is no incumbent. With policy options, each of three prospects may be assumed to dominate the existing state of affairs, the
null or do-nothing option, for all three voters. In this choice setting,
where does the voting begin?

There are two possible procedures. One of the options or motions
could simply be selected, in some nonvoting fashion, as the initial
position or as the option to be placed against the null option that is
outside the cyclical set, and the sequence could then proceed just as if
the arbitrarily chosen position were the status quo in the other setting
discussed. Or, as a second procedure, any two of the three motions or
options could be arbitrarily selected, and an initial vote between these
two elements would then determine the direction of the cyclical flow.
The selection of either one or two options from among the choice set

must be arbitrary in the pure cycle. In the configuration of preferences that are postulated, no one of the alternatives is superior to any other under any conceivable procedure that assigns equal weights to the preferences of each voter. The inference must be that the group decision process, the voting rule, "should" reflect indifference as among all of the elements in the set. This essentially normative result suggests, in turn, that the initial selection be made through the use of some random device that will ensure that each of the three possible outcomes is equally likely to emerge.

When Should the Cycle Stop?

As noted earlier, the sequence of outcomes in the pure majority cycle is predictable once a starting point is defined and the form of the cycle known. From this regularity, the specific result as of any effective stage of the cycle can be predicted. The starting point will not, of course, be decisive in determining a final outcome unless the stopping point is specified. Given any starting point, control over the number of rounds in the cycle can determine the outcome. Similarly, given any specified number of rounds of voting, control over the starting point can determine the outcome.[2]

One simple point to be made is that collective groups, committees, do make decisions, despite the widespread use of majority voting procedures, and despite the possible majority cyclicity inherent in individual preference orderings. Ambiguity has been present in some discussion that suggests that, under majority cyclicity, the committee cannot reach a decision; that the decision process is analogous to Buridan's ass, unable to choose among the alternatives confronted. This phenomenon would arise, however, only where the decision procedure evaluates the alternatives equally at each voting stage. With simple majority voting, and with pairwise comparisons between any two elements in the choice set, no such indifference or inability to reach a decision exists. (Ties are not possible in the pure cycle with an odd number of voters.) One of any two of the choice options always holds a decisive majority over the other. Indecisiveness is not a characteristic feature of the majority cycle.

This ambiguity may stem from failure to examine the temporal aspects of the choice setting. By inferring that the committee "cannot reach a decision," the analyst may suggest that, unless some arbitrary limit is placed on the number of votes, the process can go on forever. The "meeting" never ends; the cycle continues infinitely.

Empirically, cycles stop. But when "should" this point be reached? The introduction of this normative question requires resort to some criterion for determining the "best" rule for stopping the voting. I shall utilize a Rawlsian approach. We may ask the question: If a person is behind a veil of ignorance concerning his own identification, when would he desire that the cyclical sequence be truncated? Assume that a person, at some constitutional stage where rules are chosen, could not know whether he will be in the position of i, j, or k, or, similarly, does not know what his ordinal preferences will be. What constitutional constraint would he prefer to impose on pure majority voting to ensure that the "meeting" end short of forever?

To answer this question it is essential to be much more specific about the nature of the choice options than has been necessary to this point. A classification of choice settings must be attempted.

First, I shall discuss a setting in which the option, once chosen, is *permanent*. This permanence of result is important for the normative rule that is preferred. This feature refers to the length of calendar time that the decision, once made, is to remain in effect. Consider a simple illustration. Suppose that A, B, and C are three possible locations or routes for a new road that is to be constructed. Once a single route is selected and construction is complete, it will be extremely costly to relocate the facility. The decision, once made by the group, is essentially irrevocable.

In this situation, what is the preferred constitutional rule for stopping the majority cycle? If we assume that either voting itself is costly or that delay in reaching a group decision is costly, it is clear that the majority cycle here should be allowed to continue only so long as is minimally necessary to determine the regularity of the pattern over successive votes, or the symmetry of the pure majority cycle. After this point is reached, a random selection device should be introduced to settle the stopping point or, in the same vein, to settle on one of the three choice options. If a computer is used, the preference rankings can be fed into it, and with the evidence of a pure and fully symmetrical majority cycle, the computer can be instructed to pick randomly from among the options with relatively little cost. The important point is that, to a person behind the veil of ignorance, any one of the three choice options is as good as any other. *Ex ante*, expected values of the outcome for the three voters or committee members can be equalized. No institutional procedure can equalize realized values *ex post*. Hence, any continuation of the majority voting cycle as a process of choosing beyond minimal limits is inefficient.

Nonpermanence

Let us now examine a model where the decision made is not permanent but is, instead, limited in application to some finite period of calendar time. Perhaps the most familiar illustration is the election of a candidate who, once elected, will be in office for a fixed term. But it is not difficult to think of other illustrations where the choice is among motions or proposals that are comparably time-constrained. Initially, I shall assume that the length of the term, or application period, is exogenously determined, and that each successive or sequential period is of equal length.

How does this change in the model modify the choice of a preferred rule for stopping the majority cycle? In the case of risk neutrality, the use of some random selection procedure at the onset of each period or term will ensure that the preferences of each person or committee member be accorded equal weight in the *ex ante* sense. If risk averseness is introduced, however, equalization of expected values at the constitutional stage may not be sufficient. Preferred rules may also involve some equalization in realized or *ex post* results, other things equal.[3]

If the costs of change in outcomes are not prohibitively high, a rule that allows only one pairwise majority vote for each period may accomplish the desired results. The preferences of each member of the committee are equally weighted in the regularly cycling sequence of outcomes over a number of periods. Under any positive discount rate, some advantage will necessarily be granted to those committee members whose preferences happen to be satisfied in relatively early periods of the cycle. If, however, the starting point of the cycle is randomly chosen, thus ensuring *ex ante* equality in expected values, the *ex post* criterion of equality is violated only by the higher discounting of the preferences of those members whose success in majority coalition formation falls late in the continuing cyclical sequence. In the case of candidates for office, a vote each period between the incumbent officeholder and the opponent who can mount the effective challenge will ensure continual rotation in office, which is precisely the result that may be most desired in this model.[4] An alternative rule that would generate essentially the same result would be one that assigned decision-making power to separate persons sequentially in each period.

How Long Should Majority Decisions Remain Binding?

To this point, I have examined two models with defined time dimensions. In the first, I have assumed that the group or committee choice is permanent and irrevocable. In the second, I have assumed that the time period over which the results of choice apply or remain in force is exogenously fixed at some finite length and that each successive choice binds the group for a period of equal length.

The next step in the analysis involves the normative issue concerning the efficient or optimal length of period, when this length is allowed to vary. If, at the constitutional stage, the term of office or period of applicability of a majority vote can be selected, what length is preferred? How long should a candidate be allowed to remain in office, once elected? Should officeholders be required to stand for reelection monthly, annually, biannually, or at less frequent intervals? Should a city council's action on zoning ordinances remain valid one month, six months, a year, two years, a decade, or forever?

I shall not try to discuss these questions in general terms. I analyze them here only in the highly restricted setting of the pure majority cycle, as defined earlier, and I shall stay within the confines of the three-option, three-person model. I shall assume throughout the analysis that the chooser is risk averse at the constitutional stage. This assumption ensures that some attention will be paid to the variance in the results produced over the sequence of periods: equalization of expected values among the separate streams of payoffs at the constitutional level will not suffice as a criterion for evaluation of alternative arrangements. Under these conditions, if it is known or predicted in advance that the preference configurations of committee members or electors are such as to generate the pure cyclical sequence, what can we say about the length of term or period of application of a single pairwise majority choice? What are the variables that will determine the efficient term lengths in this model?

Three variables are immediately suggested: (1) the anticipated rate of discount or time preference of voters or committee members; (2) the costs of changing among the discrete choice options; (3) the differentials in the committee members' evaluations of the separate choice options. In the abstract setting for analysis here, I shall postulate that committee members or voters are equivalent with respect to these variables. That is to say, all persons are expected to have the same discount rate, to face the same net costs of change in choice options, and to exhibit the same differences in evaluation among their several choice options. The persons differ *only* in their rankings of the options available.

Discussion may be clarified by introducing the simple pure majority cycle depicted in Fig. 7-2. Numbers in the cells represent cardinally measurable and interpersonally comparable evaluations of the options, A, B, and C, by committee members i, j, and k. The familiar majority cycle: $A_pB_pC_pA$ is generated.

Two parameters must be specified before we can further discuss the normative question of period length. In Fig. 7-2, no time dimension is placed on the payoffs or evaluations. This ambiguity must be removed by defining relevant time rates. Assume for purposes of the analysis here, that the evaluations are *daily rates*, that is, they are values or payoffs that will be generated *per day* of calendar time. Further, we assume that a day is the minimum period required for any payoffs to be realized by any committee members. Having set this parameter,

Options \ Persons	i	j	k
A	3	1	2
B	2	3	1
C	1	2	3

Fig. 7-2

we must also specify the length of the *planning horizon* that informs the calculus of the constitutional decision-maker who is confronted with the prospective choice among the many possible term lengths that might be selected. For present purposes, assume that the planning horizon is *finite*, and that it is set at N *days*, with N being a very large number relative to the number of choice options.

Rate of Discount

We may now examine the effects of the three variables on the selection of the efficient term length, with length of term or period of application being measured in days. Consider, first, the effects of the discount rate that the constitutional decision-maker imputes to the committee members over the period of the cyclical sequences within the planning horizon.

Initially, assume that there is no time preference introduced. Values for differing time periods are weighted equally. In this extreme, if we allow for any costs of change above zero, the efficient minimal length of term or period over which the majority voting choices are to remain valid is N/3 in the abstract example. Since there is no discounting, the delay in allowing any person's preferences to be more fully satisfied does not put such a person at a disadvantage. Since, by assumption, N is a very large number, this result suggests that the rules should, first of all, involve a randomized starting position, to be followed by one pairwise majority voting choice each electoral period, but with very long periods, minimally of N/3 lengths.[5]

Implicitly, the results suggested require that committee members live forever, or, at least, that they live for periods longer than the planning horizon, N days. If we allow persons to live finite lives, it is plausible to suggest that *ex ante* political equality could be attained only if the planning horizon is related to expected length of life. If we assume that life expectancy at birth is seventy-two years, and that twenty-five of these years are spent in childhood and/or dotage, a planning horizon of forty-eight years (17,520 days) might be considered maximal. In this case, even with a zero discount rate, the maximal length of the minimal term of application for any majority voting choice would be sixteen years. Terms of this length would ensure that the individual elector or committee member, over his adult life of forty-eight years, would find his first preferences met in one-third of these years, his second preferences met in another third, and his least preferred option selected in the remaining third.

The finite life model suggests, however, the basic absurdity of the no-discounting assumption. Even if persons place absolutely equal weights on the payoffs promised in differing time periods, each day or year that such payoffs are enjoyed, the mere fact that the actual length of life is determined stochastically to some degree implies positive discounting. That is to say, there is a necessary "biological time preference" in any rational behavior pattern. Once any positive rate of discount is introduced, the efficient length of time or period for the application or duration of majority voting choice results is reduced, given normal ranges of values.

There is an additional reason why a positive rate of discount may need to be introduced into the constitutional selection of the optimal term length, quite apart from standard time preference. To the extent that the effects of the voting choice within any one period extend beyond the period itself, there is a rational basis for positive discounting, over and beyond the elements noted above. We are concerned here with the question of determining the optimal length of time the results of single voting choices remain in force in the temporal cyclical sequence. We have assumed that the choice made in any one period is not permanent. But this assumption is not equivalent to eliminating all of the effects of a single-period action in later periods. It is necessary to examine the characteristics of the choice options, A, B, and C, even in the highly abstract models that restrict the analysis.

Consider an illustration in which the choice options take the following form: Suppose that the "community" owns a collective facility, say, a road. The alternatives confronted in each period are: (A) maintain the road, which will require an outlay of X dollars per day, *and* improve the road, which will take an additional X dollars of outlay per day; (B) maintain the road only, which requires a total outlay of X dollars per day; (C) allow the road to deteriorate at the physically defined rate of X dollars per day. The outlays per term length under each of the three options will be (A) 2X times the number of days of the term; (B) X times the number of days in the term; (C) and zero.

Assume that the payoffs or evaluations of the alternatives are defined, as before, as rates per day. Suppose that some randomized device selects option A for the initial period (some indeterminate number of days); this becomes the starting point for the cyclical sequence. Over the course of the first period, there will be net investment in the facility. At the end of the period, however, A will be defeated by C in a pairwise majority vote, and, during a second period of the same length, there will be net disinvestment in the facility. At the end of this time, C will be defeated in a majority vote by B, which will result in a policy of maintaining the capital value for the third period. And the cyclical sequence will continue.

It is clear from this illustration that the number of days included in the term or length of period for which the pairwise majority voting choices are to be valid will determine the degree of bias introduced into the sequential results as a result of the initial randomized choice among the options. If, for instance, the length of period is limited to one day, the minimal allowed under our assumption about time rates of payoffs, the initial advantage granted to the person whose first choice is for the net investment alternative is weighted less over the whole sequence of results than would be the case should the period or term be, say, ten days.

In our earlier discussion we noted that risk averseness was required to justify the continuing cyclical majority voting sequence as opposed to the use of randomized selection at the onset of each period. In the consideration here, the presence of risk averseness also requires that the variance in the expected advantage given to those whose preferences are satisfied first in the cyclical sequence be minimized. This may be translated directly into the introduction of a positive discount rate, over and beyond that generated by positive time preference in some orthodox sense.[6]

The Costs of Change

The second major variable that will influence the selection of the preferred term length for a sequence of majority votes involves the costs of changing from one collective outcome or result to another. Again we can illustrate by taking an extreme case. If there are no costs of change, and if there is any positive discount rate at all, the optimal electoral period would be equal to the minimal time required for voters to recognize and attribute payoffs to results, which, in our example, we have assumed to be one day. A single majority vote would, in this setting, be allowed to remain in force for one day only, with each day's results being replaced during the next day by the option that wins out in an effective majority vote paired against the initial day's option.

As we introduce positive costs of change, the optimal period length is increased. The partial derivatives of optimal length of term with respect to the discount rate and to costs of change move in opposing directions over normal ranges. If the costs of change are very high (as in our initial road location example), the most efficient constitutional rule may involve some guarantee of *ex ante* fairness (equalization of expected values for each potential voter), along with explicit institutions designed to prevent the group from moving through a costly cyclical majority sequence. At very high costs of change, it may be wholly inappropriate to allow the relevant choice options to be brought up for the pairwise majority votes in successive periods, no matter how long such periods may be. At the constitutional level of deliberation, for such choice options, it may be to the best long-term interest of each potential voter to prohibit the never-ending, period-by-period, majority cycle.

For other types of options, however, majority voting that would generate the cycle through subsequent electoral periods might be desired, provided the terms are sufficiently long to allow costs of change to be absorbed by the smaller variance in payoffs among the committee members or voters. In the illustration depicted in Fig. 7-2, if each voter must accept a net cost of four units under each change or shift of outcome, day-by-day voting would be less preferred than permanence of some randomized result. If, however, pairwise majority comparisons could be allowed over electoral periods of, say, twelve-day lengths, the cyclical sequence might well be preferred to any single permanent outcome.

Differentials in Evaluations of Separate Options

There remains to be considered the third major variable that will influence the selection of the length of period. We have assumed that the valuations or payoffs of the separate voters or committee members are fully symmetrical over all options. We have not, however, done more than to specify an ordinal ranking over the separate choice options within the preferences of each voter. In the illustration contained in Fig. 7-2, we may now assume that two zeros are added to each three, one zero to each two, and nothing to the ones in the diagram. The cardinalized payoffs for each voter over the three separate choice options become (300, 20, 1) rather than the (3, 2, 1) of Fig. 7-2.

It is evident that this simple change in the differentials among the three options, even if these are uniform over all voters, will modify the constitutionally preferred length of election period. At any given discount rate and with a given cost of change between any two options, an increase in the differentials will tend to reduce the length of the optimal period over which pairwise majority voters are allowed to remain valid. An increase in differentials is similar in effect to an increase in the discount rate, effectively increasing the weight given to the voter or committee member whose preferences are more fully met early in the cyclical sequence. Through this effect, the length of the optimal period of validity, considered constitutionally and behind the veil of ignorance, is reduced.

Conclusions

My purpose in this essay has been extremely limited. I have attempted to examine some of the properties of simple majority voting when the existence of what I have called the pure majority cycle emerges from the true configuration of voters' or committee members' preferences. An understanding of these properties allows certain normative inferences to be made concerning the efficiency of majority-voting procedures in differing choice settings. In particular, the analysis has implications for the question as to the optimal or efficient length of periods over which single pairwise majority-voting outcomes should be allowed to remain in force for the whole community, affecting majority and minority members alike.

I have made no attempt to go beyond the extremely simple model with three voters or committee members and three choice options. Such extensions should not prove difficult, and the central points are probably sufficiently outlined in the simple case. Extension in the number of voters can be accomplished readily, so long as persons with preferences identical to those of the three are added symmetrically to each group. Extension in the number of options involves no difficulty so long as the preferences over all options are fully symmetrical, which requires that the number of persons be at least as large as the number of options.

I have limited analysis to the pure majority cycle, largely in order to concentrate attention on the properties of the cyclical process itself rather than on prospects for alternative arrangements for selecting collective outcomes. In order to do this, I have assumed specific cardinal and interpersonal utility indicators in the model. The conclusions of the analysis do not, however, depend critically on these restrictions. To the extent that a majority cycle is predicted on the basis of ordinal preference rankings alone, but resort to alternative selection procedures is effectively forestalled, the normative implications of the analysis hold without significant change.

I have also implicitly assumed throughout the analysis that the group or committee has only the one choice on its agenda. It is assumed to have been assigned, potentially, the choice among A, B, and C, whether this choice be long-lasting in effect or made in each period. The group or committee is assumed not to face choices among, say, R, S, and T, or X, Y, and Z, along with the choice among A, B, and C. This sort of expansion of the choice set would allow for some trade-off as among the differing pure cycles, with the result that *ex post* equalization of realized payoffs might be more fully achieved.

The analysis has been based on the assumption of unchanging preferences. In this respect, there is no departure from standard economic analysis. But, in any treatment of political decision-making, such an assumption effectively denies the relevance of the whole process of political persuasion. One possible advantage of sequential majority voting, even if preferences may initially be such as to generate a pure cycle, might be the temporal change in voter attitudes that this institution allows to emerge and to modify the pattern of results.

The substantive methodological conclusion to be drawn from the analysis of this essay reinforces that which Gordon Tullock and I advanced in *The Calculus of Consent.*[7] A majority-voting rule is one among many possible institutions that may be used for the reaching of group or committee decisions. Majority voting has costs as well as benefits when viewed from the constitutional perspective of the potential voter or committee member whose own preferences are not yet identified. In some circumstances random dictatorship may be preferable to majority-driven and unending institutional change. In other situations, the efficient choice-making institution may well be the continuously changing period-by-period majority result. But the constitutional selection between these two institutions cannot be made rationally until the length of electoral term within the majority-voting sequence is itself efficiently chosen.

Notes

I am indebted to my colleagues, and especially David Friedman, Nicolaus Tideman, and Gordon Tullock, for helpful suggestions made during a seminar presentation of this paper.

1. For a discussion along with a proposal for a sophisticated alternative rule, see I. J. Good and T. N. Tideman, "From Individual to Collective Ordering through Multidimensional Attribute," *Proceedings of the Royal Society of London*, Series A, 347 (January, 1976): 371–85.

2. Note should be made of the research by Charles R. Plott and Michael E. Levine on agenda manipulation. They have demonstrated that, by manipulating the agenda in a manner that does not seem biased, specific final outcomes can be made more likely to occur, even in the presence of the pure majority cycle. In the context of the analysis of this paper, Plott and Levine demonstrate that agenda manipulation is one means of selecting the starting point and the stopping point of the pure cycle in a nonrandom way. See Charles R. Plott and Michael E. Levine, "A Model of Agenda Influence in Committee Decisions," *American Economic Review* 68, no. 1 (March, 1978): 146–60.

3. Pauly and Willett make the distinction between *ex ante* and *ex post* equity, and they introduce several examples to suggest the applicability of each criterion for policy. See Mark Pauly and Thomas Willett, "Two Concepts of Equity and Their Implications for Public Policy," *Social Science Quarterly* 53 (June, 1973): 8–19. Reprinted in *The Economic Approach to Public Policy*, ed. Ryan Amacher, Robert Tollison, and Thomas Willett (Ithaca, N.Y.: Cornell University Press, 1976), pp. 300–12.

For a more general discussion that contains intriguing proposals for equalizing "political income" in an *ex post* sense, see Dennis Mueller, Robert Tollison, and Thomas Willett, "On Equalizing the Distribution of Political Income," *Journal of Political Economy* (March–April, 1974): 414–22.

4. This is the model that I had implicitly in mind when I suggested in my review of Arrow's work that, if the preferences were such as to generate a majority cycle, the best result would, in fact, be some such continual rotation. See my "Social Choice, Democracy, and Free Markets," *Journal of Political Economy* 62 (April, 1954): 114–23.

5. N/3 is the minimal length of period under the assumption here because, with very high costs of change, even longer periods, including infinite lengths, may be efficient. Even with risk averseness, the preferred constitutional arrangement may be one that does nothing more than equalize expected values *ex ante*.

6. Objection may be made to the restrictions imposed implicitly by the three-option model in settings where there are essentially capital investment or disinvestment aspects of single-period decisions. In the road-maintenance example, the average quality of road over the whole succession of periods will be different under differing patterns of the majority cycle, and it seems unreasonable, in one sense, to argue that individuals' preferences for road improvement, road maintenance, and road depreciation would be unchanged over changing levels of road quality. My concern is, however, not with the "realism" of the assumption of unchanging preferences, but rather with the normative implications for term length that can be variously derived while remaining within the unchanging preferences assumption, no matter how restrictive these might be in particular cases.

7. *The Calculus of Consent: Logical Foundations of Constitutional Democracy* (Ann Arbor: University of Michigan Press, 1962).

8.

Voter Choice:
Evaluating Political Alternatives

WITH GEOFFREY BRENNAN

Public choice theory is the application of the method and analytic apparatus of modern economics to the study of political processes. An
integral part of this theory is the assumption that participants in
political processes act "rationally"—that is, they act purposively to
secure their particular individual ends. The object of this essay is to
show that such an assumption is highly problematic for a major group
of participants in political processes—namely, voters in large-number
majoritarian elections. The claim is such that the strict logical connection between preferences over alternatives and observed choices,
characteristic of individual behavior in the market, is severed in majoritarian elections. In other words, basic rationality postulates applicable to market behavior are not sufficient to establish an a priori
relationship between the way in which individuals vote and their
preferences over political outcomes. Since the assumption that voters
cast their votes rationally is the point of departure for virtually every
public choice model in the literature, this claim represents a major
criticism of public choice orthodoxy. Any predictive theory of voter
behavior based on the assumption that voters vote in accordance with
their "interest" is, at best, logically arbitrary. Furthermore, normative
propositions based on the assumption of voter rationality must be
treated very skeptically: Majoritarian decision-making cannot be presumed to be a satisfactory device for reflecting the preferences of citizens over alternative electoral outcomes, for reasons quite different
from those widely discussed in public choice orthodoxy.

Our object in this article is to elaborate the argument advanced
above. We begin with a simple analogy. The analytic core of the article
is found in the two following sections, and the fourth section deals
with the implications for public choice analysis—implications that undermine several of the most basic propositions in the field. A brief
summary of the argument is offered in the final section.

Originally published in *American Behavioral Scientist* 28, no. 2 (November–December,
1984): 185–201. Copyright © 1984 by Sage Publications, Inc. Reprinted by permission.

I. A Simple Analogy

Each afternoon of every weekend of the various seasons, an enormous number of individuals watch sporting events, some on television, some directly at the scene of action. Many of these individuals appear to care who wins: They cheer for their respective teams and vociferously proffer advice (sometimes only to a television screen), and their spirits seem profoundly affected by the outcome. Indeed, those who do not really care who wins may, for the purposes of the exercise, "adopt" a team for the afternoon, taking on a partisan stance as a means of stimulating interest.

Even the most ardent of spectators would admit that intense psychological involvement in the game exercises no influence on the outcome. However precisely spectators would account for their interest and their expenditure of resources in indulging that interest, they would not claim that they watch a particular game because, in doing so, they help their team to win.[1]

Few economists would argue that the sports fan is "irrational." Economists would simply acknowledge that the spectators have a taste for watching their team play, and that would be that. Economists could, of course, use their technical tools to analyze spectator behavior. They could "explain" why, when seat prices go up, attendance declines; why, when the weather is bad, gate receipts are lower; why groups of teams will have an incentive to cartelize and restrict entry to the conference, and so on. But economists, presumably, would not find it necessary to explain attendance at events in terms of increased employment opportunities and higher incomes for supporters of the victorious team.

The analogy here with voting behavior is not entirely obvious. And, to be sure, the analogy is by no means perfect.[2] Yet, in some important respects, the activities of voting and watching sporting events are very similar. Voters do, in fact, participate in electoral processes, and they care about political outcomes. But there is no logical connection between these two facts, and the absence of this logical connection is crucial. It arises from the fact that the relation between the way any individual voter votes and the outcome of the election is virtually negligible. We cannot, therefore, explain voter behavior in terms of preferences over outcomes: Voter behavior must be explained on its own terms. People vote because they want to—period. And they vote how they want to—period. And neither the act of voting nor the direction of a vote cast can be explained as a means to achieving a particular political outcome, any more than spectators attend a game as a means of securing the victory of their team.

The fact that any individual voter has a negligible effect on electoral outcomes in large-number electorates has long been recognized by public choice scholars. The implication that the act of voting cannot, therefore, be explained as a means of securing some desired policy change has also been recognized (though somewhat reluctantly in some cases). But there appears to be a widespread conviction that, although we cannot explain why a person goes to the polling booth (except in the tautological terms that it must be utility-maximizing for him or her to do so), we can explain how he or she will vote once there. The view seems to be that although people may go to the polling booth out of a sense of moral responsibility, or because they enjoy participating in political processes as a form of spectator sport, they can be presumed to cast their votes entirely on the basis of "economic interest." This claim is, we believe, essentially misconceived.

II. The Formal Analytics

It serves clarity in exposition to begin with a formal definition of voter "rationality" as used by public choice analysts. Accordingly, we offer the following:

Definition I: Let {S} be the set of all the outcomes on which any voter can exercise his or her vote. Then, to say that the ith voter is "rational" means that he or she will vote for $s^* \in S$

$$\text{if } U_i(s^*) > U_i(s) \text{ for all } s \in S - s^n$$

and only   if $U_i(s^*) \geq U_i(s)$ for all $s \in S - s^n$,

where U_i is the ith voter's utility function.

This definition corresponds exactly to that of rational consumer choice among a set of alternatives {S}.

Clearly, the proposition that individuals vote rationally in this sense is quite a powerful one. To the extent that we can determine who benefits and who loses from particular policies, we can predict more or less precisely how particular individuals will vote. Furthermore, to the extent that electoral processes faithfully reflect the preferences of the vast bulk of the citizens, the quasi-utilitarian defense that is often offered of market processes may be extended relatively easily to the voting process (as tends to be done for the median voter theorem, for example).

Our claim, however, is that strict rationality on the part of the voter does not at all imply behavior according to Definition 1. The central element in supporting that claim is the observation that the object of choice in the election context is not the electoral outcome but, rather, the vote itself. More particularly, the expected return to any voter from exercising a vote according to the utility derived from the outcome is relatively small and, in many cases, negligible.

Consider, for example, an election in which there are exactly two options, a and b. The options in question may be two candidates for office, or yes-no votes in a referendum. The precise details are immaterial, provided the options are exogenously determined and fixed. We consider the rational calculus of some voter, i. Just as in the analysis of a market choice, we initially ignore any satisfaction that the individual derives from the act of voting per se: By assumption, the voter is taken to care solely about the outcomes of the election. Without loss of generality, assume that the ith voter prefers outcome a. Then the return to that person voting for a will be as follows:

$U_i(a) - U_i(b)$, if he or she is decisive O otherwise

Alternatively, the expected return, R, to the individual in voting for a is

(1) $R = h[U_i(a) - U_i(b)]$

where h is the probability that the ith voter will be decisive.

The parameter h is clearly crucial. It is the probability that there will be an exact tie among the remaining voters. Suppose, then, that there are $(2n + 1)$ voters, and for simplicity we can let this number be the entire population of enfranchised voters.[3] Let us initially suppose further that no voter has any idea how others may vote. Hence, the prior probability p that anyone will vote for candidate or option a is one-half, and, concomitantly, the probability that anyone will vote for b is one-half. Then, the probability of a tie between the remaining 2n voters (absent i) is as follows: the number of ways those 2n voters can be arrayed so that a will receive exactly n votes divided by the total number of ways those 2n voters might be arrayed across the two alternatives. That is,

(2) $h = \binom{2n}{n} / 2^{2n}$

More generally, if the probability p that others will vote for a is not one-half, then the probability of a tie occurring is

(3) $h = \binom{2n}{n} p^n(1 - p)^n$

Using Stirling's approximation to simplify the calculation of Equation (3), we have

(4) $h' = \dfrac{2^{2n}}{\sqrt{\pi \cdot n}} p^n(1 - p)^n$

and in the special case where p is one-half, this yields a corresponding approximation to Equation (1):

(5) $\quad h = \dfrac{1}{\sqrt{\pi n}}$

On this basis, we can now return to our central question: How large must the perceived difference in the value of alternative outcomes be in order for the expected return, R, to voter i in voting for a to be non-negligible? To give a sense of the orders of magnitude at stake here, suppose we set R at one dollar. We take the dollar amount as a notional threshold, below which it is presumed that the expected benefit from voting for a rather than b is sufficiently small to be unnoticeable. Given this procedure, we can depict in the first column of Table 8-1 the values that $[U_i(a) - U_i(b)]$ must take for varying levels of electorate size in order for the purely instrumental return from voting to be exactly one dollar. Clearly, this is simply a convenient way of depicting values of h, as 2n varies: What is shown in Table 8-1 is the inverse of h. As an example, in a U.S. presidential election,[4] in which the electorate numbers roughly 100 million voters, candidate a would have to offer the voter approximately twelve thousand dollars more than candidate b before the expected economic benefit derived by the voter from casting a vote for a is as much as one dollar.

Furthermore, it is worth pointing out that the election involved in this case is a limiting case, in which the odds are exactly 50/50 that either candidate will win. If, instead, the prior probability that a randomly selected voter will vote for a differs from one-half, even very slightly, then the probability of an exact tie among the 2n voters falls drastically when the number of voters is at all large. Suppose, for example, that we define the unexpected majority, m, as the expected number of votes for a minus the expected number of votes for b (so m can be negative), and suppose m to be nonzero. Then the prior probability of any voter voting for a is

(6) $\quad p = \dfrac{n + \frac{1}{2} m}{2n}$

Substitution into Equation (4) yields

$$h' = \dfrac{2^{2n}}{\sqrt{\pi n}} \left(\dfrac{n + \frac{1}{2} m}{2n} \right)^n \left(\dfrac{n - \frac{1}{2} m}{2n} \right)^n$$

(7) $\qquad = \dfrac{1}{\sqrt{\pi n}} (1 - j^2)^n$

Table 8.1. Voting Population Value of [U(a) − U(B)]
Required for R = $1, for Various J

(2n)	j = 0	j = 0001	j = .001	j = .01
2,001	56	56	56	62
20,000	177	177	179	481
200,001	560	566	619	12.3×10^6
10m.	4,000	6,533	60,000	~
100m.	12,500	1.9×10^6	6×10^{25}	~

where j is the expected proportionate majority for a, m/2n. Clearly, even though j is small (and $[1 − j^2]$ very close to unity) the raising of $(1 − j^2)$ to the nth power makes $(1 − j^2)$ small when n is at all large. In Table 8-1, we depict for various values of electorate size (2n) and expected majority (j) the values that [U(a) − U(b)] would have to take in order for the expected return (R) to be one dollar.

Consider again our presidential example. Suppose that the expected margin of victory for candidate a is one vote in each one thousand. Then, in order for the expected return, R, to be one dollar, the value of $[U_i(a) − U_i(b)]$ would have to be of the order of 6×10^{25}, which doubtless more than exhausts the world's total product.

Some care should be taken in interpreting such spectacular examples. When n is large, even a small deviation of p from 0.5 drastically alters the probability that a will win: For example, an expected majority of one vote in one thousand for a in an election of 100 million voters means that a is virtually certain to win.[5] This alerts us to the limited reliance of such examples. In almost all elections, even those that are not expected to be close, the odds in favor of the favored party do not suggest that the coutcome is a foregone conclusion.

More generally, queries can be raised about the appropriateness of using the analogy with a sequence of random events to determine the probability of a tie—even though this is the formulation that public choice theorists typically use.[6] We know full well that in most elections a substantial proportion of voters vote from habit, and that the corresponding proportion for whom outcomes might have weight is a significant subset of the voting population. The probability of a tie may be smaller or larger in such cases, depending on the proportions of habitual voters voting for each option. However, it must be explained why it is rational for voters to cast their votes habitually in this case, something that the traditional public choice model does not explain adequately.

In any case, the general point that emerges from all this is that in virtually all elections involving significant numbers of voters, the prior probability each voter might reasonably hold that he or she will be decisive is very small, possibly negligible. This seems entirely clear. The question at issue is what this fact implies for voting behavior. In order to indicate what is at stake, let us remove the assumption that only outcomes count in influencing voter behavior, and formulate each individual's utility function in somewhat more detail, as follows.

We ascribe to each voter a utility function of the following form:

(8) $U_i = U_i[X_i; G; X_j; V; . . .]$

where

X$_i$ is i's consumption of private goods (income)
X$_j$ is the consumption of private goods (income) by other individuals, $j = 1, . . . , i - 1, i + 1, . . . , n$
G   is the level of provision of public goods, and
V   is the intrinsic consumption benefit from casting a vote in a particular way.

The formulation in Equation (8) allows for two influences on i's behavior not allowed for in the conventional public choice model. The first is the possible presence of altruism or concern for the welfare of others, as revealed by the presence of others' incomes in i's utility function. The second is the possibility that i will derive some satisfaction directly from the act of voting for one or another candidate per se, independent of the particular outcome that happens to emerge from the political process. We set aside at this point the plausibility of this formulation; it has the virtue of being a very general one and we do not, at this stage, rule out the possibility that some of the variables in the utility function will turn out to be of no importance (that is, the marginal utility will be zero with respect to some arguments).

On this basis, we can now isolate two distinct elements that are potentially relevant in the individual's decision to vote. Let A$_i$ be the aggregate benefit measured in terms of dollars that i derives from voting for a rather than b. As our earlier analysis emphasizes, the "output-related" benefits of i voting for a are not dependent solely on how i votes, and will be so dependent only when i happens to be decisive in the election. By contrast, the satisfaction that i derives from the act of voting for some candidate per se is independent of the electoral outcome. That is:

(9) $A_i = h \cdot B_i + U_v^i$

where

B$_i$ is the benefit in dollars that i receives if a wins, and
U$_v^i$ is the money value that i places on the act of voting for a in and of itself.

Our interest here revolves not so much around explaining why i chooses to vote as around the relative significance of different elements in i's voting calculus. We seek to address the question of why, given that i does vote, he or she chooses to vote in the way he or she does. To make the implications of Equation (9) for this question clear, it may be useful to offer a slight reformulation:

$$(10) \quad A_i = h\left[B_i + \frac{1}{h} \cdot U_v^i \right]$$

What Equation (10) indicates is that considerations relating to U_v^i are $1/h$ times more important in explaining voting behavior than is the outcome-related parameter, B_i. And the values of $1/h$ are those numbers set out in Table 8-1 for various different electoral settings. If we are to explain voting behavior, therefore, there seems a very strong presumption that we ought to start with the U_v^i term, and not the outcome-related term: Even quite a modest preference for the act of voting for a (or b) becomes relatively important—in many cases, presumptively crucial—in explaining voting behavior.

If we take the assumption of rational behavior on the part of voters seriously, therefore, we must recognize that neither the act of voting nor the choice of whom to vote for can be explained solely, or even predominantly, by reference to voters' preferences over outcomes. When a voter i chooses to vote for a rather than b, it is a decision that in many cases will depend negligibly on the relation between the outcome-related terms, $U_i(a)$ and $U_i(b)$, in precise contradiction to the definition of rational behavior offered in Definition 1.

III. Market Choice, Revealed Preference, and Political "Choice"

The notion of rational behavior applied by public choice scholars to voting derives from a direct extrapolation of individuals "choosing," with a given budget, among consumption items in the market—the standard case of consumer choice. When an individual so chooses, he or she must recognize that the opportunity cost of taking more of one good (x) is the prospective utility of some of another good (y) forgone. The objects over which choice is exercised are direct or indirect arguments in the individual's preferences from the choices actually made. It is possible to speak of those choices "revealing the individual's underlying preferences." Economists are often skeptical of attempts to discern preferences through other means (such as questionnaires) because, unless the preference is revealed in the context of actual choice, there is no real cost to the individual of revealing one set of preferences rather than another. Economics is firmly grounded on the methodological conviction that individuals act purposively and that their actions reveal those purposes.

Contrast this with the voter's choice in the polling booth as to which of two handles to pull.[7] Here we may presume that the ultimate arguments in the voter's utility function include the objects of "political choice" (whether those be alternative policy packages or alternative candidates). That is, we may presume that the individual cares which outcome emerges from the voting process. But this does not permit us to presume that his or her choice in the polling booth reflects or corresponds with his or her preference over outcomes, for the voter is not choosing between outcomes: He or she is choosing between levers to pull (or marks to make on a card), and is exercising that choice in the full knowledge that the particular lever pulled bears only the most tenuous relation to the political outcome that finally emerges. When the voter pulls a particular lever, the opportunity cost of doing so is not a particular policy forgone, but simply the other lever or levers unpulled. There is a categorical difference between preferences over outcomes (the things over which basic preferences are defined) and the action of pulling one lever rather than another. An individual may or may not vote for the outcome he or she prefers: He or she simply pulls the lever he or she prefers. In no sense, therefore, can we argue that the choice between levers—the act of voting—"necessarily reveals the voter's preference over the objects of collective choice" in the same way that an analogous market choice reveals a buyer's preferences over the objects of choice in the market. There is a logical wedge driven between action and preference in the voting process exactly equivalent to, and directly resultant from, the logical gap between action and outcome.

In this fundamental sense, consumer choice in the market and voter choice in the political mechanism are entirely unlike.[8] In the more formal language of the previous section, the considerations that predominate in voter choice (which of two levers to pull) are virtually absent in market choice. In market choice, even if there are considerations analogous to those captured by the U_v term in Equation (10), they are not overwhelming, as they are in the voting case. The analogous expression for market choice of some outcome A over B is as follows.

$$(11) \quad A_i = B_i + U_c^i$$

where U_c^i is the money value that i places on the act of choosing a in and of itself, and independent of whether the purchaser actually gets a.

We do not deny that U_c^i may be positive in the case of market choice. For example, an individual may like to think of him- or herself as the sort of person who supports the great classical literature of the culture. And, in some cases, this motive may be sufficient to induce the individual to buy books he or she will never read and perhaps does not really expect to read. But in the market, the individual must pay the full price of indulging such preferences: He or she has to choose a, not b. In the voting booth, by contrast, a voter can express a preference for a by casting a vote accordingly and yet recognize that he or she is not obliged to accept a, because that one vote alone is of relatively small significance in determining the final outcome. More specifically, in the market, one dollar's worth of B_i is equivalent to one dollar's worth of U_c^i; the terms of trade are 1 to 1. In voting, however, one dollar's worth of U_v^i is, to the voter, worth $1/h$ dollars' worth of B_i —perhaps twelve thousand dollars' worth, perhaps rather more.

IV. Implications for "Public Choice"

The implications of all this for the analysis of political processes depend, in part, on the purposes for which the analysis is undertaken. Within modern public choice theory, it is possible to discern two distinct strands—one concerned with providing a predictive science of politics essentially analogous to the predictive science of markets that conventional neoclassical economics purports to provide, the other concerned with the normative evaluation of alternative institutional arrangements and possibly the design of institutional arrangements that might generate superior social outcomes.

For many scholars the distinction between these two purposes need not be finely drawn. The understanding of the way in which political institutions actually work—in the sense of providing testable hypotheses that the data do not reject—is a crucial ingredient in the choice among alternative institutions. Positive analysis is viewed as a necessary precursor to normative conclusions, and all that is required for any normative exercise is to "tack on" additional evaluation criteria to the pure science. In other work we have attacked this sort of approach as unduly casual, and have argued for a more ruthless separation of political science, thus defined, from political economy in the classical sense (which we see as primarily concerned with the exercise of comparative institutional analysis and institutional "design").[9]

In spelling out the implications of our analysis, it is useful to draw this distinction quite sharply. For purely positive, predictive political science, it is clearly crucial to have some theory of why individuals vote as they do. What we have attempted to explain is that any theory that presumes that individuals vote according to their evaluation of political outcomes, much as they choose in market settings, is extremely problematic. Since the U_v^i term, and not the B_i term, is overwhelmingly predominant in Equation (10), the choice of which candidate or policy option to vote for depends overwhelmingly on tastes for showing preferences as such, and hardly at all on the evaluation of outcomes. Voting behavior is then to be understood perhaps as "symbolic" or "liturgical" (rather like the choice of which team to support in an athletic spectacle) and hardly at all like the choice among alternative investments. We must therefore search for some theory like that which will predict why individuals support one team rather than another. In the process, we might consider the net wealth-maximization hypothesis (or something like it) as a possible contender, but on the face of things any such hypothesis seems rather implausible.

The public choice theorist might, of course, respond that the U_v^i term mainly captures the individual's desires to exercise his or her vote, and is essentially independent of the candidate for whom the individual votes (i.e., $U_v^i[a]$ and $U_v^i[b]$ are virtually identical). Such a claim cannot be rejected on purely logical grounds, but it does not seem at all congruent with even the most casual observation. Individuals do seem to care as much for the candidate for whom they vote as that they vote at all. The decision to vote is, after all, the decision to vote for someone and if the decision to vote cannot be explained in terms of outcome, then it would be surprising if the decision to vote for a particular candidate could be explained in such terms.

At the same time, one should be careful not to reject all public choice explanations out of hand: Some important pieces of public choice theory are not affected in any significant way by the foregoing discussion. Positive public choice derives its predictions about the behavior of wealthy-maximizing individuals in political institutions by appealing to two quite distinct mechanisms. One—the one that is relevant to the central point made here—depends on the action of political entrepreneurs who put together packages of public policies designed to secure electoral support from some majority of voters. To derive direct predictions about which particular policies will be selected requires both a means of determining the identity of the particular majority selected and a theory of what policies that majority will vote for. In the absence of the former means, the analysis may be able to make testable predictions about the pattern of outcomes, and perhaps say something of interest concerning the normative properties of those outcomes. But it could not develop a fully fledged predictive theory of public choice. However, it is the latter theory with which we are concerned here, and we have simply advanced the proposition that there can be no automatic presumption that voters will vote for policies that reflect their interests (however broadly those interests are conceived).

There is, however, a distinct mechanism by which wealth-maximizing individuals in political institutions interact—through lobbyists, who directly purchase particular policies from politician-bureaucrats by direct graft, by payments-in-kind, or by campaign contributions. Needless to say, hypotheses about the operation of political processes based on this mechanism remain totally unaffected by the basis on which individuals cast their votes. Purchase of policy outcomes in direct return for campaign contributions, for example, involves a more or less direct exchange of the familiar market kind. It is an exchange that has certain peculiar characteristics,[10] but there is no sense in which the contributor reveals anything other than his or her true preferences for policy outcomes. This dimension of positive public choice therefore remains entirely unscathed.

Furthermore, while it is true that voters do not necessarily vote in accordance with preferences over outcomes, we cannot reject the hypothesis that they in fact do so. The claim might plausibly be made that preferences concerning which teams to support (the U_v^i term) in some measure reflect similar considerations to outcome evaluation (the B_i term). After all, voters may well be inclined to prefer candidates who redistribute in their favor (and otherwise reflect their interests). People are, one might argue, more ready to support a party that is "nice" to them than one that is not, on the same sorts of grounds that they prefer people who are nice to them as friends. The theory of behavior that underlies such a position is not the theory of contractual exchange, but the theory of reciprocal giving. A suitor, for example, does not buy the attention of the object of his admiration when he makes her a gift: He simply symbolizes his affection and interest. She may reciprocate his gift to indicate a corresponding interest, or exhibit that interest in some other way. But there is no direct quid pro quo here, no contractual obligation of the sort we associate with conventional trade. Given this rendering, it may make sense to speak of politicians "wooing" votes, but not of "buying" votes, with policy changes. And one would surmise, as in the suitor analogy, that the magnitude of the "gift" is by no means the only relevant consideration in securing voter support, and in many cases is not an important one.

Based on this understanding, rational voting behavior (in the sense of Definition 1) becomes not a logical extension of underlying rationality postulates, but, rather, an "as if" proposition: If the predictions derived from such an assumption "fit" reasonably well, then the assumption of voter rationality (as in Definition 1) is justified by the "fact." The difficulty with such a stance is that it presupposes a great deal of knowledge as to what "the facts" are. The extent to which the interests of particular voters are totally reflected in easily identifiable things, such as subsidies received and income increases due to relative factor price changes, can easily be overstated. Normal economic interest also includes, for example, the consumption value to the individual of publicly provided goods consumed—a value that is not apparent from mere inspection. As revealed preference theory of consumer choice emphasizes, preferences generally cannot be known except to the extent that they are gratuitously revealed in the process of acting. Consequently, where the connection between action and preference is itself at risk, it is difficult to see how a decisive empirical test for that connection could be mounted.

Moreover, to the extent that political outcomes do appear to reflect constituent interests, this may be attributable not to electoral constraints on politicians' behavior but to constraints arising from the rational desire to maximize gains from lobbying and campaign contributions, which, as we have noted, is precisely analogous to ordinary market behavior.

Even the most enthusiastic defender of a method that presumes voters to vote preferences over outcomes must, therefore, acknowledge the possibility of an independent source of "noise," attributable to the logical gap between voter action and voter preference—noise that may, in particular instances, become thunderous. The pessimistically inclined may well despair of the possibility of developing any systematic theory of majoritarian electoral processes from an economic interest base. Public choice, as the political science counterpart to the neoclassical theory of market behavior, lacks the foundation of a purely logical a priori theory of voting behavior. By any reckoning, this is surely a major shortcoming.

Once the notion that individuals vote their interests is seen to be at risk, then, clearly, so is the claim of any "efficiency" properties that might be construed to attach to political outcomes. Setting aside the peculiarities of majority rule as an "aggregation" device, of which standard public choice theory makes much ado, there remains the problem that the preferences so aggregated may bear little relation to the political outcomes that citizens would prefer to prevail. For example, even where the simple median voter theorem applies, and hence where there is no cycling, there can be no presumption that the median of revealed voter preferences will bear any systematic relation to the median of those voters' true preferences over policy outcomes. If voters cannot be presumed to vote for the outcomes they prefer, there seems to be widespread scope for electoral irrationality of the most basic kind. Clearly, such irrationality is a creature of the institutional setting within which voting occurs: It does not arise in analogous market settings. The familiar normative apparatus of modern welfare economics would, on this basis, indicate a presumptive preference for decentralized markets over majoritarian electoral processes.

V. Summary and Conclusion

The central proposition of this article is that the institutional setting within which preferences are revealed makes a difference in what is revealed. The strict logical connection between individual choice and the individual's preferences over choice alternatives that exists in the market is essentially absent in large-number majoritarian elections. Because no individual voter acts to determine the social outcome (except in highly unlikely cases), voters cannot be expected to choose among alternative outcomes in the manner they do in the market. This implies that any simple extrapolation of voter behavior from market analogues is misguided. The notion that voters vote according to their preferences over alternatives is not an a priori truth emerging from the basic proposition that agents are rational. At the very best, it becomes an empirical proposition potentially subject to refutation. And, on the face of things, it is by no means an overwhelmingly plausible proposition.

Public choice theory, in simply assuming that voters behave rationally and in a manner analogous to that in which market agents can be presumed to operate, is therefore at risk entirely on logical grounds. And, although pure logic may not be sufficient to enable us to reject public choice propositions, a great deal more in the way of empirical evidence would have to be amassed before rational voting (in the public choice sense) could be presumed. What logic and a priori theorizing can do is alert us to those considerations that seem likely to weigh most heavily in voting behavior: On this basis, evaluation of the outcomes can be set aside as presumptively irrelevant.

Traditional political scientists may feel reassured by all this. To some extent, the ad hoc empiricism and casual theorizing of conventional political science may seem to be vindicated by our analysis. But one of the major thrusts of public choice theory—that the outcomes of majoritarian elections may bear little relation to what citizens really want—reemerges in a rather different form. Collective irrationality may occur, not so much because of cycling problems and the like as because of the underlying irrationality of voters' revealed preferences. Because ultimately such irrationality is a characteristic of the institutional setting within which voting occurs, simple majoritarian political processes must be recognized to be presumptively unsatisfactory, at least using any normative criteria in which voter preferences are supposed to count.

Notes

1. There is some positive relation between a fan's support of his or her team and its performance: A team tends to perform somewhat better before an enthusiastic crowd; and, in the long run, good gates and good TV ratings allow a team to spend more on resources that contribute to its record. However, the relation here is simply too vague, too small, and too indirect to constitute a rationale for spectator behavior. A spectator is a booster because he or she wants to be—no more and no less. Although spectators care about the

outcome, they do not act to determine it, and they do not conceive themselves to be so acting.

2. See, for example, H. Bowen, "An Interpretation of Voting in the Allocation of Economic Resources," *Quarterly Journal of Economics* 58 (1943): 27–48.

3. This reflects nothing other than the law of large numbers. The variance of the distribution of possible outcomes around p becomes very small as electoral size increases.

4. This analysis discounts complications stemming from the electoral college system.

5. As n becomes large, the variance of the distribution becomes very small.

6. See N. Beck, "A Note on the Probability of a Tied Election," *Public Choice* 18 (1975): 75–80; W. Riker and P. Ordeshook, "A Theory of the Calculus of Voting," *American Political Science Review* 62 (1968): 25–42.

7. For an early attempt to compare individual choice in the two settings, see J. Buchanan, "Individual Choice in Voting and the Market," *Journal of Political Economy* 62 (1954): 334–43. Some of the points made here are hinted at in the treatment, though not explicitly articulated.

8. Certain sorts of market choice, in which the outcome is very uncertain, may be rather like electoral choice as here analyzed.

9. See G. Brennan and J. Buchanan, "The Normative Purpose of Economic Science: Rediscovery of an Eighteenth-Century Method," *International Review of Law and Economics* 1 (1981): 155–66, for a fuller discussion of the distinction involved here, and for a discussion of the analytic method appropriate to "constitutional analysis" in the classical political economy sense.

10. The growing literature on "rent seeking" deals directly with this type of transaction. See J. Buchanan, R. Tollison, and G. Tullock, *Toward a Theory of the Rent-Seeking Society* (College Station: Texas A&M University Press, 1980), for much of the relevant material.

9.

Vote Buying in a Stylized Setting

WITH DWIGHT R. LEE

I. Introduction

At least since the early contributions of Downs and of Tullock,[1] public choice theorists have recognized the limits of rational behavioral models in explaining why some persons vote at all in large-number settings where outcomes are determined by majority rule, and, further, why those who do vote bother to become informed about the alternatives. Theories of rational abstention and rational ignorance have long been central in elementary public choice. More recently, and picking up an early discussion by Buchanan[2] on the absence of individual responsibility in voting choice, Brennan and Buchanan[3] have discussed in some detail the likely dominance of expressive elements in the psychology of the voting choice itself.

These results all stem from the recognition of the relative impotence of the individual in being able to influence the ultimate result in the large-number majoritarian setting, where the simultaneous behavior of many persons in choosing among alternatives generates a single outcome through the operation of the voting rule. In this paper, we propose to examine yet another implication of the probabilistic relationship between the potential choice behavior of the individual voter and the ultimate collective outcome, one that has not, to our knowledge, been fully recognized. Our concern is with mutually advantageous opportunities for the buying and selling of votes that may emerge as the probabilities of influence over collective outcomes vary. The analysis is somewhat indirectly related to theories of coalition information,[4] and also to Tullock's examination of rational behavior in rent-seeking.[5] There are also analogues between our analysis and the theories of markets for voting proxies in corporate takeover bidding.

We develop the analysis in highly stylized and abstract models. We do so without apology. We leave to others the discussion of whether or not our models have implications for the real world of politics.

II. The Basic Structure of the Model

First, consider a setting where a simple yes-no or approval referendum is to be taken on a specific proposal for spending. Approval signaled by a majority authorizes the fiscal authority of the community to spend for a designated project and to levy the taxes required to finance the spending. We abstract from the problems of rational abstention, rational ignorance, and expressive voting. We assume that all voters go to the polls, and that all vote in accordance with their own identified interests, regardless of how minuscule the influence of a single person's vote on the ultimate outcome. Further, each voter is fully informed as to the consequences of the two possible outcomes (yes-no) with regard to his own economic position. Each voter's information about the probable voting choices of other voters is summarized in a single estimate the "proclivity to vote yes" assigned to each voter, and hence to the group.[6]

Our emphasis is on the value of participation to the individual voter, and on the possible willingness of a voter to sell his vote to a potential buyer. The central assumption of our model is that a voter will sell his right of participation, his vote, for anything above its value to him. That is to say, if the value of the voting act is, say, rX to individual i, then i will sell a proxy for his vote to anyone who offers a price that exceeds rX. (We may think of X as the differential in value between the two election outcomes to i, and r as the appropriate discount factor generated by the probability that i's vote will be decisive.) We assume that transactions are costless; neither moral nor institutional considerations inhibit the potential for perfect markets in votes.

In order to complete the general model, we need to examine the buyer's side of the market. If persons stand willing to sell votes for any value over and beyond the value of participation in the process rX, who will emerge as a potential purchaser?

The basis for a mutually beneficial trade stems from the prospect that a person with two votes, any person, has more influence on the ultimate outcome than a person with only one vote. That is to say, a person with two votes will value this two-vote package at some value above rX. The question to be considered is when and under what circumstances the two-vote package is valued more highly than $2rX$. If the package is valued above $2rX$, then there are mutual gains from trade; a vote purchaser, j, can offer to a vote seller, i, something more than the value of his "right to vote" which is rX, and still secure for himself some residual value above rX, his initial position.

All persons make the same estimates for the proclivities of persons in the electorate to vote yes and no. We are not concerned with possible differentials in estimates of predicted voting outcomes. The proclivities remain, however, probability estimates; the individual knows only his own interest with certainty. Further, we postulate that all voters place the same differential in value as between the two alternatives, although the directions of evaluations must, of course, differ as between two possible sets of voters. Whether or not the "game" is negative, zero, or positive sum depends, then, both on the direction of evaluation and the predicted voting proclivity.

Initially, we assume that the vote markets are blind on both sides in the sense that neither buyer nor seller knows the voting choice of his opposite number in the exchange. The prospective vote purchaser knows, of course, the direction of his own preferences or interest, but he does not know the interests of the vote seller, from whom he receives a proxy. The latter might have been a supporter or an opponent of the outcome supported by the buyer. Similarly, the person who sells the proxy does not know the voting preferences of the person to whom he sells. He may sell his proxy to someone who seeks to further the same interest as his own or to someone who will seek to further the opposing interest. The model is, literally, one of vote buying and selling; it is not a model of sale or purchase of directed voting support for one or the other of the alternatives.

As the subsequent discussion indicates, the very structure of the vote market may be such that a fully informed voter will know the identity of the person on the other side of a purchase or sale. This modifies the result only in the small-number example of Section III (see note 7, below).

III. A Small Number Example

Although misleading if the rationality assumptions are taken to be literally applicable, it will be analytically useful to begin with a simple case of three voters who must collectively decide on an issue that will provide a net gain (or prevent a net loss) of one dollar to each of those on the winning side, and impose a net loss (or prevent a net gain) of one dollar to the single loser. Each voter knows how he will himself vote, but he has only a probability estimate as to how others will vote, described in the single proclivity-to-vote estimate. The small-number model should be interpreted as a stylized and simplified representation of a large-number model rather than one that embodies predictive implications in its own setting.

Consider first the setting where individual 1 knows that he plans to vote *for* a proposal, but in which he assigns to each of the other voters a ¾ probability of voting *against* the proposal. If 1 does nothing but vote his preference, namely "yes," he expects the proposal to lose, with probability ⁹⁄₁₆ (¾ × ¾), with an expected loss to himself of $⁹⁄₁₆. However, in this situation, if individual 1 should buy one vote, he could control the outcome. By ensuring defeat of the proposal he can ensure his personal gain of one dollar. Individual 1 will, therefore, be willing to pay as much as $⁹⁄₁₆ for a single vote.

But what is the maximum value that voters 2 and 3 place on their own votes? Assume that each opposes the proposal, and, like individual 1, each places a ¾ probability estimate on the opposition to the proposal by any voter. Each of the two voters, 2 or 3, then assesses the probability of the proposal being defeated in an untampered election as ¹⁵⁄₁₆ (¼ × ¼). The expected value of the election to each of these two voters is, therefore, $¹⁵⁄₁₆. (There is a ¹⁵⁄₁₆ probability that a loss of $1 will be avoided in the electoral choice.) On the other hand, if, say, individual 2 should sell his vote, then the probability of his side winning, and the proposal being defeated, is seen to drop to ¹²⁄₁₆. The expected value of the election has been reduced by $³⁄₁₆. (There is a ¼ probability that the purchaser of 2's vote will approve the proposal, and hence, impose the net cost of $1 on 2 by making up the majority in the election.) Vote selling will be attractive to individual 2 or 3 if a purchaser offers anything above $³⁄₁₆. And, as the example demonstrates, individual 1 will be willing to pay anything up to $⁹⁄₁₆. There are mutual gains from trade in the stylized vote market explained here.[7]

Similar logic shows the potential for trade for any voting proclivity other than ½. If, to consider a different case, the proclivity that any person in our three-person electorate will oppose a proposal is estimated to be ⅗, then the individual who favors the proposal will be willing to pay up to $0.36 for another vote, and a person who opposes the proposal will sell his vote for anything greater than $0.24. Only if the probability that any voter will vote for one outcome is set at ½ will it be the case that the value of an additional vote is the same ($0.25 in our numerical example) for all persons, and that gains from vote buying and selling are not possible.

Several points emerge in the three-voter example. First, vote buying does not depend on persons attaching differing absolute values to the differential gains and losses from the electoral alternatives. In the example, the differential in value between a favorable and unfavorable outcome was, for each voter, set at one dollar. Secondly, the closer the election is expected to be, the smaller will be the motivation to buy or to sell votes (the smaller the gains from trade). And when the two possible outcomes of the election, in an expected value sense, are equally probable (the estimated proclivity for a vote for one of the alternatives is set at ½ for each voter), there are no gains to be realized from buying or selling votes. Finally, the example indicates that only those persons who favor the outcome assigned the lower probability of winning will find vote buying advantageous.

In the following section, we turn to the more general case to see how robust these conclusions are, and also, to see if additional results can be uncovered.

IV. The General Model

Given the structure of the basic model outlined in Section II. above, we know that each individual will, in the absence of any purchase or sale of votes, place the *same* value on his own vote. This result follows from the postulates that all persons assess the voting proclivity identically and that all place the same differential value on the alternatives. In a large-number setting, this value of the individual vote will be very small indeed since the prospect that any vote will be decisive under simple majority voting is highly improbable. It is the smallness of this value that motivates the theorems of rational abstention, rational ignorance, and expressive voting. Our concern in this paper is not with computations of this value, which are well known to public choice theorists. Our concern is, instead, with the value of an *additional* vote to an individual since it is only this value that can possibly motivate a vote purchase.

Assume 2n voters who must decide either yes or no on some exogenously presented proposal. Let p be the probability that any given voter will vote yes, that is, in favor of the proposal, and q the probability he will vote no, that is, against the proposal ($p + q = 1$). Assume that each voter expects to gain (or avoid the loss of) one hundred dollars if his preferred alternative is selected. The question that needs to be answered specifically is: What is the value to any individual, say individual 1, of controlling one more vote than he is entitled to?

The answer to this question depends on the probability of a tie without the control of the extra vote. Individual 1 knows that he is going to vote in favor of the proposal; hence, he will assess the probability of a tie to be equal to the number of ways the remaining $2n - 1$ votes can be partitioned into $(n - 1)$ yes's and n no's, all multiplied by $p^{n-1}q^n$, or

$$(1) \quad \binom{2n - 1}{n - 1} p^{n-1}q^n = \frac{(2n - 1)!}{(n - 1)!n!} p^{n-1}q^n$$

Multiplying the probability in Equation (1) by \$100, or

(2) (\$100) $\dfrac{(2n-1)!}{(n-1)!n!} p^{n-1}q^n$

gives the value 1 places on being able to control an additional vote. On the other hand, considering someone who is going to vote against the proposal, the value of controlling another vote equals

(3) (\$100) $\dfrac{(2n-1)!}{(n-1)!n!} p^n q^{n-1}$

Note that if $p < q$ then (2) > (3), and therefore the individual who favors the proposal is willing to pay more for an extra vote than the individual who opposes it. Individual 1 is, therefore, prepared to offer enough for a vote to make it attractive for someone to sell him one if he favors the low probability outcome. The value of an *additional* vote exceeds the value of the single vote each person possesses initially.

If we assume that individual 1 has purchased one vote, the question then becomes: What is a third vote worth to him? Again, the answer is \$100 times the probability that the election will end in a draw given that 1 casts his two votes in support of the proposal, or

(4) (\$100) $\dbinom{2n-2}{n-2} p^{n-2}q^n = $ (\$100) $\dfrac{(2n-1)!}{(n-2)!n!} p^{n-2}q^n$

It can be seen that, for large n and $p < \frac{1}{2}$, (4) > (2) [to get (2) you multiply (4) by $p(2n-1)/(n-1)$, which is < 1, since $(2n-1)/(n-1)$ is close to 2 when n is large], which means that having purchased one vote the voter buyer will place a higher value on the purchase of a second vote. The intuition behind this result is straightforward. As a voter who supports the minority position purchases control of more votes, the probability of a tie will, at least up to some point, increase.[8] This places a minority position vote buyer in a categorically different position from that of a majority position vote buyer. If someone favoring the majority position buys votes, he will know that he is reducing the probability of a tie, and therefore, with every vote he buys, reducing the value to him of the additional vote.

If the minority position vote buyer manages to keep the extent of his vote buying known only to himself, then he will be the only one who knows how much the probability of a tie is increasing, and how much votes are worth. From his perspective, the ideal case is when each vote seller is either unaware that vote buying is taking place or, if his vote has already been purchased, believes that it is the only one that has been purchased. In this situation, the vote buyer will be able to purchase votes for a price that marginally covers the value an individual places on his vote in an untampered election. The vote buyer, in this case, continues to purchase votes until the value of the additional vote increases to some maximum and then declines to the constant supply price of votes.

Next we drop the double blind assumption, and consider a situation far less conducive to vote buying by assuming that the vote buyer does not know the implications which derive from the structure of the model. Specifically we assume that (1) the vote buyer knows nothing of the voting proclivities of those from whom he purchases votes, (2) minority position voters not buying votes know exactly how many votes the vote buyer has purchased but do not know the voting proclivity of the buyer, and (3) majority position voters know not only how many votes the vote buyer has purchased, but also how these votes will be cast.[9] Even under these conditions, there will still be a gain from trade over some range between the vote buyer and voters favoring the majority position. Consider the value the vote buyer places on an additional vote, having purchased one, given by (4), and compare that value with that of an additional vote to a fully informed majority voter. Each majority voter knows that he will vote no and that a minority voter controls two votes which will be placed in the yes column. With this information, the majority voter will assess the loss of selling his vote ($100 times the probability of a tie if his vote is not sold) as equal to

$$(5) \quad (\$100) \, \frac{(2n - 3)!}{(n - 2)! \, (n - 1)!} \, p^{n - 2} q^{n - 1}$$

Notice that multiplying (5) by

$$(6) \quad \frac{2n - 2}{n} \, q$$

yields (4). For large n, and q sufficiently greater than ½, (6) will be greater than unity, and therefore (4) will be greater than (5). The vote buyer will be willing to pay more for another vote than the minimum amount our fully informed majority voter is willing to accept. Again, the intuition is straightforward. Since the majority voter knows his own as well as the buyer's position (the vote buyer knows only his own preference), the majority voter knows that the probability of a tie is less than that calculated by the vote buyer. Note, however, that once the buyer has amassed enough votes to go beyond the point that maximizes the probability of a tie vote, then each individual who plans to vote no, and also knows that the vote buyer will cast all of his votes yes will see the probability of a tie to be higher than will the vote buyer who knows only how he is voting. In this case, when majority voters have full information on the vote buyer's activities, once the probability of a tie vote is maximized, they will no longer be willing to charge the vote buyer less for their votes than he is willing to pay.

Vote buying will occur in our model, therefore, under a wide range of informational assumptions. In the case where no one knows with certainty how any particular individual, other than themselves, will vote, and has no suspicions that vote buying is taking place on a large scale, then it will pay the vote buyer to purchase a sufficient number of votes to move into the range where the initial minority position he favors is known (by him) to be the most likely position to win. In the case where the vote buyer is not able to keep secret either his position or the total number of votes he has bought, it will still pay an initial minority position individual to purchase votes up to the point where the probability of a tie is maximized (neither position has a probability advantage over the other). Other informational assumptions are possible, but vote buying will still occur over some range. For example, a vote buyer could know the voting propensity of those from whom he buys by recognizing that those who oppose the project place the lowest value on their votes. But this would simply make vote buying more attractive to the buyer over some initial range.

The most realistic assumption would be that a vote buyer could maintain some secrecy and arrange to buy votes from individuals with one seller being unaware of the existence of other sellers. This type of purchasing could be modeled after land acquisition schemes in which a large firm amasses a large block of land in an area by using several purchasing agents, each unaware of who the ultimate buyer is, to buy up small blocks of land.[10] This type of purchasing arrangement, of course, shifts the advantage to the buyer.

To this point, we have proceeded under the assumption that there is only one buyer. If anything, this assumption makes our results all the more striking. Our one buyer is motivated to act on behalf of all those who favor the initial minority position without any help or organized support. Receiving but a small fraction of the benefits that those on his side will receive if the initial minority position wins, our single vote buyer will, if his purchases remain clandestine, buy enough votes almost to ensure that this position wins.[11] Furthermore, the result does not require that differential benefits accrue to supporters of a position.[12] Neither do we require concentrated benefits versus diffused costs to motivate action on behalf of the group receiving the benefits. In our model individuals in the benefiting group receive exactly the same amount per person from successful action as those in the losing group lose.

There is no reason, of course, to expect that there will be only one vote buyer. If one voter sees advantage in buying additional votes, others will likely do the same. The only restriction our model implies in this regard is that vote buyers will be found in what is, at least initially, the minority position. Vote buying by multiple minority voters, of course, is completely consistent with the major result of this paper: that vote buying will take place and it will switch the advantage in the direction of what, in an untampered election, would be the minority position. And if several vote buyers organize into a collective effort, this result is likely to be reinforced. It should be acknowledged, however, that an organized vote buying effort may be more difficult to keep secret and, therefore, may result in higher reservation prices on the part of vote sellers. This suggests the possibility that a single vote buyer, acting strictly on his own and in response to his own self-interest, may do more to advance the interest of a large group than will an organized group effort in which the free-rider problem has been overcome.

V. A Large-Number Example

In this section we illustrate the primary results derived from the general model with another example, this time with a relatively large, though computationally manageable, number of voters. It is assumed that the selection between two collective-choice options (yes and no) is to be made by eight hundred voters in a simple majority vote. As before, it will be assumed that each voter stands to gain (or avoid losing) the same amount if the decision made is the one he favors. The probability that any given voter will vote yes is .42, hence, .58 is the probability of any person voting no.

We first look at the value of incremental votes to a vote buyer who favors the proposal, that is, supports the low probability outcome, yes. Letting X represent the value the vote buyer places on achieving his preferred outcome (and, by assumption, the value all voters place on achieving their preferred outcome), the value of the incremental vote is given by

$$(7) \quad X \frac{(799 - B)!}{(399 - B)! \, 400!} (.42)^{399 - B}(.58)^{400}$$

where $B = 0, 1, 2, 3 \ldots$ is the number of votes the vote buyer has already purchased. In words, (7) is equal to X times the probability that exactly 400 of the $799 - B$ votes the vote buyer does not control will be cast in opposition to the proposal, or that the election ends in a tie.

When $B = 0$, the probability of a tie is .00000105. For the sake of convenience, it will be assumed that $X = \$10,000$. With this individual payoff, the value realized from the first vote purchased equals 1.05

Table 9-1. Marginal values of votes

(1) B	(2) Marginal value to buyer	Vote buying secret (3) Marginal value to seller	Vote buying known (4)
0	$ .0105	.0091	$ .0091
10	$ .0560	.0091	$ .0489
20	$ .26	.0091	$ .23
30	$ 1.07	.0091	$ .96
40	$ 3.81	.0091	$ 3.46
50	$ 11.69	.0091	$ 10.76
60	$ 30.79	.0091	$ 28.73
70	$ 69.15	.0091	$ 65.42
80	$131.50	.0091	$126.13
90	$210.12	.0091	$204.39
100	$279.882	.0091	$276.08
109	$307.65	.0091	$307.49
110	$307.86	.0091	$308.15
111	$307.46	.0091	$308.20
120	$277.19	.0091	$281.53
130	$202.16	.0091	$208.40
140	$118.11	.0091	$123.61
150	$ 54.62	.0091	$ 58.04
160	$ 19.73	.0091	$ 21.29
170	$ 5.49	.0091	$ 6.02
180	$ 1.16	.0091	$ 1.29
190	$ .18	.0091	$ .21
200	$ .0209	.0091	$ .0240
202	$ .0130	.0091	$ .0191
203	$ .0102	.0091	$ .0150
204	$ .0080	.0091	$ .0093

cents ($10,000 × .00000105), barely over a penny. As explained in the previous section, once the first vote is purchased, the value of having an additional vote increases. With X = $10,000, the value of (7) is 1.25 cents when B = 1. In Table 9-1 the marginal values of votes to the initial minority position vote buyer are shown in Column 2 for intermittent values of B. There is a steady increase in the marginal value of a vote as more are purchased until B = 110, at which point another vote is worth $307.86. Further vote buying finds the marginal value of votes declining, with the additional vote worth barely over a penny when 203 votes have been purchased.

If our vote buyer can operate clandestinely, he is the only one who will realize that the value of a vote has been altered by his purchases. In this case, he will be able to purchase as many votes as he wants for slightly less than a penny each.[13] At a price of slightly under $0.01, the rational vote buyer will, in our example, purchase 203 votes. This means that the vote buyer would control 204 votes, which he will cast in favor of the proposal. Of the 596 votes outstanding, 42 percent, or 250, can be expected to be in support of the proposal. Under these circumstances, the probability of the total vote favoring the proposal is very close to unity.[14]

The assumption that the vote buyer is able to purchase votes with complete secrecy is, admittedly, a strong one that facilitates the buying of votes. We can, however, demonstrate that vote buying will occur even with full information on the part of those voters who are initially in the majority position. Assume, now, that all voters who initially oppose the proposal know that the vote buyer seeks the yes solution; they also know when a vote is purchased and, at any stage in the sequence, they know how many votes have been purchased previously. In this situation, the value each initial opponent of the proposal attaches to his vote is given by

$$(8) \quad X \frac{(798 - B)!}{(399 - B)! \ 399!} (.42)^{399 - B}(.58)^{399}$$

where, as before, $X = \$10,000$ and B is the number of votes that have been bought. In words, (8) is equal to X times the probability that of the $798 - B$ votes that the potential seller does not know how will be cast, 399 will be cast in opposition. Therefore, (8) is the expected loss each person who prefers a no solution (and who has not previously sold his own proxy) attaches to his votes at any stage in the vote-buying sequence.

In the fourth column of Table 9-1, the value of (8) is given for different values of B. The important thing to notice is that, until the minority position vote buyer has purchased 110 votes, the value of another vote to the buyer is greater than the minimum amount each majority position voter is willing to accept for his vote. Once 110 votes have been purchased, the gains from trade have been exhausted, as is easily seen from Table 9-1. Notice also, that once 110 votes have been purchased, the election is a toss-up. With 110 purchased votes, the vote buyer controls 111 votes in favor of the proposal. Of the 689 votes outstanding, the number expected to go in support of the proposal rounds off to 289 (689 × .42), for an expected total of 400. As argued in the previous section, once it is assumed that those in what was originally the majority position have full information on the activities of the vote buyer, vote buying will only proceed until the probability that the election ends in a tie is maximized.

VI. Conclusions

As we noted in the introduction, we do not propose to discuss possible implications for the real world of democratic politics that may be drawn from the highly stylized models of vote buying that we have analyzed in this paper. To the extent that economic, legal, or moral thresholds prevent the emergence of the purchase and sale of votes among persons who initially possess property rights in the collective franchise, our whole analysis is simply inapplicable. If, however, such thresholds serve only to inhibit but not to prevent totally the emergence of such markets, there should be some value in an analysis that embodies the zero transactions costs assumption.

Notes

We are indebted to Roger Faith, Arizona State University, for helpful comments on an earlier draft.

1. A. Downs, *An Economic Theory of Democracy* (New York: Harper, 1957); G. Tullock, *Toward a Mathematics of Politics* (Ann Arbor: University of Michigan Press, 1967).

2. J. M. Buchanan, "Individual Choice in Voting and the Market," *Journal of Political Economy* 62 (1954): 334–43.

3. G. Brennan and J. M. Buchanan, "Voting Choice: Evaluating Political Alternatives," *American Behavioral Scientist* 28 (November–December, 1984): 185–201.

4. To our knowledge the analysis that most closely relates to that developed in this paper is contained in J. S. Coleman, "The Marginal Utility of a Vote Commitment," *Public Choice* 5 (1968): 39–58. Coleman is interested, however, in deriving values for individual vote commitments when the number of previously committed votes is directionally known and are allowed to vary. His analysis is more closely related to the theories of coalition formation than our own.

In the theories of coalition formation (see W. H. Riker and P. C. Ordeshook, *An Introduction to Positive Political Theory* [Englewood Cliffs, N.J.: Prentice Hall, 1973], and references cited therein), emphasis is centered on the calculus of an individual in determining whether or not to join a protocoalition which involves probability estimates of the emergence of some ultimate winning coalition. The underlying game is zero sum, whereas, in our models, the game may be negative, zero, or positive sum.

5. In his paper "Efficient Rent Seeking" in J. M. Buchanan, R. D. Tollison, and G. Tullock, eds., *Toward a Theory of the Rent-Seeking Society* (College Station: Texas A & M University Press, 1980), Gordon Tullock analyzes the value of an incremental investment in rent-seeking activity under a variety of models.

6. For a general discussion of yes-no voting, see J. M. Buchanan and Roger L. Faith's "Toward a Theory of Yes-No Voting," *Public Choice* 37, no. 2 (1981): 231–46 (chapter 6 in this volume).

7. As noted, the small-number example is misleading in that the postulated assumptions may run counter to rational behavior by individual participants. In such a setting, the individual in the position such as voter 2 in the sample would know, *from the structure*, that a prospective vote buyer would necessarily evaluate the alternatives differently from his own evaluation; that is, 2 would know that a sale of his vote would ensure defeat of the alternative that he, personally, prefers. The assumption that the market is double blind is, in this sense, inconsistent with fully informed and rational behavior.

This inconsistency disappears in the large-number setting where the individual does not, even if he can identify the directional preference of the prospective vote buyer, by his own action substantially affect the probabilities of the ultimate collective outcome.

8. Obviously, at some point enough votes will be controlled by the minority position so that it will become the majority position, and controlling additional votes in favor of the position will begin reducing probability of a tie.

9. Under these assumptions, the buyer will not be able to buy cheap, but to him worthless, votes from those who will vote the same as he. But because we have assumed that the buyer does not realize that he is buying only votes from the opposition, he will not value the additional vote as highly as he otherwise would.

10. In the early 1960s, Walt Disney purchased forty-three square miles of land through several different law firms, which were not aware that Disney was the buyer (see R. B. McKenzie, *Fugitive Industry: The Economics and Politics of Deindustrialization* [Cambridge, Mass.: Ballinger Publishing, 1984], p. 157).

11. That enough votes will be purchased to almost ensure the alternative that began as the minority position will become clear from our example in Section V.

12. Mancur Olson, in *The Logic of Collective Action* (Cambridge, Mass.: Harvard University Press, 1965), has argued that individuals may take unilateral action on behalf of a group, but only if they receive larger benefits from successful action than do other members of his group.

13. The actual value is $0.91, as will become clear later in this section. This value is shown in column 3 of Table 9-1.

14. For the vote to go against the proposal would require drawing less than 196 yes votes from the 596 outstanding votes, or 54 fewer than expected. The standard deviation of a binomial distribution with 596 trails, $p = .42$ and $q = .58$, is approximately 11.93. So a loss would require drawing a sample in which the number of yes votes was over $4\frac{1}{2}$ standard deviations below the mean.

10.
Predictability: The Criterion
of Monetary Constitutions

When we consider the alternatives for monetary policy independently of the many political-institutional-historical constraints that may serve, and have served, to inhibit discussion at many levels, we are engaged in a discussion of constitutional law; we are analyzing the alternative monetary constitutions that may be appropriate to the functioning of a competitive or enterprise economy.

If we conceive our efforts in this manner, the question of criteria emerges at the outset of our discussion. What results do we desire to see accomplished? How may the comparative performances of the separate monetary frameworks be evaluated? If we can initially agree upon, and accept, a single criterion for judging the performance of a set of monetary institutions, we should already have made a major step toward securing the required consensus on the more specific elements of monetary reform.

I submit that we can reach agreement on such a criterion, agreement not only among ourselves but among scholars generally. In other words, I am stating that the issues in monetary policy can be resolved wholly into issues of means, not ends. Contrary to other areas of economic policy, there is, or should be, no basic value conflict on matters of monetary policy. Having said this, I am now obliged to define the criterion about which I speak. I suggest that the most meaningful criterion for monetary policy, regardless of the level of discussion, is *predictability* in the value of the monetary unit, or, reciprocally, in the absolute level of prices.

I. Predictability and Stability as Norms

It will be useful to compare and contrast *monetary predictability* with *monetary stability* as the criterion of policy. As we know, the latter has been more often advanced. Note that, with monetary stability, we encounter immediately the issue of definition. What is meant by stability, even in some "ideal" sense? Is stability to be defined in terms of a product or a factor price level? These questions could, no doubt, be answered satisfactorily, and significant agreement reached among large numbers of monetary theorists. But the necessity for such questions to arise at this level of discussion can be eliminated by the substitution of predictability for stability as the appropriate monetary norm. More important for our purposes, however, is that this substitution widens considerably the consensus on criteria that are required for genuine progress. Even those who have argued in favor of creeping inflation should agree on the predictability criterion. In fact, a major virtue of predictability as a criterion lies in the obvious difficulty which confronts the serious monetary scholar who proposes to refuse acceptance. As we shall discuss in the following section, predictability in the value of the monetary unit is required for maximum economic efficiency, as normally defined, and, of course, for economic growth, which has become the modern equivalent of the efficiency norm when considered in a dynamic context.

Perhaps the greatest advantage of the proposed substitution of *predictability* for *stability* lies in the fact that it allows us to isolate problems and issues relating to the monetary constitution from those which introduce problems and issues concerned with the efficacy of monetary policy in producing specific effects on the so-called macroeconomic variables. Monetary policy, either at the constitutional framework level or at the institutionally constrained level, may or may not produce the effects called for by some stabilization criteria. The quantity of money may or may not be the key control variable in an overall macroeconomic policy model. The variation in this quantity may or may not satisfactorily explain historical experience as to fluctuations in economic magnitudes. The point is that issues such as these, regardless of individual views, *need not be raised* in the basic consideration of alternative monetary constitutions. And I think that the air would be cleared substantially if we should agree to leave aside these essentially subsidiary issues until the more basic ones are settled.

II. Predictability and Efficiency

It is difficult for me to understand how anyone could seriously reject predictability as an appropriate norm for monetary policy. And yet I think that the consensus on this norm represents much more than empty agreement on such other economic policy goals as "efficiency," "rapid growth," and the like. With the latter, the fundamental agreement on goals merely puts aside argument and dispute until problems of specifying and defining the agreed-on goals are faced. Monetary predictability is not a norm of this sort. The predictability of the value of money is quite precise as a conceptual notion. Problems of definition do, of course, arise, but these are problems that are subject to discussion and, presumably, to solution. In other words, reasonable persons can readily agree on the meaning of monetary predictability.

The analogy which comes to mind is weather. Predictability in weather is a widely accepted criterion for meteorologists, and we all know what is meant by improved weather prediction. I have seen no claim or argument to the effect that improvement in weather forecasting, in predictability, will not also "improve" overall efficiency in resource usage. The correspondence between improvements in predictability here and improvements in economic performance generally is, in fact, taken for granted and rarely mentioned explicitly at all. Improved weather forecasting is acknowledged to be one of the "desirable" results to be expected from greater investment in scientific research.

This accords strictly with common-sense notions. If man can further his skills in predicting the weather, economic resources will be more effectively employed; major mistakes will be avoided. Note particularly that this conclusion holds quite independently of the trend in the weather over time. The winters in the northern hemisphere may gradually be getting "worse" or "better" by certain commonly accepted standards of "worseness" or "betterness." But the direction of change in the weather, described in this way, is irrelevant to the conclusion that improved predictability can lead to greater economic efficiency.

Our analogy becomes even closer if we move forward in time and imagine ourselves in a situation where the weather can be deliberately controlled. It is relatively easy to see that, under such circumstances, serious disputes might arise concerning criteria for betterness. But the improvements in predictability should still be recognized as universally desirable, regardless of the particular criterion of betterness that is adopted.

The analogy, as modified, seems almost perfect, but, as with all analogies, it is treacherous unless it is carefully handled. The meteorologist can direct his efforts toward improving predictability in the current situation, quite independently of his efforts toward securing greater control over the elements. The monetary theorist can, of course, do likewise. He can accept the institutional complex as it exists and devote his energies to improving forecasting techniques. But this is clearly relatively unproductive if he can, at a lower cost, devise means of modifying the institutional structure itself in such a way as to ensure greater predictability as a result. The monetary theorist would probably have much more difficulty than the meteorologist of the future, however, in separating the predictability aspects of a proposed "constitutional" change from the "improvements in results" that he might be able to secure through the change. The situation here should, of course, be reversed when we consider the relative importance of predictability and improvements in results in the two cases. With the weather, significant "improvement" can be contemplated by most people, quite apart from improved forecasting. With a monetary framework or constitution, if predictability were to be ensured, there would seem to be relatively little difference among alternative patterns of performance. There should be relatively little difference in the social costs of organizing a monetary system that would, for example, produce stability in the product price level, one that would produce a gradual decline in the product price level, and a system that would produce a gradual increase, *provided that the predictability was equivalent in the several cases.*

This is not to suggest that the choice among alternative monetary systems, independent of predictability elements, is not an important one. I should emphasize only that this choice, when constrained to a system among those that are expected to produce substantially the same predictability, is considerably less important than the initial choice between systems expected to generate monetary predictability and those which are not.

III. Predictability and Perfect Foresight

I doubt that I have said anything up to this point with which issue could be taken. I should insist, however, that the emphasis on predictability is more important than it may at first appear. But objections may be raised on the grounds that predictability is a norm that can be useful for analytical purposes but which is unattainable and, therefore, not practicable in any policy sense. Is monetary predictability as a norm not similar to the requirement for perfect foresight when we discuss the efficiency with which the competitive economic system organizes resource use? We agree that the ideally operating competitive system requires perfect foresight on the part of all or at least a substantial number of participants, but rarely do we introduce such foresight as an organizational norm. We recognize that little can be done toward substantially increasing the "predictability" of the whole economic organization, considered over all. Such efficiency as the competitive order produces is ensured through its flexibility and adaptability to changes in tastes, in resource supply, and in technology—changes that are, almost by their nature, unpredictable. The structure of relative prices responds to such of these changes as happen to occur, and any attempt to "freeze" the future course of relative price relations in some misguided efforts to increase predictability, that is, to reduce uncertainty, would make little logical sense. The act of fixing the course of relative price movements in advance would do nothing toward reducing the uncertainties that are inherent in the movements of the wholly unpredictable exogenous variables of the free economy. Surplus disposal and rationing problems would surely arise from such an attempt to increase predictability, and, rather than accomplishing this result, the reductions in responsiveness of the system to unexpected changes would be measured in avoidable inefficiency.

The pre-fixing of the course of the absolute price level would, however, be completely different. If predictability in the level of absolute prices, that is, in the value of the monetary unit, could be introduced, net gains in efficiency would surely follow. Such predictability implies, of course, *continuous monetary equilibrium*. And if this were accomplished, the actual course of change in the absolute price level would become largely irrelevant.

In comparing positions of full equilibrium, the classical dichotomy between relative prices and the absolute price level is valid. And by imposing the assumption of predictability at the outset, I am ensuring that an equilibrium state is continuously maintained. Changes in the absolute price level may, of course, require accompanying changes in the supply or quantity of money. Implicit in my argument to this point is the idea that this variable might be employed to accomplish the goal desired. The main point is that, as the neoclassical writers emphasized, the absolute price level is independent of the structure of relative prices. It follows from this that the movements in the absolute price level over time can be varied without affecting the relative price structure. And, contrary to the situation applicable to the latter, the actual course of movement is largely unimportant in relation to the predictability of this movement.

But I am not yet in the clear, since I have not really got over the possible objection that the assumption of predictability in the absolute price level is analogous to the assumption of perfect foresight in the competitive model and, as such, useful analytically but not helpful normatively. Predictability as an appropriate policy norm must still be shown to be practicably achievable or, at the least, approachable.

The unique difference between potential predictability in the absolute price level and the potential satisfaction of the perfect foresight condition lies in the Walrasian recognition that one commodity or service in an interrelated economy must be selected as a *numéraire* in order to prevent underdetermination in the solution of the system of equations describing the economy. Until and unless one such commodity or service is selected, relative price relations can be expressed only in ratios or relatives; no common denominator of value exists. The selection of such a *numéraire* does not reduce the flexibility or the adaptability of the system to changes in the exogenous variables. Quite the contrary; agreement on a *numéraire* becomes a necessary condition for organizational efficiency. It follows directly from this that the imposition of predictability in the value of this *numéraire*, when computed in terms of other commodities and services, does not substantially reduce the flexibility allowed the other variables in the system.

IV. "Ideal" Aspects of Price-Level Predictability

If the predictability norm is accepted as appropriate for monetary policy, and if it is accepted that this represents a meaningful and conceptually attainable norm, the next question to be faced involves the choice of means to implement it. In one sense, everything I have said to this point is introductory to this latter question, which is the main part of my discussion. For it is on the means of attaining monetary predictability that the various students of constitutional monetary policy may, and do, differ sharply. Before discussing some of these differences, I should like to emphasize again that the attainment of predictability, under any monetary framework, is more important than the means through which the goal is accomplished. Despite the amount of discussion devoted to arguments for or against various means of introducing monetary predictability, the underlying and central importance of ensuring predictability, *by any means*, should never be overlooked.

The result we seek is not difficult to define. What we want a monetary framework to produce is predictability in the value of money. We desire a monetary system that will allow the individual decision-maker, whether that is consumer, entrepreneur, seller of productive services, or speculator, to remove from his calculus uncertainty about the future course of the absolute price level. He will face quite sufficient and necessary uncertainty in his efforts to predict the future course of relative prices, uncertainty which, quite properly, should enter directly into his calculus.

We define the result desired in terms of the value of money, or reciprocally, the absolute price level. These are conceptual abstractions, however, not physical units of measure. These magnitudes assume arithmetical meaning only after some averaging process is undertaken, a process that utilizes movements in the prices of real physical commodities and services. The predictability about which we speak is predictability in the movement of an average over time. This average can be expressed in terms of an index number, but this number can never be expected to serve for more than an arbitrary scale factor. As such, movement in the index number can provide a criterion to suggest the suitability of action being taken on *other* variables, real or physical variables. The index itself cannot be acted upon in any direct manner.

We may provide an illustration by an analogy with temperature. The thermometer measures temperature, but temperature as such can do nothing other than to provide us with a criterion for taking action directly on other variables. We cannot directly increase temperature; we must instead take action on other variables, such as the quantity of coal in the furnace, which will, in turn, influence the heat index, or temperature, that we are observing.

Fundamentally, there exist two ways in which predictability in the movement of a price index can be incorporated into a monetary constitution. First, we may utilize the price index as the *instrumental* criterion for policy changes, changes that must involve action taken on other variables of the system. Second, and alternatively, we may try to organize the institutions of private decision-making in such a way that the desired monetary predictability will emerge spontaneously from the ordinary operations of the system.[1]

It is easy to see that the first approach possesses somewhat greater appeal when the problem is conceived in its "ideal" sense. If, in fact, the "ideal" or "norm" can be defined with some precision, as we have said is the case with monetary predictability, it can always be achieved by "ideal" men operating under "ideal" conditions. Hence the tendency in this area, as in others, is for students to jump somewhat too quickly into support of the first approach suggested above. When, however, we recognize that in all matters of economic policy specific actions can be taken only by individual human beings, and that these human beings are fallible and subject to mistakes and error, we begin to sense the merit of the second, alternative, approach, that which aims at securing the desired results spontaneously rather than instrumentally.

V. Managed versus Automatic Systems

This represents the difference between what we call a "managed" monetary system and what we call an "automatic" monetary system. I am aware that these terms introduce still further questions; all monetary systems are, in a sense, managed; none can be wholly automatic. For our purposes, however, we may think of a managed system as one that embodies the instrumental use of price-level predictability as a norm of policy, either loosely by discretionary authorities possessing wide latitude for independent decision-making powers, or closely in the form of specific rules constraining discretionary authority within narrow limits. On the other hand, we may think of an automatic system as one which does not, at any stage, involve the explicit use of the absolute price level, the price index, or any other macroeconomic variable, in guiding monetary policy.[2] In the automatic system, monetary policy as such consists solely of the designation of a single commodity or service as the basis for the monetary unit, as the standard, and the firm fixing of the future course of the price, in money units, of this commodity. Note that I do not, in this description of an automatic system, require that the money price of the commodity chosen as the standard be stabilized over time. All that is required is that this price be fixed at each particular moment in time and that its level be known in advance. The price of the standard commodity may, of course, be stabilized, which is the case usually analyzed, but my point is that the normative argument for such stability arises at a level of discussion different from that considered here. Predictability is the important normative element that must first be incorporated into either a managed or an automatic system.

The ultimate policy decision as between a managed monetary system and an automatic system should be made only after a careful analysis of the relative costs and benefits expected from the operation of each system. Comparisons must be made on the basis of the expected properties of the alternative systems in the real world, not on the basis of properties of ideally constructed models. But we do not get very far until and unless we specify quite carefully and precisely the nature of the alternative systems that we propose to compare. There are many institutions described by the term "managed system," and there are many different commodities and services that are possible standards. Too often generic evaluations will be made as a result of comparisons between a particular managed system and some poorly working automatic system or between a particular automatic system and some poorly working managed system.

VI. The "Ideal" Managed System

We may avoid this difficulty, to some extent, by commencing with a comparison between the best or "ideal" managed system and the best or "ideal" automatic or commodity-money system.

I do not propose here to argue the case for any particular managed system. I shall state my conviction that some such scheme as that proposed by Henry Simons and Lloyd Mints would come closest to introducing predictability in the absolute price level. That is to say, I should opt squarely in favor of some predetermined, quasi-constitutional "rule" that would define quite precisely the task of the monetary authority, the "managers." This authority would then be charged with the responsibility of following the rule or set of rules. This system would, ideally, produce divergencies between observed and predicted values for money only as a result of errors and miscalculations stemming from the attempts of the authorities to follow the predetermined rules. By contrast, under a discretionary managed system, divergencies between observed and predicted values would arise not only from this source but also from the additional one involving departures of the actually followed rules from predicted ones. But, as suggested, it is not my function to argue this point.

VII. The "Ideal" Automatic System

Those monetary theorists who generally tend to favor managed systems of one sort or another have not, as a rule, specified the alternative automatic standard or system with which their mental comparisons are made. Too often, I suspect, they have dismissed automatic systems, generically, because they associate all such systems with one specific member of a very large set, a member that is known to have produced undesirable results when it was partly operative. I speak here, of course, of the gold standard. As we know, the historical gold standard was not even a good model of a monetary system based on the commodity gold. But this need not concern us here. My point is that we should always specify carefully the characteristics of the alternative monetary system under consideration, and until and unless we have examined the "best" practicable automatic system, we should not opt for managed systems out of hand.

I propose, therefore, that we think first in terms of the characteristics of an "ideal" commodity system of money. If it could be found, what commodity or service would "ideally" accomplish the goal of monetary predictability? Viewed in this light, it seems that we should seek some commodity that is perfectly representative of the production of goods and services over the whole economy. That is, we need to locate some commodity whose production embodies some appropriately weighted set of coefficients that are representative of production processes for all goods and services in the economy. The elasticity of supply of this ideal monetary commodity would be equivalent to that possessed by production as a whole. The production of this ideal monetary commodity would be in a real sense an image of the whole economy in operation. Or, to use a mathematical metaphor, the whole economy would be "mapped" into the single production process.

The weights that would be implicit in this ideal commodity must in some manner reflect the relative importance of the various goods and services produced. But this relative importance can be judged only in terms of values. We must introduce market prices as the only meaningful reflection of consumer evaluation. We are led in this way to the conclusion that the ideal commodity for a monetary constitution utilizing some automatic or indirect means of achieving monetary predictability must be some commodity whose price, in the absence of its designation as the standard commodity, would move *pari passu* with movements in the absolute level of prices, that is, with the price index.

If there should exist such a commodity, that is, one whose price varies in perfect correspondence with the absolute price level in the absence of its designation as the monetary standard or basis, the achievement of monetary predictability to the degree desired would require a relatively simple institutional change. The government could state simply that the monetary authority, in this case, the Mint, would stand ready and willing to buy and to sell for money units unlimited quantities of this ideal commodity at a schedule of prices fixed in advance (and not necessarily to be stabilized over time). The economy would, as a result, be operating on a basis of monetary predictability, since the decentralized and impersonal forces of the competitive mechanism could be depended upon to produce and to destroy "money" as the economy required. If the absolute price level fell below predicted values, production and sale of the ideal commodity would take place. The quantity of money units in circulation would increase, and this increase would continue until observed and predicted values for the absolute price level roughly coincided. Conversely, if the absolute price level rose above predicted values, purchase of the ideal monetary commodity from the Mint would be stimulated. This purchase would continue until observed and predicted values for some price index were roughly in equivalence. Note that predictability under this system would be achieved without the instrumental usage of any price index as a criterion of policy action. The primary virtue of any "automatic" or commodity standard of money lies in the fact that only in such a system would the forces of the competitive market be directly utilized to achieve monetary predictability. In one sense, there would be no explicit monetary policy involved in the operation of such a system.

VIII. The Price-Level Rule as a Simulated Ideal Commodity Standard

For purposes of comparative analysis, we may conceive the operation of the Simons-Mints rule for price-level predictability in terms of such an "ideal" commodity standard. In one sense, the system of managed money in accordance with this type of rule is designed to simulate the more automatic system. Under such a rule-oriented system, the government is essentially "selling" units of an ideal composite commodity at a schedule of predetermined prices and "buying" units of this commodity at the same schedule of prices. If the administrators of such a managed system make few errors, the results will be substantially equivalent to those produced under the operation of an actual ideal commodity standard. But there are no market checkreins on the behavior of the monetary authorities. This important control feature of an actual commodity standard is missing. Decisions must be centralized.

Some of the monetary theorists who support such a rule for monetary management will argue convincingly that, given some predictability in the future course of the absolute price level, the forces of the competitive market mechanism will become operative. The profit-seeking actions of speculators will tend to ensure that the predictability implicit in the rule-as-directive to the monetary authorities will, in fact, characterize the rule-as-result. The phenomena here have been referred to as self-reinforcing expectations. If people are sufficiently sure that a particular result is to be achieved, their own private actions will tend to guarantee that their prediction becomes true. I do not want to go further into the interesting philosophical issues raised by the question of rules as predictions.

There is, however, one important factor that prevents self-reinforcing speculation from being fully effective under the operation of a rule for monetary predictability. Even if we can discount the major problems involved in crossing the "belief threshold," that is, the problems of convincing speculators that the predetermined rule will in fact continue to be employed as the overriding criterion for policy, the force of competitive counterspeculation will be reduced because individuals are unable to buy or sell "an average," "a price level," or "a price index." The general expectation that the overall price level will, for example, rise to some predicted value (as indicated in the rule-as-criterion) from some currently observed value will cause speculators to shift their asset holdings from money into real goods, but in such a shift, the absence of any ideal composite commodity necessitates taking on relative price uncertainties. Some choices must be made among the many possible real assets that may be purchased. On the other hand, if there exists a general expectation that the price level will decline to some predicted value from some currently observed value, speculators will shift from real goods into money, thereby shedding some relative price uncertainties. The actions of speculators will, on balance, seem to exert a slight downward bias on the price-level that the monetary authorities would have to discount, assuming of course that individuals, on the average, prefer certainty to uncertainty. I do not want to explore here this interesting area of speculation in a system characterized by a set of rules for ensuring monetary predictability. I think that I have discussed self-reinforcing speculation sufficiently for it to be compared briefly with that which would take place under a regime of an ideal commodity standard.

IX. Stabilizing Speculation under an "Ideal" Commodity Standard

Let us now examine again the monetary system that bases the value of the monetary unit on the "ideal" commodity discussed above. Leave aside for a bit longer the attempt to locate such an "ideal" commodity. Assume that one such commodity does exist. In effect, this system utilizes the forces of the free market to ensure predictability. The market price for the designated standard commodity cannot diverge significantly from the Mint price, which is predetermined. The absolute price level can, of course, move above or below a certain predictable trend value. But the phenomena of self-reinforcing expectations will be equivalent to those arising under a system of predetermined rules for monetary management. But these market forces, which should not be underestimated in either case, become *secondary* to the main competitive force in the automatic standard, this main force being represented by the direct shifts into and out of the designated standard commodity as its price in relation to other prices (costs) moves upward or downward. The speculative forces, secondary to this main force, increase predictability to the extent that speculators in the nonstandard commodities share a general faith in the strength of economic motives in the calculus of those individuals who are potential direct traders in the money commodity. In other words, the relevant comparison here is the one between the average or representative speculator's faith in the forces of the market as stabilizing devices and his faith in the monetary authority's success in following a predetermined rule.

X. Common Brick as the Standard Commodity

Having gone through ten sections of this essay, I come now to the place where I had intended to begin. I hope that by this time some of the groundwork has been laid for a more careful consideration of what must seem, at first glance, to be the proposal of a monetary extremist.

There exists no "ideal" commodity for purposes of achieving monetary predictability under an automatic system. There is no single real commodity or service that serves at all adequately to represent composite production over the whole economy, or that could appropriately be used as an image of the economy. Having recognized this, however, we should not dismiss all automatic or commodity money systems as unworkable and impracticable. There are still better and worse commodity standards, "better" and "worse" being measured in terms of the degree to which specific real commodities possess the characteristics required of the "ideal" commodity discussed above.

It is in this sense that the use of common brick as the standard commodity should be considered. Among existent real commodities, a good argument can be made out for common building brick as the best practicable commodity that could be employed as the basis for an automatic monetary system. The ingenious proposal that the value of money be based on common building brick was first advanced by Dr.C. O. Hardy, one of the seminal minds in monetary theory during the interwar and early postwar years. So far as I can discover, Dr. Hardy never published the proposal in a formal paper.[3] It has, however, come to be recognized as one of his many important contributions to monetary theory, and its substance has been passed along in an oral tradition by several scholars, among them Professor Lloyd Mints and a few of his former students, who have been impressed by the logical completeness and, confessedly, by the shock value of the common-brick proposal.

It will be useful to consider the advantages and disadvantages of common brick as the basis for an automatic monetary system. First let us specify briefly but carefully the structure of the system as it is expected to operate. The government sets a schedule of money prices for common building brick of specified quality. For simplicity in exposition, let us assume that this schedule of prices can be represented by a single price that is to be held constant over time. Again I should emphasize, however, that neither a single price nor constancy over time is significant to the proposal. At the same time that this price is announced, a public authority, which we shall call the Mint, announces its willingness to buy and sell units of common brick at the specified price in unlimited amounts. Money is issued from the Mint only in exchange for common brick, and money proceeds from the sale of common brick by the Mint are impounded in the Mint. Every individual has the assurance that he can, at any time, take a common brick, or any quantity of common brick (or a certificate of ownership of brick) to the Mint and receive in exchange a monetary unit, say, a paper dollar. He also knows that he can, at any time and in any desired amount, go to the Mint and purchase, for paper dollars, common brick of the specified quality. No additional monetary or fiscal policy need take place. Having no powers to create or to destroy money other than those implicit in the rules governing the operations of the Mint, the government has to finance expenditures through taxation or through real borrowing. Commercial banks may be assumed to operate on the basis of 100 percent reserves behind deposits, although this assumption is not essential to the analysis of the brick standard itself.[4]

This sort of monetary system could be predicted to work in a manner analogous to any other monetary system based upon a commodity standard. When the general level of prices rises above some presumed initial or "equilibrium" level, it becomes profitable for traders in common brick to *purchase* physical units of the standard commodity from the Mint. They can do so readily by exchanging paper money for brick or certificates of ownership of brick. As these traders turn in units of paper money to the Mint, the money supply outside the Mint is reduced, since the Mint is obligated to destroy or neutralize paper so received. As the supply of money in the system is reduced, the upward pressure on general prices is changed into downward pressure, and the price level begins to fall toward a predicted value. At the same time, of course, the brick-production industry becomes depressed in relation to other industries. The rate of brick production is reduced and resources tend to shift to other industries. This induced increase in the supply of nonstandard commodities and services does, of course, exert an effect that is substantially less significant than the demand effect resulting from the monetary contraction generated by the expansion of brick purchases from the Mint. Both the demand and the supply processes continue until they, along with supporting speculation in nonstandard commodities, are successful in bringing the absolute price level back into some accepted relation with a generally expected or predicted value. This result is accomplished, however, without any agency, authority, business firm, or single individual paying explicit attention to the absolute price level as such. Traders and potential traders in the standard commodity, brick, are guided by profit-maximization criteria, not by any private or public concern for monetary stability.

The system is fully symmetrical in the case of a fall in the absolute price level below some predicted value. This fall generates offsetting equilibrating behavior. Firms find it profitable to sell brick to the Mint. As this takes place, additional money finds its way into the payments stream of the economy. This primary effect tends to increase aggregate demand for all nonstandard goods and services. It is supplemented by a supply-side effect generated by the shift of resources away from the production of nonstandard commodities, reducing the excess supplies forthcoming, and into the production of brick, the standard commodity. Again, the process continues until the absolute price level returns to some expected or predicted value or, to state the same thing in terms of the criteria directing private actions, until the relative profitability of production and sale of brick to the monetary authority disappears.

To this point, the same analysis might be applied to any physical commodity designated as the standard for an automatically operating monetary system. Indeed one of the points in discussing this analysis in terms of an everyday commodity like common building brick is the demonstration that a commodity standard need not be conceived in terms of precious metals. But we may go much further than this.

There are many positive advantages of the brick-standard system in comparison with other possible commodity systems. In reviewing some of these advantages, it is useful to compare and contrast common brick with gold as the basis for an automatic monetary system.

First of all, common brick can be produced advantageously in almost every local area in the United States. The required adjustments in the industry producing the standard commodity would not, therefore, be localized in particular regions or areas. When general inflationary or deflationary pressures in the economy imposed depression or boom on this brick-producing industry, the dispersion of production over space would tend to prevent differential regional impact. Contrast this situation with one involving a standard commodity, such as gold or anthracite coal, which is produced only in highly localized areas. In periods of incipient depression or recession, the employment effects of the brick-standard system would be noteworthy. Opportunities for employment in local brickyards would tend to mitigate the necessity for the accelerated labor mobility that would be required in the shifting of resources into a regionally localized industry. This advantage is symmetrical with respect to the unemployment effects during periods of inflation.

A second major advantage lies in the fact that production processes for common brick do not seem to be overly complex, although I plead technical ignorance here. Efficient producing plants probably need not be of extremely large size, and entry into and egress from the industry should not be difficult. For these and other reasons, reactions to relative price and cost changes should take place rapidly and without serious dislocation of resources. A closely related third advantage is that production seems to require relatively few highly specialized resources. These three features combine to ensure that the elasticity of supply would be reasonably high.

A final advantage that should not be overlooked is that common building brick would probably not be suitable for adjusting international balances of payments. The system would, in this way, facilitate rather than hinder the separation of the domestic monetary system from the international payments mechanism, a separation whose impossibility would seriously restrict the use of gold as the standard commodity. The brick-standard system would be a suitable companion to a system of floating exchange rates.

On each of the four counts noted, a monetary standard of common building brick would seem superior to one of gold or any other precious metal.

There would, of course, be some offsetting disadvantages to the brick-standard system. Any commodity standard must involve some storage costs not present under managed systems: some proportion of the resources of the economy must of necessity be devoted to maintaining a stock of the commodity designated as the monetary standard, a stock over and above that which would be normal for nonmonetary uses. With brick, there would be little deterioration or depreciation involved in storage over time, but the sheer bulk of the commodity could make storage costs substantial. Economic resources would be tied up in maintaining unused a sizable stock of common brick. This stock need not go entirely unused, however. A substantial proportion could be devoted to the construction of government buildings. If in fact it could be predicted that the system would operate effectively on some fractional-reserve withdrawal, that is, if it could be predicted that the required responses to general upward or downward pressures would involve no more than, say, one fourth of the existing stock of "money brick," then three-fourths of this stock, against which the Mint would at some time have issued dollars, could be employed in the construction of government buildings. In this way, the general taxpayer would secure some indirect benefit. As a recognized ultimate reserve or backing for the outstanding money issues, the brick used in such construction projects would have to be carefully distinguished from those government bricks acquired through ordinary market channels, and a potential withdrawal of this "money brick" would have to be acknowledged. Should a general wave of dishoarding on the part of the public generate serious inflationary pressure, thus making it highly profitable for private buildings to be constructed with brick purchased from the Mint, then offsetting destruction of some government buildings might have to take place. It is difficult to imagine that such major swings around a predicted norm would take place, however, once a monetary system of this nature came to be in full operation. For this reason there would seem to be little grounds for concern about the periodic possible destruction of private or public buildings.

One of the major disadvantages of any commodity standard, especially when viewed in the light of the predictability norm, lies in its vulnerability to unpredictable changes in the relative costs of producing standard and nonstandard commodities. A major technological improvement in production processes in the brick industry could, for example, be the source of serious inflation in the economy. We know that one of the disadvantages of the historical gold standard was its subjection of general economic conditions to the sometimes fortuitous discoveries of new goldfields. While brick would on this count clearly be superior to gold, the possible inflation that could result from a differential technological breakthrough should not be neglected in any thorough comparative evaluation. There would seem to be little chance of such a depletion of suitable raw materials as to make deflation from this source a serious possibility.

A second disadvantage of any commodity standard lies in its potential vulnerability to unpredictable shifts in the nonmonetary demand for the standard commodity. For example, an upsurge in the fashionableness of brick houses would, under the operation of a brick standard, impose deflationary pressure on the economy generally. To some extent, however, these unpredictable shifts in the private demand for the monetary commodity could be offset by variations in the government demand. In so far as such demand shifts occur and are not effectively offset, the commodity standard will not be able to produce monetary predictability. But broadly considered, such shifts are different in degree only from shifts in the desire to hold money, that is, hoarding and dishoarding, which seem to reduce the predictability of any monetary system.

XI. A Labor Standard of Value?

It seems clear that common brick would be a more desirable monetary commodity than gold. But are there other commodities or services that might serve the desired purposes as well as, or perhaps better than, common brick? Before and after the time of Adam Smith, economists have been intrigued with and attracted by the idea that, of all existent commodities and services, common labor provides the best single measure of value in an economy. I should like to explore briefly the idea of utilizing common labor as the basis for an automatic monetary system.

In thinking about pedagogical devices for clarifying the logic of such a standard, I have toyed with an idea jokingly suggested by Professor Armen Alchian. He proposed that the general unemployment problem could be solved quite simply by installing money machines on each street corner. Each machine would be equipped with a crank or foot pedal, and upon turning the crank or pumping the pedal anyone could secure money at a fixed rate in exchange for effort measured solely by energy inputs. The energy generated by turning the crank or pumping the pedal could, perhaps, be turned into electricity by tying each machine into a power grid of some sort. This proposal represents one side of an automatic monetary system that bases the value of money on common-labor units. As a substitute for the Alchian machine, we could think of the Mint purchasing common labor at a fixed price in unlimited quantities. The labor so purchased could then be "sold" at auction to private entrepreneurs, or used to construct public works.

The other half of a common-labor-standard system is somewhat more difficult to conceive. Labor is not a storable commodity but a service. A fully automatic system would require that the Mint stand ready to sell as well as to buy units of the service. How could the Mint "sell" labor in unlimited quantities during times of threatened inflation? The idea is not wholly implausible. We could think of a scheme in which the government obligates itself to "sell" common labor to business firms without a stock of labor being maintained. For example, if the market price of common labor should rise above the "standard" price, the business firm could "purchase" labor services from the government. To meet this demand the government would have to purchase, at the market wage rate, sufficient labor services to meet business demands on it. This public outlay would have to be financed wholly from general tax revenues. The government would be obligated to neutralize the fixed money sum turned in by the business firm in "purchasing" each unit of labor service. I do not have the space to discuss further the interesting features of a scheme such as this, but I should emphasize the importance of considering all possible alternatives.[5]

XII. Predictability and Constitutional Attitude

I am convinced that an automatic monetary system utilizing some basic commodity or service, such as common brick or common labor as the standard of value, would work. And by this I mean that such a system would embody a high degree of predictability about the course of movements in the absolute level of prices, in the value of money. I am also convinced that a managed system characterized by some specific rules for action would work; and I make no strong argument for one alternative over the other. Both alternatives will work, or both will fail, for the same reason.

I recall a statement once made by Professor F. A. Hayek to the effect that "nothing is inevitable but thinking makes it so." I should paraphrase this to apply here as "nothing is predictable, but thinking makes it so." The implementation of a monetary constitution that will produce predictability requires more than consensus among experts. Even if we could substantially agree on the most practicable monetary reform, and even if we were given the power to institute such reform, we would have no assurance that the continuing monetary problem would be solved. We should never lose sight of the fact that the average man knows little of economics and, worse than this, he does not know how little he does know. Man has, throughout modern history, tended to blame the monetary system for many of his economic ills, and he has been quite right on many occasions. But by now he has learned through observation that his own actions, or the actions of men acting "for him," the government, can change, modify, and reform the monetary system. Thus, with respect to monetary matters, we find the average man able to raise objections, to criticize, without being able himself to provide rationally motivated alternatives to existing institutions. No longer is the average man willing to adopt a quasi-fatalistic attitude, to attribute the workings of the monetary system to the gods, to accept some mythology of money. To some small extent, such a mythology, such an attitude, was engendered by the operation of the historical gold standard. This system was to many people sacrosanct, and even today there is within all of us some of this mythology of gold as the appropriate monetary metal. It is this mythology that makes us look upon any such proposal as the one for a brick standard as amusing, and which causes us to dismiss such a proposal before we have seriously considered its working properties.

Careful observation should convince us, however, that even the mythology of the gold standard is substantially gone, and once gone, a mythology can never be reconstructed. If it could be, it would, by definition, not constitute a mythology. Nor can the wisest of monetary reforms create a monetary mythology surrounding a brick standard, a price-level rule, a Federal Reserve Board, or whatever.

Yet without something that serves the same purposes, *no* monetary reform can be expected to work, to ensure the predictability in the value of money that we all should accept as the appropriate norm. I suggest that what is required, what is essential here, is a "constitutional attitude"; that is to say, people must agree on the basic rules that define the operation of a monetary system and then agree to abide by these rules as adopted. The attitude of which I speak is one that prevents continual tampering with the rules as adopted. This constitutional attitude seems to me to be one of the most difficult of human behavioral characteristics to adopt, or even to explain and to understand. Since the Enlightenment men have refused to acknowledge the validity of any absolutes, either in terms of ethical principles or in terms of social institutions. Ideas, laws, social structures: all have been subjected to discussion and to question, and through these, to deliberately organized modification and change. Chaos is likely to result if change is made too quickly and for reasons that are not rational. Until and unless we know what changes are in fact "best," it is far better to accept certain "relatively absolute absolutes," both in ethics and in the rules defining the social order. And we cannot really know what fundamental or constitutional changes are needed until we are able to observe the working of a given set of institutions over time, through a long succession of events. The willingness to do this, to play a series of games by the same rules in order to evaluate properly the rules themselves, is the essential attitude that is required. The need for this attitude is not, of course, confined to the monetary problem. The monetary problem does serve, however, to point up sharply the general relevance of the attitude that is more generally required for the maintenance of orderly civilized life.

Specifically, with the emergence of a genuinely constitutional attitude, there are many possible monetary systems that would work well, that would ensure an adequate degree of monetary predictability. Without the emergence of this attitude, there is no monetary system that will work well, and continued monetary chaos, of sorts, can be expected to prevail.

Notes

1. An analogy with economic efficiency, defined in the orthodox way, will be useful. Insofar as such efficiency is a norm for competitive economic organization, it is achieved as a result that emerges from the operation of the economy and not as a result of instrumentally oriented attempts to achieve this goal in any direct manner.

2. A system characterized by the *exclusive* attention of stabilization authorities being given to other macroeconomic variables, such as an employment index, could hardly be called a monetary system at all. Nevertheless, insofar as it should become necessary to classify such a system, it would clearly fall within the managed set.

3. In my search for some published version of the original proposal, I am indebted to Mrs. Myra M. Hardy of Washington, D.C., and to Dr. William H. Moore of the staff of the Joint Economic Committee.

4. I should point out that the brick standard proposal as outlined here, and the analysis of its operation that follows, represent my own version of the original proposal. I should like to give Dr. Hardy the full credit due him for originating the proposal without attributing to him any of the possible errors that might be present in this version.

5. Dr. Francesco Forte has suggested to me that the proposal for a labor standard has been discussed at length by P. Jannaccone. I have not, however, been able to consult Jannaccone's work.

11.

An Outside Economist's Defense of Pesek and Saving

I am not an "inside" monetary economist in this time of subdisciplinary specialization. I have neither mastered the intricacies of modern monetary theory nor kept abreast of recent empirical investigations. Be this as it may, my professional soul was stirred and my curiosity aroused by the almost-adjacent reviews by Stephen W. Rousseas and William G. Dewald in the December, 1968, issue of the *American Economic Review*, reviews of two separate books by Boris P. Pesek and Thomas R. Saving. Rousseas's attack alone was sufficient to make me want to defend a book I had not read, especially since I had myself been entangled with roughly the same set of intellectual adversaries in the debt-burden controversy a decade past. Dewald's contrasting praise added to my interest because he placed such praise midst agreement with Rousseas concerning a Pesek-Saving error on the central point at issue.

Are the demand deposits of commercial banks properly treated as liabilities? Pesek and Saving reject the conventional wisdom and deny that deposits embody liability characteristics. By so doing, they provide a direct and explicit basis for recognizing that bank-money issue adds to net wealth. In this note, I shall concentrate on this question. I shall suggest an extremely simple means of clarifying the discussion, a means which, had it been adopted by Pesek and Saving, might have spared them from some of the more extreme criticisms that their work has generated.

Initially, let us forget about banks. Suppose that I ask you for a loan of one hundred dollars, with an agreement that I shall pay you back in one year's time. No mention is made of an interest charge. In absolute simplicity, let us examine how this transaction would be recorded by our accountants. The T-accounts would look as in Table 11-1. No change in net wealth is recorded, either for the individual accounts, or in total for the community.

This is economic nonsense. The transaction has transferred wealth from you to me, and this would be indicated on the T-accounts if en-

Table 11-1. T-accounts, I

Me		You	
Assets	Liabilities	Assets	Liabilities
Cash $100	Notes payable $100	Cash $(-)$ $100	
		Notes receivable $100	

tries were made to reflect *expected present values.* Economically meaningful T-accounts would appear as in Table 11-2, the precise entries being, of course, dependent on the rate of discount. The net transfer of wealth is, of course, effected because of the neglect of interest on the loan.

Consider now a second and different transaction. Suppose that I borrow one hundred dollars from you, as before, but that I agree to pay you back at any time that you demand repayment. As before, we assume that no interest is charged, and that transactions costs are zero. There is a major difference between these two simple transactions. Because you know that you can now call the loan at any time, it is proper that you record the asset under "Notes Receivable" at full face value. For this is the *expected present value* of my obligation to you. For me, however, it remains wholly irrational to record the full face value as a liability item. Even should I know nothing whatever of your behavior patterns, there would only be some positive probability less than one that you would call the loan immediately after the contract is made. Hence, the expected present value of the liability, to me, must be less than full face value in all cases. If I know something about your behavior, and especially if I make it a business of entering into such contracts with large numbers of persons, I can place reasonably accurate estimates on the expected present value of the liability which I will enter into my accounts. Economically meaningful T-accounts might appear as in Table 11-3. In the transaction, note that the net wealth of the community has increased by eighty dollars, the difference between the face value of the loan and the expected present liability that the loan represents to the debtor.

Implicitly, this is the model that Pesek and Saving employ in their argument. In my view, this would have been a better means of presentation than theirs which denies the liability aspects completely. In the simple model here, I am similar to the money-issuing bank. Instead of stating that demand deposits *are* liabilities, with expected present values that *should* be explicitly recorded, Pesek and Saving record the approximate twenty dollars as a "Repurchase Reserve." The result is the same, but less shock is imposed by my suggested procedure on those who adhere to the conventional wisdom. The economic meaning of the T-account entries is more clearly revealed. The approach has the advantage of emphasizing the inherently sub-

Table 11-2. T-accounts, II

ME

Assets	Liabilities
Cash $100	Notes payable (expected present value) $90
	Net Worth $10

You

Assets	Liabilities
Cash (−) $100	
Notes receivable (expected present value) $90	
	Net Worth (−) $10

Table 11-3. T-accounts, III

ME

Assets	Liabilities
Cash $100	Notes payable (expected present value) $20
	Net Worth $80

You

Assets	Liabilities
Cash (−) $100	
Notes receivable (expected present value) $100	

jective nature of behaviorally meaningful deposit liabilities. Expectations modify present values of liabilities and, residually, net wealth. In liquidity crises, banks become less wealthy even if no deposits are withdrawn.

The conventions of double-entry bookkeeping can help or hinder the economist. These conventions can prove of great value when confusion arises about the assignment of assets and liabilities among persons and groups, as was the case with the debt-burden controversy. They can be of great hindrance when the problem is one of showing how new wealth is generated, as the history of recent monetary theory amply demonstrates. Many economists have explicitly recognized the limitations that simplistic balance sheet consolidations impose on monetary theory. And from the work of McKean, through Patinkin, Gurley and Shaw, and Leijonhufvud, to mention only a few, attempts have been made to offset the elementary fallacies of balance sheet consolidations by resort to distributional effects and differential behavioral adjustments.[1] Even with the most sophisticated of such attempts, however, there remains the apparent dependence of formal monetary theory on "adventitious institutional and historical details," to use Harry Johnson's terminology.[2] The distinguishing feature of Pesek and Saving is their boldness in attacking the central accounting paradigm. The simple suggestion that I advance here may be classified either as an extension or a defense of their effort.

If pushed to their extreme limits, accounting conventions "prove" that gains from exchange are impossible. Subjectively conceived by the parties to the contract, any trade must increase wealth or else it would not be made.[3] However, only by ignoring this elementary fact can wealth measurements be objectified. Broadly speaking, this procedure is acceptable so long as all transactions are assumed to be made in full equilibrium and at the individual margins of adjustment where there are offsetting transfers of expected present values between contracting parties. The unique feature of the call-loan is that no such offsetting transfers take place. In the language of public goods theory, exclusion is replaced by nonexclusion; objectively measurable wealth must be increased in the process.

Notes

I am indebted to Joseph M. Burns, William Gibson, Benjamin Klein, and Gordon Tullock for helpful comments.
1. R. N. McKean, "Liquidity and a National Balance Sheet," *Journal of Political Economy* 57 (December, 1949): 506–22 (reprinted in *Readings in Monetary Theory* [New York: Richard D. Irwin, 1951]); Don Patinkin, *Money, Interest, and Prices*, 2nd ed. (New York: Harper and Row, 1965); John G. Gurley and

Edward S. Shaw, *Money in a Theory of Finance* (Washington, D.C.: Brookings Institution, 1960); Axel Leijonhufvud, *On Keynesian Economics and the Economics of Keynes*, esp. chapter 4 (New York: Oxford University Press, 1968).

2. Harry G. Johnson, "Monetary Theory and Policy," *American Economic Review* 52 (June, 1962): 335–84.

3. In one sense, trade represents an awareness of wealth that exists, rather than its creation. Applied to deposit creation, this approach suggests that the bank is realizing its net worth, which previously exists in potential form. This approach has powerful explanatory value in many areas of economics.

12.

Can Policy Activism Succeed?

I. Introduction

The question posed in the title assigned to me presupposes the existence of an ordering of options along some scale of presumably agreed-on preferredness or desirability. Only if this presupposition is made does it become appropriate to ask whether or not politics, as it operates, can be expected to select the most preferred option on the ordering, or, less ambitiously, to select, on average, options that would allow the pattern or sequence of "choices" to be adjudged "successful." The generalized public choice answer to the question, given the required presupposition, is reasonably straightforward, and it is essentially that of classical political economy. Those who make political decisions can be expected to choose in accordance with agreed-on or "public interest" norms only if the institutional structure is such as to make these norms coincident with those of "private interest." The public chooser, whether voter, aspiring or elected politician, or bureaucrat, is no different in this role than in other roles, and if incentives are such that the coincidence of interest is absent, there will be no "successful" political ordering over the feasible options. I shall return to the possible coincidence of interest following Section II.

The more fundamental question to be asked, however, involves the appropriateness of the required presupposition, that concerning the possibility of any meaningful ordering of policy options, quite independently of any problems of implementation. This question has been obscured rather than clarified by those economists who resort to "social welfare functions." These functions impose a totally artificial and meaningless ordering on "social states" without offering any assistance toward facilitating choice from among the set of options feasibly available to the public chooser. Section II examines this fundamental question in the context of the issues that prompted the assigned title.

II. Is It Possible to Define an Ordering of Policy Options?

In this section, I propose to ignore totally all problems of policy implementation—all public choice problems, if you will. For simplicity, assume the existence of a genuinely benevolent despot, who sincerely seeks to do that which is "best" for all of those who are members of the political-economic-social community. How can we describe the utility function of this despot? It is easy, of course, to list several desired end-states. Full employment, stable and predictable value in the monetary unit, high and sustainable rates of economic growth, stable international order—these may be mutually agreed-on objectives for policy action. But there may be conflict among the separate objectives (to raise a topic of much debate and discussion in the 1950s but which has been relatively neglected in the 1980s). How are we to model the trade-offs among the objectives within the utility function of the benevolent despot if indeed such conflicts should arise?

I presume that the despot can act so as to influence macroeconomic variables in the economy; I will not discuss possible rational expectations feedbacks. But how "should" the despot act, and, in this model, how "will" he act? There is no definitive answer to these questions until and unless the utility function is defined more fully.

There is, of course, an empty response to the question posed in the title to this section. Clearly, if the despot can, by our presumption, influence macroeconomic variables by policy action, then, by some criterion of his own, he can be "successful." But presumably we seek to employ a more objective criterion for success, one that can at least conceptually be observed by others than the despot himself.

For simplicity, let us assume that the despot is concerned only about domestic employment and monetary stability; we ignore all non-domestic considerations and we put aside problems of growth. Further, let us restrict attention to standard macropolicy tools. The despot here is assumed to be unable, at least in the time frame of the policy under consideration, to modify the structural features of the economy. With these simplifications, we can go further and specify the objective function more precisely. Let us assume that the despot seeks to guarantee that level of employment that is consistent with stability in the value of the monetary unit, given the institutional structure of the economy. The objective reduces to a single price-level target.

Even in his highly restricted setting, which is by no means that which might command consensus as a normative posture, the despot cannot simply "choose" the ultimate end objective from an available set of options. That is to say, "stability in the value of the monetary unit" cannot be selected as if from a policy shelf. The despot is further restricted by the tools of policy available, which in this setting are those of the familiar fiscal (budgetary) and monetary instruments. Nominal demand can be increased, directly or indirectly, or reduced, directly or indirectly, by the use of fiscal-monetary tools, either separately or in some mix. Even if we ignore, as indicated, the expectational-induced feedbacks generated by resort to any instrument, there remains the task of predicting accurately the relationship between the instrument, economic structure, and ultimate objective. The structural features of the economy are not invariant over time, and a policy thrust that might be successful under one set of conditions, say in t_0, may fail in, say, t_1, because of structural shifts. At best, therefore, the truly benevolent despot can be only partly successful, even given the most clearly defined target for policy.

III. Monolithic and Nonbenevolent Despot

The presumption of benevolence on the part of political agents is not, of course, acceptable within a public choice perspective. It is precisely this presumption that has been a central focus of the overall public choice critique of the theory of economic policy. Political agents must be presumed to maximize personal utilities in a behavioral model that is invariant as between public and private roles or capacities. The structure of decision-making may, however, affect utility-maximizing behavior through shifts in the effective constraints on choice.

In this section, I shall discuss briefly the simplest possible decision structure, one in which political decisions are lodged within a single monolithic authority (in the limit in one person) which (who) is not directly accountable to or subject to constituency pressures, whether or not these be explicitly "democratic" (electoral) in nature. In this model it is evident, quite apart from any historical record, that the despot will find it advantageous to resort to money creation over and beyond any amount that might characterize the "ideal" behavior of the benevolent counterpart considered above. This result emerges, quite simply, because incentive effects must be taken into account, and the despot, even if totally immune from constituency pressures, must reckon with individual adjustments to alternative revenue-generating instruments. Through a policy of revenue-maximizing inflation, defined in a dynamic sense, the despot can extract the full value of monetary structure (that is, the value differential between a monetary structure and a barter structure).[1]

The amount of revenue that may potentially be raised through money creation is, of course, finite. And the uncontrolled despot may seek to utilize the taxing and debt-issue power over and beyond the inflationary revenue limits. The precise features of the despot's policy mix will depend, in part, on his time horizon in relation to the behavioral reactions of the population. These features need not be examined in detail here. It is sufficient, for my purposes, to conclude that the monolithic despot will be successful only in terms of his own criteria, and that by any of the more familiar criteria for policy success, the failure would be manifest.

IV. Monolithic and Nonbenevolent Agent Subject to Electoral Constraints

The analysis becomes more complex once we introduce electoral feedback constraints on the behavior of the monolithic political agent. Assume now that decision authority remains concentrated, but that the holder of this authority is subject to potential electoral replacement at designated periodic intervals. In this model, the "governor" cannot expect to use his authority for personal enrichment for any extended period. Under some conditions, simple wealth-maximizing strategy might involve revenue-maximizing exploitation during the period of office, with no attention to possible reelection. In other conditions, the wealth-maximizing strategy might involve the effort to remain in office, in which case short-run revenue maximization via inflation, debt creation, and taxation will be mitigated. If the agent is modeled as a simple revenue-maximizer, it seems unlikely that his pattern of behavior would be adjudged "successful" by external criteria under either of these circumstances.

The more interesting model is one in which the agent is motivated by other considerations than wealth, the simplest model being that in which political position is itself the single maximand. The agent's behavior will, in this case, be constrained by expectations of electoral support. The question then becomes one of determining to what extent voters, generally, or in a required winning coalition, will support or oppose patterns of policy outcomes that might be deemed "successful" by external criteria. Given the postulated motivation here, the agent will base behavior strictly on constituency response.

Consider this question in the terms introduced earlier, that of a unique objective of monetary stability. Will a sufficiently large voting constituency support a regime that seeks only this policy objective? This question may be examined in the calculus of the individual voter, or potential voter.

Two separate difficulties arise. The first involves the absence of individual voter responsibility for electoral outcomes in large-number constituencies. Even if the individual knows that the agent elected is fully responsive to the electoral process, because he knows that his own voting choice will rarely, if ever, be decisive, the individual may not vote. And if he does vote, he has little or no incentive to become informed about the alternatives. And if he votes, and even if he is reasonably well informed, there is little or no incentive for him to vote his "interests" rather than his "whims." Hence, there is only a remote linkage between what might be defined by the observing external "expert" as the "interest" of the voters and the support that be given to a prospective political agent who promises these externally defined "interests." This difficulty alone suggests that political agents cannot be "held responsible" by the electoral process nearly to the extent that is suggested by naive models of electoral feedback.

A second difficulty emerges even when the first is totally ignored. Even if all individuals are somehow motivated to vote and to do so in terms of their well-considered interests, these interests will not be identical for all voters. There are differentials among persons in the relative benefits and costs of any macropolicy action. Even the ideally responsive political agent will meet only the demands of the relevant coalition of voters, as determined by the precise voting rules.

Consider a single political agent who must satisfy a simple majority of constituency voters. If voters' interests in the employment-inflation trade-off can be presumed to be single-peaked, the political agent's optimal strategy requires satisfying the median voter. It seems likely that this median voter will tend to be myopic in his behavior in the electoral process. He will place an unduly high value on the short-term benefits of enhancing employment relative to the long-term, and possibly permanent, costs of inflation. He will do so because, as a currently decisive voter, he can ensure the capture of *some* benefits in the immediate future. By forgoing such short-term benefits in a "rational" consideration of the long-term costs, the currently decisive voter *cannot* guarantee against the incurrence of such long-term costs in future periods. This asymmetrical result follows from the potential shiftability of majority voting coalitions. A subsequent period may allow a different median voter or coalition of voters to emerge as dominant, a decisive voter or group that may choose to inflate from strictly short-term considerations. To the extent that this takes place, all of the initial benefits of policy prudence may be offset. In the recognition of this prospect, why should the decisive voter or coalition of voters in the initial period exhibit nonmyopic "rationality" in the sense indicated?[2]

The ultimate answer to the assigned question is clear in this highly simplified model for "democratic" politics. Policy activism cannot be successful if the criterion of success is long-term monetary stability, a criterion that seems most likely to emerge consensually in a constitutional process of deliberation.[3]

V. Nonmonolithic and Nonbenevolent Agents Subject to Varying Electoral Constraints

The political models examined in Sections III and IV above were over-simplified in the assumption that authority was placed in a single agent or agency. As we approach reality, it is necessary to recognize that policy-making authority is likely to be divided among several agents or agencies, who (which) may be subjected to quite different electoral controls or constraints, and hence potentially affected by differing electoral pressures. For example, fiscal or budgetary policy may be made in a wholly different process, institutionally, from monetary policy, and, even within the institutional structure of budgetary policy authority may be divided between executive and legislative branches of government, subjected to varying electoral constraints as defined by such things as breadth of constituencies, length of terms of office, voting structure within agency (in legislatures and committees), legally defined responsibilities, and so on.

The direction of difference in effects between this more realistic political model and the monolithic model previously examined seems evident. To the extent that policy-making authority is divided, the proclivity toward response to short-term pressures is increased. Any array of results along the success criterion indicated would indicate that the divided-authority model ranks well below its monolithic counterpart.

VI. Nonbenevolent and Monolithic Agent Subject to Constitutional Rules

If there is little or no basis for expecting political agents to express benevolence in their policy behavior, and if, as suggested, the standard "democratic" controls will not themselves ensure patterns of outcomes that meet reasonable criteria of success, alternative institutional structures must be analyzed. Consider, first, a model in which decision-making authority is lodged in a single agent or agency and one that is specifically divorced from the electoral process, an agent or agency that does not face continual electoral checks. To prevent that potential for excess under the model discussed in Section III above, however, suppose that the agent or members of the agency are placed within enforcible legal-constitutional limits with reference to his or their personal or private enrichment, either directly or indirectly. That is to say, the agent or members of the agency cannot use the money creation and/or taxing power to finance their own private consumption needs or accumulation (e.g., Swiss bank accounts) desires. Beyond this restriction, however, we shall assume that the agent or members of the agency is (are) not limited in behavior except in the overall and general mandate to carry out "good" macroeconomic policy.

This model can, of course, be recognized as one that is closely analogous to the monetary authority of the Federal Reserve Board in the United States. Some elements of the model discussed in Section III, that of the nonconstrained despot, describe the existing structure, and, more important, some political controls are exercised, but for my purposes the existing monetary authority fits the model reasonably well.

The problem becomes one of predicting the behavior of such an agent and of assessing this behavior in terms of the success criterion introduced. Neither economic nor public choice analysis is capable of being of much assistance in this respect. To make a prediction it would be necessary to get inside the utility function of the agent (or of those who participate in agency decisions). In particular, it would be necessary to know something about the internal rate of time preference that will characterize behavior. If, as we have assumed, demand-enhancing action is known to generate short-term benefits at the expense of long-term costs, the behavior of the monopolistic and discretionary agent in making this trade-off will depend strictly on his own private rate of time preference, as expressed "for" the community. That is to say, under the conditions indicated, the agent will not personally secure the benefits or suffer the costs. By definition, the agent is not *responsible* in the sense of a reward-penalty calculus.

This absence of responsibility itself suggests that the behavior of the discretionary agent is likely to be less carefully considered, to be based on less information, and hence to be more erratic than would be the case under some alternative reward-penalty structure. The model suggests, further, that the agent here is more likely to be responsive to the passing whims of intellectual-media "fashion" than might be the case in the presence of some residual claimancy status. To the extent that the agent is at all responsive to interest-group pressures, such response seems likely to be biased toward those groups seeking near-term benefits and biased against those groups that might be concerned about long-term costs, if for no other reason than the difference in temporal dimension itself. Organized pressures for the promotion of short-term benefits exist while there may be no offsetting organization of long-term interests. This bias might well be exaggerated if the agent or agency is assigned functions that cause the development of relationships with particular functional groups in the polity (e.g., banking and finance). In sum, although there is really no satisfactory predictive model for behavior of the genuinely discretionary agent or agency, there are plausibly acceptable reasons to suggest that policy failures will tend to take the directions indicated in the discussion here.

Viewed in this perspective, and in application to the Federal Reserve agency in the United States, and perhaps notably after the removal of international monetary constraints, there should have been no surprise that the behavior exhibited has been highly erratic. Any other pattern would indeed have required more explanation than that which has been observed. From both analysis and observation the ultimate answer to the question concerning "successful" policy activism in this model, as in the others examined, must be negative.

VII. Nonbenevolent and Monolithic Agent Subject to Constitutional Rules That Direct Policy Action

The generally negative answer to the question posed in the title prompts examination of still other institutional structures that do not involve attempts at "policy activism" as such but which instead embody sets of predictable and directed policy actions in accordance with constitutionally specified rules. In familiar terminology, if "policy activism," when applied in a setting of *discretionary authority*, must fail to meet the success criterion, can a setting of *rules* do better? It would be inappropriate to discuss at length the relative advantages of alternative regimes or sets of rules. But it is clear that almost any well-defined set of rules would eliminate most of the incentive and motivational sources for the failure of discretionary agency models as previously discussed.

In a very real sense, there is no agency problem in an effectively operating rule-ordered regime. A fiscal-monetary authority, charged with the actual implementation of policy, but only in the carrying out of specified rules, defined either in terms of means or objectives, cannot itself be judged on other than purely administrative criteria of success or failure. More ultimate criteria must now be applied to the alternative sets of rules, with success or failure accordingly assigned. And working models of such alternative sets might be analyzed, just as the models of discretionary agency have been analyzed here. But there seems to be a closer relationship between the rules that might be selected and the success criterion adopted than there is between the latter and the pronounced goals of discretionary agency.

The potential for success of rule-guided macro-policy depends, in large part, on the *absence* of policy activism, not only for the removal of the potential for self-interested behavior on the part of discretionary agents, but also for the built-in predictability of such action that is inherent in the notion of rules, as such. The relative advantages of rule-guided policy over agency discretion could be treated at length, but this effort would carry me well beyond the intended scope of this essay.

VIII. Fiscal Policy and Monetary Policy

There are two distinct policy instruments, or sets of instruments in the familiar textbook terminology: fiscal policy instruments and monetary policy instruments. To this point, I have made no distinction between these two sets, and I have avoided altogether any discussion of relative efficacy as well as relative vulnerability to the sorts of influences on behavior that are emphasized in a public choice approach. It is time to explore some of the differences that are directly relevant to the arguments that I have advanced above.

Fiscal policy involves budgetary manipulation, and hence a necessary linkage between any macropolicy objectives and the whole process of public sector allocation. Given this necessary linkage, and given the institutional-political history, it seems totally unreal to suggest that any shift of authority over fiscal policy would be delegated to either discretionary or even to rule-bound authority. It seems highly unlikely that fiscal policy, in any sense, would be removed from the ordinary procedures of democratic decision-making, with divided legislative and executive responsibilities and roles in its overall formulation. It becomes unrealistic in the extreme to presume that we, in the United States, would transfer to an agency immune from electoral constraints any authority to manipulate either side of the budget in accordance with rules or intentions to improve macroeconomic performance. Decisions on tax rates, spending rates, and, in consequence, deficits and borrowing requirements, are likely to remain within the responsibility of "democratic" determination, with the predicted result that any meaningful success criterion will fail to be satisfied. There will be a bias toward "easy budgets," with higher than desired deficits, to the extent that any considerations of macroeconomic policy enter the policy argument.[4]

Given this predicted bias, and quite apart from any consideration as to the independent efficacy of budgetary policy in effecting desired results, any genuine hope for "success" in macroeconomic policy must involve a reduction or removal of budgetary manipulation from the potentially usable kit of tools.[5] If "fiscal policy" can be isolated so as to ensure that its operation does not make the task of monetary management more difficult, a major step toward genuine reform will have been made. It is in this context that the argument for a constitutional rule requiring budget balance becomes important in macroeconomic policy discussion.

If fiscal policy is so isolated, the task of policy action is left to the monetary agency or regime. A monetary agency can be made effective if the discretion of the agent is limited by the imposition of legally binding and enforcible rules for policy actions. These rules may take on any one of several forms, and it would be out of place to discuss these alternatives in detail here. The monetary agency can be directed to act on the defined monetary aggregates so as to ensure prespecified quantity targets (as in some Friedman-like growth rule). Or the authority might be directed to act so as to achieve a specifically defined outcome target, such as the maintenance of stability in the value of the monetary unit. In either case, the structure of the rules must be such as to invoke penalties for the failure of the authorities to act in accordance with the declared norms. Some allowance for within-threshold departures from targeted objectives would, of course, be necessary.

But only with some such feedbacks in place can the persons in positions of responsibility as monetary agents be expected to perform so as to further the success criterion that is implicit in the imposition of the rules. It seems at least conceptually possible to build in a workable reward-penalty structure for the compensation and employment of rule-bound monetary agents. And, in the limiting case, such a reward-penalty structure, appropriately related to the achievement of the desired policy target, may obviate the need for explicit definition of a rule for policy action. For example, if the compensations of all employees of the monetary authority should be indexed so as to ensure personal penalty from any departures from monetary stability, perhaps nothing more need be required by way of rules. (Such a scheme might involve the maintenance of fixed nominal salary levels against inflation, and double indexing of salaries against deflation, or some more sophisticated formulas.)

If no incentive-motivational structure is deemed institutionally and politically feasible, under the operation of any fiat money regime, the argument for more basic regime shift in the direction of an automatic or self-correcting system based on some commodity base is substantially strengthened. The relative advantage of all such systems lies in their incorporation of market-like incentives to generate behavior that will tend to generate at least long-term stability in the value of the monetary unit.

IX. Conclusion

In this discussion, as elsewhere, the primary implication of public choice theory is that institutional-constitutional change or reform is required to achieve ultimate success in macroeconomic policy. There is relatively little to be gained by advancing arguments for "better informed" and "more public-spirited" agents, to be instructed by increasingly sophisticated "economist-consultants" who are abreast of the frontiers of the "new science." All such effort will do little more than provide employment for those who are involved. It is the *political economy of policy* that must be reformed. Until and unless this step is taken, observed patterns of policy outcomes will continue to reflect accurately the existing political economy within which these outcomes are produced. And we shall continue to have conferences and discussions about the failures of "policy activism."

Notes

1. For further elaboration and analysis, see Geoffrey Brennan and James Buchanan, *The Power to Tax* (Cambridge: Cambridge University Press, 1980), chapter 6; and *Monopoly in Money and Inflation* (London: Institute of Economic Affairs, 1981).

2. For further elaboration of the analysis, see Geoffrey Brennan and James Buchanan, *The Reason of Rules: Constitutional Political Economy* (Cambridge: Cambridge University Press, 1987), chapters 5 and 6.

3. I shall not develop the argument in support of the contractarian-constitutional criterion for measuring policy success or failure. Let me say only that such a criterion must be used unless we are willing to introduce external and nonindividualistic standards of evaluation.

A more controversial position is the one that suggests that the monetary stability criterion would, indeed, be the one that would emerge from the ideally constructed constitutional setting. I shall not develop the argument in support of this position, although I think it can be plausibly made.

4. For an early statement of this point, see my article "Easy Budgets and Tight Money," *Lloyd's Bank Review* 64 n.s. (April, 1962): 17–30, reprinted in *Theory of Public Choice*, ed. James M. Buchanan and Robert Tollison (Ann Arbor: University of Michigan Press, 1974), pp. 62–75. For a more extended discussion, see James M. Buchanan and Richard E. Wagner, *Democracy in Deficit* (New York: Academic Press, 1977), and *Fiscal Responsibility in Constitutional Democracy*, ed. James M. Buchanan and Richard E. Wagner (Boston: Martinus Nijhoff, 1978).

5. Keynes and the Keynesians bear a heavy responsibility for destroying the set of classical precepts for fiscal prudence that had operated to keep the natural proclivities of politicians in bounds. By offering what could be interpreted as plausible excuses for fiscal profligacy, modern politicians have, for several decades, been able to act out their natural urges, with the results that we now observe. For further discussion, see my paper, "Victorian Budgetary Norms, Keynesian Advocacy, and Modern Fiscal Politics," prepared for Nobel Symposium on Governmental Growth, Stockholm, Sweden, August, 1984 (Fairfax, Va.: Center for Study of Public Choice, Working Paper No. 4-02, 1984).

13.

Ideas, Institutions, and Political Economy: A Plea for Disestablishment

I. Introduction

In early 1985 President Reagan seriously considered abolishing the Council of Economic Advisers, either temporarily through failure to make appointments, or permanently by seeking legislative approval for formal disestablishment. The Council was not abolished, and the inclination of any administration to do so does not seem likely to recur. The Council of Economic Advisers survives, and as the institution ages, pressures for continuation strengthen, quite independently of purpose or function.

The Council of Economic Advisers should have been abolished. The Council is an institution that finds its origins in a set of political and economic ideas that are no longer accepted. In the context of its originally claimed purpose, the Council is irrelevant. Any productive output now generated is peripheral to the primary objective. The institutional heritage that defined this objective, however, carries sufficient weight to the uninformed, and notably to the media, to ensure counterproductive influence on the economic policy of the nation.

In supporting these arguments, I shall *not* introduce directly any of the three familiar complaints about the operation of the Council. (1) I shall not dust off the hoary notion that, given the Council's political setting, it cannot refrain from advancing the partisan objectives of the administration that it serves. It cannot, so the complaint goes, present its recommendations or findings with sufficient "scientific objectivity." (2) I shall not, on the other hand, reject the general claim of "economic science" that the institutionalization of the Council seems to advance. There is a science of economics, but this science, properly defined, tends to be weakened rather than strengthened by the formalization of advice that the Council represents. (3) I shall not, finally, base my position on the more sophisticated modern notion that governmental economic policy is rendered ineffective by the predictive competence of rational citizens.

My recommendation that the Council be abolished as an institution is based on its political history and its relationship to the ideas that were important in shaping that history. The argument for disestablishment is not analogous to the argument for deregulation that has motivated efforts in transportation, communication, and finance. There has been no interest-group capture. Nor does the argument emphasize inefficiencies of bureaucratic apparatus. The damage or harm wrought by the Council is indirect and arises from the Council's very existence rather than from any efficacy or inefficacy in what it does. Its existence, as an institution, distracts the attention of political leaders and the public from structural features of the political economy and ensures the politicization of economic policy, either in reality or in appearance. Implicitly, the existence of the Council postulates a role for government that involves active participation within the rules of the political-economic game as opposed to government's more appropriate role in modifying the rules themselves.

I have leveled strong charges at an institution that has a very modest budget and which seems to exercise relatively little influence on politics. Admittedly, I am using the institution of the Council as the focal point of a whole mindset that should be disestablished. It is, of course, possible that major features of this mindset would persevere even if the Council should be abolished. On the other hand, so long as the institution continues to exist, as such, the mindset that it embodies cannot be fully dislodged.

There are two separate elements in my inclusive argument. One of these is within the corpus of economic analysis and it will be broadly familiar to modern economists. The other is based on elementary application of public choice theory to the institutions of democratic politics. The first element is more significant in assessing the role of the Council in the context of its own origins and history. The second element is more important when assessing the legitimacy of the Council of Economic Advisers as an institution designed to offer professional guidance to political decision-makers. These elements are discussed separately below. I shall then examine the broader issue of professional guidance in the conduct of economic policy, and I shall emphasize the categorical distinction between advice to political decision-makers who act within existing rules and advice to citizens who take part in a continuing discussion of possible changes in the rules (i.e., constitutional reform).

II. The Keynesian Theory of Policy

The Council of Economic Advisers, as an institution, was established in the Employment Act of 1946. There is no question but that the Council, and the more inclusive legislation that set it up, was intellectually grounded in the Keynesian theory of economic policy that had literally conquered the academic/intellectual community of Washington during the early 1940s. We need only recall the several projections of massive postwar unemployment generated by the application of simple macroeconomic models that now seem so grossly naive. But events occur in their own historical settings, and the events of 1946 were produced out of the ideas that were current at the time.[1]

The United States had experienced the great depression, and it was widely held that only the armaments industry boom of the 1940s had pulled the otherwise stagnating national economy into high gear, with high employment. The "natural" state of the economy was widely thought to be characterized by excessive saving relative to investment opportunities with accompanying high unemployment and excess industrial capacity. There was general acceptance of the normative principle that positive action by the national government should be taken with the precise objective of achieving and maintaining desirable levels of income and employment. This normative principle was itself based on the theory of relationships among economic aggregates that we associate with the descriptive term Keynesian. A genuine revolution in the thinking of economists had occurred. Keynes had provided a framework within which the whole economy, not just the actors within it, could be analyzed. Economists were duped into thinking that they could "understand" the operation of a complex economic interaction process by the use of hydraulic-like models that embodied the interdependencies among a relatively small number of macroeconomic variables, with macroeconomic equilibrium being defined independently from that which described incentive-compatible states in the behavior of participating actors.

The macroeconomy equilibrium need not, however, embody, as any necessary consequence, the full employment of resources. Hence, the theory seemed to explain that which had been observed in the 1930s without direct references to the neoclassical hypotheses concerning market clearances. Attention was diverted from the operation of markets, whether for resource inputs, final products, or financial instruments, and toward the operation of the macroaggregates, as a system, and also toward the prediction and measurement of the gap between observed output and that which might be potentially attained if the equilibrating variables should assume values different from those emerging.

The step from Keynesian theory, as macroeconomic analysis, to economic policy, as the normative application of the theory, was a natural one that could scarcely have been resisted by economists who accepted the former. To anyone whose thinking was indeed revolutionized by the Keynesian theory, there could have been no pulling up short before the policy applications. Who could forswear effort to attain the objectives of full employment and high income? The real opportunity costs of underutilized resources seemed nonexistent, and the use of the budget to fill in the gap between predicted and desired levels of aggregate demand seemed to follow as a matter of course. Lerner's regime of "functional finance" was self-evidently the policy ideal.

At this point, it is necessary to examine the Keynesian impact on the theory of economic policy in a more inclusive historical context. With the acceptance of the Keynesian analysis, the role and responsibility of the central government in maintaining target levels of employment and output were made explicit. And the assignment of a major share of this task to the instruments of fiscal or budgetary policy again seemed a natural extension. What is missing from the narrative to this point is any reference to the pre-Keynesian or even to the Keynesian theory of monetary institutions or to the assigned task of government in maintaining stability in the value of the monetary unit. An active policy role had been assigned to government in these respects prior to the 1930s. Keynes had, himself, discussed this role in detail in his early writings. The theory of central banking, developed in the 1920s, embodied an idealized policy norm along with implicit instructions to the monetary decision-makers. In practice, this theory of policy failed in the Great Depression, for reasons to be discussed later. The impact of the Keynesian teachings of the 1930s was to divert attention almost totally from the workings, and the failures, of basic monetary institutions, and to build a theory of macroeconomic policy as an appended superstructure to an existing central-bank foundation that had been flawed in its origins.

The stage was set, at the end of World War II, for the institutionalization of the Keynesian theory of economic policy. The macroeconomic models were in place; improvements had been made in the collection and processing of data necessary for prediction. The responsibility of government for maintaining high employment was widely accepted in the setting where the achievement of the more specific war objectives was observed as reality. Legislation was required only to make the objective explicit, and to establish in the executive branch an agency charged with the functions of assessing the data, making the predictions, and offering the advice of the political decision-makers.

We know, of course, that the Council of Economic Advisers was unable to fulfill its promise from the very beginning of its existence. We know that the mid-1940s predictions of the Keynesian macromodels were almost uniformly in error, while the simpler classical predictions proved basically accurate. There was no shortage of investment opportunities in the postwar years; there was no excessive saving. Inflation rather than unemployment was the economic policy problem.

Both ideas and their institutionalized embodiments, however, once created, tend to assume quasi-permanence, regardless of their empirical validity or demonstrated achievement. This characterization is especially descriptive when the ideas in question are comprehensive rather than piecemeal, when they reflect a whole mindset rather than particularized hypotheses. It is not surprising, therefore, that the Keynesian theory of macroeconomics, along with the theory of policy, was not simply abandoned as a result of its early record of predictive failure. The late 1940s and 1950s were years in which this dominant mindset was adjusted, modified, and extended, all with the aim of making the basic models offer more plausibly acceptable "explanation" of observed economic reality. Difficulties in prediction were acknowledged; lags between the implementation and the effects of policy action were recognized; differences in results of differing policy instruments were analyzed; possible conflicts among desired objectives were emphasized. The early Keynesian neglect of money and financial instruments along with the necessary complementarity and substitutability between fiscal and monetary instruments became the subject matter for intensive research inquiry.

The Council of Economic Advisers shifted its role from that originally envisaged to one that was in keeping with the changing content of macroeconomic theory. Its reports collected and presented data on macroeconomic aggregates; they assessed the record of performance *ex post*; they made cautionary projections of future movements; they presented briefs for the policy stances of the administration in office. The difficulties of translating ideas directly into policy formulation were acknowledged both by academic economists and by members of successive Councils.

The national economy is a much more complex reality than that incorporated into the models of the early American Keynesians. The function and purpose of any agency assigned the task of proffering economic advice in the sense initially intended was lost almost from the start. By the end of the 1950s, almost all economists were "Keynesian" in the sense that macroeconomic tools were used to "explain" the aggregates. At the same time, almost no economists were "Keynesian" in the sense that they retained the faith in the efficacy of simplistic macromanagement that had been expressed a decade earlier.

In the late 1950s and 1960s, the Phillips trade-off dominated macroeconomic policy discussion, and argument centered on the relative weights to be placed on the employment and monetary objectives, along with some debate as to the relative efficacy of fiscal and monetary instruments. The apogee of economic advice, as such, was perhaps attained in the early 1960s, when the political decision-makers seemed to act as economists suggested, when taxes were deliberately reduced for macroeconomic policy rather than for budgetary policy purposes, and with surprising success.

By the middle and late 1960s, however, the Keynesian neglect of monetary elements forced itself into recognition as inflationary dangers appeared. Economists, meanwhile, had commenced looking for the microfoundations of macroeconomic action. The historical record of the 1930s was reassessed and the Keynesian low-employment trap was called into question. Milton Friedman (1968) and E. S. Phelps (1967) introduced the "natural rate" of unemployment as that rate which could at best be only temporarily shifted by fiscal and/or monetary manipulation.[2] Martin Bailey (1971) questioned the efficacy of fiscal policy in its claimed ability to accomplish any macroeconomic objective.[3]

Historically, the national economy moved from the low-inflation, high-growth years of the early 1960s into the accelerating-inflation, low-growth years of the 1970s. "Stagflation" was upon us, and the Keynesians had neither a satisfactory explanation nor a plausible policy suggestion for escape.

The monetarists gained the high ground in some academic citadels. Their testing was to come later. But the monetarists, at least in their early years of return to respectability, were almost as simplistic as the early Keynesians. And, had their substitute models been proven fully descriptive, there might have emerged an argument for the institutionalization of monetarist advice. However, the early monetarists did not shift attitudes to an extent remotely comparable to the Keynesians of the 1940s. At best, monetarist influences indirectly entered into the Councils' reports, but almost always through the language and data of the Keynesian macromodels. The results could scarcely have been otherwise. The Council of Economic Advisers was a product of the Keynesian mindset, and this mindset must be embodied in the institution itself, independently of the particular economists who may be chosen to serve and also independently of the economic stance of the administration in office.

In the mid-1980s (as this is being written), macroeconomic theory is in disarray. The aggregative relationships described in neither the most sophisticated Keynesian models nor in the most advanced monetarist hypotheses described the experience of the early 1980s. On the other hand, the severe recession of 1982 essentially refuted the extensive claims made by the rational expectations advocates. There is no macroeconomic theory, as such, upon which economic policy advice might be based. The Council of Economic Advisers is a redundant agency, a leftover from the Keynesian era, an agency that could, at its best, present the case for its own ineffectiveness.

III. The Politics of Policy

A different, and perhaps even stronger, indictment can be developed, independently of the validity or invalidity of the whole macroeconomic "scientific" enterprise. Even if macroeconomic theory, whether in its pristine Keynesian simplicity or in its modern expectational feedback variants, should be acknowledged to be descriptively adequate, the bridge between analysis and policy would still have to be crossed, and efficacy in policy would require resort to instruments that embody incentives compatible with the roles assigned to decision-makers within the governmental structure. The whole Keynesian edifice was constructed on the preposterous supposition that economic advice is offered to a genuinely benevolent despot, an entity devoid of its own interests, and presumably willing and able to implement, without resistance, the advice offered to it. The early monetarist challenge was directed to the Keynesian analysis and, in itself, did not question the implicit political supposition.

Policy decisions emerge from a process in which persons participate in accordance with established rules governing their behavior and authority. In order to advance any normative theory of policy at all, it is necessary to model the decision process. As noted above, the implicit Keynesian supposition is starkly simple; there is no decision process. An argument for a policy change need not go through a model of decision, either in terms of potential incentive compatibility for the individual or in terms of the reconciliation of possibly divergent individual interests.

For purposes of initial discussion here, I shall assume that there does exist a theory of the macroeconomy that allows economists to offer agreed-on policy advice. Further, I shall assume that the economists, themselves, are not directly motivated by their own career objectives in the governmental structure. Under these assumptions, the advice offered will be invariant over differing political decision structures, and it will, presumably, reflect the whole community's long-term interests. The same "independent" advice will be forthcoming whether or not the political authority is responsive to the preferences of an electorate.

These assumptions allow me to focus attention on the behavior of the political agent when economic advice is offered. Only if the interests of the agent are coincident with those of the community would we expect quasi-automatic acceptance of the advice. Effective authority lodged with an hereditary monarch might represent the closest historical parallel to the implicitly presumed Keynesian model of politics. In all assignments of authority that are impermanent and that are not convertible into private-wealth equivalents, there will arise a necessary conflict between the interests of the agent and those of the citizenry. The impermanence of tenure along with the nonmarketability of the "policy regime as a capital asset" ensures that the interests of any designated political agent will be myopic relative to those that would be appropriate for the community. The agent would, therefore, tend to reject the advice of the economists when it embodies considerations of long-term gains at the expense of short-term sacrifice.

Applied to the whole set of choices among instruments and targets for macroeconomic policy, the political agent's decisions will tend to be biased toward demand-side rather than supply-side adjustments. More specifically, the agent's decisions will reflect biases toward public spending increases as against tax reductions, toward deficit as against surplus financing, toward monetary expansion as against monetary contraction.

This myopia exhibited by political agents will be accentuated if they are required to compete with potential replacements through electoral processes.[4] An authority or agent who is genuinely independent of politics possesses more flexibility in choice, and this may be exercised by closer adherence to the economists' advice. The absence of electoral feedbacks must, however, also allow more latitude for deviant behavior on the part of the agent.

Any plausible descriptive model of the political decision process must yield the prediction that policy advice of economists will get, at best, only a biased acceptance. If political agents are to be made to conform more closely to the genuine "public interest" (on the presumption that there are no difficulties in defining such interest), their range of discretionary authority must be reduced, or their incentives must be modified so as to induce closer conformity. The second of these prospects is severely restricted in democratic structures; politicians cannot readily be provided with effective incentives that run contrary to their survival in elected office. Meaningful prospects for reform may be limited to reduction in the range for discretionary action, to some introduction of *rules* within which action must take place.

To the extent that such constraining rules take the form either of specifically defined targets or instruments of policy, there is little left for advisory economists to do. As an extreme case, what would be the role for a Council of Economic Advisers in a setting where there exists a constitutional amendment for budget balance along with a Friedman-like rule for monetary growth? We do not, of course, have any such rules in place as a part of our constitutional structure. If constitutional reform is impossible, and hence if arms and agencies of government are to continue to be empowered to take policy actions that will exert effects on the economy, is there a residual role for an agency designed to offer expert advice? Could it be argued that such an agency might exert a force, even if a limited one, toward policy directed in the community's interests?

My judgment is that such a potentially constructive role is more than offset by the delusion of effective policy activism that the very existence of such an agency tends to foster. This judgment is strengthened when we drop the provisional assumption, advanced above, that an agreed-on theory of the macroeconomic exists. The existence of an agency of experts in the context of 1985 creates the appearance that there exists a basis for agreed-on policy action which politicians could, ideally, implement but for their own narrowly defined interests.

In this setting, individuals will attempt to base their own economizing decisions on expectations concerning how political agents will, in fact, behave, both against the idealized policy set and in terms of their own interests. The political agents in office will encourage the delusion by claiming credit for economic improvements, and their opponents out of office will reinforce the argument by blaming incumbents for economic disappointments. The very appearance of macroeconomic policy effectiveness or ineffectiveness on the part of an activist government tends to shift political debate to artificial if not false grounds of argument. The primary task of the Council of Economic Advisers—presenting an annual economic report—implies the assignment of "grades" to the stewardship of the national economy. Could we expect a council of economists to use the report for truth-telling? Could we expect them to expose the reality behind the appearance?

IV. Economics: Positive and Normative

I have not based my argument for the disestablishment of the Council of Economic Advisers on any claim that economics lacks scientific standing in the proper meaning of the term. There is a science of economics that yields testable hypotheses and allows conditional predictions to be made. Economists can predict the effects of shifts in the constraints within which persons act. These predictions are possible because of uniformities in the nature of man, who remains both natural and artifactual. At this level of inquiry, the science of economics is no different from the science of chemistry or biology. And the professional standards of the discipline operate similarly. An economist who advances a claim that trade restrictions increase the value of national product loses his credibility as a scientist. But, as noted earlier, there exist no comparable agreed-on standards in macroeconomics.

The comparison with other sciences is suggestive, however, because we do not observe agencies of government carrying the labels Council of Chemical Advisers, Council of Biological Advisers, and so on. It is more or less taken for granted that the predictive properties of these basic sciences are utilized as inputs in any discussion of governmental action. But there is no call for the elevation of the practitioners in these disciplines to positions of particularized political influence. The role of such institutions as the President's Science Advisory Council or the Office of Technology Assessment is much more limited than that occupied by the Council of Economic Advisers. In general, it is taken for granted that scientists will do their work in academic and research communities, and it is also presumed that such work is best performed in relative isolation from the political forum.

Economists, as positive scientists, can contribute much to our understanding of the interactions among us and of the institutions within which such interactions take place. But what of the role for the economist reformers, for those who seek to use the predictions emergent from positive economics to suggest what governments "should" do? Even if there is no agreed-on "science" of macroeconomics, the predictions of macroeconomics offer a basis for normative advice to governments, or so it may seem. Consider the simple case of minimum-wage legislation. Economic science predicts that increases in the level of real minimum wages, legally enforced, will increase unemployment, and especially among low-skill workers. This prediction has been empirically corroborated. Does it not follow directly that the economist, armed with these findings of his science, can suggest to governmental decision-makers that such legislation be repealed? Can the economist not use the familiar efficiency criterion to advance this argument?

The economist who takes this position must, however, place himself in the arrogant role of assuming a private knowledge of the preferred "social" rankings of alternative policy steps. And in this position, there is nothing whatsoever in the economist's "science" that allows his own value rankings to be superior to those of anyone else in the polity. Enhanced employment of the low-skilled workers, increased value of real product in the economy, extended sphere for voluntary contractual exchanges—these may be valued results, but they may well be relegated to rankings below those of maintaining higher wages among the employed, or maintaining the existing geographical dispersion of employment, by members of certain groups. The economist who implies that his "science" enables him to call for the repeal of minimum-wage legislation is on all fours with the nuclear physicists who imply that their "science" enables them to call for nuclear disarmament. In both cases, the genuine authority of the positive science is seriously undermined by the advancement of such false claims.

My own efforts in what we now call "constitutional economics" has often been classified as "normative economics." Does this suggest that I have been guilty of that which I have admonished against? Careful reading of my position would suggest otherwise. I have called on my fellow economists to devote more attention to the working properties of alternative sets of rules within which persons, and especially those charged with political responsibilities, act. My continuing frustration has been with the refusal of so many of my fellow economists to recognize that the behavior of persons in public-choice roles is also subject to the predictions of our science. With Wicksell, I have urged those who seek reforms in policy, not as economists but as socially responsible citizens, to look to changes in the constraints placed on those we charge with political authority as opposed to changes in their behavior within existing constraints.

In one sense, again with Wicksell, my central purpose has been that of ridding our discourse of the benevolent despot image, in all its forms. The Keynesian half-century in which this image was politically institutionalized through the creation of the Council of Economic Advisers, is behind us. It seems time that we eliminate this relic of a past that has failed on so many counts, and that we get on with our business of engaging in constructive dialogue on the potential for reform in the framework of rules within which we may, both privately and publicly, pursue our individually defined purposes.

Notes

1. See Herbert Stein, *The Fiscal Revolution in America* (Chicago: University of Chicago Press, 1969), for the definitive history here.

2. Milton Friedman, "The Role of Monetary Policy," *American Economic Review* 58 (March, 1968): 1–17; E. S. Phelps, "Phillips Curves Expectations of Inflation, and Optimal Unemployment over Time," *Economica* n.s. 34 (August, 1967): 258–81.

3. Martin Bailey, *National Income and the Price Level: A Study in Macroeconomic Theory* (New York: McGraw-Hill, 1971).

4. For a discussion of the differing effects of alternative political structures, see my essay, "Can Policy Activism Succeed?" presented at the Federal Reserve Bank of St. Louis, October, 1984, and published as chapter 12, this volume.

14.

The Evaluation of Public Services

WITH FRANCESCO FORTE

I

Specialists in the construction and use of national income and product accounts have been unable to agree upon the appropriate evaluation of public or governmental goods and services. In a recent conference, this problem was said to represent "the chief and perhaps the only really serious point of disagreement" among these specialists, and the lines of communication among the adversaries were said to be "notoriously defective."[1] Despite the general recognition that the issues are conceptual in nature, the fact that specialists in national accounting have been so closely associated with instrumental problems of measurement per se may have served to prevent the clarification that seems so obviously to be required. Nonspecialists may be able to contribute toward such a clarification because of their very detachment from the complexities of statistical estimation.[2]

Although generalizations concerning the two sides of any debate are difficult to support, the fundamental cleavage in this particular case seems to be based on the fact that the adversaries are approaching the whole issue of measurement with two separate purposes or goals in mind. National income or national product can, on the one hand, be taken to reflect an evaluation of *existing* output for the purpose of making comparisons of "welfare" among communities and through time. On the other hand, national income or product can be taken to measure the value of *potential* output that might be produced with existing inputs of resources. In either case, consistent procedures for measurement can be developed, but only after the purpose is made definite. The distinction between these two approaches will, we hope, be made clear in what follows.

If the circular-flow conception of the economic process is accepted, income payments received by factor owners must equal the value of total output produced. This dual manner of conceiving national income or product has served to introduce an important element of confusion into national accounting, a confusion that directly affects the evaluation of public services. Income, as received by factor owners, has been measured at factor costs, whereas output or product has been measured at market prices. Despite these two distinctly different means of valuation, the attempt has been made to force the aggregative results into the equality suggested by the circular-flow identity. There seems to have been some failure to recognize that costs do not measure the same thing as do market prices. Costs provide a measure of the market value of resources in *alternative* uses; only indirectly do cost values provide some measure of the value of resources in existing uses. And there is no reason why a measure of national income at genuine factor costs need be equal to national product at market prices. The circular-flow identity can be ensured only if all residual rents are included in costs. But this procedure makes the whole distinction between market prices and factor costs meaningless. As Bowman and Easterlin point out, consistent evaluation at cost *or* at market price can restore the definitional identity between the two sides of the account.[3]

The particular discussion concerning the evaluation of the public services does not seem wholly to have escaped from the confusion and the ambiguities of the diamond-water paradox. Participants have not consistently embodied in their measurement proposals adequate recognition that economic values for output are set at the margins and that a market price always reflects the purchasers' evaluation of a little more or a little less of a good or service rather than any evaluation of a total quantity. Prices multiplied by quantities and summed over all goods and services provide an evaluation of the *particular* composition or output mix that is purchased and nothing more.

The fact that both sides in the debate have chosen to discuss the evaluation of public services within an overly restricted frame of reference has prevented progress toward a solution. First of all, discussion has been centered on the proper treatment of those goods and services, provided collectively, that serve as *intermediate* products or inputs to private buiness firms or upon those governmental activities that supply environmental or framework services for the private production process. If an attempt had been made to extend the analysis to the evaluation of public services generally, a more satisfactory meeting of minds, if not an agreed-upon solution, might have been achieved. A second weakness has been the widespread reliance on the application of the so-called invariance test. Argument has proceeded on the assumption that the net product of the economy should not be changed by the shift of an activity from the private to the public sector, or vice versa. However, when it is recognized that the institutional shift of an activity from private production, which embodies a positive output price, to public production, if this embodies free provision of the service in question, must generate some reallocation of economic resources, the change in the output mix and its distribution must be expected to involve some change in the real value of net output. The whole problem of appropriate quantity weighting for deflating money measures of output to obtain real values is introduced.

In Sections II and III we shall examine critically the two opposing positions: first, that taken by the Department of Commerce in its actual measurement procedures and stoutly defended by departmental spokesmen and, second, that taken by Professor Simon Kuznets and his followers. We shall demonstrate that neither of these positions is fully satisfactory. In Section IV we shall present an alternative proposal that is valid for the evaluation of both intermediate and final public services. Finally, in Section V, we shall try to show that the Department of Commerce position can be rationalized more readily if we shift the purpose from that of measuring the value placed on existing output to that of measuring the potential output value that might be produced from existing resource inputs.

II

The Department of Commerce, in estimating the total value for net national product, adds the cost value of all governmentally provided goods and services (except for those that are directly priced) to the values for final output of privately produced goods and services. This practice has been subjected to a long and continuing criticism. The method has been said to be based on the assumption that all public goods are equivalent to final products for consumers. The spokesmen for the Department have responded by stating that the relevant distinction, for the public sector of output, is not that between intermediate and final goods; it is, instead, whether or not the goods are "resold" through ordinary market channels. If the goods provided by government are not resold (that is, if they do not again enter the market process), they are freely consumed and must be considered, in this sense, as final goods and services. Department spokesmen have illustrated this position with reference to the now familiar example of free flour. If the government should provide free flour to all bakers, the bread subsequently produced would be sold to consumers at prices which *do not* include a cost price for flour. The consumer would receive the value of this flour free of direct charge. The baking firms would only serve to "transmit" this final good to consumers. Therefore, every publicly provided good or service that is not directly priced, that is provided free, becomes final. And, since the acknowledged final goods and services received by individuals from government are to be included in estimates of national product, there is no reason why the so-called intermediate goods and services should be treated differently.

This analysis seems unsatisfactory, but not primarily for the reasons advanced by its opponents. The value of goods sold in the market, when computed at market prices, is the value placed upon them by purchasers *at the margin*. What is the value at the margin for public goods and services that are provided to purchasers free of direct charge?

At the risk of oversimplification, we propose to examine the evaluation of intermediate goods and services supplied by government in carefully restricted analytical models. For the time being, we shall assume a fully competitive economy. Resources are assumed freely mobile as among alternative employment opportunities; no specialized resources exist, and all production is carried out under conditions of constant returns. Now let us assume that, through an international agreement with another country, the government purchases a technological advisory service affecting a particular industry and embodying a cost-reducing innovation. It then makes this service freely available to the firms in the domestic industry. This is clearly an *intermediate* service provided by government. Under the circumstances described, the mechanism of competitive adjustment will ensure that more resources enter the industry affected. Prices of output to consumers will fall by the full value of the freely provided service. At the new industry and firm equilibriums, the product price will be fully exhausted by marginal productivity payments to *priced* resource inputs. No imputable value for the free technical service will remain in the price of final output.

Intuitively, this analysis seems consistent with the position of the Department of Commerce. The firms in the industry act merely as "transactors" that pass along the free service to final consumers. The departmental spokesmen are in error, however, in that they reach wrong conclusions from a position that can be made internally consistent. They have been quite correct in emphasizing that the values of freely provided intermediate products *do not show up* in final product prices under the competitive adjustment model *because they are free*. But this also suggests that, precisely because the services are free, they are not positively valued by users at the relevant margins. The free provision of services by government, under the conditions of this model, guarantees that resources will be adjusted in such a manner that the services will be treated *as if* they were, in fact, "free" in the broader, zero-cost sense. And, since "free" goods have no economic value, they should not be counted in estimates for national output. The fact that the government actually uses up resources in acquiring these services and, in order to finance this acquisition, levies charges on the general taxpayer, is not relevant at all. For purposes of measuring national output at market values, these services must be treated in the same way that any geuinely free good, say air, is treated.

On one point the Department of Commerce spokesmen are quite correct: that there are no reasons for treating the intermediate services provided by government any differently from final services. The analysis above can be applied without change to freely provided final goods and services. We may demonstrate this by the introduction of a simple illustration. Let us assume that a municipality provides water to residential consumers free of direct charge and that it places no restrictions upon the amount of water that each consumer may use. Despite the fact that this water will cost something in resources and that this cost will be distributed among individual citizens through the tax system, the utilization of water in the community will proceed *as if* it were genuinely *free* in all respects. The individual consumer will use water to the point at which the marginal utility becomes zero, since there will be no marginal price connected with his own decision to use a little more or a little less. It is relatively easy to see that, under circumstances such as these, the individual will place no marginal value on the water provided by the municipality. Water will be treated in precisely the same way that a genuinely costless (free) good is treated. To impute a value to water by measuring it at some cost-price for purposes of including this value in estimates of community output would amount to measuring a part of "consumers' surplus," something that is not done for other goods and services. Since the individual will use the freely available water to such an extent that one unit has no value, the total valuation of water would be zero.

These conclusions suggest that both intermediate and final goods and services supplied by government without charge should be excluded from estimates of national output at market values insofar as they are made available to consumers (individuals or firms) in unlimited quantities. But there remains the question concerning those intermediate or final goods and services provided by government without direct charge to consumers but in limited amounts. In this case, despite the fact that the goods or services are not directly priced, a positive marginal utility may exist in any final equilibrium. Let us continue, for now, to assume a fully competitive economy with resources freely mobile among separate employments and all production carried out at constant returns.

First we may examine a model in which a limited quantity of a public good is made available; this good is known to generate differential effects on the separate sectors of the economy but is made freely available to all firms that might potentially employ it.[4] Here we may rely on the famous Pigou-Knight "narrow but good road" for all illustrations.[5] Competition among the using firms will act so as to increase the non-collective inputs in the affected industry. The market price charged to consumers will fall to some extent, but not by the full amount of the costs of the collective input. This stems from the fact that, relatively, too many private resources will be drawn into the industry for efficient operation. At a final equilibrium, output price in the industry will be barely sufficient to pay for the services of the privately supplied resource inputs employed. No part of the input price can be imputed to the publicly supplied input that is made available without charge. The total production of the industry differentially affected will, of course, be larger after the instrumental public good is made available than before. The marginal value of this production will be smaller than before, and this value will be fully exhausted in meeting marginal productivity payments to priced resource inputs. The publicly supplied input has no marginal value. The only means of including the value of this publicly supplied input in estimates of national output is to include the value of the larger private production in differentially affected industries at the new prices. This is accomplished, of course, simply by counting the whole value of private output at market prices.

Let us now examine a different model. Return to our former example and assume that, instead of making water available without charge in unlimited quantities, the municipality provides each resident with a definite quantity of water. Assume further that the freely provided public water amounts to less than the average residential use in the case of unlimited availability. Under these circumstances water will, of course, have some positive marginal utility to the average or the representative consumer. If water rights to this limited quantity are allowed to be marketed freely among separate individuals, a price will come to be established for these rights. Note, however, that this valuation, which should be included in output estimates, will be wholly divorced from the costs of supplying the water to the municipality. These prices for water rights will depend on the amount of water that is made available freely by the municipality and on the marginal evaluation of water by the citizens. In this case, it seems clear that a cost valuation for the municipally supplied water should not be added to the market valuation of water rights. Only the latter should be included in national output estimates. If the rights to free water are not marketable, however, this positive utility will not be represented in a market value. The evaluation of water in national output should, however, be wholly divorced from the average cost or the marginal cost of providing this free public good.

Let us now consider an intermediate good or service that is made available without direct charge, that does generate some differential effects among the separate industries, and that is not freely accessible to all potential users. We may think of the government making some good available to all firms in a perfectly competitive industry but rationing the limited quantity among the firms. Water for irrigation purposes might be the example. In this case, the provision of the free inputs will result in the creation of differential rents for those producers who receive the ration coupons that enable them to utilize the free inputs. This rent may serve to reduce the costs of production for the benefited producers. Because of the free public good, the productivity of priced resources will be greater for the affected firms. But this increased productivity will not be reflected through an increase in resource prices because the marginal productivity of priced resources in "non-subsidized" employment will tend to determine resource prices.

This model, embodying the formation of differential rents as a result of free provision of a public intermediate good, may seem somewhat extreme under the assumptions of an ideally competitive economy. However, when this latter assumption is dropped, the differential rent model becomes perhaps the most general one. If the mechanism for competitive adjustment is imperfect, if monopoly is allowed to be present, in greater or lesser degree, the creation of differential rents as a result of governmental provision of intermediate goods and services must be carefully considered. Even if an input service should be made available in unlimited amounts, or if a fixed amount should be made freely accessible to all potential users, the failure of full competitive adjustment to take place may allow some of the benefits from the free government input to be retained by producing units. The full benefits may not be shifted forward to final consumers, and, as a result, some part of the final product value will tend to reflect the marginal value of the government input.[6]

When we combine all these models, we must conclude that the procedure for evaluating public goods and services that is followed by the Department of Commerce is conceptually incorrect. Insofar as public goods and services are made available without direct charge in unlimited quantities and competitive adjustment takes place, the value of these goods and services at the margins of use becomes zero. There is no reason to include any cost valuation for these goods and services in any proposed measurement for the market value of national output. Insofar as public goods and services—intermediate or final—are provided to users free of direct charge, but either they are unequally distributed among users or fully competitive adjustment does not take place—or both—producers' rents may be created. Such rents may arise for firms in industries supplied with a governmental intermediate product or for firms in industries supplying goods that are complementary with a freely provided final good or service. To the extent that such rents replace private costs of production, at the margin, as imputable distributive shares, the market value of the free public goods is included in the market value of private output. Double-counting or duplication is indeed involved here when the cost value of public goods is added to the market value of final output.

There remain situations in which public goods, although provided without direct charge to consumers, retain a positive value at the margin and in which this value is not included in the market value of some final output. These situations are represented in those cases where the quantity of the public good is limited but where the benefits of this limitation are transmitted forward to final consumers. Even for these cases, however, an inclusion of the public goods at values at the margin has no relation to the cost of production, and the unit value may be above or below marginal or average cost. This is reminiscent of Jevons: cost can influence marginal value only through its influence on supply; and, in this case, the supply of the public good made available is not directly influenced by cost considerations.

III

Simon Kuznets has been the most important and persistent advocate of the thesis that intermediate and environmental public goods and services should be excluded from estimates of national product.[7] In his view, current procedures of measurement result in an overstatement of the contribution of the public sector because of the failure to introduce some downward adjustment for the value of the intermediate goods supplied by government. The inclusion of the publicly provided "intermediate" goods and services involves a clear case of double-counting; these goods and services do not represent net additions to national output.

This general position has perhaps been most clearly outlined by Bowman and Easterlin.[8] In specific reference to the line of reasoning advanced in opposition by Department of Commerce spokesmen, the double-counting argument has perhaps been most fully developed by Shoup and Musgrave.[9] To counter the Department's argument that firms act merely to "transmit" the values of freely provided intermediate goods to final consumers, these writers rely on the deflation of money measures of output to offset collectively induced changes in output prices. If, as in the example of free flour, the market price of bread should fall as a result of the initiation of collective provision of an intermediate good, flour, the general price level is presumed to fall. Thus, when measured values for output are appropriately deflated to reflect real values, national product should remain invariant under the particular change postulated.

A somewhat broader approach has been taken by Kuznets with reference to those environmental or framework services that are not fully analogous to inputs in the private production processes but which nevertheless constitute a part of the setting essential for private production. (Typical examples are external defense and the administration of justice.) Kuznets' argument for excluding any valuation for these "environmental outputs" from national income is that these goods and services, by making private production possible, must be reflected in the value of final output for the private sector. In other words, private output assumes a certain size because of the existence of collective provision of defense, justice, and so on. To count both the preconditions of production and the production itself, argues Kuznets, involves duplication.[10]

Let us consider these arguments: first, that of "adjusted income" employed in opposition to the inclusion of those strictly intermediate goods and services supplied by government, for example, free flour. If the flour is provided to firms in the baking industry without charge, the results may be represented in one of two limiting cases or any combination thereof. In the first extreme, no competitive adjustment takes place at all because of monopolistic or other conditions. The price of bread (final product) may remain invariant. In this case there is no reason to include the value of the flour at cost in estimates of national output, since this value will already be embodied in the price of bread, being now imputable as a distributive share to producers and classified properly as producers' differential rents. In the second extreme, the full competitive adjustment will take place, and the market price of bread will fall by the full amount of the value of the free government input. Here, the proponents of the "adjusted income" argument say, the general price level also goes down. If national production in any given year (or community) has to be compared with that of another year (or community), money measures for output must be deflated by some appropriate price index in order to obtain comparable "real" incomes. When two situations are compared—one in which a good, say flour, is provided free of charge and in which the price of output, bread, is lower; another situation in which the same good is priced through the market and the price of output, bread, is for this reason higher—*if the same amount of bread is produced in both situations,* the proper deflation will yield identical "real" incomes for both situations. To add a cost value of the free flour to the value of the bread, in the public-good situation, continues this argument, will result in double-counting because the value of this free input is reflected in the price-deflator that must be applied to reduce money values to real values.

The important, and essential, step in this analysis is the assumption of invariance, that is, the assumption that the production of the differentially affected commodity or service remains the same when the intermediate good is provided free and when it is priced through the market. It is, however, clear that this invariance assumption is not supportable. When an intermediate good is provided freely to firms in an industry, surely the output of the industry must be increased, provided only that there is some variation in the coefficients of production. If, in fact, output could not increase, then the price could not fall and the whole idea of adjusted real income to reflect price changes would be meaningless. If the production of the differentially affected commodity is increased as a result of the free provision of a single input, the production of other goods and services normally must be decreased. The whole output composition of the community is modified. And, once this is allowed to happen, the central problem of index numbers is introduced. Weighting with the output mix of one situation will lead to a different result from weighting with the output mix of another situation. *Ceteris paribus*, weighting an index with the quantities of final output produced in the situation in which the intermediate good is priced through the market will tend to produce, relatively, a lower "real" income for the public-good situation than will the weighting of the index by those quantities of output produced in the situation when the intermediate good is provided freely by government.[11]

Let us turn to the broader argument of Kuznets for the exclusion of the "framework" intermediate public services from output measures. If the purpose is that of measuring "welfare" by the market evaluation of present consumption and capital goods useful for future consumption—Kuznets holds—all items of expenditure that are not in themselves final consumption or investment must be excluded. But the dividing line between framework goods and other public goods, as traced out by Kuznets, seems arbitrary. He asserts that those goods, with counterparts in the private sector, which are provided freely by government are not part of the "framework" of production. But it seems questionable to classify public schools, which do have counterparts in private schools, as falling without the "framework" and external defense, which has no private counterpart, as within the "framework." Logically, this argument suggests that the institutional structure of the country, which will determine the presence or absence of many counterparts to public goods and services, may affect the evaluation procedures.

From the discussion of Section II, and from what follows in Section IV, it should be clear that, for some purposes, we should support Kuznets's recommendations as improving currently employed measurement procedures, but both the adjusted income and the framework arguments in support of these recommendations seem to be of questionable conceptual validity. Neither the specific recommendations of Kuznets nor the arguments in their support lead to a wholly satisfactory resolution of many of the difficulties inherent in the evaluation of public services.

IV

As we have said, the methods of evaluating social income and, through this, the contribution of the public sector, depend upon the purposes that the evaluation is designed to accomplish. J. R. Hicks has distinguished two ends or goals of income measurement: welfare and productivity.[12] If either of these is to be adopted, some value scale must be introduced through which a whole set of heterogeneous goods and services may be compared and summed. Market-established prices provide the basic value scale in an enterprise economy. Since the individual consumer presumably adjusts his behavior to an established set of prices, the total expenditure that he makes on all goods and services reflects his evaluation of the whole pattern of his consumption. The total expenditure of all consumers thus provides us with some composite evaluation of the whole output mix, and, because of this, we can accept this as an indicator of "welfare" in one highly restricted sense.

We propose to exclude all valuation for government product that is not directly priced. This seems to follow directly from this "welfare" criterion. Since individual users (firms and final consumers) are not charged for public goods and services, their behavior is adjusted to *zero* prices for these services. Hicks accepts the proposal that publicly provided goods and services should not be valued in national output if they are made available in unlimited quantities (our first model). He does not accept this procedure when the total supply of the goods and services is limited. The legitimacy of extending the exclusion even to these cases can, perhaps, best be shown by analogy. There are many "free" goods in nature that are strictly limited in supply. The sun shines only four hours per day on the average in some communities; clearly, "welfare" could be increased by more sunshine. But no effort is made to place a positive value on sunshine because no market transaction can produce more of the output. Instead, we assume implicitly that the adjustment processes of the economy act so as to take the differential availability of such "free" goods into account. Publicly supplied but limited goods and services seem no different. If the individual secures the enjoyment of these goods without direct charge and cannot resell them through some sort of a market transaction, no value should be included in national output estimates.

The two supposedly contradictory arguments that have appeared in the debate—the first that government intermediate services should not be counted (double) in national product and the second that "free" intermediate and final services cannot be distinguished and should not be differently treated—are not contradictory at all when considered properly. Both extend to the logical conclusion that all free public goods and services must be excluded from any consistent evaluation of national product for the purpose of measuring "welfare" in the restricted sense. From one point of view all public goods and services are, in fact, intermediate. From another point of view they are all final. They are intermediate because, being freely provided, they must to some extent be reflected in the values of other goods and services. In this sense, their inclusion in measurements of output implies overstatement. From another point of view all public goods are final because they must be considered to provide some measure of satisfaction to the population. This remains true despite the fact that, in many cases, they may provide zero marginal value to consumers. But any attempt to measure the extent of this total satisfaction by including these public goods at cost is not consistent with valuing private goods at their marginal (market) prices. In those cases where the freely provided goods retain positive marginal values, there are no means of determining what these values are and to what extent they are reflected in the market prices of other goods and services. The inclusion of public goods, supplied free of direct charge, at some cost valuation implies, therefore, both an inconsistency and an overstatement. Total exclusion, on the other hand, may imply an understatement of "welfare" in a certain sense. But it must be kept in mind that even the valuation of privately produced goods and services at market prices measures "welfare" in a very restricted definition of this term since only marginal values are incorporated. A measure of "total welfare" is unattainable. We are reduced to using the measurement of output valued at market prices because it is internally consistent and because it does have *some* significance for welfare. This consistency as well as the limited significance for welfare that is present is lost when the market values of privately produced output are added to the cost values for publicly supplied output. The only consistent measure of national output with current welfare significance at all seems to be that which includes only the valuation of goods and services actually sold on markets at positive prices.

It is important to note that this approach does not prevent useful comparisons of "welfare" between communities with different amounts and kinds of goods provided free through the collectivity. The exclusion of those goods and services provided free from the total value of output at market price means only that the items in question have zero prices. A total valuation of zero is put on such goods. However, the quantities of these goods are not necessarily excluded from the collection of items that may be relevant for making comparisons with communities in which these same goods have a positive price because they are sold through organized markets.

Again, let us proceed by simple examples. Community 1 is assumed to have no public police force; certain private individuals and firms hire police services through ordinary market channels. Community 2, assumed to be similar to Community 1 in other respects, taxes its citizens in order to provide police protection collectively. Under our proposals for the evaluation of community real output, the value of police protection would be included in the measurement of real product in the first community but excluded in the second community. Community 1 would, therefore, seem to show a higher real output solely due to the difference in organization. This implication is not correct, however, even in this specific example. To show that it is not, take the extreme assumption of invariance. Assume that private individuals in Community 1 hire the same number of policemen that the whole community does in 2. Assume further that the whole scheme is financed by income taxes that do not alter prices (another extreme assumption). Measured output in Community 1 would exceed that in Community 2 by the amount of the valuation placed on police services. But the price level is lower in Community 2 by virtue of the fact that police services *are priced at zero*. With the income generated in Community 2, consumers should be able to purchase, at Community 2 prices, all the goods consumed in Community 1, including police services that may be secured at zero prices. Obversely, with the income generated in Community 1, at Community 1 prices, consumers should be able to purchase all goods purchased in Community 2, including police services which are available only at market prices.[13]

In the normal case, however, with police protection being assumed genuinely collective, Community 1 would tend to utilize fewer police services than would Community 2. The "private" solution for Community 1 would, therefore, involve fewer resources devoted to police protection and more resources devoted to other uses than in Community 2. How does this change influence the problem of comparing real incomes in the two communities? Since the composition of production is no longer identical, the problem of quantity weights is introduced. The output of Community 1 will contain fewer police services and more alternative goods and services. If the quantities of goods and services actually consumed in Community 2, *including the amount of police services freely provided*, could be purchased by the income generated in Community 1, at Community 1 prices, *which must include some positive price for police services*, then Community 1 clearly has a real output at least as great as Community 2 has. On the other hand, if the quantities of goods and services actually consumed in Community 1, including the amount of police services purchased by private individuals and firms, could be purchased at Community 2 prices, which must include a zero price for police services, by the money income generated in Community 2, then real output in Community 2 must be at least as great as that of Community 1. By this procedure, Community 2 can, of course, show a lower money income but a higher real income than Community 1.

Unambiguous results could be expected to follow from such direct procedures only in limiting cases. Beyond these, nothing definite can be said about the relative size of real incomes in the two separate communities without the introduction of an explicit value judgment concerning the appropriate weights to be employed. Our purpose here is not, however, that of discussing the complexities of index-number construction and application to the evaluation of real product in making comparisons among countries or through time. The simple examples presented here have been designed to show only that no bias in such comparative measurement needs to be systematically introduced by our proposals for treating the governmental sector of output. Although resources are, of course, utilized in the production of governmental output, the exclusion of any valuation for this output from estimates of national product does not necessarily affect the comparison among communities that may organize their economic structures differently. That is to say, no difficulties that are not already present when such comparisons are attempted are introduced by the exclusion of any evaluation of public services.

V

A wholly different approach is suggested if the aim is that of measuring, not "welfare," even in the limited sense embodied in the attempts discussed above, but the value of the *potential* output that might be produced by the resource bundle in existence at any period of time. In this approach the relative evaluations placed on final goods and services are irrelevant except insofar as product prices reflect genuine marginal costs of production. Ideally, this approach would involve the addition of genuine resource or factor costs for all goods and services produced, including public as well as private goods. Immensely difficult problems arise, however, when any attempt is made to break down final product prices into the separate components of resources costs and true rents. Recognizing this difficulty, the analyst is tempted to adopt the simplifying assumption that, in competitive economies, product prices do, in fact, tend to approximate marginal costs. For the private sector, therefore, the addition of output values, yielding total expenditure, provides a measure of productive capacity.

Something of this approach seems to be implicit in current Department of Commerce practices, or, at least, this enables us to rationalize these practices more easily. If, in fact, market prices in the private sector could be assumed to equal marginal costs, the total value of privately marketed goods and services, minus indirect taxation, *plus* the cost values of publicly provided goods and services, would yield one acceptable measure for productive capacity of the economy. Market prices will, in this pure model, reflect only *private* marginal costs to firms; no cost value for publicly supplied intermediate or environmental services could possibly be included in market price. Therefore, no adjustment along the lines of Kuznets' theory would need to be made for these. But indirect taxes would clearly act to insert a wedge between product prices and genuine marginal costs; hence, some downward adjustment must be introduced to account for this. Since resources are also employed in producing governmental output, consistency requires that a direct cost-valuation be added to the indirect cost valuation (through market price) for those resources employed in the private sector.

Conceptually, this is a consistent approach, and comparisons among separate communities or through time could be made. If consistent practices are followed in measuring the relevant magnitudes in each of two separate communities, meaningful comparisons of real productive potential should be possible despite the differences in the organizational breakdown between the public and the private sectors in the two communities. Note here, however, that the price index which should be used to deflate measured income estimates must include the quantities of publicly supplied output *valued at cost prices*, not zero prices, as in the other "welfare" measurement approach.

But let us now try to see precisely what such a "productivity" measure means. If, when appropriately reduced to constant-dollar totals, Community 1 is shown to have a higher "productive capacity" than Community 2 has, what does this suggest? In the purely private economy (without any collective action) the answer seems clear. A "higher" productive potential means that, if the market economy should be "optimally" organized, total output will be greater in Community 1 than in Community 2. The production surface over the relevant area lies outside that for Community 2. When we introduce a public sector of the economy, however, the analysis becomes more complex. If it is legitimate to employ market prices, net of indirect taxes, to reflect marginal (equal average) costs of goods and services produced in the private sector, and if it is legitimate to use average cost to reflect marginal cost of public goods and services, the transformation curve between private and public goods and services must be linear. A shift of resources from private to public production could never change average and marginal costs under the restrictive assumptions required by this model. Thus, even at this purely conceptual level, the highly restricted nature of this model must serve to reduce seriously the value of any comparative results that might be obtained.

The primary difficulty with this cost model, however, lies in its practical failure to measure real opportunity costs. Market prices, even after these are adjusted for indirect taxes, do not reflect marginal costs except in a very rough sense in the real dynamic world economy of less-than-perfect competition. Some improvements might be made by viewing the separate components of cost from the factor side and trying to isolate genuine opportunity costs from true rents. This would be a most difficult task. The failure of any realizable measurement procedures to incorporate the required adjustments in market prices that would make this cost approach fully acceptable makes any unambiguous estimation of "productive capacity" practically impossible.[14]

Quite apart from the difficulties that arise from any attempt to measure opportunity costs in the market sector alone, the different treatment of entrepreneurial remuneration in the private and the public sector creates complex theoretical and practical problems. The practical result of any overall cost approach must surely be some bastard combination of a "welfare" and a "productivity" measurement which tends to compound the theoretical difficulties of both.

The "welfare" approach that we have advanced, in which the values of all publicly supplied services are excluded except those that are directly priced, is internally consistent. No addition of cost values and market values need be made, directly or indirectly. No problem arises of classifying public goods into final, intermediate, and environmental. And, with this approach, meaningful, even if somewhat restricted, international and intertemporal comparisons of real output, with some "welfare" significance, can be made. The "cost" approach covers a wider range of questions; but in its practical application it is less consistent and much more ambiguous. It seems reasonable to suggest that this latter approach be introduced, on grounds of expediency, only when the first, and more rigorous, approach is not considered sufficient for the task at hand.

We find the current practices of measuring national output justifiable on neither theoretical nor practical grounds. No effort is made to eliminate the inconsistency of adding the value of public goods at costs to the value of private goods at market prices. The admitted correction for the indirect tax wedge is meaningless, unless current practices are assumed to follow the costs approach suggested. In any attempt to measure the total market value of existing output, such a correction is clearly not in order. The only significant measure of national output at market prices is that which we have suggested: the price value of output that is effectively sold in organized markets. The addition of the private and the public sectors may have meaning, in a rough and ready sense, only when made in terms of input or cost values and when designed for the purpose of approximating to the total opportunity costs of producing the existing output mix.

Notes

This paper was completed when Mr. Forte served as research fellow and visiting associate professor at the University of Virginia.

1. National Bureau of Economic Research, Conference on Research in Income and Wealth, *A Critique of the United States Income and Product Accounts: Studies in Income and Wealth*, vol. 22 (New York: National Bureau of Economic Research, 1958), pp. 17, 304.

2. R. A. Musgrave's published treatment of this may be taken as a case in

point. His analysis has advanced the state of the debate, but controversial issues remain, and additional clarification of some of the conceptual problems seems possible; see R. A. Musgrave, *The Theory of Public Finance* (New York: McGraw-Hill, 1959), chapter 9.

3. R. T. Bowman and R. A. Easterlin, "The Income Side: Some Theoretical Aspects," in *Critique of United States Income and Product Accounts*, p. 170. Some of the inconsistencies that arise from the use of the factor-costs approach have been pointed out by Douglas Dosser in his unpublished paper, "The Status of National Income at Factor Costs."

4. Samuelson has provided a rigorous definition for a purely collective good, although he discusses collective consumption goods only; see Paul A. Samuelson, "The Pure Theory of Public Expenditure," *Review of Economics and Statistics* 36 (November, 1954): 386–89. J. Margolis has shown that the purely collective-good case of Samuelson is a limiting case ("A Comment on the Theory of Public Expenditure," *Review of Economics and Statistics* 37 (August, 1955): 347–49. Even services like external defense do have usually differential effects on separate sectors of the economy.

5. A. C. Pigou, *The Economics of Welfare*, 1st ed. (London: Macmillan & Co., 1926), p. 196; F. H. Knight, "Fallacies in the Interpretation of Social Costs," *Quarterly Journal of Economics* 38 (August, 1924): 582–606, reprinted in *Ethics of Competition* (London: George Allen & Unwin, 1935), pp. 217–36. Note that the road case may be used to study both "intermediate" and "final" public goods, because roads are used both for purposes of production and for final consumption.

6. Once the assumption of full competitive adjustment is dropped, the free provision of intermediate goods and services can result in the elimination as well as the creation of producers' rents. If, for example, firms receive a free input service and as a result are led to expand production, this may cause a general reduction in rents previously enjoyed by those resource owners not directly benefited by the government action. Insofar as the availability of free water reduces the cost of producing new crops on marginal lands, the price of the agricultural products concerned will fall, the rents of previously existing inframarginal lands will be reduced, and the benefits of the free public good will be transmitted forward.

7. See especially his "National Income: A New Version," *Review of Economics and Statistics* 30 (May, 1948): 151–79; and his "Government Product and National Product," in *Income and Wealth*, ser. 1 (Cambridge, Mass.: International Association for Research in Income and Wealth, 1951).

8. R. T. Bowman and R. A. Easterlin, "An Interpretation of the Kuznets and Department of Commerce Income Concepts," *Review of Economics and Statistics* 35 (February, 1953): 41–50.

9. Musgrave, *Theory of Public Finance*, chapter 9; and C. S. Shoup, *Principles of National Income Analysis* (Boston: Houghton Mifflin, 1947), chapters 4 and 6.

10. See Kuznets, "Government Product and National Product," pp. 192–96.

11. An additional difficulty in the invariance approach involves the implicit assumption that it is possible to compare situations with and without public goods and services. But a perfectly anarchistic model is wholly unrealistic. The relevant comparisons must be between situations in which different amounts of public goods and services are provided. No deflator is able to ex-

clude fully the impact on prices of money caused by the public services exist-ing in the initial base situation.

12. J. R. Hicks, "The Valuation of Social Income," *Economica* 7 (May, 1940): 105–24.

13. Note that our employment of the invariance test in this extreme model is not inconsistent with our earlier criticism of this test as it has been normally introduced in the discussion. In a sense, our approach here considers all gov-ernment output as final product but includes this at zero prices in computa-tions of index numbers. This is wholly different from assuming that govern-ment intermediate product, insofar as its value is transmitted forward to consumers, will reduce final prices of products on the market. In this latter case output cannot remain invariant.

14. On some of these problems, see G. Warren Nutter, "On Measuring Economic Growth," *Journal of Political Economy* 55 (February, 1957): 51–63, esp. 57 ff.

15.

A Note on Public Goods Supply

WITH MILTON KAFOGLIS

The theory of economic policy upon which arguments for the collectivization of any activity must be based embodies the prediction that the behavior of individuals in markets does not produce socially desirable results. In the orthodox analysis, this prediction stems from the presence of significant externalities that the market is presumed unable to internalize. In his independent behavior, the individual is assumed to take into account only the effects of his actions on his own utility or that of the family group. From this it follows that, if private behavior exerts Pareto-relevant external economies, the market-generated supply of resources to the activity in question falls short of the "social optimum," as this is defined by the Paretian criteria.[1] For example, if the citizens of a social group secure, generally, genuine benefit from the existence of a healthy, disease-free population, the behavior of individuals in purchasing health services independently in private markets appears to commit, relatively, too small a share of total community resources to the provision of such services.

In this note, we shall demonstrate that this orthodox policy implication is not completely general and that in certain circumstances it may be in substantial error. Independent or market organization of an activity that is acknowledged to embody relevant external economies need not result in an undersupply of aggregate resource inputs, relative to that amount required to satisfy the necessary marginal conditions for Pareto-optimality.

We shall examine alternative institutional arrangements through which one particular service may be provided. For expository purposes, we may consider the utilization of a type of medical care that will reduce the probability that the individual will catch a communicable disease. We analyze two separate cases. In the first, the consumption of the service by one person, say B, is assumed to exert relevant external economies on another person or persons, say A, but this relationship is *not reciprocal*. The consumption of the same service by

A does not exert relevant external economies on B. For example, A, the "rich man," may find his utility affected by B's consumption of the service, whereas B, the "poor man," may not be affected, marginally, by the extent to which A himself purchases the service. The second case is that in which the relationship is *reciprocal*. The utilization of the service by B exerts relevant marginal economies on A, as in the first case, but, also, A's consumption of the same service exerts relevant marginal economies on B.

The first and most obvious point to be made is that if an individual receives external or spillover benefits from the activity of others, this affects his utility and may lead him to change his allocation of income among the various goods and services available. If the activity of others generating the spillover benefit is a substitute for some of his own, he will reduce the latter as the activity of others is increased. An increase in the level of immunization privately undertaken by B will tend to reduce the purchase of medical services, say vaccinations, by A. The degree to which the alternative institutional arrangements facilitate the mutually desirable adjustments of consumption in the presence of such substitutability determines their relative efficiency in the exploitation of the external economies. It will be convenient to discuss the nonreciprocal and the reciprocal cases separately and with different tools of analysis.

I. Nonreciprocal Case

We discuss the nonreciprocal case in terms of a two-person geometrical model. We shall, however, treat this model as representative of the n-person model, and we shall not be concerned with considerations of strategic behavior. In Fig. 15-1, the curve, D_a, represents the marginal evaluation of individual A for a final output which, in this model, we label "Healthy Days per Year." Throughout the analysis, we neglect income effects, allowing us to use marginal evaluation curves as demand curves. This demand curve, D_a, can also represent the demand for health-service inputs, which we define in units of the size necessary to provide one healthy day. The ordinate measures the price of these inputs, along with A's marginal evaluation. Input units are available at constant marginal cost. Assume, initially, that A considers himself to live in isolation from B. He will purchase a quantity, Q_m, of health-service inputs, yielding an output, Q_m, of healthy days per year.

By assumption, B does not experience any spillover benefits from A's action. He will purchase a quantity, q, of health-service inputs, shown in Fig. 15-2, providing to him a like amount of final output. This is clearly not an equilibrium for the group, however, since A will

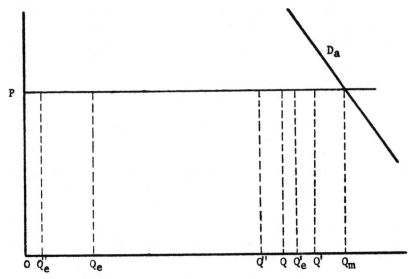

Fig. 15-1

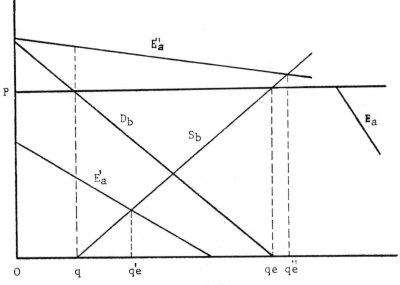

Fig. 15-2

recognize that B's performance of the activity is providing him with certain spillover benefits at the margin, and, under the assumptions of the model, these are substitutes for A's own purchases of health services.

Initially, we assume that A considers B's utilization of an input unit to be a perfect substitute for his own direct utilization of a like unit. That is to say, B's use of one additional input unit allows A to maintain the same quantity of healthy days per year by reducing his own direct use by one unit. Thus, A will reduce his own direct consumption from Q_m to Q, as shown in Figs. 15-1 and 15-2, with this difference being exactly equal to q. This position, described by A's purchasing Q and B's purchasing q, is the equilibrium that is attained through wholly independent adjustment.

We now compare this position with that which might be attained under an alternative institutional arrangement that allows full advantage of the external economies to be taken. If interpersonal markets should become activated, this would provide a means of exploiting such externalities, and the analysis will be developed in terms of such markets. More traditionally, we may assume that some "ideally" operating collective arrangements produce the same results. Individual A will recognize that, at the independent equilibrium, he can secure additional benefits through some extension of B's consumption. Retaining the assumption that B's use of an input is a perfect substitute for his own, we now examine A's evaluation of B's activity. In this instance, A would be prepared to pay any amount below the price of an input to himself in exchange for B's marginal extension of the activity. The marginal evaluation curve—that is, A's demand for B's activity— would lie along the horizontal marginal cost or price curve, out to the point at which this intersects with A's demand curve for final output.

How much compensation will be required to encourage B to extend his direct purchases of health-service inputs? The supply curve for B's services that confronts A may be derived by subtracting B's own demand curve from the marginal cost curve, constant at the given price per input unit in this model. This supply curve is shown as S_b in Fig. 15-2. Equilibrium is attained when B purchases q_e units of health service. A will, in this solution, reduce his own direct input purchases to Q_e, which is less than Q by exactly the difference between q_e and q.[2] The answer to our basic question in this set of circumstances is clear. The solution that allows the full exploitation of the external economies embodies the same total resource use as that which is involved in the independent market adjustment, provided that, in the final solution, A continues to utilize directly some positive quantity of inputs. The distribution of resource use and the total amount of final output are, of course, different in the two solutions. B enjoys more healthy days than under independent adjustment, and A enjoys the same amount, although his own direct purchases of inputs have been reduced *pari passu* with the expansion in B's purchases.

The analysis indicates that, in this type of model, it is necessary to distinguish carefully between *units of resources supplied* and *units of final output* that may be consumed. In ordinary market organization, because of the assumed divisibility of benefits in consumption, these two dimensions are equivalent; a unit supplied to the consumer by the seller is identical, physically, to the unit that is consumed. Thus, the total number of units supplied to all purchasers is equal to the total number of units consumed by all persons. This direct relationship between inputs and outputs is, however, modified when some interpersonal substitutability in consumption is allowed, as must be the case with external economies. The very word "economies" suggests that a great quantity of final output can be achieved with a given quantity of resource inputs when these economies are exploited.

We may now extend the analysis to allow for either less-than-perfect or more-than-perfect substitution between the inputs by B and those by A, in the utility function of A. If A recognizes that B's utilization of health-service inputs will yield external benefits to him, but that these still are not so productive of health as those stemming from his own utilization of inputs, his marginal evaluation curve for B's activity will lie below the price. One such curve is shown as E_a' in Fig. 15-2. In this situation, equilibrium is attained with B's purchase of the amount, q_e', subsidized by A over the range beyond B's own desired independent purchases. In this case, A will find it possible to reduce his own direct purchases, but he will not reduce these sufficiently to offset the expansion in B's resource use. Hence, A will reduce his own direct resource use from Q', the position reached under independent adjustment in this case, to Q_e'. Total resource commitment will be expanded as a result of the exploitation of the externalities.

If, however, B's utilization of health services should prove to be more-than-perfect substitutes for A's own direct consumption, these results are reversed. The marginal evaluation curve of A for B's activity will lie above the price, as is shown by E_a'' in Fig. 15-2. Here equilibrium is attained with the amount q_e'' being provided by B. Individual A will, in this instance, reduce his own activity by more than the amount of additional activity undertaken by B. The final result will embody a smaller resource use, a smaller total expenditure, than that produced under independent adjustment. As in the other two models, A will continue to enjoy the same total quantity of final services, healthy days per year, and B will, of course, enjoy substantially increased amounts of final services as he utilizes directly more inputs. Because of the extreme substitutability that is present, however, this result can be attained with a smaller total outlay than before.[3]

This third model is not nearly so implausible as it might initially appear. In the immunization example, it seems clear that, under certain conditions, private organization would generate an overextension of immunization on behalf of some groups in the population that might be more than proportionately reduced in response to an extension of immunization on behalf of other groups.

II. Reciprocal Case

We now turn to the case where reciprocal external economies are present. In the two-person model, the consumption of A yields relevant external economies to B while, at the same time, the consumption of B yields relevant external economies to A. As we did in the analysis of Section I, we assume that there are no scale effects present in the utilization of inputs. That is, were A and B to act jointly, they could not purchase the inputs more cheaply than they could with each acting privately.

As in the nonreciprocal case, we examine the process through which the various members of a group attain equilibrium when we assume that only independent action is possible. The individual will not take into account here the external benefits that his own decisions impose on others. However, he will adjust his own behavior in the light of actions taken by others. As in the earlier model, we limit analysis to the situation where the relationship is one of substitution. Each individual will extend his own independent activity in purchasing inputs in some inverse relationship to the quantity of activity that he expects others in the group to generate.

We have, in this model, an example of "nonseparable" externality, defined by Davis and Whinston, and, as their analysis suggested, the familiar economic policy analysis cannot be readily applied.[4] In all such nonseparable cases, it is essential that the interactions among individual decisions be carefully examined. The tools of game theory can be usefully employed in this respect. The details of analysis and the determinacy of solution need not be explored in this note since we seek only to demonstrate that collective organization, even if ideally operated, *need not* result in greater total outlay on provision of the final service than that which independent adjustment would generate. This, of course, does not deny that, in many cases, the satisfaction of the necessary marginal conditions for Pareto optimality may require greater total outlay. In some cases it will surely do so; in others it will not.

The demonstration is presented in the numerical example shown in Fig. 15-3. The example is presented for the two-person case, but the results can be generalized without difficulty; and, throughout, we use the two-person model as representative of an n-person model, allowing us to eliminate considerations of strategic behavior. Each of two

A \ B	b_0	b_1	b_2	b_3	b_4
a_0	100 <u>200</u> (100) 0 100 (0) (100)	60 <u>120</u> (50) 0 60 (10) (60)	45 <u>90</u> (25) 0 45 (20) (45)	30 <u>76</u> (16) E 0 30 (30) (46)	29 <u>77</u> (8) 0 29 (40) (48)
a_1	60 <u>140</u> (70) 10 70 (0) (70)	45 <u>110</u> (45) 10 55 (10) (55)	35 <u>85</u> (20) 10 45 (20) (40)	28 <u>81</u> (13) 10 38 (30) (43)	25 <u>82</u> (7) 10 35 (40) (47)
a_2	40 <u>110</u> (50) 20 60 (0) (50)	32 <u>91</u> (29) 20 52 (10) (39)	23 <u>78</u> (15) M 20 43 (20) (35)	19 <u>77</u> (8) 20 39 (30) (38)	18 <u>84</u> (6) 20 38 (40) (46)
a_3	29 <u>99</u> (40) 30 59 (0) (40)	23 <u>86</u> (23) 30 53 (10) (33)	18 <u>82</u> (14) 30 48 (20) (34)	17 <u>83</u> (6) 30 47 (30) (36)	16 <u>91</u> (5) 30 46 (40) (45)
a_4	20 <u>90</u> (30) 40 60 (0) (30)	17 <u>89</u> (22) 40 57 (10) (32)	16 <u>89</u> (13) 40 56 (20) (33)	15 <u>89</u> (4) 40 55 (30) (34)	14 <u>97</u> (3) 40 54 (40) (43)

Fig. 15-3

persons in the group, A and B, is presumed to be able to take any one of five separate actions, as indicated by the five-by-five matrix. For simplicity in exposition, an example similar to the earlier one will be helpful. Suppose that the activity in question is that of getting a series of immunization shots that provide partial, but never complete, protection against some communicable disease. Each person can either do nothing, as indicated by the a_0 row and the b_0 column in the matrix, or he may get one, two, three, or four shots.

It is convenient here to measure payoffs in negative terms, that is, in terms of expected costs rather than expected benefits. Hence, players will attempt to minimize the payoffs shown in the matrix. In the upper left-hand corner of each square, we measure the expected value of the costs that catching the disease will impose on each of the two persons, A and B. These are determined by the probability of getting the disease, given the level of immunization undertaken by each person, along with the costs of the disease, if it is contracted. These costs, for A, are shown without parentheses; those for B are shown with parentheses. Since the two individuals are not assumed to be identical, these costs will differ.[5] Note that, as the example is constructed, expected costs fall, for each individual, as either one or both of the two persons get additional shots. Individual behavior exerts external economies throughout the range of action illustrated.

There are direct resource costs involved in securing the services. In the example, immunization shots are available at ten dollars each. In the lower left-hand corner of each matrix square in Fig. 15-3, the total costs of purchasing shots for each individual are shown, again with those for B placed in parentheses. The expected costs of catching the disease plus the costs of getting the shots must be added to provide a single negative payoff for each individual. This addition is indicated in the lower right-hand corner of each matrix square. This total payoff will provide the basis for individual decision under independent adjustment.

Examination of Fig. 15-3 suggests that there is neither row nor column dominance. Neither A nor B will choose his own level of immunization independently of the action taken by the other. If A gets anything less than three shots, B will purchase two for himself. However, if A gets three shots, B will get only one, and, if A purchases four shots, B will go without immunization of his own. The indicated behavior of A is similar. If B gets no shots, A will get three. If B gets one shot, A will get two. If B gets either three or four shots, A will not seek any immunization on his own account. The matrix is specifically constructed so that a position of equilibrium is attained only when each of the two persons gets two shots; this is shown as the (a_2b_2) box, labeled as M. This is the only position where the independently chosen plans of the two persons are simultaneously fulfilled. Should the private behavior of the two result in any other position being attained, at least one of the two persons would have some motivation for independently changing or modifying his behavior. This is, therefore, the equilibrium position under wholly independent adjustment processes.[6]

It will be useful to examine this equilibrium position more carefully. Note that, at equilibrium, the behavior of each party continues to impose marginal external benefits on the other. Also, in one of the two cases, this marginal external economy is Pareto-relevant. This is shown by comparing (a_2b_3) with the equilibrium, (a_2b_2). If negotiations between the two parties could be introduced, A presumably could compensate B sufficiently so that B would take an additional immunization shot. The private advantages to B from getting the additional shot are not sufficient to cover the marginal cost of ten dollars, but the combined advantages to both A and B, from B's getting the additional shot, are greater than ten dollars. This is proved by the fact that the figure in the upper right-hand corner of the squares is lower in (a_2b_3) than it is in (a_2b_2). This is the group or collective payoff. Note that, although A's action, at the position of equilibrium, continues to impose marginal external economies on B, there is associated with A's action no Pareto-relevant external economy present. That is to say, the shift from (a_2b_2) to (a_2b_3) cannot be made without damaging at least one of the two parties.

At independent equilibrium, four units of input are being utilized in providing immunization. Total outlay on shots is forty dollars. Now assume that the two persons merge into a collective group for the provision of immunization. If we then assume that the "government" acts perfectly or ideally, the new solution will be located where the total group payoff is minimized. This is shown in the square (a_0b_3), labeled as E. Only in this position, Pareto optimality is attained with B being given three shots and A none, with both persons sharing the total costs. Total outlay on inputs is now thirty dollars, less than the forty dollars spent under private or market equilibrium. Fewer resources are being devoted to immunization than under the independent adjustment alternative. The position of cooperative or collective equilibrium could, of course, be attained also by the operation of interpersonal markets. That gains from trade could be realized over the change from M to E is indicated by the fact that total group costs are lower in the latter position than in the former.

In the numerical example of Fig. 15-3, Pareto optimality is attained with smaller total outlay on the service, but, also, with smaller total "consumption" of final output, in this case, immunization, than under independent adjustment. This is shown by the fact that, in E, expected costs of catching the disease are thirty dollars for A and sixteen dollars for B, whereas these are reduced to twenty-three dollars and fifteen dollars in M. This suggests that, under independent adjustment, the consumption of final output is overextended.

This conclusion need not, of course, follow, and it is easy to modify the example to produce results similar to those shown for the nonreciprocal case. It is possible that the ideal cooperative result may involve smaller total outlay while at the same time providing a larger quantity of final services consumed. This possibility may be illustrated in Fig. 15-4, which simply substitutes partially new numbers for the upper-right three-by-three corner of the matrix in Fig. 15-3. Remaining parts of the initial matrix remain unchanged and are not reproduced in Fig. 15-4.

Note that, as before, private equilibrium is attained only in the position M, while the position of overall cost minimization is reached in E. However, with the revised numerical payoffs in Fig. 15-4, the quantity of final output is actually increased in the "efficient" solution, de-

B \ A	b_2		b_3		b_4	
a_0	45 (23)	88	21 (14)	65	20 (8)	68
				E		
	0 (20)	45 (43)	0 (30)	21 (44)	0 (40)	20 (48)
a_1	35 (20)	85	20 (13)	73	19 (7)	76
	10 (20)	45 (40)	10 (30)	30 (43)	10 (40)	29 (47)
a_2	23 (15)	78	19 (8)	77	18 (6)	84
	20 (20)	M 43 (35)	20 (30)	39 (38)	20 (40)	38 (46)

Fig. 15-4

spite the fact that, as before, the total outlay is below that attained in the private solution. Note that the expected costs of catching the disease are reduced from twenty-three dollars and fifteen dollars for A and B, respectively, in M, to twenty-one dollars and fourteen dollars in cooperative or collective equilibrium, even though a smaller total outlay is made.

It should be repeated that the matrix illustration introduced is not designed to show that the "efficient" solution necessarily, or even normally, involves a smaller resource outlay and/or a smaller or a larger consumption of final services than that which independent or private adjustments would produce. The purpose of this analysis, as well as that of the earlier geometrical construction, is primarily negative. It is aimed at showing that the implications concerning aggregate resource use that are normally drawn from the orthodox analysis of collective or quasi-collective goods are not universally correct.

The commonsense explanation of the point made in both the non-reciprocal and in the reciprocal case is straightforward. The means of producing final output are altered when a shift is made from wholly independent adjustment to cooperative or collective arrangements. Insofar as the utilization of inputs is characterized by relevant external economies which stand in a substitute relationship, the individual can, under cooperative or collective arrangements, in one sense, "purchase" the consumption of others. By contrast, under wholly private adjustments he can only modify his behavior in response to the behavior of others. And whereas here, too, he can utilize the consumption of others as a partial substitute for his own, he cannot, through his own independent efforts, modify the quantity of others' consumption.

If negotiations among all parties to the externality relationship are allowed to take place—that is, if side-payments in interpersonal markets are introduced—the "optimal" solution will tend to be reached through the emergence of private agreements. Such negotiations will surely take place to some extent in any case, and especially when the interacting group is reasonably small. However, when the interactions extend over a large number of persons, the costs of attaining voluntary agreements may become prohibitive, and any approach to the "optimal" solution in this fashion may be precluded. It is in reference to such situations that collectivization arguments are applied. A complete analysis would, however, take into account the costs of reaching collective or political decisions, and, when this set of problems is included, there is no a priori way of determining whether or not the "optimal" solution may be approached through this means.

III. Conclusions

In presenting both the geometrical and the numerical illustrations above, we have referred to the example of health services, especially those that provide immunization from communicable disease. There are several other practical examples that come to mind and reinforce the relevance of the analysis. If a municipal government should cease, forthwith, to provide any collective police protection, individuals would, surely, respond by hiring private policemen, guards, night watchmen. It seems quite likely that, in such a situation, total resource outlay on providing protection to life and property would be greater than under collectivization. The analysis here suggests that this might be true, even in the absence of scale factors. In other words, even if private policemen should be empowered to arrest thieves on property other than that of their employers, and even if police protection is not provided at increasing returns to scale, collectivization might well reduce total outlay on policemen.

The same broad conclusions apply elsewhere. If there were no municipal fire departments, it is likely that total outlay for fire protection would exceed the costs of maintaining the fire departments. Such general conclusions as these will not be questioned. The difficulty in reconciling them, at least initially, with the standard implications drawn from the Pigovian policy analysis seems to be based on the failure of this analysis to have considered adequately the nature of the externality relationship.[7]

Our interest in the particular comparison was stimulated by an attempt to "explain" the comparative record of Great Britain and the United States in the provision of medical care services in the last fifteen years. Over this period, medical care has been collectivized in Great Britain, while it has remained largely organized under market processes in the United States. Naive extensions of the orthodox economic policy analysis would suggest that, under collectivization, if decisions are made at all "rationally," total resource outlay on the provision of health services should have been substantially increased over that which might have been generated under market organization. An examination of the comparative performance of the United States and Great Britain over this period does not support this crude hypothesis. Even when adjustments are made for the substantially higher levels of provision in the United States over the whole period, for the relative growth in GNP in the two countries, and for relative price changes, there remains the fact that total outlay on medical services has increased more rapidly in this country, and that the gap has been expanded during the period of the National Health Service.[8] There seems to have been no demonstrable effect of nationalization, per se, on the trend of aggregate medical expenditures in Great Britain in comparison with the United States.[9]

There are, of course, other hypotheses that might be developed to "explain" this same experience. We make no particular claims that the consumption of medical services is even approximately described by relationships analogous to those presented in the illustrative analyses of Sections I and II. That some aspects of medical services are of this sort is suggested by the "realism" of the communicable disease examples employed. To some extent, at least, it is surely true that, to any particular individual, the utilization of medical services by others reduces his own private requirements for similar services. Nevertheless, other and more sophisticated hypotheses involving institutional differences between the two countries may prove more satisfactory in "explaining" the comparative record. Minimally, we can say that the facts do not contradict the illustrative analysis presented in this note. The same cannot be said for orthodox Pigovian analysis of external effects.

Notes

The authors are indebted to W. C. Stubblebine and Gordon Tullock of the University of Virginia for their comments at various stages of this paper's development.

1. For definition of Pareto-relevant externalities, see James M. Buchanan and W. Craig Stubblebine, "Externality," *Economica* 29 (November, 1962): 371–84. Briefly, an externality is Pareto-relevant when the party or parties enjoying an externally imposed benefit (suffering an externally imposed damage) can be made better off without the acting party or parties being made worse off. Favorable interpretation of the literature suggests that economists have, generally, meant to refer only to Pareto-relevant externalities when they discuss external economies and diseconomies. Otherwise, most of the orthodox analysis is seriously deficient.

The discussion in this note is limited to the external economies case, since it is upon this that the collectivization is normally based.

2. The analysis of individual adjustment in the presence of external economies has been developed in a somewhat different context by Milton Z. Kafoglis (*Welfare Economics and Subsidy Programs* [Gainesville: University Presses of Florida, 1961], pp. 33–38).

3. It is, of course, possible that B's activity might be a more-than-perfect substitute for A's own at certain levels of provision and a less-than-perfect substitute at other levels. In this case, the appropriate E_a curve in Fig. 15-2 would cut the marginal cost curve, and the final solution might embody either more or less aggregate resource use depending on the particular configuration.

In each of the models considered, individual A continues to enjoy the same quantity of final services, "healthy days per year," as indicated by Q in Fig. 15-1. As B's direct utilization of inputs is allowed to substitute for his own, the average price per unit of final service consumed, to A, falls. This decline in average price might suggest that A would move down his demand curve for the final service as this substitution takes place. His decision will depend, however, on marginal price, not average price, and, so long as he continues to purchase directly for himself any health-service inputs, "healthy days" are available to him only at the marginal price shown by P. Thus, since marginal price does not change, total amount of final services demanded does not change, given our previous assumption that income effects may be neglected. If the relationships were such that, as B's utilization of inputs substitute for his own, A could cease all of his own direct input purchases, marginal price would decline. In this case, the elasticity of A's demand for final services as well as the elasticity of substitution between B's resource use and his own would be relevant in determining the direction of change in resource outlay that the cooperative solution would generate.

4. Otto A. Davis and Andrew Whinston, "Externalities, Welfare, and the Theory of Games," *Journal of Political Economy* 70 (June, 1962): 241–62. In an unpublished manuscript ("Some Foundations of Public Expenditure Theory," November, 1961), Davis and Whinston utilize game theoretic models similar to those that we introduce here. They do not, however, address themselves specifically to the issue here analyzed.

5. These expected costs may be converted into objectively determinate values, at least conceptually, if we think in terms of the costs of purchasing in-

surance policies guaranteeing complete payments for all damages that might be suffered. This point, as well as several others in the development of this example, we owe to Gordon Tullock.

6. The matrix of Fig. 15-3 is, of course, deliberately constructed so as to include a unique equilibrium position. In the general case, either in the two-person or a larger game, there need not be an equilibrium in pure strategies, and there may also be multiple positions of equilibria. Such questions as these need not, however, concern us here since our purpose is one of constructing an example that will embody the standard relationships while refuting the orthodox implications concerning resource use.

7. The theory here is being corrected, in the light of recent critical contributions. In addition to the papers previously cited, the basic article by R. H. Coase ("The Problem of Social Cost," *Law and Economics Journal* 3 [October, 1960]: 1–44) should be mentioned.

8. For an examination of the comparative record see John and Sylvia Jewkes, *The Genesis of the National Health Service* (Oxford: Oxford University Press, 1961).

9. "The effect is to channel additional money and resources into the health services." This early statement concerning the National Health Service made by Seymour Harris in 1951 has not been supported by the facts. See Seymour Harris, "The British Health Experiment: The First Two Years of the National Health Service," *American Economic Review* 41 (May, 1951): 652–66.

16.
Breton and Weldon on Public Goods

Albert Breton's paper, "A Theory of Government Grants," along with the subsequent discussion between him and J. C. Weldon, suggests that the modern theory of public goods, often associated with Paul A. Samuelson and R. A. Musgrave, has not yet attained the status of rigid orthodoxy.[1] The Samuelson polar case, the purely public good defined to be equally available to all members of the community, is acknowledged to be of very limited application. To develop his theory of optimal structure for multilevel government, Breton was forced to introduce a category of "nonprivate goods," provided publicly but not equally available to members of the inclusive political jurisdiction. Essentially his procedure was that of subdividing the community so that the polar model would apply in each particular case.

Weldon raises objections to Breton's analysis of public goods, and by inference to the received doctrine. He attempts to bring both purely public and "nonprivate" or intermediate goods within a broad theoretical framework based on external economies. I am on record as sharing Weldon's objectives in this respect.[2] His discussion is helpful at critical points, but it does not, in my opinion, satisfactorily resolve all of the issues. In addition, Weldon's criticisms of Breton are inappropriate in application to certain problems of interest. In the course of developing materials for a graduate seminar over several years, I have, at this point, settled on an approach that provides, in one sense, a synthesis between the positions of Breton and Weldon.[3]

The standard treatment gets on the wrong track when the polar Samuelson model is employed as a means of *classifying* public goods. Helpful suggestions toward some eventual classification are one of the purposes of the whole theory, but, initially, the public goods model should be used in quite a different fashion. The model supplies allocative norms (and, in certain highly restricted situations, predictions as to political results) for the provision of *any* good or service that happens to be supplied *publicly* rather than privately. Used in this way, the theory derived from the polar case can be applied to all goods along the spectrum, as these may be described in terms of inherent "publicness" characteristics. The Samuelson conditions define norms for optimality which allow us to treat all goods "as if they were public" in the descriptively meaningful sense. My general position here is related to that of Weldon, as expressed in his concluding footnote. I should, however, reverse his emphasis and say that anything which produces public intervention in the supply of a good ensures its *public* quality.

To demonstrate this point, I propose to apply the theory to a good that is acknowledged to be purely private in the descriptive sense. In itself, this demonstration would have little relevance, but it will be useful in the later extension to those goods that lie between the polar extremes. Consider "shoes" which are, for some reason, publicly, not privately, supplied. *With the proper definition of units,* the Samuelson model allows us to treat this good as purely public. What is required here is that we identify the final consumer of each item of the good. Once we define the good with which we are concerned as "*my* shoes," the allocative norms hold without question. The necessary conditions for Pareto optimality in the provision of "my shoes" are defined in the equality between summed marginal rates of substitution over all persons and marginal cost. Note that, "as *my* shoes," this good is equally available to all members of the group. In the summation process, of course, a whole string of zeroes is added to my own marginal evaluation of the good. The solution is identical to that generated in the competitive market process.

The critical step in the analysis lies in the proper definition of units. The basic distinction that is necessary is one between *units of production* and *units in consumption.* Unfortunately, Weldon slips over this point when acceptance and elaboration would have greatly clarified his own argument.[4] The distinction tends to be obscured, for different reasons, in the two polar cases of the purely private and the purely public good. With the former, a single unit that is produced embodies a unit that is available for consumption, by some *one* person. The total quantity of production units adds up to the total quantity of consumption units. "Shoes" can be discussed without identification, which would, in the normal theory of markets, be redundant. With a purely public good, the unit of production is equally available to all consumers. The quantity of consumption units available to *each* person is measured by the total production. In this case, the distinction clearly exists, as Weldon recognizes explicitly, but the usefulness of making the identification is not apparent.

In all situations of genuinely joint supply, a unit of production may embody two or more units of consumption, as witness the classic Marshallian examples. A single steer, the unit of production or supply, embodies both meat and hides, two separate consumption components, defined on the production unit. Almost by definition, public provision of a good implies that the demands of several persons are met jointly. A single unit of production embodies within it consumption units for all members of the appropriately defined group.

This joint supply approach facilitates the incorporation of the whole range of externalities into a single theoretical framework and makes unnecessary some of the awkward devices resorted to by Weldon in his efforts. Consider now an impure good. Defined in production units, this good will enter the utility functions of several, not necessarily all, members of the political community. The evaluations placed on this good will vary among individuals, not only because of differences in the utility functions, but also because of differences in the physically measurable service flows to separate persons, differences in *consumption units*, defined in terms of homogeneous quality. In his attempts to incorporate such goods in his model, Weldon introduces unnecessary complexity. He states that the arguments in an individual's utility function take on a dimension that measures the total quantity available *to all persons*, a summation, and not the quantities that are available to the individual as a particular consumer. My suggested distinction between units in production and units in consumption provides a more satisfactory means of getting around the problem with which Weldon is concerned. As units of production, the total quantities available to the whole community enter each individual's utility function. The individual's evaluation on any particular quantity will depend on his own projected utilization. To add an argument measuring this utilization, as Weldon suggests, seems redundant.

Weldon attempts to bring all of the distinctions among separate categories of goods into individual utility functions, and he explicitly rejects Breton's proposed separation of "objective benefits" from subjective evaluations. Weldon charges that this proposed distinction is not needed and that it is nonoperational. As earlier paragraphs here may have implied, a utility-inclusive approach can be fully general, and it can be applied to any good. My quarrel with Weldon at this point is limited to the specification of arguments in individual utility functions, not with the essentials of his approach.

Precisely because of its generality, however, the utility-inclusive approach does not allow us to tackle problems beyond those already developed in the standard models. Breton's primary interest lies in a set of different problems, those relating to the determination of optimal structures of multi-level governments, and he has intuitively recognized the extreme limitations of the tools of public-goods theory. His attempt to separate "objective benefits" from subjective evaluations is based on his recognition of the need for a modified set of tools. Weldon's charge that this distinction, properly made, is not needed and is not operational is, I think, in error once we move beyond the formal limits of the general public goods models. Breton's treatment, and particularly his "objective benefits" language, may be criticized, but I shall show that a closely related distinction is relevant, and, indeed, essential when variability among consumption components in a single production unit is allowed.

Consider fire protection, one of Breton's examples of a nonprivate good. If a single fire station in a municipality is fixed in location, it will yield differing quantities of consumption services to different persons who live at different distances from the facility. These differences can be measured, in physical terms, by external observers. These differences in physical service flows, measured by the objective probability of fire, can be distinguished from differences in tastes for the service. Even if two persons have identical utility functions, thus ensuring that the same evaluation will be placed on equal quantities of homogeneous-quality consumption services, their marginal evaluations of the production unit, the facility, will differ with their distances from the facility.

Weldon is correct, however, in saying that this distinction is not needed under the assumption of the example.[5] If the fire station is *fixed in location*, there is no need of making any distinction between objective service flows and subjective evaluations. Assume, however, that the fixity in location is not present, and, instead, that the community is faced with the additional problem of determining the optimal location of the facility. In this case, a distinction between measurable service flows and subjective evaluations is necessary, and also clearly operational. It becomes possible to modify the mix among separate consumption components by changing the location of the unit of joint supply, the production unit, independently of changes in utility functions. This brief comment is obviously not the place to develop the analysis in detail, but the general validity of Breton's proposed distinction seems clear.[6] In the illustration here, of course, "location" is the only characteristic of the production unit that is allowed to vary. In the real world, many such variables may exist for any one publicly supplied good.

The theory of public goods remains interesting precisely because it has not yet attained rigid orthodoxy. No single treatment is likely to stand rigorous scrutiny as the concepts are extended to new problems. This comment applies as fully to the "joint supply-externality" approach that I have advanced as to the models of Breton and Weldon. Both of these scholars have made contributions to an ongoing discussion that will, we hope, eventually produce a "theory of publicly supplied goods" that will, despite the inherently greater complexities, be comparable with the "theory of privately supplied goods."

Notes

1. See Albert Breton, "A Theory of Government Grants," *Canadian Journal of Economics and Political Science* 31, no. 2 (May, 1965): 175–87; J. C. Weldon, "Public Goods (and Federalism)," *Canadian Journal of Economics and Political Science* 32, no. 2 (May 1966): 230–38, 238–42; Paul A. Samuelson, "The Pure Theory of Public Expenditure," *Review of Economics and Statistics* 36, no. 4 (November, 1954): 3870–89; "Diagrammatic Exposition of a Theory of Public Expenditure," *Review of Economics and Statistics* 37, no. 4 (November, 1955): 350–56; R. A. Musgrave, *The Theory of Public Finance* (New York: McGraw-Hill, 1959), esp. chapter 4.

2. See my "Theory of Public Finance," *Southern Economic Journal* 26 (January, 1960): 234–38. This is a review of Musgrave's book.

3. My approach is fully presented in my book *The Demand and Supply of Public Goods* (Chicago: Rand McNally, 1968).

4. "But it seems to me that at this stage it is not necessary to draw a distinction between production (and possession) and consumption" (Weldon, "Public Goods," p. 237).

5. The question of operationality is somewhat different. Conceptually, it would be possible to make the distinction by shifting persons from one location to another and observing their changed evaluations in relation to the measured variations in service flows, provided, of course, utility functions could be assumed stable over the process.

6. For further discussion of this analysis, see my "Joint Supply, Externality, and Optimality," *Economics* 33 (November, 1966): 404–15.

17.
Public Goods in Theory and Practice

Practical examples lend both interest and credibility to abstract theory, but these advantages are not without their own opportunity cost. Illustrative applications may be taken seriously, both by the theorist and by his critics, with the result that analytical constructions of value are lost in the fury of policy argument. This seems to have been the case in the recent exchange between Professors Minasian and Samuelson.[1] The attention of both was concentrated on the relative advantages of pay and free TV, with TV signals being one allegedly practical example of a public or collective good. In the shambles, any hoped-for consensus on the theory of public goods itself was made less, not more, probable. In this note, I shall try to reconcile the two positions within the context of a *meaningfully constructed and deliberately* artificial example, still confined to the TV-signal illustration, but explicitly divorced from real-world applicability.

Consider a community of persons living on an island, somewhat outside the normal TV signal range of shore-based stations. By constructing a receiving antenna at the highest point on the island, signals from *one* distant station can be picked up and these can, in turn, be retransmitted to local residents. There is no possibility of local control over program content.

The quantity of output of the receiving-retransmitting facility can be expressed in minutes per day of retransmission, and we shall assume that the total costs of operation are a linear and homogeneous function of this quantity. This simplification eliminates troublesome problems about initial investment and returns to scale.

Let us now examine the results of an ideally operating, tax-financed collective facility. The retransmitted signals will be free to direct users. Users will finance the services through a set of tax-prices. These will be set so as to equate, at the margin of provision, individual marginal evaluation and individual marginal cost (tax-price). The necessary conditions for Pareto optimality are satisfied when the summed marginal evaluations equal the marginal (average) cost of retransmission. Note that, in this ideal solution, users are paying the opportunity cost for the service. At the margin, they are required to pay, in tax-price, precisely what they are willing to pay, as measured in money, neither more nor less. Note also that users are "purchasing," through their tax-prices, the services of the facility that is known to be equally and freely available to members of the whole community. They cannot, under this arrangement, purchase divisible units of service.

Once again the artificiality of this illustration should be emphasized. But it is, I submit, this ideal-type situation, or one closely resembling it, that Samuelson initially had in mind in his reference to TV signals as an application of his theory of public goods, although his zeal for stirring practical interest may have led him into the seemingly more general statements of the sort instanced by Minasian in his footnote reply.

Let us now examine an alternative organization of the service in which tax-financing is not employed. Since, by assumption, there can be only one facility, this means a private or a public monopoly. Let us assume that the community grants sole operating rights to a single entrepreneur. Lacking the power to impose tax-prices, the entrepreneur is forced to resort to direct user prices. To collect user prices, he must be able to exclude individuals from the retransmitted signals as the penalty for nonpayment. To avoid additional problems arising from the costs of various excluding devices, let us assume that the community gives the entrepreneur property rights in the signals and allows him to sue for damages all those who use his property without proper compensation.[2] The monopolist faces two related decisions. First, he must determine how much output to supply (in this model, how many minutes per day to transmit). Secondly, he must determine the number of users to whom service will be extended. The first decision involves, on the cost side, a straightforward computation. In our extreme example, service can be extended at a constant average or marginal cost. Conceptually, the monopolist will seek to equate this cost with marginal revenue. But marginal revenue is not so easy to compute, even conceptually, in this model because each unit of output is *jointly supplied* to a number of users, with this number to be determined. If he is somehow required to charge all users the same price, he can, given a knowledge of all user demand curves, compute a "market" demand curve for his output and reach a joint decision on output and number of users. This solution will clearly violate the necessary conditions for Pareto optimality, as Samuelson initially suggested, since some users will be excluded despite the fact that they can be added at no additional cost to the monopolist. Nor will this inefficiency be eliminated by forcing the monopolist to act as if he were competitive and to equate marginal cost with price, thus reducing net profits to zero. It will, however, be eliminated, and monopoly organization will be fully efficient, if the monopolist is allowed to and is able to discriminate perfectly among separate users. In this case, the monopolist will have no incentive to exclude anyone from the service, and he can take into account all of the differences in individual demands. This discriminating-monopoly solution is Pareto-optimal, and is identical with the ideally collective solution, provided we assume away the feedback income effects on the allocative outcome itself. There is, of course, a major distributional difference in the two solutions, and this may, in itself, imply different allocative outcomes if income-effects are allowed. Even here, however, the two solutions represent two separate points on the Pareto-welfare surface.

In either the ideal collective solution (free usage financed by tax-prices) or the ideal "private" solution (perfectly discriminating monopoly) the jointness or commonality features remain. These are not modified by the form of organization. A single unit of output, a minute of transmission, supplies many persons simultaneously, and each person must adjust to a *single* quantity of output. In essence, the "theory of public goods" is one particular extension of the Marshallian theory of joint supply.

We may now drop some of the extreme simplifications imposed on our example. Suppose that the single receiving antenna can retransmit only one signal at a time, as before, but that it can receive signals from any one of several shore-based stations. The necessary conditions for Pareto optimality in the extension of output of a commonly shared good tell us nothing at all about this choice. The theory of public goods, in this limited sense, is of no assistance in determining which one, from among a set of mutually exclusive alternatives, should be provided. This decision requires a consideration of the total conditions, some conceptual or actual measurement of consumers' surplus. There is, as such, no means of measuring this, and Minasian's point is well taken when he suggests that the ordinary profitability criterion, whether applied by a private or a public monopolist, would be a more instructive guide than the opinions of a governmental authority. The monopolist owner of the antenna, seeking out his highest net revenue, will tend to select that signal (or that mix of signals) which most closely satisfies consumer demand. Care must be taken, however, not to claim too much for the superior allocative judgment of the profit-seeking monopolist. The argument hinges on his ability to discriminate more or less perfectly among users and over quantities. Through this discrimination, the monopolist can secure all of the consumers' surplus. If by necessity, by convention, or by law, the monopolist is prevented from discriminating and is, instead, required to charge uniform prices, his profitability criterion will no longer serve as an appropriate guide for aggregative allocative decisions. In other words, the perfectly discriminating monopolist may find it profitable to select quite a different signal-mix from that which the nondiscriminating monopolist would find most profitable.

We may modify our initial simplification in one further way. Instead of only one receiving antenna located as the single highest point on the island, let us now assume that there can be many such antennas erected. Let us further extend this assumption and say that the retransmission of signals can be *competitively supplied*. Many separate retransmitting firms can technically operate with each supplying a different signal to users. Here we confront a model where many *separate* purely collective goods can be supplied competitively if privately organized. These separate goods may be very close substitutes one for the other in the users' utility functions. This is the extremely interesting model that has been fully explored by Professor Earl Thompson.[3] He shows that, in this model, private organization will violate the necessary conditions for optimality due to an *overinvestment* in facilities, an *oversupply* of the goods.

Many other interesting, and instructive, variations in the initial assumption of the example could be made. In carrying out these exercises, useful theory might emerge. In each case, however (and this is the point I want to emphasize), the example or illustration is *artificially constructed* to be helpful to us in developing our theoretical tools and concepts, and not vice versa. We have learned a great deal from Adam Smith's deer and beaver example, much that is helpful in an understanding of real-world market processes, but it is essential that we recognize always the artificiality of the construction. Hard thinking about such real-world problems as the pricing of TV signals can lead to the development of useful theoretical tools, which, we can, often, illustrate with oversimplified examples depicting idealized conditions. In the critically important discussion about the actual solutions to real-world problems, no set of theoretical tools is likely to be fully adequate. Such problems are, almost by definition, too complex to allow theory to be applied simply and straightforwardly. This acknowledged difficulty should not, however, cause us to reject any set of tools, which may be wholly correct within the context of the models for which they were developed.

Minasian is correct when he states that the modern theory of public goods does not allow us to make institutional decisions about organizational alternatives independently of other considerations, only some of which he mentions. Only the most naive of the theory's advocates should have made this claim, although it seems clear that the theory was interpreted in this sense by some scholars. On the other hand, Minasian extends his criticism beyond acceptable limits when he suggests that the allocative norms contained within the theory are incorrect, within properly constrained models. His demonstration that other considerations may be dominant in certain real-world circumstances has little relevance to the validity or invalidity of the theory of public goods.

It is unfortunate that Minasian failed to separate more fully the theory of public goods from the organizational problems in the TV case. It is equally unfortunate that Samuelson chose to keep the discussion on the same ground. Finally, it is distressing that Samuelson, who could have had the better of the argument, threw his own advantage away by bringing ideological overtones into what should be a reasoned debate. In so doing, he placed an ideological cloud over the whole theory of public goods, to which he has contributed so much. Surely this theory can be, and should be, wholly *wertfrei* in an explicit sense, as Samuelson states in his last sentence. His charges against Minasian may, I fear, prompt the response: "Methinks thou dost protest too much."[4]

Notes

1. Jora R. Minasian, "Television Pricing and the Theory of Public Goods," *Journal of Law and Economics* 7 (1964): 71; Paul Samuelson, "Public Goods and Subscription TV: Correction of the Record," *Journal of Law and Economics* 7 (1964): 81.

2. This arrangement is not nearly so far-fetched as it might seem in this context. In a decision reached in early 1966, a United States District Court in New York held that televised motion pictures cannot be intercepted by CATV companies without payment of royalties to producers. *United Artists Television, Inc.* v. *Fortnightly Corp.*, 255 F. Supp. 177 (S.D.N.Y., 1966).

3. Earl A. Thompson, *The Perfectly Competitive Allocation of Collective Goods* (Los Angeles: Institute of Government and Public Affairs, University of California, 1965).

4. After completion of this note, I have had occasion to see a more recent paper by Samuelson, in which many aspects of his approach to the theory of public goods are clarified. See Samuelson, "Pure Theory of Expenditure and Taxation," July, 1966 (Massachusetts Institute of Technology, mimeographed).

18.

Convexity Constraints in Public Goods Theory

WITH ANTÓNIO S. PINTO BARBOSA

Convexity constraints create problems in the pure theory of public goods that need not arise in the theory of private goods. These
problems have not been fully recognized. Aside from a somewhat
vague and remotely related discussion by Samuelson himself in his
1966 Biarritz paper, along with a comparable indirect treatment by
Bradford in 1970, the point made in this paper has not been explicitly
discussed.[1] Specifically, we shall demonstrate that under convexity
constraints analogous to those normally introduced in the analysis of
allocation in private or partitionable goods markets, the satisfaction
of the familiar Samuelson second set of conditions *may not* lead to
Pareto-efficient allocations. The analysis suggests, somewhat more
restrictively, that even if individual marginal tax prices are equated to
individual marginal evaluations of the public good (i.e., a Lindahl tax-
share distribution) violations of second-order conditions may generate inefficient solutions.

It will be useful to begin with Samuelson's treatment in his initial
1954 paper.[2] He developed his analysis utilizing two polar categories,
purely private goods and purely public goods, which he called "collective consumption goods." Using his notation, the former goods, X_1
..., X_n, are characterized by the additive relationship,

$$(1) \quad X_j = \sum_{i=1}^{s} X_j^i$$

whereas the public goods, $X_{n+1}, \ldots, X_{n+m}$, are characterized by the
equality relationship, $X_{n+j} = X_{n+j}^i$, so that each and every person in
the community of persons $(1, 2, \ldots, i, \ldots, s)$, has available for consumption or use the same amount of good.

Samuelson placed what appear to be quite ordinary restrictions on
his model as regards utility and production functions. For the former,

he states: ". . . I assume each individual has a consistent set of *ordinal preferences* with respect to his consumption of all goods (collective as well as private) which can be summarized by a regularly smooth and convex utility index $u^i = u^i(X_1^i, \ldots, X_{n+m}^i)$ (any monotonic stretching of the utility index is of course also an admissible cardinal index of preference) [italics in original]."[3] For the production side Samuelson stated: ". . . I assume a regularly convex and smooth production-possibility schedule relating totals of all outputs, private and collective, or $F(X_1, \ldots, X_{n+m}) = 0$, with $F_j > 0$ and ratios F_j/F_n determinate and subject to the generalized laws of diminishing returns."[4]

Samuelson then proceeds to lay down his set of "optimal conditions," with our particular interest here being, of course, in his statement of his famous set (2), written as:

$$(2) \quad \sum_{i=1}^{s} \frac{u_{n+j}^i}{u_r^i} = \frac{F_{n+j}}{F_r} \quad \begin{matrix} (j = 1, \ldots, m; r = 1, \ldots, n) \text{ or} \\ (j = 1, \ldots, m; r = 1). \end{matrix}$$

He amplified his analysis in 1955 in his "Diagrammatic Exposition" paper. In this paper there is only one point of interest to us here. In a footnote, Samuelson states:

> Even though a public good is being compared with a private good, the indifference curves are drawn with the usual convexity to the origin. This assumption, as well as the one about diminishing returns, could be relaxed without hurting the theory. Indeed, we could recognize the possible case where one man's circus is another man's poison, by permitting indifference curves to bend forward. This would not affect the analysis but would answer a critic's minor objection. Mathematically, we could, without loss of generality, set $X_2^i = $ *any function* of X_2, relaxing strict equality. [Note: here X_2 is the notation for the public good; italics supplied].[5]

As we shall see, the critic's objections may turn out not to have been so minor, after all. But we shall return to this footnote later, and also notably to Samuelson's 1966 Biarritz paper.

We shall demonstrate that with public goods it is inappropriate to assume convexity in preference orderings, or more basically, in the consumption set, in a manner analogous to that employed in the analysis of private-goods interactions. Nonconvexities may emerge from the "nature of publicness," so to speak, with consequent welfare implications. Even with polar public goods, defined strictly in Samuelson's initial terms, there is no need that the second set of Samuelson conditions ensure Pareto optimality. In terms more familiar to some readers, we shall demonstrate that individual marginal evaluation curves may be upward rather than downward sloping, with the welfare implications that may be inferred from this result.

We commence by concentrating on *dimensionality*. Recall the Samuelson definition of his polar case, $X_{n+j} = X^i_{n+j}$. Recall, also, that he assumed a convex utility index $u^i = u^i(X^i, \ldots, X^i_{n+m})$. There is, of course, nothing wrong in this, but our point is that the convexity assumption here is not so simple as it might seem, and as it has apparently seemed to most economists.

What is in the individual's utility function? The conventional response suggests that, in its most general form, the utility function describes a person's tastes or preferences for all potentially available goods and services. (The poor man may include an argument for diamonds in his general utility function, despite the fact that his income constraints may keep diamonds forever beyond his reach.) We do not, at least in the conventional models, include in utility functions *only* those goods and services over which actual choices are to be exercised. This distinction becomes important when we look at the role of convexity assumptions in public goods theory.

Buchanan (1966, 1967) stressed the usefulness of distinguishing carefully between what he called *production units* and *consumption units* in public goods theory.[6] He emphasized that the necessity of making this distinction arises from the central "publicness" feature itself. Consider the opposing polar case, that of the purely private or partitionable good, say, apples. In this case, there is no need to worry about dimensionality, no need to distinguish between an apple, as produced, and an apple, as consumed or available for consumption. An apple is an apple, and we have no qualms about putting "apples" directly into the individual's utility function, the same "apples" that enter directly into the producer's production function. But consider the polar public good. The essential feature of "publicness" is the simultaneous availability of something to all persons in the community. But what is "something"? It is the unit as produced, as made available, the *production unit*, which in itself embodies several consumption services, the consumption unit, that is contained within that which is provided.

For clarification, we may use uppercase X's to define production units and lowercase x's to define consumption units. Hence, a single unit of X has within it several units of x, say $(x_1, x_2, \ldots, x_s)$.

We may introduce an example, Tullock's familiar model of mosquito abatement.[7] In order to get away from possible initial ambiguity involved in differential evaluations, we assume that all persons in the community have identical utility functions. Further, to get away from other complexities, we assume initially that all persons are located at a single point in space. What is the public good in this example? What is it that the members of this community must consume jointly in order to capture the potential efficiency gains? What is it that they must "purchase" from public goods suppliers, or else, produce for themselves? How about *pounds of insecticide per week sprayed on the swamp?* In our terminology, this is a good defined in production units, in uppercase X's.

In "purchasing" this good, however, what are the individuals evaluating? They are indirectly placing values on X, values that are derived from those placed directly on the x's, which, in this case, are the *reduced likelihood of mosquito bites*. To which of these two goods should the standard convexity properties be applied? The appropriate response would seem to be the small x's, the consumption units, the reduction in mosquito bites. An individual's utility function should tell us how much bread, milk, and dollars he would be willing to trade off for reductions in mosquito bites or the probabilities thereof.

But convexity over this set of goods, so defined, need not imply convexity over the X's, over the production units over which fiscal choices must be exercised. To ensure that convexity is maintained when the X's are substituted for the x's in individual utility functions, particular restrictions must be imposed on the functional relationship between the production and the consumption units, or $x^i = x^i(X)$. However, there seem to exist no logical or technological bases for imposing the required restrictions. In this case, it must be concluded that individual utility functions, normal over the x's, may be nonconvex over the X's.

We may readily show this by introducing an example. Suppose that, for any individual i, the relationship $x^i = x^i(X)$ is characterized by $\partial x^i / \partial X > 0$, and $\partial^2 x^i / \partial X^2 > 0$. So long as the first derivative of this function increases more rapidly than the marginal rate of substitution between x^i and the numeraire good decreases, individual i's marginal rate of substitution between X and the *numéraire* will increase rather than decrease. The latter term will embody two separate components, the evaluation of x (the good that enters the utility function) and the *numéraire,* and the "production" relation between x and X. Fig. 18-1 illustrates the situation. Holding a person at a specific level of utility, given convex preferences between the lowercase x^i and a *numéraire*, and given the relationship between x^i and X as depicted, the resulting indifference curve between X and the *numéraire* is concave to the origin.

The normative welfare implications are clear. Setting the summation of marginal evaluations equal to the marginal cost of providing the public good, defined as the uppercase X, which is the only good that can be "purchased" collectively, may actually describe a minimal rather than a maximal position.

Under the formal conditions of the model presented above, we might restore the standard convexity constraints on utility functions, or, if desired, on consumption sets, defined appropriately on the lowercase x's, the consumption units, by the device of incorporating these x's in the production functions in lieu of the X's. If this sort of

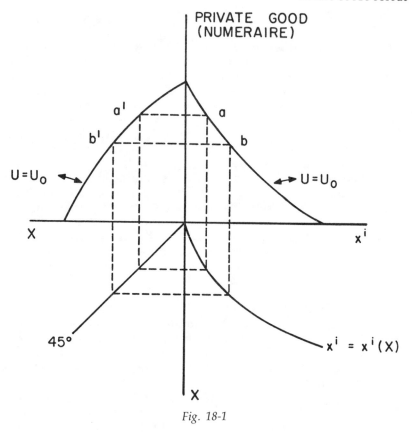

Fig. 18-1

transformation is accomplished, then the lowercase x's, the consumption units, are produced under increasing returns, and nonconvexity characterizes the production set with the familiar welfare implications. That is to say, the consumption units are produced under declining marginal cost conditions throughout the relevant ranges in question. The question that arises from this procedure concerns the appropriateness of placing consumption units in production functions, which is, of course, the dual of that involved in placing production units in utility functions. That which is available for joint or collective consumption is that which is produced, the composite result of combining inputs. If we think of the technological basis for the standard assumption of nonincreasing returns, the relevant unit would seem to be that which physically results from the combination and use of inputs, such as insecticide sprayed on the swamp. As in its dual, to extend convexity constraints to that which is physically received by consumers seems to be logically and analytically lacking in foundation.

We should also note that this procedure is available only in the *very special case* that we have postulated in our initial formal model. To demonstrate this, we need change only this one feature. The remaining conditions may be restated. The public good, defined as X, remains purely collective or public in the sense of the equality condition, $X = X^i$. We can still retain the assumption that all persons in the group have identical utility functions. And we can assume that there exists only one way, technologically, that the good can be produced. Each unit of X embodies s consumption units, $x^1, \ldots, x^i, \ldots, x^s$, provided simultaneously to all persons in the community.

However, consider the possibility that, as between any two persons, i and j, the relationship between $x^i(X)$ and $x^j(X)$ is nonlinear. Specifically, let us assume that, for either i or j, the conditions previously stated hold. That is, $\partial x^i/\partial X > 0$, $\partial^2 x^i/\partial X^2 > 0$, or $\partial x^j/\partial X > 0$, $\partial^2 x^j/\partial X^2 > 0$, and that the two functions, $x^i = x^i(X)$ and $x^j = x^j(X)$ cannot be linearly transformed one into the other. In this setting, there may be no way that the lowercase x's, the consumption units, can be transformed so as to allow them to be entered appropriately into the production functions faced by firms, by producers. The difficulty arises, of course, because a unit of X does not contain within it the same mix of consumption components as production varies.

Note that we have in no way departed from the polar public good constraints. There is no rivalry in consumption; additional consumers can be added at zero marginal cost, regardless of the quantity of X that is produced. There is no "crowding," no "congestion." The range of publicness is unlimited; there is no "local government limit" to efficiency in sizes of the sharing group. Exclusion is not possible. Despite these very severe definitional constraints, we have shown that the familiar conditions deemed to be necessary for allocative efficiency need not produce such results, under plausible assumptions of convexity in utility and production functions.[8]

We are surprised that the point made here has not been noticed by those who have worked in formal public goods analysis. To our knowledge, Samuelson himself came closest to a recognition of our point in his 1966 Biarritz paper. Included in that paper is a footnote that warrants quotation at some length:

> Whether the same good appears in two utility functions can be affected by definitions and symbolisms used to represent variables. Thus, we may have fireworks in your function and mine; but, without changing the substance of the case, suppose we redefine as distinct variables, fireworks exploded in the sky, y; fireworks observed (or observable) by you, z; fireworks observed by me, v. Then it might be misleadingly said that there are no variables entering literally into more

than one utility function and we have here "purely private" goods. However, by such a change in symbolism all public good phenomena could be defined out of existence. This shows the need for some such word as "irreducibly" (enters utility functions) in any formal definition. In the last analysis, we can diagnose the existence of the private good phenomena which can be optimally handled by the market only by a simultaneous scrutiny of the variables and of how they enter in both the utility functions and the technological side constraints.[9]

Samuelson was really almost there. He was correct in suggesting that a procedure which defined each and every lowercase x as a different variable would result in a model with nothing but "purely private" goods, yet, at the same time, a model that would carry no implications at all for the potential comparative efficacy of institutions. In order for his formal analysis to have implications for market failure, Samuelson was required to stick to the uppercase X's, which we have called production units, as "public goods." In terms of his example, he should, of course, have seen that the fireworks exploded in the sky, y, is the only variable that can enter *both* utility functions, but that the standard convexity properties, which are appropriately applicable for the z's and v's, do not extend readily to the y's without *additional* constraints.

In the appendix to his Biarritz paper, Samuelson once again, and in a different way, comes very close to a recognition of our point. Here he states that: "Even if, semantically, a variable can be put in more than one individual utility function, we shall not have a *standard* public good case unless it enters the production possibility frontier and industry production functions in the standard way. Moreover, the variable in question may not have the returns and other properties of an ordinary good, private or public."[10] Following this statement, Samuelson proceeds to present an example of a good that has both a separable cost and a joint cost aspect: electricity supplied to summer homes on a peninsula. In this example, he recognizes that there may arise convexity problems. In this, and other examples in the appendix, however, Samuelson seems to imply that such issues arise only with departures from his polar models, and not with "ordinary public goods."

We now return to the footnote to the 1955 paper cited earlier. By allowing forward-bending indifference curves, Samuelson seems to be saying only that, over some ranges marginal evaluations of public goods might be negative for some members of the community, and, if they are, the negative values must be incorporated in any final aggregate solution. But the last sentence of the footnote, in which Samuelson states that "Mathematically, we could . . . set X_2^i = any function of X_2, relaxing strict equality," seems highly ambiguous and wholly unrelated to the preceding parts of the note. As our analysis has shown, if the physical flows to all consumers are linearly related, production can be defined on the consumption units, but with the questions raised about convexity in the production set. If the consumption flows are not so related, which seems to have possibly been in the mind of Samuelson's unnamed critic, the possibility of nonconvexities in the consumption set must be recognized.[11]

In his 1966 paper on joint supply, and particularly in his 1967 comment on the Breton-Weldon controversy, Buchanan specifically looked at models in which measurable consumption flows among persons differed, while being produced by commonly available production units meeting all criteria for publicness. But he overlooked the convexity-constraint problem because of his interest in deriving the set of conditions for optimality when the technology allowed for explicit variance in the mix among these consumption components. That is, Buchanan was basically interested in the question: "Where should we locate the fire station?" and, as a result, he jumped too readily away from any exhaustive examination of the model which assumes that the location of the station is technologically determinate and not subject to change. Bryan Ellickson seems to have done something analogous in his 1973 paper, in which he stressed the possible nonconvexities that might emerge when "crowding" is allowed on public goods facilities, when the nonrivalry attribute is limited over some ranges of membership.[12] Ellickson apparently failed to note the possible presence of nonconvexities even when no such departures from the polar model are introduced.

To our knowledge, all of those economists who have included public goods pricing in a general equilibria setting have accepted the initial Samuelson formulation without recognition of the significance of the dimensionality issue. For instance, Duncan Foley, in both his early 1967 essay and in his 1970 paper, simply postulates an economy that contains both private and public goods, defined analogously to Samuelson's initial statements, and he assumes that preference orderings and production functions over these goods are convex.[13] In his proof of the existence of a Lindahl equilibrium, Foley constructs an all-private goods economy by extending the commodity space so that each person's "bundle of public goods becomes a separate group of commodities."[14] These separate bundles seem to correspond to the lowercase x's in our model. However, in Foley's treatment these bundles must stand in a one-to-one relationship to the public goods, as initially defined. That is to say, there is a perfect mapping between any person's "private goods bundle" in Foley's associate economy and the corresponding public good in the initial model. In our terms, he does not allow for *any* variance between the quantity of X and that of *any* x^i. The nonconvexity possibilities identified in this paper restrict the settings within which sustainable Lindahl equilibria exist below those limits implied by this invariance.[15]

Notes

1. David F. Bradford, "Benefit-Cost Analysis and Demand Curves for Public Goods," *Kyklos* 23, no. 4 (1970): 775–91.

2. Paul Samuelson, "The Pure Theory of Public Expenditure," *Review of Economics and Statistics* 36 (1954): 387–89.

3. Ibid.

4. Ibid.

5. Paul Samuelson, "Diagrammatic Exposition of a Theory of Public Expenditure," *Review of Economics and Statistics* 37 (1955): 351.

6. James M. Buchanan, "Joint Supply, Externality and Optimality," *Economica* 33 (November, 1966): 404–16; and "Breton and Weldon on Public Goods," *Canadian Journal of Economics and Political Science* 33, no. 1 (February, 1967): 111–15.

7. See Gordon Tullock, *Private Wants, Public Means* (New York: Basic Books, 1970).

8. There is an analogy, of sorts, in the relationship between dimensionality and convexity constraints in public goods theory and that which emerges in the theory of composite consumer commodities, associated primarily with Gary Becker and his colleagues ("Economic Theory"). In the latter, the person demands a composite commodity, Z, but in order to secure this Z, he must resort to a household production function that allows him to combine inputs, x_1, x_2, x_3, some of which may be market goods. Each unit of Z, as consumed, therefore, embodies the several x's; seemingly analogous to our X, x_i, x_j relationship. In a sense, the composite-commodities model is the obverse rather than the parallel of the public goods model. That which is purchased in the marketplace is the lowercase "input"; that which is ultimately consumed is the composite of these. Convexity in preferences over the latter need not imply convexity in preferences over the former; in this respect, the analogy holds. However, we do have the broad empirical evidence from individual behavior in markets to suggest that the implied functional relationships between the x's and the Z's are of the appropriate form to ensure convexity. There is no such evidence at hand in the theory of public goods. And, indeed, the whole purpose of analysis is different here. The general theory of public goods is not positive; it is explicitly normative. The objective is that of laying down the formal requirements that must be met for the attainment of allocative efficiency. We should perhaps note that some of the writers in the theory of composite commodities (e.g., J. Muth ["Household Production and Consumer Demand Function," *Econometrica* 34 (1966): 699–708] and R. Willis ["A New Approach to the Economic Theory of Fertility," *Journal of Political Economy* 81 (March–April, 1973): part II, 514–64]) have explicitly imposed restrictions on the curvature of the relevant production functions. Other writers have not done so. However, the microempirical perspective of this body of theory requires relatively less emphasis on formal constraints of the sort discussed in this paper.

9. Paul Samuelson, "Pure Theory of Public Expenditure and Taxation," in *Public Economics*, ed. J. Margolis and H. Guitton (New York: Macmillan, 1969), p. 108.

10. Ibid., p. 115.

11. David Bradford ("Benefit-Cost Analysis and Demand Curves") indi-

rectly recognized the difference in the convexity assumptions as between private goods models and public goods models. His interest was directed toward the instrumental use of benefit-cost analysis, however, and he apparently did not sense the implications for formal public goods theory.

We are indebted to David Rees, who brought Bradford's paper to our attention after we had completed the substantive draft of this paper.

12. B. Ellickson, "A Generalization of the Pure Theory of Public Goods," *American Economic Review* 63 (June, 1973): 417–32.

13. Duncan Foley, "Resource Allocation and the Public Sector," *Yale Economic Essays* 7 (1967): 43–98; and "Lindahl's Solution and the Core of the Economy with Public Goods," *Econometrica* 38 (January, 1970): 66–72.

14. Foley, "Lindahl's Solution."

15. Other writers who have made contributions to the general-equilibrium approach developed initially by Foley, have not, in our interpretation of their analyses, substantially modified Foley's treatment of this respect.

19.

Fiscal Choice through Time: A Case for Indirect Taxation?

WITH FRANCESCO FORTE

I. Introduction

How should taxes be paid? This question has been discussed for centuries. It has not been resolved, either in the formal theory of public finance or in the institutional structure of modern fiscal systems. The direct-indirect tax comparison continues to occupy a central position in the literature of fiscal theory, and the choice between these two institutions of taxation confronts governments of all states, new and old.

We do not propose to develop further refinements in the analytical models that have become familiar to scholars in public finance. The familiar "excess-burden" theorem, initially stated by Barone,[1] along with the more recent criticisms that have been advanced against it, will not concern us here except insofar as the theorem proves useful in explaining our own model. Broadly speaking, it seems correct to say that, despite the acknowledged relevance of "second-best" arguments, most modern theorists accept the view that, other things equal, direct and general taxes are to be recommended over indirect and specific taxes on both equity and efficiency criteria. We shall challenge this position, and we shall demonstrate that from a different, and apparently new, approach to fiscal choice, a case can be made out for specific commodity taxation. We do not claim that the case is a definitive one, and, as is noted, other considerations can be introduced that tend to oppose those stressed in this paper. Our primary purpose is not that of defending specific indirect taxation per se, but, instead, that of utilizing this traditional problem to illustrate the efficacy of a proposed analytical approach to fiscal institutions.[2]

II. A Methodology for Tax Analysis

There are two separate, but closely related, elements in our approach which contrast sharply with methods traditionally employed. First, we base the analysis on an individual calculus; that is to say, on the choice of the individual as he participates in a collective decision process. We examine his behavior as he tries to choose the "preferred" means of meeting his tax obligations. In one sense, this method is implicit in much Paretian welfare analysis, including the Barone theorem, but the central position of individual choice is made explicit in our model. Instead of conceiving the fiscal problem as that of determining the results of alternative institutions on individual and group behavior patterns, we conceive it as the choice confronted by the individual when he is required to choose among these alternative institutions.

In this setting, the second major element emerges as a natural order of events. By concentrating initially on the individual's choice among tax instruments we are led, almost necessarily, to think of these instruments as *institutions*, and not as mere analytical devices without spatial or temporal dimension. This should not suggest that we propose to lapse into the methodology of traditional "institutionalism." But we do propose to incorporate into the analysis the quasi-permanency of fiscal institutions, and to recognize the lasting impact of fiscal decisions once they are made.

Almost without exception, the direct-indirect tax discussion has proceeded from the assumption that a choice must be made only in a one-period setting. To our knowledge, no attempt has been made to extend the comparison to the multi-period setting; no one has assumed that the tax instrument chosen shall remain in effect over several income or accounting periods. The model that introduces such a temporal sequence is both more logical and more realistic than the orthodox one-period model. If we look, however casually, at the fiscal experience of almost any government, we must recognize that decisions tend to be relatively long-lived in effect. Tax institutions and spending programs alike tend to remain in force over a series of accounting and budgetary periods. Nor does this observed political history reflect irrational collective choice. The making of collective or group decisions is costly and time consuming. The agreements and the compromises that may be finally incorporated in a single apparent decision emerge from a many-stage process of discussion, debate, bargaining, mutual and marginal adjustment to complex circumstances. Quite similarly, it is costly to organize changes in institutions that are in being. If the results of analysis are to have even remote applicability to real-world problems, collective choice, and individual participation in its formation, must be examined in a long-run institutional context.

III. The One-Period Argument Summarized

Barone demonstrated that, for the individual, a direct tax "should" rationally be preferred to an indirect tax of equal yield if a one-period model is accepted. The argument has been elaborated many times through the indifference curve apparatus and it need not be repeated here. Little demonstrated that, strictly speaking, the Barone conclusions follow only when a lump-sum tax is compared with a specific commodity tax.[3] Friedman and also Rolph and Break showed that the Barone theorem could be extended from the single individual to the community only if all of the remaining conditions necessary for Pareto-optimality should be satisfied.[4] These latter criticisms of the basic analysis need not concern us here, however, since, initially at least, we shall remain at the level of individual choice. In this restricted one-period model, the rational individual will always prefer the direct tax over the indirect tax, of equal yield, for the simple reason that he can, in this way, enjoy the widest range of choice.[5]

In order to relate it to our subsequent analysis, we shall state the problem, applied in the one-period setting, as follows: "Should" the rational utility-maximizing individual, confronted with a determined tax obligation, choose to meet this obligation through a lump-sum payment, a proportional tax levied on his income, a progressive tax on his income, a general tax on total consumption expenditure, or a specific tax on the consumption of one commodity? In such a model as this, the first alternative provides the individual with the widest area of choice. It will be preferred over the proportional tax on income which does, of course, discriminate between measured and non-measured income. This proportional tax will, in its turn, be preferable to the progressive tax which introduces an additional element of discrimination. This tax alternative will, in its turn, be rationally selected over the even less general tax on expenditure. And, finally, the tax on the single specific commodity or service becomes the least desired of the lot. These familiar conclusions are relevant, however, only if the individual is allowed to select among alternatives in each discrete period of time, or if the results of the one-period model can be generalized to apply for a sequence of periods.

IV. The Introduction of Time

Let us now ask the same question as before, only now let us assume that the individual recognizes that the tax instrument, once chosen, will remain in force, not for a single period only, but over a whole series of periods, which we can identify as $t_0, t_1, \ldots, t_n$. The results may be different from those in the one-period model.

We want, first, to develop a model under the assumption of certainty. The individual, whose choice calculus we examine, is assumed to know with certainty, at t_0, the time or moment of decision, what his income will be in each of the periods, $t_1, t_2, \ldots, t_n$. We shall also assume that his current decision process reflects some consideration of expected fluctuations in wants or needs over time. Viewed from t_0, his wants in each of the subsequent periods is also known with certainty, although these need not be stable over time.

Before posing the fiscal choice issue specifically, it will be useful to establish some general principles of rational behavior for the individual. For convenience, we may assume that the individual saves only in order to retire debt or to accumulate funds for future consumption. This is in accord with a life-cycle model of saving behavior that has been suggested by several economists in recent years.[6] In such a model, the present value of the income stream, at t_0, is equal to the present value of the consumption expenditures stream.

To avoid confusion, it is first necessary to distinguish spending on items of consumption and actual consumption of such items. For simplicity, we shall assume that these acts are simultaneous. This implies that the services of all durable consumption items are purchased or leased as consumption actually takes place. Let us now break down consumption into two categories, which we do not propose to define rigorously at this time. The first category includes those services that are aimed at fulfilling what may be called "basic needs." The second category includes those services that are purchased with a view toward fulfilling what may be called "residual needs," which are in some sense less urgent than those in the first category. Despite the arbitrariness of any specific dividing line, some such division exists for each individual or family. Some needs must be met in the normal order of affairs; others may be met only if the opportunity (largely determined by income) should arise.

Orthodox rationality criteria suggest that the individual will equalize the utility per dollar spent on each consumption service in each period. This may suggest that any attempt to distinguish between "basic" and "residual" services is misleading. If income fluctuates over time, however, casual observation indicates that residual items may be consumed only during periods of relative affluence. Such behavior will be irrational in a certainty model, however, since the individual "should," through his saving activity, attain results approximating those observed under a stable income flow. He should, in other terms, equalize the marginal rates of substitution between any two items of consumption service for all time periods, viewed from t_0, independently of predicted fluctuations in income or in needs, on the assumption that price ratios remain constant. If needs should vary as among separate periods, this equalization need not, of course, imply equal consumption flows of either service in each period of time.[7]

Viewed from the moment, t_0, the individual will plan a pattern of saving and spending over the several periods such that, in each period the marginal rate of substitution between any two goods, say, bread and coal, is equal to the price ratio. If as an example, we consider a two-season year as a sequence, the rational individual will plan his spending over the whole year to ensure that his needs for bread and coal will be equally satisfied, in a relative sense, in each season. He will not skimp on bread during the winter season merely because his needs for coal are great. Nor will he gorge himself in the summer because he need make no expenditure on coal. He will, of course, save some portion of his income during the summer in order to meet his varying need for coal over the sequence. This example suggests that either income or need can vary over a temporal sequence and that the individual must take these variations into account as he attempts to maximize the present value of expected utility.

Now return to the problem of individual fiscal choice. We ask the same question as before, but this time in the multi-period setting. How will the individual choose to pay a specific tax obligation? In order to simplify the issue, assume that the government must service a deadweight public debt. This allows us to isolate the tax question, per se, from the public expenditure side of the fiscal account. Secondly, we seek to eliminate the problem of the distribution of the tax load among separate persons in the group. We assume here that each person has assigned to him a predetermined share in the aggregate tax liability. By this set of assumptions, we arrive, finally, at a model which substitutes an equal-present-value tax obligation for the equal-yield obligation in the one-period, orthodox analytical model.

If he is allowed full freedom of choice, the individual should prefer to pay the tax when and how he wants to pay it, without temporal or institutional restriction. This undesignated tax is equivalent, in this multi-period model, to the more familiar lump-sum tax introduced in the discussions of the one-period model. If he can select both the timing and the method of payment, the individual can adjust his spending plans over time optimally. Aside from the income effects that result from any payment of net taxes, no temporal distortions are introduced.

This most preferred alternative is explicitly ruled out in the problem as posed to the individual. We allow him to consider only the following: (1) a tax of equal sum each year, defined independently of fluctuations in income or need, (2) a proportional tax on income received in each year, (3) a progressive tax on income received in each year, (4) a proportional tax on all consumption spending in each period, and, (5) a proportional tax on a specific item of consumption spending in each period. Under either one of these second-best alternatives, some distortion will be introduced in the consumption-saving pattern over time. The question is which of these institutions, each of which describes a real-world tax instrument, involves the minimum distortion? Which alternative "should" the individual select?

V. Exchange through Time

If the capital market works perfectly, and costlessly, in a restricted sense that we shall define in a moment, the orthodox conclusions are not modified. The specific tax on a single item of consumption remains the least desirable of the lot. If the individual should be able, without additional institutional cost, either to borrow or to lend at the rate that is used in discounting the aggregate tax liability—that is, at the government borrowing-lending rate—there need to be no temporal distortion introduced under any of the tax institutions. Hence, they can be arrayed in order of preference based on minimizing behavioral or pattern distortions within each single period, the setting for the one-period model. By entering the loan market, the individual can borrow or lend funds so as to maintain an undistorted pattern of consumption spending over time; he will be uninfluenced by the form of the tax instrument.

The required assumption of perfection in the capital or loan market is, however, extremely severe. Individuals may be able to lend funds, and thus to employ saving for future consumption, at the government borrowing rate. They do so by purchasing government securities. On the other hand, it seems wholly unrealistic to assume that, as individuals, they can also borrow at this same rate even when incomes are predictable with certainty. Lenders need not have access to the sources of information possessed by potential borrowers, and, if they do not, risk considerations alone make private borrowing rates exceed those for government. In addition, institutional factors make borrowing against future income expected from human capital possible only at differentially higher costs than borrowing against nonhuman capital. Also, in normal circumstances, the very process of entering the capital market, either as a lender or as a borrower, involves some positive conversion cost for the individual.

When such imperfections as these are allowed in the model, the private or individual rate of discount that is appropriate for the decision among the tax alternatives may be different from the "objective" rate that is employed by government in presenting the alternatives. In such circumstances, the rational man must try to select that tax instrument which requires the least amount of conversion through the capital market; that is to say, requires that he make the smallest number of exchanges of income through time. The objective of the individual is not changed. He will try, after the imposition of the tax, to retain, insofar as is possible, the desired equalities through time for the relevant marginal rates of substitution.[8]

Let us now assume that, before the imposition of any tax, the individual has attained a position of "planning" equilibrium. That is to say he has formulated a pattern of saving and spending over time that will equalize the relevant marginal rates of substitution in the different periods, always viewed from the moment, t_0.[9] We now confront him with the tax obligation, which we define in present-value terms computed on the basis of the government discount rate. The rational individual will try to select that tax alternative which minimizes resort to the market. He will choose that tax instrument that introduces the least initial disturbance in his planned "equilibrium" pattern of consumption over time. If both income and needs are expected to be equal in each period, the orthodox conclusions continue to hold. If, however, we allow for some predicted fluctuations in either incomes or needs, these conclusions must be modified in the light of specific temporal distortions. If needs are expected to be more stable over time than income, the progressive tax on income earned in each period will tend to be preferred over either the annual tax or the proportional tax because of the temporal distortion factor. Here the intrusion of possible temporal distortion must be added to the "pattern distortion" that has commanded almost the exclusive center of attention in orthodox analysis of the relative efficiency of the various tax instruments. It is, of course, impossible to state, a priori, which of these two elements will be the more important in any particular circumstances. It is clear, however, that when the temporal distortion factor alone is considered, the progressive tax will be preferred over alternative taxes levied on income. This tax allows the tax liability to be concentrated in periods when, failing recourse to the loan market, the marginal utility of spending is expected to be low.[10] The question we seek to examine now is whether or not the general or the specific tax on consumption expenditure might not be preferred, on similar grounds, even to the progressive income tax. The answer seems clearly to be in the negative. Either of these taxes on consumption would, in this case where needs are expected to be more stable over time than income, clearly introduce the familiar pattern distortions. And, at the same time, they would not be preferred over the progressive income tax in terms of the temporal distortions introduced.

If, however, we should assume that predicted needs over time fluctuate more than predicted income, these conclusions do not follow. For simplicity, assume that income is expected to be the same in each period, but that consumption needs are predicted to vary sharply from one period to the other. The second factor ensures that, without recourse to the loan market, the marginal utility of spending will vary sharply over time. If imperfections in the capital market introduce differential costs, the final adjustment made by the individual may involve a consumption sequence over time which allows for considerable variation in the per period consumption of residual services. In this case, the specific consumption tax, levied on an item of residual consumption, may well involve less overall distortion than even the progressive income tax due to the possibility that it allows for reducing temporal distortion.

It is rational for the individual, who expects both his needs and his income to fluctuate over time, to adjust temporally his consumption of residual consumption services so as to "bunch" these in periods when the marginal utility of spending is low. That is to say, he will plan to satisfy residual consumption needs only when his overall level of needs is, relatively, low or when his level of income is high. This behavior need not violate rationality norms, even in the most restricted sense, when it is recognized that substitution among services in different periods is clearly possible in many instances. Certain items of residual consumption are postponable, necessarily so. For example, the individual "needs" only one holiday a year. It is rational for him to plan this holiday for a period when either income is higher than usual, or "needs" for remaining services are lower than usual.[11]

If we allow for such bunching of residual consumption, which is surely descriptive of human behavior, it is clear that, when the fiscal choice is posed, the tax on specific consumption services may, in certain cases, be the most desirable of the alternatives. The orthodox pattern distortions may be more than offset by the added advantage of bunching tax payments, which only this tax makes possible, during periods of low expected marginal utility for spending, and, in this way, minimizing temporal distortion. When specific consumption taxes are discussed, a familiar theorem states that distortion is minimized when the tax is levied on an item characterized by a relatively low price elasticity of demand. When some recognition of temporal distortion is made, this theorem must also be amended. The most preferred tax should be that levied on an item that combines low price elasticity of demand, thus reducing pattern distortion, with high income elasticity of demand, thus minimizing temporal distortion.

As compared with a progressive tax on income in each period, a tax on a single item of postponable residual consumption can allow adjustment in tax liability not only due to fluctuating incomes over time but also to fluctuating levels of need for basic consumption goods and services. To demonstrate this point assume, initially, that income is expected to be stable, but that needs for basic consumption services are predicted to fluctuate. Let us say that a family expects to receive an annual income of fifteen thousand dollars over the next decade, which is the assumed relevant period for planning. During this decade, t_1 through t_{10}, a son is expected to be in college during the years, t_3, t_4, t_5, and t_6. Without adjustment through the capital market, the marginal utility of spending in these four years will be higher than during the other years of the decade. The progressive tax would, in this model, require payment of the same sum each year. But the family, if allowed to choose, might well "prefer" to bunch tax payments in the years, t_1 and t_2, and then again in t_7, t_8, t_9, and t_{10}. They may be able to do so, without recourse to the capital market, either as net lenders or net borrowers, if the tax could be imposed on some item of residual consumption that they plan to postpone for purchase and use only in those years. For example, holidays in Europe may be "planned" only for those noncollege years. Despite the orthodox pattern distortions that a tax on holiday expenditure would surely involve, such a tax might, over time, actually expand the range of choices open to the individual as compared with the other tax instruments considered.

Interestingly, in this model, when the various tax instruments are arrayed in terms of the temporal distortions introduced, the general tax on all consumption expenditure becomes the least desirable of all instruments. The specific tax on an item of residual consumption allows tax liability to be bunched in periods when the predicted marginal utility of spending is low. The income tax, whether proportional or progressive, allows the liability to be spread equally over time. The general expenditure tax, by comparison, requires a higher total payment precisely in those years when the need for basic consumption items may be greatest. This conclusion is perhaps noteworthy, for it runs counter to the argument that the general expenditure tax may be more "efficient" in some ways than the income tax because of the removal of the discrimination against savings. This contrast in result illustrates the basic difference in our approach and the more traditional one.[12]

Many other models, or examples, could be constructed by using different assumptions concerning predicted fluctuations in incomes and in needs for basic consumption services over time. These need not be elaborated here, however, since our main purpose is that of demonstrating that under some conditions the individual may choose to meet a tax obligation through the payment of a specific commodity tax.

These conclusions are, of course, strongly reinforced when we relax still further the rationality assumption. If moral scruples influence behavior in the direction of making individuals "live within their incomes," and causing them to consider "eating up capital" or "going into debt" to be repugnant, or at best, imprudent, the marginal adjustments necessary for achieving any "equilibrium" pattern of planned consumption do not take place. The marginal rates of substitution between items of consumption will not be equal in separate time periods, even when viewed from a single moment. As such departures from any rationally planned equilibrium become more significant, the advantages of the specific consumption tax become greater.

The rationally planned equilibrium pattern of consumption spending is, of course, the normative version of the permanent-income hypothesis, either in the limited horizon, life-cycle version, or in the unlimited Ricardian version. To the extent that empirical data lend support to the hypothesis, in either form, the advantages of the specific consumption tax in minimizing temporal distortions are reduced. To the extent that empirical data suggest that individuals plan consumption on the basis of measured income in each period, and not on permanent income, the relative advantages of an indirect tax instrument are enhanced.

VI. Certainty Relaxed

To this point we have assumed that the individual, whose calculus we examine, chooses under certainty regarding future income prospects, future needs, and the expected life of the fiscal institutions considered. In any plausible real-world situation, such choices would not be possible. Yet individuals must, in some manner, make selections among fiscal instruments as participants in some collective decision process. It will be helpful to see how the general conclusions reached under the assumption of certainty may be modified when this assumption is dropped.

When the individual is uncertain as to future income prospects and as to future needs or wants for goods and services, it is not possible to present him with a choice among a set of equal-present-value fiscal alternatives. If his income is expected to fluctuate, but the magnitude and the directions of such fluctuations are not predictable, there is no means of determining the present value of an income tax obligation. Similarly, if his consumption pattern is expected to change over time, but in some unpredictable way, we cannot determine the present value of either a general or a specific tax on consumption. The individual must choose among the several possible fiscal institutions without knowing which of these will, in fact, impose the greatest overall tax liability upon him. Obviously, this factor becomes important in his choice calculus. Quite apart from those considerations discussed above as well as those present in the more orthodox tax analysis, the individual will, other things equal, try to minimize aggregate tax liability. His behavior in so doing will depend on his expectations concerning future income and future needs. It is significant, however, that precisely to the extent that the individual is uncertain as to his prospects, he will also be uncertain as to which fiscal instrument will minimize his own personal liability. Thus, distributional considerations, which admittedly cannot be eliminated, even conceptually, from any uncertainty model, loom less important than they might appear. If the individual does not know which tax alternative will, in fact, minimize his aggregate tax liability, he will tend to choose on the basis of nondistributional considerations, such as the temporal "efficiency" calculus previously discussed.

The time element alone tends to reduce the importance of purely distributional considerations. The longer the period over which the institution chosen is expected to remain in force, the less important distribution becomes relative to the more limited criteria of efficiency. For this reason, the analysis that we have developed under the assumption of certainty retains its relevance for an uncertainty model. An example may be useful. Assume that a man is uncertain as to his income prospects over time, and also as to his basic expenditure needs. He may, however, accept that there are certain criteria which will, roughly and approximately, measure his unadjusted marginal utility of income in particular future periods. He may say that, for instance, "if my income is either high enough or my needs for basic consumption items low enough, I shall probably find myself wearing tailored suits and my wife wearing mink capes. Such items seem to me to be reasonably good independent measures of the marginal utility of income. Hence, if a tax is placed on such items, I can maintain some insurance against being subjected to burdensome tax liability during periods when the marginal utility of income is highest, either because my needs of basic services are unexpectedly high or because my income is, for some reason, unexpectedly low." In one sense, the choice of the indirect tax on residual and postponable consumption items reflects the same sort of mental calculus that might go into a decision to exempt from income taxation certain basic consumption items. We consider this point further below.

In the uncertainty model, we need to make no particular assumption about the perfection or the imperfection in the capital market in order to derive a logical individual preference for the specific commodity tax. With future income and needs uncertain, the whole conception of an "optimal" or "equilibrium" pattern of consumption over time loses much of its meaning. The individual will, more or less as a natural order of events, expect the marginal utility of his expenditures to vary from one period to another. In the case of complete certainty, the individual may prefer, because of the orthodox in-period distortions, the direct tax to the indirect tax because his resort to the loan market can effectively remove the temporal distortions and smooth out his consumption pattern as desired. If uncertainty is introduced, however, he may be observed to select the indirect tax.

To this point, the individual has been assumed to be motivated by ordinary utility-maximizing considerations. A somewhat broader conception of individual choice allows us to introduce other elements into the analysis that tend to support the conclusions reached. The first concerns the subjective or the "felt" burden of tax payment over future time periods. At the moment of choosing among various tax instruments, the individual may be influenced in this choice by his predictions regarding his own reactions, in later periods, to the decision that he makes at present. He may realize, for example, that on each payment date, the income tax will impose upon him a genuine "felt" burden. On the other hand, he may recognize that, since he pays the tax along with the price of a specific commodity, such a burden may be absent in the consumption tax. This is a fiscal illusion, and the individual, in his more rational moments, may recognize it as such. But he may, nonetheless, deliberately choose to impose future taxes on himself in such a way that the subsequent subjective burden of payment is minimized.

A second consideration involves the individual's own ethical attitudes toward his consumption of residual items. He may well recognize that he is, on occasion, the slave of his passions, and, because of this, he may, quite rationally, choose to place obstacles in the way of specific consumption patterns. Sumptuary taxation can be derived from an individual calculus of choice. Nevertheless, great care must be taken here to distinguish this attitude from the paternalist one, through which the individual attempts to lay down standards, not for himself, but for others in the social group.

VIII. Problems of Aggregation

Individuals are not, of course, allowed to choose separately and independently the fiscal instruments through which their collective financial obligations may be discharged. At best, they are allowed to participate, directly or remotely, in the group choice which must, once made, impose standard or uniform institutions on all members of the collectivity. To what extent can an analysis of individual choice, as described above, be employed in a discussion of group choice?

The consistency of individual decisions, one with the other, must be examined. While it may be rational for the isolated individual to prefer a privately levied tax on a specific commodity, he may not want the collectivity to impose uniform taxation on the consumption of specific items. Substantial agreement on the commodity or the service to be taxed may not be present. What one man considers as a superfluous or "luxury" good, and its purchase a reasonably good independent criterion for the marginal utility of income, a second man may consider to be a basic consumption item, essential to life, happiness, and well-being. If wide divergencies of this sort exist, the individual participant in group choice may well abandon any support for indirect taxation. On the other hand, social groups are reasonably homogeneous in many respects, and substantial, if not total, agreement might be attainable on a relatively small group or set of specific commodities that might be subjected to a set of specific consumption levies. To the extent that such homogeneity exists, indirect taxation of specific commodities may emerge from a group choice process, in part at least based on considerations such as those we have discussed. The individual participant in such choice may, for example, consider his own consumption of champagne to be a good indicator of his relative "welfare" position. On the other hand, another individual may consider his wife's consumption of mink capes or French perfumes a better choice. After the predicted discussion, argument, and compromise, they may well agree that a bundle of commodities, including champagne, mink capes, and French perfumes, provides a reasonably good index for the marginal utility of expenditure for the average man.

The problem of aggregating individual choices in attaining group decisions suggests the relatively greater applicability of indirect tax institutions for local units of government. The smaller the collective group, the more homogeneous are its members and hence, agreement on the specific commodities or services to be taxed. In addition, the open-ended nature of small collective groups provides the safety valve that is essential to prevent sumptuary exploitation of dissident minorities.

Elements of paternalism cannot, of course, be wholly eliminated from a collective choice among tax instruments. Each participant in a collective decision, be he voter, political leader, or bureaucrat, has a set of preferences, of "values," not only for himself but also regarding the behavior of others in his social group. The point to be stressed here is not the absence of such elements, but rather the fact that these need not be present to drive a collective preference for specific commodity taxation. "Externalities" of this nature are not necessary. Alcohol may be taxed heavily in most jurisdictions because voters and political leaders think that the average man "should" be discouraged from drinking. But, also, alcohol taxes may be accepted because the average man, himself, knows that he can always escape taxation by refraining from drink. In a basic, philosophical sense, indirect taxation of specific commodities allows the taxpayer more ultimate choice than direct taxation precisely because it is specific. He retains an additional faculty of choice over time, so to speak, because he has available a wider range of alternatives than he would retain under direct taxes. This faculty may never be exploited; indeed, the individual will hope that he will never find it necessary to reduce his tax obligation in this way. But the existence of this wider range of potential choice may be decisive for the individual.

VIII. Taxes and Public Spending

The argument has been developed within the orthodox setting for tax analysis. By assuming that the government is obligated to meet a fixed interest charge on a deadweight debt, we have been able to discuss the choice among tax instruments independently of the choice among public expenditure programs. In a more general setting, taxes and expenditures are simultaneously selected. If the latter are considered to be such that they can be appropriately financed by "general charges against the whole community," such as, for example, spending for national defense, much of the analysis remains valid. However, additional elements enter into the individual calculus, even in these cases, and these should be discussed briefly. We shall limit the discussion to the financing of general-benefit programs. We assume that total spending is not, however, fixed in advance, as in the interest-charge model, but that the level of spending may be at any level that the group chooses.

Here the individual must consider the additional question concerning the *aggregate* tax liability. His own share will depend, in part, on how much the group chooses to spend publicly. And there may exist important interdependencies between the decisions made on tax institutions and the decisions made on the size of public expenditure programs. The individual wants, *ceteris paribus*, the largest possible general-benefit program combined with the lowest possible personal tax liability. If he values public spending benefits relatively more than his fellows, he may choose indirect taxation, quite independently from other considerations, if he thinks that the fiscal illusion involved will lead to an expanded public sector. On the other hand, should he be relatively more interested in his own personal tax liability, he may support direct taxation for the same reasons.

These and other considerations are important, but they can only be noted, not examined, in this paper. Only one further element should be mentioned. The individual may recognize that collective decisions to spend are likely to be more favorable when revenues from existing taxes are available. The indirect tax on specific commodities or services of residual consumption becomes, in this light, a means of ensuring an automatic or quasi-automatic expansion of public spending along with the expansion of private spending on residual consumption items, and, similarly, a quasi-automatic reduction in public spending when private spending on residual items is reduced.

IX. Generalizations

This essay does not present a generally applicable normative theory of indirect taxation. We have shown that a case can be made out for the imposition of specific consumption taxes on the basis of an individual choice calculus. The departures from orthodox fiscal analysis are represented by this concentration on individual choice and upon the introduction of fiscal instruments as institutions that are costly to select and costly to modify once they are selected. The explicit introduction of time into the model, and the individual's choice among institutions that are expected to remain in being over time, allows us to show that the indirect tax may be the most preferred instrument under certain conditions. The result may be generalized for the community, but this step depends critically on the existence of some reasonable consensus on a set of commodities or services, the consumption of which provides a criterion for the marginal utility of income in separate periods.

At one point the close similarity between the imposition of specific levies on items of residual consumption and the exemption of items of basic consumption from the income tax was noted. It will be useful to examine these two devices more carefully, since both are to be found in modern fiscal systems. Both of these schemes have been introduced to include some recognition of fluctuating needs for basic consumption goods and services in the tax base. The exemption of such basic consumption items as medical care and education from the income tax base involves the acknowledgment that, during the periods when such expenses are high, income alone does not provide an adequate criterion for computing relative tax liabilities. In either case, the taxpayer retains somewhat greater freedom of action than he would have retained under the general income tax without exemptions. The freedom of the taxpayer to adjust his own liability through a modified pattern of consumption is present, but different, in the two cases. Under the exemption scheme, the individual can reduce his tax liability only by consuming the specific items, say, medical services. Under the specific commodity tax, he can reduce his liability by reducing his consumption of one or a few items, leaving him a broad range of alternatives upon which to spend.

One of the interesting by-products of the analysis is the relatively low ranking that is placed on the *general* consumption or expenditure tax. The case that has been made out for specific consumption taxation depends, strictly, on the specificity of the objects taxed. On the basis of an individual choice calculus, it is difficult to see how any argument for general indirect taxation could be derived. The orthodox distortions in static consumption patterns are, of course, smaller than they would be with specific levies. But such distortions can always be minimized with taxes on income which are also preferred on the temporal distortion scale.

Notes

1. E. Barone, "Studi di economia finanziaria," *Giornale degli economisti* 2 (1912): 329–30 in notes.
2. Essentially the same approach used here has been applied, more generally, to the choice among various political decision rules by Buchanan and Tullock. See James M. Buchanan and Gordon Tullock, *The Calculus of Consent* (Ann Arbor: University of Michigan Press, 1962).
3. I. M. D. Little, "Direct vs. Indirect Taxes," *Economic Journal* 61 (September, 1951): 577–84.
4. Milton Friedman, "The 'Welfare' Aspects of an Income Tax and an Excise Tax," *Journal of Political Economy* 60 (1952): 25–33, reprinted in *Essays in Positive Economics* (Chicago: University of Chicago Press, 1953), pp. 100–16; Earl E. Rolph and George F. Break, "The Welfare Aspects of Excise Taxes," *Journal of Political Economy* 57 (1949): 46–54.
5. Lancaster has shown that the whole analysis can be derived in terms of expanded individual choice instead of the more usual indifferent curve apparatus. See K. Lancaster, "Welfare Propositions in Terms of Consistency and Expanded Choice," *Economic Journal* 68 (September, 1958): 464–70.
6. For a summary discussion that contains references to the other works, see M. J. Farrell, "New Theories of the Consumption Function," *Economic Journal* 69 (December, 1959): 678–96.
7. For each period, the standard necessary conditions hold. That is,

$$(1) \quad \frac{MU_i}{p_i} = \frac{MU_j}{p_j}, \text{ for any two goods, } i \text{ and } j, i \neq j, \text{ in a set } i, j = 1, 2, \ldots, m.$$

In the model that includes several periods, the standard income constraint does not apply. Over the periods of the appropriately determined life cycle, the individual acts so as to satisfy (1) in each period. If we assume that the price ratios among separate goods or services are to remain constant over time, necessary conditions for multi-period "equilibrium," at the moment of planning, become,

$$(2) \quad \left(\frac{MU_i}{MU_j}\right)_{t_0} = \left(\frac{MU_i}{MU_j}\right)_{t_1} = \ldots = \left(\frac{MU_i}{MU_j}\right)_{t_n} = \frac{p_i}{p_j}$$

where the subscripts outside the parentheses refer to periods of time, t_0 to t_n.

No explicit discounting factor need be introduced in (2), since, by assumption, prices are not paid until consumption takes place. Thus, for periods later than t_0, marginal utilities and prices are discounted by a common factor. Note particularly that the satisfaction of (2) does not require that tastes remain constant over time. The equalization of the marginal rates of substitution can be achieved by widely differing "mixes" of the two items.

If we assume that the individual has no control over the income to be earned, and, further, that income payments are lagged by one period, the overall income constraint becomes,

$$(3) \quad A_{t_0} + \frac{Y_{t_1}}{(1+r)} + \frac{Y_{t_2}}{(1+r)^2} + \cdots \frac{Y_{t_n}}{(1+r)^n} =$$

$$\left[\sum_{i=1}^{m} p_i q_i\right]_{t_0} + \frac{\left[\sum_{i=1}^{m} p_i q_i\right]_{t_1}}{(1+r)} + \cdots \frac{\left[\sum_{i=1}^{m} p_i q_i\right]_{t_n}}{(1+r)^n}$$

where A_{t_0} measures initially held assets, p, q, and r, the prices, quantities, and rate of discount, respectively.

If the individual is allowed to vary his income (earnings) over time, (3) is not relevant, and it must be replaced by a set of production constraints. The fundamentals of the analysis do not, however, require this generalization. Hence, in the discussion the individual is presumed to act on the basis of the income constraint defined by (3).

8. The type of imperfections in the capital market that are introduced here are similar to those discussed in a recent paper by Frank H. Hahn. See his "Real Balances and Consumption," *Oxford Economic Papers* 14 (June, 1962): 117–23.

9. We are concerned here only with the individual's calculus at t_0. The fact that, when t_1 arrives, he may have a different set of "optimal" plans need not concern us. On this latter point, see Robert H. Strotz, "Myopia and Inconsistency in Dynamic Utility Maximization," *Review of Economic Studies* 23 (1956): 165–80.

10. This "defense" of progressive income taxation is developed and discussed at some length in a paper by James M. Buchanan (pp. 225–40 in *Public Finance in Democratic Process: Fiscal Institutions and Individual Choice* [Chapel Hill, N.C.: University of North Carolina Press, 1967]).

11. Care should be taken to distinguish postponable items of residual consumption from durable consumer goods. The durable goods-nondurable goods distinction need not concern us here, and we have assumed that all services are purchased as they are used. A postponable service is characterized by nonrecurrence of "need" over time.

12. The relationship between our analysis and the "double taxation of savings" argument should be explained. This argument, developed by J. S. Mill, Irving Fisher, Luigi Einaudi, and others, supports the imposition of a general expenditure tax relative to a general income tax on grounds of efficiency because the income tax discriminates against savings. This argument assumes meaning only when the *distribution* of the tax load among separate persons in

the group is introduced. It is not relevant to our model since we limit the analysis, specifically, to the calculus of the single person when faced with a determined tax obligation defined in present-value terms. In the life-cycle pattern of savings behavior postulated, the present value of expenditure must equal the present value of income. If the individual is taxed on income received in each period, including the fruits of income saved in previous periods, the rate of tax will tend to be somewhat lower than the rate that would be necessary to produce the same present-value under the general expenditure tax.

20.
Efficiency Limits of Fiscal Mobility

WITH CHARLES J. GOETZ

I. Introduction

In 1956, Charles M. Tiebout published "A Pure Theory of Local Government Expenditures," a paper that has become a classic in the public finance theory of local government.[1] Perhaps largely in response to practical reality, economists have since devoted increasing attention to the provision of goods and services by local units of government. The traditional discussion has been recognized to be lacking in rigor, consisting as it does in a crude mixture of equity norms and immature analysis. Since the Tiebout model offers something of apparent substance in this confused and complex jungle, it is not surprising that its limits have often been neglected.[2]

Our purpose is to provide a critical reexamination of the Tiebout model for local public goods provision. The efficiency properties of the model are familiar, and these will be noted indirectly here, but the less-familiar efficiency *limits* will be emphasized. We shall demonstrate that there remain inherent inefficiencies in the Tiebout adjustment process, even when this is interpreted in a conceptually idealized form. Specifically, we neglect (1) the problems of fiscal spillovers among local communities and (2) all problems of discreteness that locational groupings almost necessarily introduce.[3] Our aim is to examine the Tiebout adjustment in its most favorable setting.

Tiebout tried to demonstrate that so long as local governmental units are appropriately assigned the task of providing certain public goods and services and so long as individuals retain freedom of personal migration among jurisdictions, there are efficiency-generating processes at work, despite the "publicness" of the goods provided. His analysis was presented in partial but positive response to the negative proposition advanced by Samuelson that, with nonexcludable public goods, there exists no means of using market-like decentralization to attain tolerably efficient results. Tiebout recognized and acknowledged that institutional rigidities will make the fiscal mobility adjustment process even more imperfect than its market analogue. Nonetheless, he swept these imperfections away in an admittedly extreme model in which the fiscal shopper guarantees that the Pareto efficiency frontier will be reached in equilibrium. Just as the careful shopper of market goods and services tends to ensure that the necessary conditions for optimality are met, the careful migrator in choosing among alternative communities which offer him assorted packages of local public goods and services, tends to ensure that the necessary conditions for Pareto optimality are met in the localized public sector of the economy.

To our knowledge, there has been no exhaustive criticism devoted explicitly to the Tiebout model, and his analysis has secured wide acceptance. In an appendix subsection to his 1958 paper, Paul A. Samuelson briefly discussed "local finance and the mathematics of marriage."[4] Although he acknowledged that Tiebout's solution "goes some way toward solving the problem," Samuelson rejected it in more general terms. He did so in part on the existence of migration thresholds in individual decision-making and in part on the absence of demonstrable nonoptimality under restricted voluntaristic choices. In an interesting potential marriage-partner model, he showed that maximum efficiency need not result from simple pair-wise combinations of ordinally preferred partners. Although his discussion was characteristically cryptic, Samuelson seemed to suggest that fiscally induced migration would amount to marriage of like-with-like, which he apparently rejected on efficiency grounds. It is perhaps unfortunate that this critique was not elaborated either by Samuelson himself, by Tiebout, or by others.

We shall concentrate on two features which eliminate or at least reduce severely the normative efficiency properties from the equilibrium generated by the Tiebout adjustment process. The first is the *fact of location*. Both in the private-goods or market sector of the economy and in the local public goods sector, spatial dimensions are relevant to any allocation of resources. To ignore these dimensions or to assume that they are nonexistent is to remove a central part of the problem. The second feature is the *absence of proprietary ownership—entrepreneurship* in the spatially defined scarcities relevant for local public goods. As our analysis will demonstrate, local political communities cannot act in the particular profit-maximizing role dictated by allocative efficiency criteria.

II. Locational Fixity

The absence of proprietary entrepreneurship imposes a severe constraint on any adjustment process. Nonetheless if we could disregard locational fixity, adjustment toward a market-type equilibrium with optimality properties would take place. In such a model, individuals would make choices among relevant alternatives which do not embody geographical dimensions. One way of illustrating an absence of locational fixity would be to introduce a setting of either consuming or producing clubs.[5] We assume that private profit-making in the formation or organization of clubs is prohibited. If there are gains to be secured from either joint consumption or joint production, these must be discovered and exploited by the participating members. Individuals would, within limits, voluntarily reach agreements on the joint efforts that efficiency criteria might dictate, and some proximate "clubs" equilibrium might be attained. In the idealized setting for this model, the individual would find himself confronted with a large number of clubs for each activity on either the consuming or producing side.

The characteristics of the conceptual-equilibrium approach in this model are in all respects parallel to those of competitive equilibrium. Different persons would be charged equivalent "prices" for similar services or facilities. Within each club, payments made by each member would be identical so long as services provided are identical. The total gains that are potentially realizable from joint or cooperative action would be exhausted in equilibrium. The necessary conditions for Pareto optimality would be satisfied.

In our view, Tiebout's analysis may best be interpreted as an early and pioneering attempt to describe the adjustment process in an essentially *nonspatial* world of voluntary clubs. It seems clear that Tiebout did not actually intend that his analysis of the local public goods problem be interpreted in this fashion. He formulated his analysis to be applicable in a local public goods setting. Despite this, he sensed the difficulties that locational fixity would introduce. In his formal model, therefore, he introduced the assumption that all personal incomes are from dividends. This provides a means of virtually eliminating locational fixity from the model of adjustment. If all income should be received from dividends, the individual's actual choice of location in space would be independent of the allocation of resources in the private sector of the economy. The implications of this interpretation should, however, be noted. In choosing among clubs in this model, the individual presumably is not making a simultaneously locational adjustment in his private sector activities in the economy. To him, the clubs are means of securing particular services more efficiently, and there is no requirement that he modify his private-sector behavior in any compensating sense. There is no "voting with the feet" in the adjustment, no migration or mobility as such. Demanders of various club services and facilities stratify themselves voluntarily in accordance with their relative preferences for quantity-quality of those services, including preferences for privacy. Geographic stratification or classification is not implied nor is stratification by income and wealth level necessarily embodied, except indirectly. Note that, in this world of voluntary clubs, individuals can locate in space strictly in accord with criteria of maximal individual productivity in the private goods sector of the economy. That is to say, there is nothing in the model which prevents the simultaneous maximization of the value of strictly private goods product and the value of joint goods product.

The setting within which local governments provide public goods and services to their citizens is quite different, conceptually, from this idealized Tiebout model. Individuals locate themselves in space. Their incomes are not exclusively drawn from dividends, and their allocation over space does influence the total value of private goods product in the economy. Local governments have geographic as well as membership dimensions. This fact of location along with the absence of proprietary entrepreneurship must be systematically incorporated into any model that purports to represent the forces at work in any adjustment process, even at the most abstract and rarefied level of analysis.

III. Models of Migrational Adjustment

Fiscally induced migration of persons among separate communities will take place in a setting where local units of government provide at least some goods and services collectively. Individuals will "vote with their feet," at least within limits, and their choices among locational alternatives involve a Tiebout-like process of adjustment. When locational fixity and the absence of proprietary entrepreneurship are taken into account, however, the equilibrium solution of this interaction is *not* characterized by efficiency properties.

When public goods, which embody jointness efficiencies, are produced along with private goods in an economy, resources should be allocated so that the total value of output, from private *and* public goods, is maximized. The criterion for optimality is that individuals should locate themselves in space in such a fashion that each person's contribution to total value, private and public, is the same in all locations. If all persons are in this situation, gains from trade in the most inclusive sense will be fully exhausted. More important, in making any movement from a competitive private goods equilibrium, the individual does not exert an external economy or diseconomy on other persons. In equilibrium, the individual's private returns are identical to his marginal *social* product in all alternatives, including locational ones.

This result does not carry over when we introduce locally provided public goods and services. There will normally be fiscal externalities, both with respect to benefits and costs, involved in any shift of a person between two communities. A person's tax dollars, wherever they are collected and used, generate public goods inputs for *others* in the appropriate sharing group as well as for himself and allow the per-unit cost of public goods to fall for each individual as group size expands. Hence, any move imposes an external diseconomy on all those who remain in the original sharing group and an external economy on all those in the jurisdiction that the migrant enters. This direction of effect is the same for all cost or tax-side externalities. The benefits side of local fiscal accounts may also become a means through which migration exerts externalities. These may parallel and reinforce the tax-side effects when "publicness" attributes of locally provided goods and services are sufficiently strong so that the addition of an immigrant's demand permits mutual net benefits from some increase in the quantity of the public good. They may, however, offset or oppose tax-side externalities when the local goods exhibit nonpublicness or private goods features (e.g., congestibility).[6]

The necessary conditions that must be satisfied for Pareto optimality are that, for each person i and for each pair of locational alternatives, X and Y,

$$(1) \quad MVP^i_X + MVG^i_X = MVP^i_Y + MVG^i_Y$$

where the MVPs refer to marginal private goods value or product and the MVGs refer to marginal public goods value or product generated by an individual location in the subscripted community. Designating the number of persons in a local fiscal community by N,[7] the total benefit that the person secures from the public good or service made available by that community by B, and the total tax payment made by the individual by T, the MVG terms may be broken down in detail:

$$(1a) \quad MVP^i_X + (B^i_X - T^i_X) + \left[\frac{\partial(\Sigma B^j)}{\partial N_X} - \frac{\partial(\Sigma T^j)}{\partial N_X} \right] =$$

$$MVP^i_Y + (B^i_Y - T^i_Y) + \left[\frac{\partial(\Sigma B^j)}{\partial N_Y} - \frac{\partial(\Sigma T^j)}{\partial N_Y} \right]$$

$$i, j = 1, 2, \ldots, N$$

$$i \neq j.$$

As he migrates from one community to the other, or as he considers the locational alternatives, the individual will be cognizant of the benefits and the taxes that he, personally, will share. Just as MVP incorporates the "consumer surplus" achievable through market transactions, the terms in parentheses ($B^i - T^i$) measure the "fiscal surplus" that the person secures from location in the designated jurisdiction. The fiscal externalities noted earlier are summarized in the bracketed terms in (1a). The individual will *not* take these values into account in his own decision process.[8] Instead, the following conditions will be satisfied in a Tiebout-like adjustment equilibrium:[9]

(2) $\text{MVP}^i_X + (B^i_X - T^i_X) = \text{MVP}^i_Y + (B^i_Y - T^i_Y)$,

for all *i*.

Model 1.

In order to demonstrate the efficiency limitations of fiscal mobility, we may look briefly at several models. Consider a situation where each of two communities, X and Y, provides the *same* quantity of a Samuelson-pure public good. Each local unit undergoes the same total outlay. The interesting feature of this model is that the allocation of individuals between communities that satisfies the conditions for optimality remains unchanged with the introduction of local public goods into the economy. That is to say, Pareto-optimality is attained when,

(3) $\text{MVP}^i_X = \text{MVP}^i_Y$.

This result arises because of the assumption of the fixed and identical quantity of public good provided in each of the two communities. The assumption of pureness not only ensures that $B^i_X = B^i_Y$, for any and all allocations of persons, but also guarantees that

$[\partial(\Sigma B^j_X)]/\partial N_X = [\partial(\Sigma B^j_Y)]/N_Y = 0$.

Further, we know that, in this model

$T^i_X = [\partial(\Sigma T^j_X)]/\partial N_X$, and that $T^i_Y = [\partial(\Sigma T^j_Y)]/\partial N_Y$.

Hence, the general statement for optimality (1a) reduces to (3).

In this model, any fiscally induced migration that might be necessary to satisfy (2) will be inefficient.[10] The manner in which the Tiebout mechanism may fail in this model is apparent if the private productivity functions differ at the two public goods provision sites. Then, in order to equalize the marginal private products, as demanded by the optimality condition (3), the values of N_X and N_Y must be unequal. In turn, an implication of the different values of N when $\text{MVP}_X = \text{MVP}_Y$ are equal is that individuals in the larger community enjoy lower tax shares and higher values of the fiscal surplus ($B - T$). Under these circumstances, the optimality condition (3) is inconsistent with the equilibrium condition (2) and individual migration would have the effect of inducing overconcentration at the site with the more productive private returns function. On the other hand, if the sites are identical in all respects, conditions (2) and (3) will be satisfied simultaneously so that the distribution of people among the two communities will be optimal.[11]

Model 2.

Here we retain the assumption of Model 1, except that we now allow the communities to adjust their provisions to *differing* levels of the public good or service in accord with the number and preferences of the resident individuals.[12] The general conditions for Pareto-optimality or efficiency remain as stated in (1a) above. These conditions cannot now, however, be simplified to (3) as was the case with Model 1. The Pareto-efficient allocation of persons will not be characterized by the equality of marginal private goods product. As in Model 1, the Tiebout adjustment process will attain an equilibrium when (2) is satisfied. Individuals will neglect the bracketed terms in (1a). The question concerns the direction of the distortion that this neglect will introduce.

Assume that the Tiebout process has produced the equilibrium allocation (2) but that the local units of government, X and Y, are observed to be offering differing quantities of the public good or service. In both communities, however, the good or service remains within the range of pure "publicness." Consider the shift of a single person from Y to X in this setting. Will this shift improve or worsen the allocation in accordance with Paretian criteria? This requires an evaluation of the fiscal externalities on each side of (1a).

Under the assumptions of this model an immigrant cannot impose any net costs, and we know that the values for each of the bracketed terms are positive for any increase in population. This means that a shift of a person from Y to X will exert a net fiscal benefit on the recipient community and a net fiscal harm on the community which loses population. There is no means, however, of specifying relative absolute values for the two bracketed terms in (1a). Although their analysis was concentrated on the situation to be discussed in Model 3, Buchanan and Wagner argued that a higher-valued bracketed term for the community with the larger public goods output would be the normal outcome for Model 2. They based their analysis on a geometric construction, and they implicitly assumed that real-world examples would fall within the adjustment ranges generating this result. In this case, the Tiebout adjustment process stops short of inducing an optimal concentration of population in the community that is relatively affluent in public goods and services.[13] In the converse case, where X is observed to be providing a larger quantity of public goods *and* the value of the terms in the X-subscripted bracket is less than that in the Y-subscripted bracket, the Tiebout adjustment mechanism produces an overconcentration of persons in the community with the relatively affluent local government budget.

Model 3.
   We now drop the restriction that the goods or services provided by local communities must be *purely* "public." These remain "public" in the strict sense of nonexclusion. A unit that is available to any one person in the relevant local community or jurisdiction is available to all persons. But the evaluation that is placed on specific physical quantities of these goods is now allowed to depend on the number of persons with whom the goods are to be shared. This category of "impure" public goods seems descriptively characteristic of many items in local government budgets (e.g., fire protection, police services, health facilities, water and sewage facilities, etc.).[14]
   The statement for the necessary conditions that must be met for Pareto-optimality remains that in (1a) above. This model does, however, modify the fiscal externalities that are included in the bracketed terms. As noted, tax-side externalities always work in the same direction. In-migration must reduce tax cost per unit of public good to other persons in the community, and out-migration must increase tax cost per unit of public good to other persons. Benefit-side externalities are unidirectional, however, only under the strict pure publicness assumptions of Model 2.[15] In that setting, the in-migrant's tax share (at any value above zero) produces some public goods benefits to all other persons in the jurisdiction to which he moves, and, by assumption, these persons are indifferent as to the number of persons in the sharing group. If we introduce impurity, however, this result no longer holds.
   Formally, we may state the effects of in-migration on members of the community in the following way. For any person, j, in the community, his public goods benefits function now includes an argument for numbers, that is, $B^j = B^j(Q,N)$, where Q refers to quantity of the public good. The effect of an in-migrant on j's utility becomes,

$$(4) \quad \frac{dB^j}{dN} = \left(\frac{\partial B^j}{\partial Q} \frac{dQ}{dN} \right) + \frac{\partial B^j}{\partial N} .$$

In Model 2, there is no explicit argument for numbers in the utility function of j, in which case only the first term on the right-hand side of (4) exists. And, since public goods are presumed to retain positive value over relevant ranges, the effects on j's utility are positive for the benefits side considered in isolation. In Model 3, however, the last term in (4) must be evaluated, and this term normally will be negative when congestibility of facilities and services is present. Moreover, the sign of the first term now depends on whether dQ/dN is positive or negative. The negative change in output may occur if the price effect due to increased cost-sharing is swamped by the downward shift in marginal evaluation schedules as the good becomes more congested.

It remains impossible to generalize concerning the direction of distortion that the Tiebout process will produce, even in this model. To the extent that public goods impurities in the form of congestibility become important, it seems plausible to suggest that the Tiebout process here is likely to lead to an overconcentration of population in those communities where public goods quantities are large. This would, in turn, suggest that there may be an overconcentration of persons in the larger communities and in the communities with higher than average income levels.[16]

Our purpose in this paper is not that of deriving policy implications concerning the socially desired direction of adjustments in population distribution among local units of government, important though this may be. As the analysis has indicated, within the descriptively plausible Models 2 and 3 no such implications can be derived in the general case. To take this step would require that empirical estimates be made of the actual values for the fiscal externalities that we have identified. Our purpose here is the much more restricted one of assessing the efficiency limits of the Tiebout-like adjustment process. The question we have put is: Does the prospect of "voting with their feet" ensure that individuals will locate themselves among local jurisdictions so as to satisfy Pareto efficiency criteria, at least to some close approximation? We have not thrown in the "noise" that distorts any economic adjustment process; we have not incorporated moving costs, search costs, decision thresholds, and so on. We have examined the Tiebout process in its conceptually idealized form. As the examination of the models indicates, our answer to this question is negative. Our overall conclusion is, therefore, consistent with that reached by Samuelson in his brief comment. Unfortunately perhaps, the world with local public goods is not an analogue to the competitive market in private goods.

IV. The Absence of Proprietary Institutions

In the analysis of Section III, goods and services provided by local governmental units are "public" in the nonexcludability sense. This assumption ensures that the B terms in (2) do not change in value for an individual as he might assume different roles in a temporal locational sequence for a community; "pioneers" and "late-comers" enjoy the same benefits. The B terms need not, of course, take on identical values for all persons, but the nonexcludability requirement guarantees that, for any given person, his temporal role in the formation of the sharing group is irrelevant.

No assumption was made about the values for the T terms in (2), and, in this respect, the migrational adjustment analysis was deliberately left ambiguous. The necessary conditions stated in (1a) are fully general and involve no ambiguity. But we did not specify the T terms in (2), and we did not say how these were derived. Until we do so, we cannot be sure that Pareto-relevant fiscal externalities exist at all.

We showed that, under certain implicitly assumed values, the Tiebout process generates an equilibrium that is not optimal. Gains from trade in their most inclusive sense are not exhausted. Will not "trades" emerge to eliminate all potentially realizable gains? Will not the fiscal externalities, if these exist, be internalized?

A Regime of Private Cities

Such internalization might, in fact, occur if proprietary ownership arrangements should characterize the institutions through which localized public goods and services are provided. Suppose that persons jointly consuming nonexcludable goods and services, locationally defined, find themselves purchasing these goods and services from private supplying firms, from "private cities."[17] Consider a setting in which all nonexcludable goods are offered privately, and assume that the characteristics of Model 2 above prevail. Recall that the value of the terms in the brackets are positive in this model. In this case, should we not expect that the firm supplying community X would offer a subsidy to the potential in-migrant, and, in the limit, would we not expect that competition among separate community-supplying firms would equal the value of the externality? This could be treated as a negative item in the value of the T term in the migrant's decision calculus. The firm supplying community Y, could, of course, take the same action and offer a subsidy to the potential out-migrant to stay where he is. If this sort of adjustment should take place on both sides of a potential migrant's decision account, his choice would then be made on the basis of socially correct evaluations, and migrational adjustment would produce Pareto-efficient results.

Collective Internalization of Fiscal Externalities

It may seem that a collectivity might similarly differentiate among persons so as to internalize all fiscal externalities. It could do this, however, only if it divorces individual tax shares from all objective criteria that reflect internal demands for the nonexcludable goods. Tax shares would have to be related to the size of the *locational rent* component in individual income receipts. Locational rent is the surplus, if any, that an individual gains from being in his present location as compared to his next most favorable location. The possible existence of such rents requires us to revise slightly the conditions described in Section III above by substituting $>$ for each $=$ sign in the equations. That is, for a person's efficient location to be community X, his returns in X must be *at least* as high as in any other location Y. In the theory of the firm, such locational rents are eliminated in equilibrium because there are always a large number of identical potential bidders for the locational advantages concerned. In the case of consumers, however, utility functions of individuals may be unique and a person making a locational selection need only pay as much as the next highest bidder.

It is the absorption of locational surpluses through differentially higher tax shares which provides the principal rationale for bargaining over the individual values of T. Under the conditions of Model 2, for instance, one would expect the fiscal surpluses in a local jurisdiction to vary *inversely* with the importance of locational rents in individuals' private returns.

Consider a two-person community under Model 2 conditions, where there are positive benefit-side as well as positive tax-side external economies derived from in-migration. In the community, one person, A, secures all of his income from locational rents (from "land" or some other spatially defined resource). The second person, B, secures all of his income from wages, no part of which represents locational rents. The income receipts of the two persons are the same, and they hold total assets of equal value. Furthermore, they both have identical preferences for the public good supplied in the community. Under these conditions, simple equity norms would dictate that total tax shares be equal as between the two persons, and standard efficiency norms would dictate that marginal tax rates also be equal. Let us suppose, however, that a potential in-migrant appears, who is himself identical in all respects to B. Both A and B recognize the favorable fiscal externality that this in-migrant would exert on the community, and that they agree to share equally in the subsidy required to induce C to move into the community.

Once this move is made, however, B could clearly observe that C, who is in *all* respects his equal, is more favorably treated than himself. Since B is a "marginal" member of the community who secures no locational rents, he can readily threaten to withdraw from the community unless he is treated on equal terms with C. This system becomes completely unstable until and unless A recognizes that his receipt of locational rents is the only source for payment of the subsidy to C. In order to keep both B and C in the community and on an equal footing, A must agree to bear a larger share in total taxes, despite the identity between his objectively measured income-wealth position and those of B and C, and despite the identity of public goods preferences over the three persons. A will, however, accept this apparently disadvantageous fiscal treatment since he will secure some net gain under the conditions postulated. Note, however, that no gain would be forthcoming if B and C should be absolved from *all* tax payments. This situation would eliminate all tax-side external economies and A would clearly be in a worsened or at least no better position with a larger than with a smaller community size.

The relationship of total tax shares to locational rents under the Model 2 conditions examined here does not modify the criteria for Pareto-optimality in the community. Given any size of sharing group, these criteria are summarized in the equality between summed marginal evaluations over all taxpayer-beneficiaries and marginal cost. But this condition for optimality in public goods quantity must be supplemented by a condition for optimality in the location of persons over space in the world of local public goods, and that this second condition may and normally will involve differences in *inframarginal* tax shares even when the satisfaction of the standard Samuelson criteria, interpreted in individualistic terms, suggests equality in marginal tax shares.[18]

The relationship between total tax shares and locational rent shares in personal income receipts is unidirectional only so long as we remain within the pure "publicness" range, as defined for Model 2. If we consider the provision of local public goods and services where congestibility is present alongside nonexcludability, the externality terms in (1a) may be negative rather than positive in absolute value. In this case, the recipients of locational rents become residual claimants in this conceptually efficient internalization process, not residual payers as before.

V. The Realities of Fiscal Mobility

The difficulties that a local fiscal unit would face if it tried to follow strict efficiency norms should be apparent from the discussion in Section IV. Even if all goods and services remain fully nonexcludable, nondiscriminating taxes would not be suitable to finance their provision. Nor would the common forms of discrimination, based on income, asset, or expenditure criteria, result in efficient tax shares. Total taxes of persons would have to depend on relative fiscal alternatives, and these need bear no relationship to incomes, assets owned, or expenditures on private goods. Indeed, it seems likely that, for many local units, relatively high-income recipients will have more effective fiscal alternatives (will secure less in the way of locational rents in a relative sense) than their low-income counterparts.[19] In this instance, total taxes might have to be lower for the high-income, high-demand member of a local fiscal community than for the low-income, low-demand member. (Marginal taxes may, of course, still be higher for the former.)

It should be evident that local governmental units simply do not, and cannot, behave in the manner that efficiency criteria would dictate. The organization and operation of a fiscal sharing group on this basic violates the central notion of *free migration*, the notion upon which the models of the Tiebout adjustment process are initially founded. Freedom of migration means that a person may choose among local governmental jurisdictions on the basis of nondiscriminatory fiscal treatment. That is to say, a person is ensured that, if he moves into a local community, he will be allowed equal access to non-excludable goods and services made available in that jurisdiction and, further, that he will be taxed for these goods and services on the *same* basis as residents of the community who are his equals in an objectively measurable sense. The fiscal discrimination between old residents and in-migrants or new residents that would be required for efficiency violates the central meaning of resource mobility. If nothing else, constitutional provisions would surely prevent local governments from adopting policies that would be aimed exclusively at promoting locational efficiency. Individuals are guaranteed "equality before the law," and as this has been interpreted by the courts, any overt tax discrimination among persons that is not directly related to an objectively measurable base such as income or assets would be held illegal.

Quite apart from constitutional issues, the very meaning of local *government* makes efficient fiscal adjustment difficult. If the ultimate franchise is open to all citizens in a local community, it becomes almost impossible to trace out a plausible public choice sequence that will generate an efficient policy mix. If recipients of locational rents are in the minority, and if the conditions of Model 2 hold, it becomes relatively easy to think of a sequence where the sources of fiscal subsidization might be found in locational rents. In such a model, however, there is nothing that ensures the utilization of other fiscal sources, without which the appropriate adjustments will not even be proximately realized. If the conditions of Model 3 are present, and if these are such as to make for fiscal external diseconomies, efficiency dictates that entry fees be collected. But an open franchise could hardly be expected to limit the rebates of these funds to recipients of locational rents. If we allow for franchises limited to the recipients of locational rents, the opposing results would be predicted for the two cases noted. There seems to be no escaping from the fundamental contradictions between the discriminatory distribution of costs and benefits as between persons who secure locational rents and those that do not, the distribution required for allocative efficiency, and the nonexcludability or genuine "publicness" of goods and services supplied by governmental units.

While we do not emphasize the point in this paper, there remains the final difficulty that, even in the absence of any operational limits on a local government's ability to discriminate, there is no mechanism from which the government can derive the information upon whose basis the optimal type of discrimination must be calculated. Although we speak of locational rents which accrue to certain individuals, the existence or nonexistence of such rents may be calculable only with considerable knowledge of the utility functions of the individuals involved.[20] A government may know that it can and should discriminate, but against whom and by how much?

Somewhat circuitously, we have arrived at a precise conceptual definition for the T terms in the equations of Section III above. We would expect the total tax bill for any person to be a pro rata share of the total taxes assessed by the community on all persons in the group who are classified as belonging to the same fiscal category by legally acceptable criteria of equality.[21] This means that individualized tax shares in the real world of local public finance cannot be adjusted to incorporate fiscal externalities. Hence, the analysis of the models in Section III holds without qualification.

VI. Conclusions

If locational rents in the private goods sector did not exist (Tiebout's model of dividend income), the locational dimension of nonexcludable local public goods would create no problems for migrational adjustments. Individuals with similar demand patterns would simply form themselves into efficient "fiscal clubs." On the other hand, if those goods and services exhibiting nonexcludability did not simultaneously embody locational attributes (the world of voluntary clubs), the presence of locational rents in the private sector of the economy would not be a source of inefficiency in allocation. Individuals would, once again, form themselves into an efficient set of consuming-purchasing units. But locational rents do exist and nonexcludable goods and services carry a locational dimension. Even this combination of circumstances might not, however, generate inefficiency except in the absence of proprietary ownership of locational or spatial scarcities. If all valued "space" should be privately owned and if competition among proprietary ownership units were effective in all respects, allocational efficiency might emerge. In general, however, internalization of migration-produced externalities requires interpersonal discrimination in tax shares of a type which local governments are unlikely to be able either operationally to impose or even to calculate correctly.

The conclusions of our analysis must be nihilistic. There are elements at work in fiscally-induced migration of persons among local communities that are efficiency-generating, and perhaps these dominate those that are efficiency-retarding. If we broaden our objectives somewhat and introduce available but unused options in individual utility functions, the protections offered to the individual in the opportunity of "voting with his feet" have intrinsic value quite apart from the standard efficiency properties examined in this paper.[22] Samuelson said that the Tiebout process "goes some way toward solving the problem." This can surely be accepted if the alternative to fiscal decentralization in the provision of spatially limited nonexcludable goods and services should be increased fiscal concentration at central government levels. But, also with Samuelson, we must conclude that there "remain important analytical problems of public-goods determination that still need investigation at every level of government."[23]

Our analysis is perfectly consistent with the important and relevant hypothesis advanced by Buchanan and Wagner to the effect that fiscally induced migration is responsible for an undue concentration of persons in the large and growing conurbations of America in 1971. Their particular hypothesis cannot be rigorously supported on analytical grounds in the most general model where the *direction* of the inefficiency is indeterminate. Nonetheless, before meaningful attempts are made to examine the implications of the hypothesis empirically, it seemed necessary to analyze the pseudo-paradigm embodied in the Tiebout hypothesis. There is nothing in the Tiebout solution that rules out the possible validity of the overurbanization hypothesis.

Notes

Research on this paper was partially supported under the auspices of a Ford Foundation grant.

1. *Journal of Political Economy* 64 (October, 1956): 416–24. Essentially the same analysis was developed, at about the same time but less rigorously, by George J. Stigler. See his "The Tenable Range of Local Government," in *Federal Expenditure Policy for Economic Growth and Stability* (Washington, D.C.: Joint Economic Committee, 1957), pp. 213–19.

2. For papers that, on balance, stress the explanatory potential of the Tiebout hypothesis rather than its limits, see Bryan Ellickson, "Jurisdictional Fragmentation and Residential Choice," *American Economic Review* 61 (May, 1971): 334–39; Martin McGuire, "Group Segregation and Optimal Jurisdictions," prepared for a meeting of the Committee on Urban Economics,

Toronto, 1971 (mimeographed); Wallace Oates, "The Effects of Property Taxes and Local Public Spending in Property Values: An Empirical Study of Tax Capitalization and the Tiebout Hypothesis," *Journal of Political Economy* 77 (December, 1969): 957–71.

3. The spillover problems have been widely discussed. On these, see Alan Williams, "The Optimal Provision of Public Goods in a System of Local Government," *Journal of Political Economy* 74 (February, 1966): 18–33; Burton Weisbrod, *External Benefits of Education* (Princeton, N.J.: Princeton University Press, 1964). For a critique of the Tiebout process that calls primary attention to discreteness problems, see Charles J. Goetz, "Fiscal incentives for the cities" (mimeographed; paper prepared for meeting of the Committee of Urban Public Economics, Philadelphia, 1970).

4. Paul A. Samuelson, "Aspects of Public Expenditure Theories," *Review of Economics and Statistics* 40 (November, 1958): 337–38.

5. James M. Buchanan has examined the normative efficiency requirements for individual club equilibrium, with his emphasis centered on consuming clubs with congestible facilities or services. See his "An Economic Theory of Clubs," *Economica* (February, 1965): 1–14. Buchanan's model has been interpreted to be applicable to the theory of local public goods, notably by Mitchell Polinsky. See his "Public Goods in a Setting of Local Governments." Working Paper, pp. 705–77 (Washington, D.C., The Urban Institute, October, 1970). As will be noted in this section, the clubs model cannot readily be extended in this fashion, precisely because of the locational fixity problem.

6. "Publicness" is not an attribute that inheres in the technology of a good or service independently of the numbers of persons who secure benefits. A good that is purely public for a small group may become effectively private for a larger number of persons. For background discussion of these points, see James M. Buchanan, *Demand and Supply of Public Goods* (Chicago: Rand McNally, 1968).

7. For expository convenience, we treat the number of individuals at each location as a continuous variable rather than one which may take only integer values. This greatly simplifies the statement of equilibrium conditions without affecting the practical conclusions in any important respect.

8. The explicit role of spatial rents as an equilibrating device should be clarified. In their simplest and most abstract form, our two communities may be thought of as two islands, each of which is sufficiently large to satiate all potential demands for space. This extreme case, in which space itself cannot command any positive price is, of course, one model in which spatial rents cannot serve as adjustment devices even though the model incorporates genuine locational differentiation between the two communities. More realistically, however, assume that privacy, the consumption of space, is a scarce good which commands a positive price, a "rent." How does this affect our equations developed above? If we wish to bring space explicitly into the equations, we need only add an additional term both to (1a) and to (2).

Letting S equal a migrant's total evaluation of the space he consumes in a community and R the total rent paid (quantity of space X rent per unit), it is clear that $(S\text{-}R)$, properly subscripted, should be added to both sides of (2) in order to reflect the net benefits of space consumption in each community. In the optimality equation, (1a), the change, S, in private values created by the migrant is counterbalanced by one of opposite sign for all other members of the community whose use of space has implicitly been altered. It would seem, then, that

$$\left(S_i - \sum_j \frac{\partial j}{\partial N} \right) \quad i \neq j$$

should be added to both sides of (1a). Provided that the space consumed by an immigrant is small and the number of preexisting residents from whom the space is bid away is relatively large, we can say that

$$R \approx \sum_j \frac{\partial S_j}{\partial N} \quad i \neq j$$

because the marginal rental rate (marginal evaluation) of the land approaches, in the limit, the average evaluation of the space consumption to those who have surrendered it. Thus, the same $(S-R)$ terms may be added to both (1a) and (2), in which case our results are unaltered. Alternatively, we prefer to regard this effect as being subsumed in the generalized MVP private net product term.

9. Strictly speaking, this condition involves the sign $>$ rather than $=$, assuming that X is the equilibrium location. See the discussion of locational rents in Section IV.

10. This is the model that was implicitly used by Martin Feldstein in his critique of the Buchanan-Wagner analysis, and his conclusions are identical to those reached here. See Martin Feldstein, "Comment," in *The Analysis of Public Output* ed. J. Margolis (New York: National Bureau of Economic Research, 1970), esp. p. 160.

11. Note, however, that optimal distribution among clubs does not necessarily imply the correct number of clubs. If the private returns at a site decline very slowly or not at all, then it is perfectly possible that optimality in the most general sense may require that public goods be produced at only one site.

12. The necessary conditions for efficiency in public goods provision in any single community are,

$$\sum_{i=1}^{n} \frac{\partial B}{\partial Q} = \frac{\partial F}{\partial Q} \; ;$$

that is, summed marginal evaluations equal marginal cost. But the quantity of the public good (Q) which will satisfy these conditions will itself be dependent on the size of n. Immigration will increase the efficient quantity of a pure public good in a community; outmigration will decrease it. Cf. Paul A. Samuelson, "The Pure Theory of Public Expenditures," *Review of Economics and Statistics* 36 (November, 1954): 387–89.

13. Note that a community would normally be predicted to supply a larger quantity of localized public goods and services under either one or a combination of two conditions: (1) a larger population, and/or (2) higher average incomes and wealth. See James M. Buchanan and Richard E. Wagner, "An Efficiency Basis for Federal Fiscal Equalization," in *The Analysis of Public Output*, pp. 148–50.

14. For a general discussion of the taxonomy here, see Buchanan, *Demand and Supply of Public Goods.*

15. Benefit-side externalities are nonexistent in Model 1 because of the combined assumptions of pure publicness and unchanged goods quantity.

16. This is the conclusion reached by Buchanan and Wagner and upon which they placed policy emphasis. While this conclusion seems highly plausible in terms of existing reality in the United States, it depends critically on whether or not the existing population distribution falls within certain ranges. This is at base an empirical question.

17. Certain retirement and resort communities are organized on proprietary bases.

18. The local public goods model considered in this paper offers only one of several examples of the failure of orthodox marginal-cost pricing norms to provide complete prescriptive norms in the presence of nonexcludability in any form.

19. For an elaboration of this possibility in the context of the modern central city-suburban migration problem, see James M. Buchanan, "Principles of Urban Fiscal Strategy," *Public Choice* 11 (Fall, 1971): 1–16.

20. The persistence of the preference-revelation problem is developed at some length by Charles J. Goetz in "Fiscal Structure for the Cities," Committee on Urban Public Economics Seminar Series, November, 1969.

21. In terms that are more familiar to economists, we can say that taxes must be assessed in terms of some *average* per person value, whereas efficiency criteria would require that net taxes (and/or benefits) should be assigned in terms of *marginal* values. This is one way of conceptualizing the approach used by Buchanan and Wagner in their paper. We have avoided using these terms in the discussion here because, as the analysis indicates, the fiscal externalities vary as among different fiscal categories, and any average or marginal value would have to be applied only to members of defined categories.

22. See Burton Weisbrod, "Collective-Consumption Services of Individual-Consumption Goods," *Quarterly Journal of Economics* 78 (August, 1964): 471–77.

23. Paul A. Samuelson, "Aspects of Public Expenditure Theories," p. 338.

21.

Tax Instruments as Constraints
on the Disposition of Public Revenues

WITH GEOFFREY BRENNAN

> . . . *public services are never performed better than when their reward comes only in consequence of their being performed, and is proportional to the diligence in performing them.*
>
> Adam Smith

I. Introduction

In an earlier paper, we examined one facet of a "tax constitution" for Leviathan.[1] There we were concerned primarily with ways in which the constitutional selection of tax institutions might be used to limit the overall *level* of public activity, the relative withdrawal of financial resources from the private sector of the economy. In order to concentrate on this aspect of constitutional choice, we assumed that the *disposition* of governmentally collected revenues was set exogeneously (that is, independently of the tax system itself).[2] By "disposition" here we refer to the mix between those revenues devoted directly to the production or provision of goods and services valued by the taxpayers and consumers and those revenues directed to the provision of perquisites to the politicians and bureaucrats. The *disposition* of revenues, as here defined, is clearly an important element in the overall efficiency of the fiscal system, and not obviously less important than the *level* of revenues, previously analyzed.[3] Our objective in the current paper is to focus primarily on the disposition-of-revenues issue.

The analysis shares some crucial features with our earlier discussion. Again, we analyze the choice calculus of an individual at a constitutional stage, where he is in some sort of "original position" behind a Rawlsian-like "veil of ignorance." As before, this constitutional choice is to be exercised over alternative sets of basic tax arrangements which governments in postconstitutional periods are to be allowed to utilize. And, as in our earlier treatment, we pose this choice problem in a setting in which governmental activity in postconstitutional periods is predicted to be characterized by Leviathan-like proclivities. That is, we assume that the government—once allowed access to the coercive power that is implied by the power to tax—will exploit this power for its own ends. In such a model, individual voters and taxpayers exert control over the fiscal system only at the constitutional stage; they are essentially powerless to affect the government's fiscal activities in postconstitutional political settings.

Our objective is to apply this basic model of political process to the prospects for control over the disposition of revenues. Even if the potential taxpayer-beneficiary can, by means of constraints built into the tax constitution, restrain the total revenue demands of Leviathan-like governmental institutions (that is, even if the overall *level* of revenue collections is appropriately constrained), how can the potential taxpayer ensure that the revenues collected will be devoted to the provision of goods and services that he values? Once given the taxing power, what is to prevent Leviathan from utilizing revenue to further its own particular purposes (a lavish court at one period in history; high salaries, perks, and congenial working conditions for politician-bureaucrats as a class of another)?

A variety of enforcement mechanisms may, of course, be conceived. Here we focus primarily on those that may be built into the *tax structure*. The particular virtue of tax constraints, as opposed to most of the obvious alternatives, is that they build into the very structure of Leviathan's coercive power an automatic interest in wielding that power for the "common good": the natural appetites of Leviathan are mobilized to ensure that, to a substantial extent, revenues are used in the manner that taxpayers desire. The fiscal constitution becomes, in this basic sense, self-enforcing. The central ingredient in this element of a self-enforcing fiscal constitution is a particular form of earmarking; and the aim of our discussion is to indicate the line of argument that generates this earmarking result. To our knowledge, this is an argument that has not been recognized in the traditional analysis.

The paper is organized as follows. In Section II, we develop the basic model. In Section III, we examine this model in its simplest variant, and we derive our central result from the elementary geometry for that case. In Section IV, we introduce slightly more complex algebraic treatment, and we then proceed to a more realistic model in Section V. Section VI includes both a summary of the analysis and an attempt to relate it to practical issues in tax policy.

II. The Model

The quantity of the public good (or public goods bundle), G_s, provided by the monopoly government (Leviathan) is determined as

(1) $G_s = \alpha R$,

where R is total tax revenue collected and α is the proportion of that revenue devoted to outlay on the public good, G. In the earlier paper, we examined limits on R that could possibly be achieved by appropriate constitutional restrictions on the tax base and rate structure, with the value of a α given exogenously. In such a context, it is apposite to ascribe a revenue-maximizing objective to Leviathan, whether the latter is best conceived in a Niskanen-type bureaucracy model,[4] or as a "pure surplus" model, in which the maximand is the excess of revenues collected over outlays on the public good. The fact that α is fixed implies revenue-maximizing as a rational course of action in either case. (In the "pure surplus" model, the maximand becomes $(1 - \alpha)R$ which, for given α, is maximized simultaneously with R.)

However, it is evident that the value of α may depend on the tax institutions selected, and it is this relationship that we shall examine in this paper. Let us suppose that we envisage the constitutional process as one which establishes a "monarchy," under which a "king" may be treated as a utility-maximizer in the standard manner.[5] There seems to be no particular reason, in this context, for imagining the "king" to be anything other than an income-maximizer. So we ascribe to him the maximand, Y_k, where:

(2) $Y_k = R - G_s$

(3) $= (1 - \alpha)R.$

Given (3), the "king" will aim to maximize R and to minimize α (that is, to set α at zero), if R and α are unrelated. If, however, α can, in some way, be positively related to R, the maximization of Y_k may not involve the minimization of α. Recognition of this facet of the king's maximization problem provides the setting for the potential taxpayer-beneficiary's constitutional strategy in choosing tax instruments to assign to the "king" in the first place.

Before exploring this strategy in some depth, it is necessary to specify carefully the relationship of the "king" to other members of the political community. If the goods and services expected to be provided by government, G, are genuinely "public" in the nonexcludable sense, and, further, if the "king" shares in these benefits along with other consumers, α will not be reduced to zero, even if its value remains wholly within control of the "king." That is to say, if his utility function, U_k, contains an argument for G, as well as for privately divisible goods that can be enjoyed exclusively, a strict utility-maximizing calculus will involve some provision of G, and, hence, some value for α. Largely for purposes of simplifying our argument here, we shall initially assume that the "king" is wholly external to other members of the community in the sense that he does not secure any positive benefits from the provision of G, even though the latter may be described as a pure collective-consumption good for all other members of the group. A somewhat more complex model which allows the "king" to be among the sharers of public goods benefits and/or which allows for G as a direct argument in the "king's" own utility function is presented in Section V.

We should also reconcile our assumption concerning the "king" as a surplus maximizer with that which places the individual in some original position behind a veil of ignorance. In the model that follows, we treat the "king's" surplus as a potential cost to the potential tax-payer-beneficiary. It might be argued that in the genuine state of ignorance required for a constitutional perspective, each person would reckon on his own chances to be king, in which case postconstitutional transfers in the "king's" favor might be perceived to be costless, at least in some expected value sense. Several responses may be made to this possible criticism. First, it seems reasonable to suppose that extensive redistributions in favor of the "king" or "ruling class" will run counter to the direction that would be preferred by individuals behind the veil of ignorance (whether those preferred distributions exhibit Rawlsian or other characteristics): such "perverse" redistributions imply an expected cost, though not necessarily up to the full amount of the transfer involved. Secondly, the surplus which accrues to the "king" may give rise to wasteful "rent-seeking," which, in the limit, will dissipate the full value of the surplus itself (and indeed, under some assumptions about individuals' behavior, might exceed it). Thirdly, the process by which the surplus is attained may involve welfare losses, against which no welfare gain from collective goods supply can be set. Finally, there is some historical evidence that "kings" have been conceived to be entirely separated from the community, to be outside the "constitution"—rulers (and armies) have been imported, sometimes voluntarily.

Thus, except where we explicitly indicate otherwise, we shall assume that the king does not benefit from public goods supply, and that the surplus that accrues to the king is pure loss to the society. Both assumptions can be considerably weakened without the central results being lost, but initially it is convenient to deal with the more extreme case.

III. Public Goods Supply under a Pure Surplus Maximizer: Geometric Analysis

The characteristic feature of our Leviathan model is that, in the absence of any constraints that force him to act differently, the "king" will set α at zero. That is, he will provide none of the public good, G, valued by citizens. He will simply maximize tax revenues, R, and he will utilize all of these for the funding of his own privately consumed goods and services. The question to be posed is as follows: Is there any way in which tax institutions may be selected, at the constitutional stage, so that α will not be set at zero—so that at least some G will be provided?

By our Leviathan-like assumptions about political process in post-constitutional periods, the potential taxpayer-beneficiaries have no direct control over the quantity of G provided by government. How can the "king" be induced to supply some positive quantity as a part of his own utility-maximizing behavior? Such inducement may be provided if, by supplying G, total revenue collections are increased sufficiently to increase Y_k. That is to say, an increase in α, the proportion of revenue devoted to the financing of G, may, in certain cases, increase the value of $(1 - \alpha)R$, provided there is a positive relationship between α and R.

Total revenues, R, are a function of the tax base and rate structure. In order to generate the required positive relationship between R and α, therefore, the base and rate structure, the essential determinants of R, must be variable and somehow related to the provision of G. This suggests that the tax base, whether it be an expenditure item or an item of income, must be *complementary* with the provision of G, as reflected in the independent behavioral adjustments of the taxpayer-beneficiaries.

The tax-base variable, B, may be arranged so that it is subject to some direct control by the taxpayer-beneficiaries. The public goods variable, G, is, by our assumptions, under the direct control of government. Hence, we have a reaction-function sequence that may be illustrated in familiar diagrammatics. In Figure 21-1, we measure G along the abscissa, and B along the ordinate, both in dollar units. Consider now the curve NN', which is drawn to be horizontal over the range out to the production constraint. This represents the locus of equilibrium consumption levels of B as the quantity of G increases, or alternatively, the reaction curve (line of optima, ridge line) traced out by the utility-maximizing reaction of taxpayer-beneficiaries in "supplying" B for each possible level of G. Over the relevant range along NN', note that the "supply" of taxable base, B, is invariant with the provision of G. In such a situation, the government would have no incentive at all to use any tax revenues collected to provide a positive quantity of G. It can maximize R by levying the highest allowable

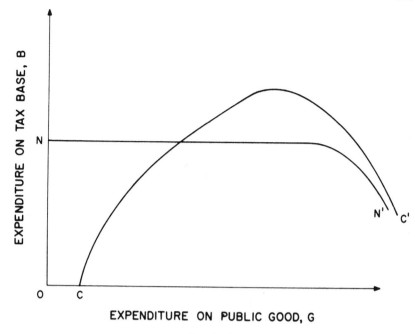

EXPENDITURE ON PUBLIC GOOD, G

Fig. 21-1

tax rate on B and then maximize Y_k by using all of the R to satisfy its own strictly private needs. Note that this seems to be the relationship that would essentially prevail under a fully comprehensive income base for taxation, where the base for allowable taxation is the full income of persons.

Contrast this situation with one in which B is highly complementary with G. The curve CC' in Fig. 21-1 depicts this case. Note that here the amount of taxable base "supplied" by the taxpayer-beneficiaries increases with the amount of G provided by government, at least over a substantial relevant range. And, as Fig. 21-1 suggests, there may be situations where any revenue collection is impossible without some positive provision of the public good: individuals will simply not spend money on B unless there is some G to consume with it.

In order to determine how much G will be provided, it is necessary to specify the relationship between tax revenues and the tax base. For this purpose, we assume that the government is limited to a specific rate structure, which for ease of treatment we take to be proportional.[6] This allows us, in Fig. 21-2, to depict a relationship between the equilibrium amount of B consumed by individuals and the level of G, in the presence of the revenue-maximizing proportional tax rate, t^*, applied to the designated base, B. This is shown by QQ, which will in general differ from $C'C$ in Fig. 21-1. The curve, QQ, traces out

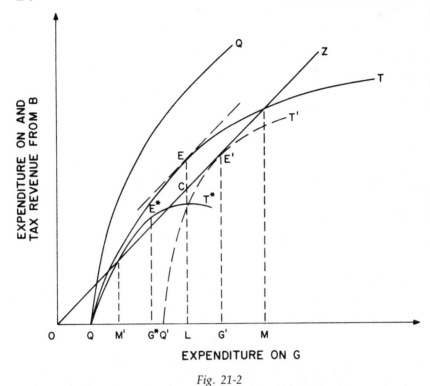

Fig. 21-2

the behavioral adjustments of taxpayer-beneficiaries in generating taxable base under the imposition of the maximum-revenue tax. (*QQ* may lie above, below, or be coincident with *CC'* over any part of the relevant range, with the precise relationship being primarily dependent here on the income elasticity of demand for the base variable.) The curve, *QT*, in Fig. 21-2 relates the tax collections derived from the revenue-maximizing tax on *B* to levels of *G* provision. For each level of *G*, the vertical distance from the abscissa to *QT* represents total tax revenue. The vertical distance between *QT* and *QQ* represents net-of-tax expenditures on *B*.

On the basis of the set of relationships indicated in Fig. 21-2, what level of spending on *G* will the surplus-maximizing "king" opt for? Given that he is restricted to tax base *B* and a proportional rate structure, we can answer this question by constructing a 45-degree ray, *OZ*, from the origin. Since all variables are measured in dollar units, the location of a position on the 45-degree line implies that *all* revenues collected from the tax are required for spending on the provision of *G*. There is no net surplus. Clearly, if *B* is the only tax source available, points to the left of *M'* are infeasible: the maximum revenue that can be raised from taxing B cannot, over this initial range, sustain the levels of G that are required to generate such revenues in the first place. Positions to the right of M' and below M *are* feasible in the sense that the levels of outlay on G required can be financed by levies on the designated tax base, B. If the relationships are as depicted in Fig. 21-2, the "king's" surplus is maximized at E, where the "marginal cost" of producing more G is equal to the "marginal revenue" generated by that provision (where the slope of QT is unity). At this point, spending on G is measured by OL (equal to LC), and total revenue collections are LE, with a maximum surplus of EC. The proportion of revenue spent on G, the α previously noted, is LC/LE. This illustration demonstrates that tax institutions—and specifically the selection of an appropriate tax base—may serve to ensure that the "king" (or, more generally, the monopoly government) will spend a share of tax revenues on financing valued output in order to maximize his own utility, without any enforcing agency, in a setting where, without the tax-base constraint, spending on G would be nil. The surplus-maximizing solution for government or the "king" may, however, generate varying levels of G, depending on the tax base selected and on the precise shape of the complementary relationship between the base and the public good. Suppose, for example, that a tax base, B^*, is selected such that QT shifts to the shape shown by QT^* in Fig. 21-2. Net surplus is maximized at E^*. But G^* may not be the predicted efficient level of outlay on the valued public good; such a constitutional arrangement may succeed in raising α only to ensure that an unduly restricted level of outlay be undertaken by government.

The construction does suggest, however, that, if there should exist an unconstrained choice among possible tax bases, with varying degrees of complementarity between these and the public good, an optimum optimorum solution might be imposed constitutionally. This would require that the tax base be selected such that, when the "king" levies the allowable revenue-maximizing proportional tax rate on this base, the only viable budgetary position requires that virtually all funds collected be spent on providing the good, and further, that these finds will purchase precisely the efficient quantity, as predicted at the constitutional level. Such a solution is shown at E', where G' is the predicted efficient level of outlay on the public good, and where $Q'T'$ suggests that the position at E' is the only possible position for viable budgetary behavior on the part of the government. There is no surplus left over for exploitation by the revenue-maximizing, perquisite-seeking "king." Under such constitutional "fine tuning" as this, the problem of ensuring the predicted efficient level of outlay is incorporated into the problem of ensuring that revenues collected will be disbursed efficiently.

Possible criticism of the analysis at this point involves the unconstrained-choice assumption. Such "fine tuning" may not be pos-

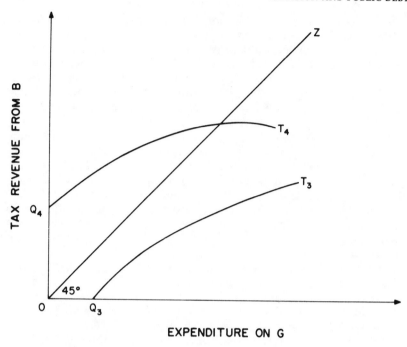

EXPENDITURE ON G

Fig. 21-3

sible, especially when it is recognized that the complementarity relationships for feasible tax-base usage may be severely restricted in number, and, even among the feasible set, the relationships may be narrowly confined. Constrained optimization for the potential taxpayer-beneficiary will in general require trade-offs between allowing the king additional surplus on the one hand, and accepting levels of public goods outlay which differ from that desired.

Indeed, far from there being an unconstrained choice over tax base each generating a different level of G and amount of king's surplus, we must face the possibility that there will be *no* tax base available which constrains the king to produce any G at all. Thus, to demonstrate some of the effective limits on the central proposition, consider Fig. 21-3. If a tax base selected is too narrow, in relation to the public good in question, a viable budgetary solution may prove impossible. For example, consider a situation like that depicted by the curve Q_3T_3 in Fig. 21-3, which nowhere touches the 45-degree line. As an illustration, suppose that an attempt were made to finance highways exclusively by taxes on automobile air-conditioners. It is probable that the revenue-maximizing tax on such a narrow base would generate far less revenue than would be required even to maintain a road network, much less construct it. A second possibility might be that the complementarity between a selected base and the public good might be insufficiently strong to offer any incentive for public goods provision by the surplus-maximizing "king." Consider a situation as depicted in the Q_4T_4 curve in Fig. 21-3. Unless otherwise constrained, and despite the complementarity between the tax base and the public good, the "king" will maximize his own surplus by providing none of the good, by keeping α at zero.

What is required for the disciplinary influence of selected tax base constraints on governmental fiscal behavior in disposing of tax revenues is a tax base that exhibits a *strongly* complementary relationship with the public good *and* is sufficiently broad to finance its provision. It is not entirely obvious that such a tax base will be available for each of the public goods that the taxpayer-voter might demand. We can, however, think of some examples where the required relation does hold—and the highway–public road case is one such. In the absence of a road network, few automobiles would be privately purchased and used. In the presence of a road network, automobile usage is "supplied." Hence, a general constitutional requirement that roads be financed exclusively by taxes levied on automobiles (perhaps along with other privately purchased road-using inputs—gasoline, oil, tires, etc.) will ensure that the government, even in the model of the pure surplus-maximizing "king," will spend some part of its tax revenues on road construction and maintenance.

IV. The Surplus Maximizer: Algebraic Treatment

The basic relationships inherent in our central proposition, along with the limits within which these relationships must operate may be more fully captured in a simple algebraic treatment.

In the model, the "king" seeks to maximize

(4) $Y_k = R^* - G.$

We have specified that the tax base be chosen so as to depend on public outlay on G, so we may write,

(5) $R^* = aB^*(G),$

where B^* is the aggregate value of tax base B, gross of tax, when the revenue-maximizing proportional tax is imposed, and where a is the proportion of B^* collected in tax revenue. Then, substituting (5) into (4) and differentiating with respect to G, we get,

(6) $\dfrac{dY_K}{dG} = a\,\dfrac{\partial B^*}{\partial G} + B^*\,\dfrac{\partial a}{\partial G} - 1.$

In order for the constraining effect on governmental behavior to be present, this expression must, somewhere, be greater than zero, or in the limit, equal to zero.

Complementarity between B and G implies

(7) $\dfrac{\partial B^*}{\partial G} > 0.$

But this is not sufficient to ensure that

(8) $a\,\dfrac{\partial B^*}{\partial G} + B^*\,\dfrac{\partial a}{\partial G} > 1$

particularly since the only requirement on a is that

(9) $0 < a < 1.$

Under reasonable assumptions, however, we should note that $\partial a/\partial G$ is likely to be positive, and, further, that the second term on the left-hand side of (8) may dominate. Hence, it seems likely that the condition (8) will hold for some value of G above zero. It is possible to construct cases in which the revenue-maximizing tax rate, t^*, declines as G rises without violating the complementarity assumption, but on balance it seems unlikely.

Let us suppose, however, that the condition (8) is not satisfied. Is there a simple way of increasing the likelihood that it may be met? We may first observe the effect of *tying extra or supplemental revenue from general sources* to the particular revenue that the "king" (bureau) is able to derive from the particular base, B. Hence, in lieu of (5), we have

(10) $R^* = (1 + \beta)aB^*(g)$

where $\beta > 0$, and

(11) $\dfrac{dY_K}{dG} = (1 + \beta)a\,\dfrac{\partial B^*}{\partial G} + (1 + \beta)B^*\,\dfrac{\partial a}{\partial G} - 1.$

Clearly, if both $\partial B^*/\partial G$ and $\partial a/\partial G$ exceed zero, (11) exceeds (6) for $\beta > 0$, for a given value of G in the relevant range, and there exists *some* value for β which will guarantee that (11) is positive for positive values for G. Moreover, the higher the value of β is, the larger the value of G for which (11) is zero.[7] Therefore, by increasing the value of

β, we can both ensure that the "king" will want to provide some G, and increase the amount of G thereby obtained (at least up to the point where the complementarity relationship ceases).

While accepting this emendation analytically, it may be challenged on the grounds that it seems inconsistent with the underlying institutional assumptions. While one can imagine the possibility that the "king's" ability to raise *general* revenue might be tied to the revenue from base B, it does seem as if, once he has been allowed access to some more general tax source, he would use that source exclusively and spend all the revenue on private goods. In a more realistic institutional setting, however, it may be possible to establish a bureau whose sole function is to raise revenue from some general source, under the constraint that it be handed over directly to other public goods-supplying bureaus in direct relation to the latters' revenue-raising activities from the assigned complementary tax bases.[8]

If even this seems implausible, roughly the same effect might in any case be achieved by assigning to the "king" several tax bases, *all of which* are complements to the public good, G. Suppose that there should exist a whole set of potential bases, $B_1, B_2, \ldots, B_n$. Consider assigning both B_1 and B_2 for usage as possible tax bases to the surplus-maximizing "king." In this case,

(12) $\quad R^* = a_1 B_1(G) + a_n B_2^*(G)$

and

$$(13) \quad \frac{dY_K}{dG} = a_1 \frac{\partial B_1^*}{\partial G} + a_2 \frac{\partial B_2^*}{\partial G} + B_1^* \frac{\partial a_1}{\partial G} + B_2^* \frac{\partial a_2}{\partial G} - 1,$$

where

$$(14) \quad \frac{\partial B_1^*}{\partial G}, \frac{\partial B_2^*}{\partial G}, \frac{\partial a_1}{\partial G}, \frac{\partial a_2}{\partial G} > 0.$$

As before, (13) exceeds (6) for values of G in the relevant range, and the value of G for which (13) is zero (if it exists) exceeds the comparable value of G in (6). Hence, by adding bases to the government's taxing retinue, all of which are complements to G, we both increase the possibility that it will prove profitable to provide some public goods, some G, and increase the level of G that will be provided.

The preceding arguments may be synthesized in simple diagrammatics. In Fig. 21-4, *DD* represents the potential taxpayer's prediction of the aggregate demand curve for the public good G (or public goods bundle) that will prevail in postconstitutional periods. This prediction represents his best estimate from behind the veil of ignorance in a genuine constitutional setting. The *MC* line indicates the (predicted)

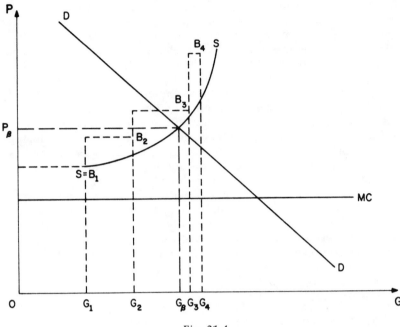

Fig. 21-4

"physical" cost of public goods provision (the opportunity cost of a unit of G in terms of private goods forgone). The public good can, however (as our whole analysis has been designed to discuss) be provided only under some arrangement that involves an additional institutional cost, reflected by the "king's" surplus.

The supply curve for G lies, therefore, above the MC line at all points, and this curve can take two forms. If supplementary revenue from the complementary base with tied funds (i.e., some sort of dollar-for-dollar arrangement) raised from general funding is institutionally feasible, then the "supply curve" may be as depicted by the smooth curve SS in Fig. 21-4, a curve that is continuous, upward-sloping above MC and which allows for a single optimal value of G, namely, G_β. At this point, the "king's" surplus is maximized, at a value of $(P_\beta - MC)G_\beta$.

If supplementary revenue from the assigned base is institutionally infeasible, as seems possible, then the alternative strategy of assigning a *number* of bases, all of which are complementary with G, may be used. The "supply curve" in this case connects a number of disjoint points, B_1, B_2, B_3, B_4, in Fig. 21-4, which will also trace out an unsloping sequence. In this case, the preferred level of G will have to be selected from the two alternatives, G_2 and G_3, with the precise marginal adjustment being precluded by the nature of the institutional constraints assumed. It is of course possible that the point B_1 will lie *above* DD, in which case the constitutional choice involves an option between a base assignment that will allow for too much G at too high a price (in terms of the withdrawal of surplus)—or none at all. In a sense, Fig. 21-4 depicts the basic elements of the constitutional decision on the size of the public sector, given the assumptions made about the postconstitutional political process and given that tax bases have been assigned to the "king" in the most "efficient" manner, as here indicated.[9]

V. The Nonsurplus Maximizer

Before turning to possible policy implications, it will be useful to modify the analysis in the direction of a more widely shared image of government. What effect will be exerted on rational constitutional choices among tax instruments if the model is changed so as to allow the institutions that supply public goods—be these kings, bureaucrats, politicians, or judges—to be somewhat less intractable than the earlier treatment makes them appear? The most selfish of kings or bureaucrats may supply *some* public goods, even from purely self-interested motivations, and especially if they themselves secure shares in the nonexcludable benefits. Some law and order, some defense, some fireworks, will be supplied by a king for his own benefit; and the masses can then be expected to secure spillover benefits. Beyond this, political decision-makers, even if unconstrained directly by the citizenry, may be honorable men and women motivated by a genuine sense of public duty; kings may care about their subjects.

We now want to allow for this, while still retaining the assumption that the government will attempt to maximize revenues from any tax base or bases assigned to it. We want to examine a model in which some G will be provided due to the "king's" utility function. In Fig. 21-5, assume that some arbitrarily chosen tax base yields a maximum revenue to the "king" of $O\overline{X}$. If the "king" is a pure surplus maximizer as previously analyzed, he will, of course, retain all of this revenue for personal usage. If, however, G is included as an argument in his utility function, he will want to provide some G. The "king's" preferences in this case may be represented in a set of indifference contours defined on B and G and exhibiting the standard properties. The rate at which a dollar's worth of revenues in the "king's" hands can be transformed into a dollar's worth of outlay on public goods is, of course, unity. Hence, the "price line" faced by the "king" is the 45-degree line drawn southeasterly from $\overline{X}$. Equilibrium is attained at

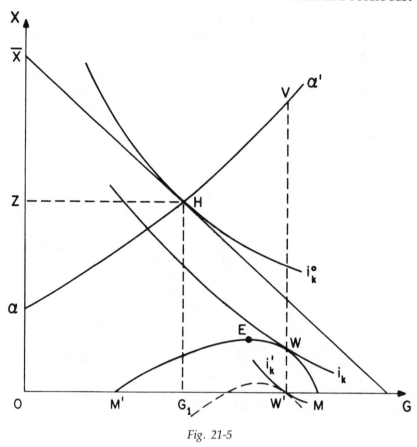

Fig. 21-5

H; the amount of revenue "given up" to provide the public good is $\overline{XZ}$; the amount of revenue retained as surplus is OZ, with the ratio $\overline{XZ}/\overline{OX}$ being the α previously discussed. This ratio is simply the "king's" average propensity to consume G out of revenues collected.

The curve $\alpha\alpha'$ in Fig. 21-5 is the locus of equilibrium positions as the "king" is assigned more comprehensive bases for tax levies, all of which are independent of spending on G. (Note that an α of unity would imply that this curve lies along the abscissa.)

In the setting depicted in Fig. 21-5, what is the effect of substituting a tax base that is complementary to G for the independent tax bases assumed in tracing out the $\alpha\alpha'$ curve? To answer this question, we may transform figure 2 into Fig. 21-5 by relating surplus to levels of G. Recall from Fig. 21-2 that, at M', there is no net surplus, and that this rises to a maximum at L, while falling back to zero at M. We simply translate these results into Fig. 21-5, with the same labeling. The curve $M'EM$ now represents the transformation possibilities facing the "king." He will attain equilibrium at W, with W' being the total outlay made on G. Note that this solution involves more public goods and less surplus than the equilibrium at E reached in the surplus-maximizing model.

The dramatic difference between this complementary tax-base constraint and its absence can now be indicated by comparing the costs (in terms of surplus retained by the "king") of securing the amount of G shown at W'. In the constrained model, these costs are measured by the vertical distance $W'W$. But, for the same G, these costs rise to $W'V$ in the unconstrained case. If the potential taxpayer-beneficiary is assumed to be confronted with an unlimited set of choice alternatives, he will conceptually be able to reduce the retained (wasted) surplus to zero in the limiting case, while at the same time ensuring that a predicted efficient level of outlay on public goods will be made. In Fig. 21-5, if we assume that W' is the efficient level desired, a tax base may be selected that exhibits the complementarity properties required to generate a curve like the dotted one drawn through W'. Note that, in contrast to the comparable curve in the surplus-maximizing model, this curve can lie above zero along a part of its range. Surplus is reduced to zero (assuming the required properties of the "king's" utility function) because the "king" places an independent marginal valuation on G.

VI. Toward Tax Policy

The analysis of this paper indirectly supplies an efficiency argument for a particular form of earmarking. The normative implication is that each activity of government, each budgetary component, should have assigned to it a specified tax instrument, or set of instruments, designed not merely to ensure a level of revenue adequate to and appropriate for a predicted desirable level of the activity, but more particularly to introduce complementarity between the tax base and the governmental activity—and the stronger the complementarity the better. We have already referred to the most obvious real-world example—the financing of roads from gasoline and/or automobile taxes. Government broadcasting financed by taxes on receivers offers another. When possible, the argument suggests that fees and tolls should be used in the governmental sale of partitionable services, perhaps even at the costs of some underutilization of facilities; it is unlikely that there could be tax bases for a good more complementary than the good itself.

Less conspicuous examples are worth mentioning. Earl Thompson has recently argued for taxes on capital to finance defense on the grounds that capital accumulation leads to the threat of external aggression.[10] A similar argument might be made as concerns internal law and order. Thompson's argument is that there will be excessive accumulation of coveted capital in the absence of capital taxation. One implication is that capital and defense outlay are complementary. Hence, our analysis points toward a similar conclusion to Thompson's, but for somewhat different reasons, and with the different extra requirement that revenue from the tax on capital be explicitly earmarked for defense against external aggressors and for internal provision of law and order.[11]

Our purpose in the above is to suggest examples for possible application of our analysis. We have made no attempt to determine whether or not the norms suggested for tax policy can be extended to cover all components in the budgets of modern governments. And we have not examined the severe informational requirements necessary for rational choice in a genuine constitutional setting. However, the general institution of earmarked taxes is familiar. The conventional wisdom in normative public finance theory has condemned earmarking essentially on the grounds that any restriction on revenue usage tends to reduce the flexibility of the budgetary decision-maker who is charged with the responsibility of allocating total governmental outlay among activities. This normative argument against earmarked bases is conceived in a benevolent-despot image of governmental process, one that envisages a centralized decision-maker divorced from the citizenry but always motivated to act strictly in the interests of the latter, in the "public interest." Such an image is not consistent either with models of democratic decision-making or with models that allow some role for the self-interest of politicians and bureaucrats. Once the government is perceived in an institutional setting that bears any remote resemblance to reality, the role of earmarking as one means of securing more efficient fiscal outcomes must be reexamined.

An argument in support of earmarked taxes has been advanced in post-Wicksellian, public choice theory,[12] and it will be useful to compare this with that argument which emerges here. If decisions on public spending are assumed to be made democratically even at the postconstitutional level, there is a self-evident argument for requiring that benefits be tied directly to costs. Voters, or their representatives, are likely to choose outcomes more rationally, more efficiently, if they can compare costs and benefits for each separate activity rather than for a multicomponent budget. General-fund financing ensures that fiscal choices are made under almost maximal uncertainty.

Our analysis differs from the standard public choice model in its basic assumption about postconstitutional political process. We explicitly drop the central assumption that budgetary spending and taxes are determined through an effectively democratic voting process in postconstitutional periods. The argument for earmarking that emerges is derived directly from the political model in which in-period fiscal decisions are made by revenue-maximizing politician-bureaucrats who may have at least some power to secure a share of tax revenues as surplus for themselves. A constitutionally imposed tie-in between the tax base and the provision of the public good becomes a means of exerting discipline on those who do make fiscal decisions. As such, it is not at all out of place in a democratic decision model, and it may be interpreted as reinforcing other arguments noted above. One plausible model of democracy involves attempts by rotating majority coalitions to maximize net fiscal transfers to their members at the expense of members of minorities. The disciplinary argument for earmarking applies equally well to this model as to the more cynical model of bureaucratic domination. All that is required is that the words "majority coalition" be substituted for the word "king" in the earlier parts of the paper.

Our base argument is indeed simple. Effectively designed earmarking may limit the extent to which government, any government, can exploit the tax-paying public; government may be given a *positive* incentive to provide the goods and services that taxpayers want. The decision-makers, whoever these may be, can be kept "honest." Given the nature, size, and diffusiveness of governmental activities and institutions that we currently observe, such considerations are surely relevant.

Notes

We are indebted to members of the Public Choice Seminar at Virginia Polytechnic Institute for helpful comments, and especially to Mark Crain and E. C. West for useful criticism.

1. "Towards a Tax Constitution for Leviathan," *Journal of Public Economics* 8 (December, 1977): 255–73.

2. This setting was explicitly designed to bring our earlier discussion into conformity with the traditional treatment of tax reform. This procedure allowed us to relate our analysis to the familiar issues in tax policy—comprehensiveness in tax bases, progressivity in rate structure, and so on.

3. A third element determining the overall efficiency of the expenditure structure, over and beyond both the *level* and the *disposition*, is the *composition* of budgetary outlay as among separate public goods components. We do not discuss this element explicitly here, though our analysis does have some implications for it.

4. In the Niskanen model, α is effectively unity by virtue of constraints inherent in the political process. Leviathan achieves its surrogate equivalent of "surplus" by producing excessive quantities of G. See William Niskanen, *Bureaucracy and Representative Government* (Chicago: Aldine, 1971).

5. Both the "monarchy" and the "king" here are, of course, artifacts constructed solely for convenience in exposition. The latter can be interpreted as

a shorthand expression for the appropriately chosen collection of politician-bureaucrats whose behavior generates fiscal outcomes in postconstitutional political settings, or even for the decisive majority in a context of revolving coalitions where that majority exploits the minority. In this latter setting, Section V is probably more relevant.

6. For a discussion which bears on the relation between rate structure and maximum revenue yield, see Brennan and Buchanan, "Towards a Tax Constitution for Leviathan."

7. Given the second-order conditions implied by the shapes of CC' and NN' in Fig. 21-1, i.e., $\partial^2 B^*/\partial G^2 < 0$.

8. There is an analogy of sorts between such an arrangement as here described and the return of bloc grants or revenue shares to local units based on "fiscal effort" criteria. The purpose in the two cases could, however, scarcely be more opposed. With the "fiscal effort" criteria, the purpose is to ensure that local governments levy sufficiently high taxes on citizens. With our model, by contrast, the underlying purpose is to ensure that tax monies are expended on public goods rather than on bureaucrats' perks.

9. Although their normative emphasis is quite different from that of this paper, Atkinson and Stern introduce the complementarity between public goods and the tax base as a determinant of the allocatively optimal budget. See A. B. Atkinson and N. H. Stern, "Pigou, Taxation, and Public Goods," *Review of Economic Studies* 41 (April, 1974): 119–28.

10. Earl Thompson, "Taxation and National Defense," *Journal of Political Economy* 82 (July–August, 1974): 755–82.

11. In this general sense, it is clear that the analysis is related to the discussion and analysis of the capitalization of public goods benefits and taxes into land values, and especially in the context of a set of local governments among which persons may move.

12. See James M. Buchanan, "The Economics of Earmarked Taxes," *Journal of Political Economy* 71 (October, 1963): 457–69. Also, see James M. Buchanan, *Public Finance in Democratic Process* (Chapel Hill: University of North Carolina Press, 1967), esp. chapter 6.

22.
Dialogues Concerning Fiscal Religion

WITH RICHARD E. WAGNER

I. Introduction

In writing and publishing *Democracy in Deficit* (1977), we were aware that we would arouse antagonism from many camps. We attacked the Keynesian orthodoxy in macroeconomic policy, yet for expository purposes we accepted the central features of the Keynesian model. We did this because we wanted to focus on the manner in which the Keynesian precepts would be applied within democratic political institutions. The Keynesian theory of policy proceeds as if policy is enacted by benevolent and omniscient despots. Our primary inquiry concerned the probable conduct of policy once we allowed for the obvious reality that results emerge through democratic processes. Our main emphasis was not on macroeconomic analysis as such, though aspects of our presumptions about macroeconomics appear in several places in *Democracy in Deficit*. As we acknowledged in the book, we do not deny that major unsettled issues remain in macroeconomic analysis, treated independently of the implementation of policy. And, of course, these issues deserve the efforts and attention of economists. But does not the "political economy" of policy also merit notice?

Our macroeconomic position cannot be simply described by Keynesian, Monetarist, or Marxist. It is not, therefore, surprising that we have attracted the attention of a disparate set of critics. Before responding to the critics specifically, we should express our gratitude to Professor Karl Brunner, as well as to the critics who have made contributions. When all is said, the worst treatment authors can receive is neglect. Intelligent criticism carries its own mark of mutual respect. We hope that this brief response lives up to the standards of our critics.

II. Who Were the Keynesians?

Professor Tobin reacts personally to our criticism of American Keynesians and in so doing he seriously misinterprets our argument. If we can be allowed the occasional rhetorical flourish that may well have been misleading, we did not intend to suggest that Keynesianism arrived full-blown in Washington in 1961. Keynesian economics was not really brought in denim carpetbags from Cambridge, Minneapolis, and New Haven. The policy advice of the *1962 Economic Report* did not sweep out the long stagnant swamps in one blow. Had this interpretation described our reading of the historical record, we should have named more names, given credit where due, and we should have tried to cite line and verse. But surely such an interpretation gives far too much influence to the particular policy advisors of the early 1960s or of any other time. Keynesian economics came to Washington and to the consciousness of our politicians in fits and starts from the 1940s, through the 1950s, and into the 1960s. It came via the textbooks read by budding politicians of the whole postwar era; it came in the academic and intellectual discourse of the 1950s; it came in the financial and economic journalism of this period.

We do not suggest that the Camelot economists pulled off a monumental coup and took control over the implementation of economic policy, as Tobin seems to think we do. Camelot economics merely represented the culmination of a process in which the understanding of economic reality that informs public policy changed essentially from the classical vision to the Keynesian. The dominant belief about our economic order came to be Keynesian. Our critique, therefore, was aimed at a generation of economists rather than at a handful of readily identifiable persons who, perchance, may have been in the vanguard when the politicians finally began to act out the repeated messages they had been receiving.

III. The Theory of Public Debt

At least three of our critics question the theory of public debt that our book embodies. Tobin charges that our argument is "factually false" in attributing the "no future burden" position to the Keynesian economists. This charge is again related in part to Tobin's misinterpretation of our targets. We challenge anyone to read the elementary textbooks of the 1945–65 period and to find more than the occasional passing reference to the future burden of public debt. The overwhelming preponderance of the discussion is on the other side, discussion that suggests the fallacy of the classical position rather than its elemental truth. Interestingly, in this respect, we could scarcely do better than to cite Tobin himself who, in 1965, asked, and answered: "Does debt-financing . . . place a 'burden' on future generations? The answer has long been . . . 'no' among academic economists."[1]

Exegesis aside, however, do the Keynesians, even today, accept the theory of debt burden that we have tried to present, in *Democracy in Deficit* and elsewhere? If Tobin correctly summarizes the Keynesian view, it seems clear that they do not. He acknowledges the presence of "future burden" only to the extent that capital accumulation is affected adversely by debt issue. But this possible effect of debt finance is only a by-product of its primary influence. By comparison with taxation, debt issue reduces the charges on current-period taxpayers, on voters, on legislators who are sensitive to voters' wishes, and increases charges on persons who will live and vote in future periods. This fact is too elementary to warrant repetition save for the continuing refusal of highly sophisticated economists to accept its logical consequences.

Robert Barro fully appreciates the central issue in debt theory, and we welcome his constructive criticism of our thesis. We are encouraged that the long-forgotten Ricardian equivalence theorem has found an elegant modern defender. Barro's suggestion that our own model of public debt is closer to the Keynesian than to the Ricardian is only partially correct, however, for the relations among the Ricardian, the Keynesian, and our theories of debt entail consideration of two separate dimensions. The Ricardian theory, as well as our own, says that public debt will shift the temporal location of the tax burden from taxpayers in the present to taxpayers in the future. In this respect, we stand with the Ricardians in opposition to the Keynesians. Taxpayers in the future will, of course, be either the same people as taxpayers in the present, only older, or children of taxpayers in the present. Barro suggests that present taxpayers will take full account of the future tax liability entailed by debt finance, in which event debt finance will be indistinguishable from tax finance in its impact. This identity results because present taxpayers will increase their saving in response to debt finance, and will do so in an amount sufficient to amortize the debt when it comes due.

We differ from the Ricardians because we do not think that future taxes are fully discounted. We think that public debt is different from taxation precisely because we, unlike Barro, do not think that people act with an infinite-lived perspective. While the debate between us and the Ricardians should be open to empirical examination, let us be careful to avoid adding to existing confusion here. We are not concerned with the differential impact of these alternative financing instruments on the private economy. Our main concern is with how the issue of debt differs from taxation in its impact on the *public economy.* Niskanen is correct in noting that our proposition that debt finance will increase public spending because of its effect in reducing the perceived price of government entails the proposition that debt finance will increase aggregate spending. Nonetheless, our book is about the public sector import of debt finance.

Our thesis suggests that an expanded use of debt finance will lower the perceived price of government, thereby producing a larger public budget. Niskanen presents evidence to support this thesis. Within a model of federal spending, Niskanen finds that a relative decrease in the importance of tax finance (a relative expansion in the use of debt finance) lends to an increase in federal spending, and with an elasticity of about 0.6, meaning that a one hundred dollar replacement of taxation by debt would increase public spending by about sixty dollars.

Where does Niskanen's evidence leave Barro's proposition in support of the Ricardian Equivalence Theorem? If debt is viewed as less costly than taxation, why would tax finance be used at all? Perhaps we should distinguish between average and marginal perceptions here. If public expenditure is viewed as less costly when financed by debt than when financed by taxation, there would seem to be strong tendencies for borrowing to take place. Suppose we postulate the reasonable proposition that the perceived cost of any source of revenue rises with the use made of that source. An equilibrium distribution between debt and taxation would result when the marginal perceived costs were equal. At this margin, the Ricardian Theorem would come into effect. Yet in total terms debt finance will have increased public spending.

In closing this section we may discuss briefly the empirical indications that are used to signify a proclivity toward debt finance. Both Barro and Gordon suggest that we have interpreted the post–World War II period incorrectly because the ratio of debt to GNP has been declining over this period. Barro further suggests that the identical pattern of declining debt/GNP ratio holds for all postwar periods and uses this observation to suggest there has been no change in the historical pattern of debt finance.

We contend that debt/GNP ratios are inappropriate for the analytical task at hand, and that actual amounts of debt are the appropriate magnitudes. What we are concerned with is action by individuals in a political context. The patterns of a debt/GNP ratio are irrelevant to such rational political action. What is relevant is that the ability to borrow reduces the price of government below what it would have been had only tax finance been used. This, and only this, is what is relevant to our thesis. That the ratio of debt to GNP is declining is of no behavioral relevance.

The observed behavior of politicians and the observed patterns of policy discussion also support our central hypothesis. We do not find politicians generally indifferent in their reactions to tax finance and debt finance. This absence of indifference would seem to suggest that the Ricardian Equivalence Theorem is not fully descriptive of economic reality. Historically, the discussion of public debt in the pre–Keynesian era was accompanied by discussion of sinking funds to provide for debt amortization. A sinking fund is, in fact, an institutional arrangement that has the effect of approximating the results described by the Ricardian Theorem. Moreover, we still observe debt limits at all levels of government. These considerations suggest that, in all ages, political action has been on our side of the issue in question, recognizing the need for constitutional-institutional arrangements to constrain the tendencies toward debt finance.

IV. Rational Expectations and Public Choice: A Cautionary Criticism

Barro's reconstruction of the Ricardian Theorem on public debt is derivative from the rational expectations hypothesis in the theory of macroeconomic policy, a development to which Barro himself has made major contributions. As we noted in our book, we do not accept the thesis that the implications of rationality are the same for both private choice and public choice. We submit that the particular manifestations of rational economic conduct depend on the institutional setting within which choice takes place. People may be basically rational in all conduct, but the outcomes of choice will still vary as between market choice and public choice.

We shall limit our remarks here to Barro's extension of rational expectations to public debt theory. In the theory of market exchange, so long as a sufficient number of participants possess the knowledge to act efficiently, the results are equivalent to those that would emerge if all participants should possess this knowledge. So long as a sufficient number of traders possess information and act in response to it, the marginal adjustments will insure movements toward equilibrium positions that are indistinguishable from those produced under universal omniscience over all traders.

When, however, we extend the usage of economic tools to the explanation of behavior in nonmarket situations, the generalization of the rationality postulate must be made with considerably more prudence. It is not that people are necessarily less rational, but that the informational foundations for economic conduct are weaker. Relatedly, the absence of a profit motive in government weakens the incentive to act on the knowledge that is possessed. These differences mean that there may not exist opportunities which enable those participants who possess the appropriate information to act so as to generate equilibrium results equivalent to those produced by universal omniscience.

Consider a simple example. In a competitive labor market for carpenters and plumbers, there may be no more than 5 percent of the workers in the total community who may detect a difference in returns to the two occupations, and be willing to change occupations in consequence. But the willingness to shift to this small number may be enough to ensure that wage rates of carpenters and plumbers will be equalized, a result that would, of course, also be produced if all workers in the community should know about the wage difference and be willing to shift employments in response. Consider now, however, a setting in which individuals must "vote" on a pair of alternatives, say, between the debt financing and the tax financing of a specific governmental outlay. Assume, as in our market example, that 5 percent of the voters are fully informed in that they, and only they, realize that the two alternatives are equivalent in present-value terms. The remaining 95 percent of the voters do not sense the equivalence, but instead view the debt alternative as being less costly than tax finance. Do there exist opportunities through which those whose actions correspond with the predictions of economic theory can bring the results into equivalence with those that might be forthcoming in a market setting? It seems to us that such opportunities are indeed limited, and that the median voter will likely be among the uninformed in the public choice that must be made between taxation and debt creation.

We should never lose sight of the fact that traditional economic theory works so well, in spite of the questionable status of the usual presumptions about knowledge, because values are set at the margins. In public choice theory, by contrast, there is little room for arbitrage through the actions of a few people at the margin, at least in the simple models of democratic process. A recognition of this basic difference between market and political institutions suggests that propositions derived from a model of market choice cannot be applied automatically to public choice. Consequently, much more attention should be given to the way in which information flows, learning motivations, and institutional constraints may make political or public-choice outcomes different from those that would be predicted to emerge under market choice.

V. The Two Hypotheses

William Niskanen empirically examines two hypotheses that are suggested in our book. While his evidence supports the thesis that deficits increase public outlays, it rejects the thesis that deficits produce inflation via the stimulus given to money expansion. Barro similarly finds no support for the proposition that deficits influence the supply of money. Ultimately, of course, we need a theory of the money supply process if we are to understand the relation between deficits and monetary expansion. Our examination of the relation between Federal Reserve actions and the desires of the legislature is not, of course, a theory of the money supply process. Rather, our observations on this topic simply express the importance of recognizing that the Federal Reserve is not truly independent of the legislature. Hence, legislative desires to outspend revenues will generally not, when combined with a desire not to let the increased demand for loanable funds that results from the government's borrowing requirements drive up interest rates and crowd out private investment, be neutralized by the Federal Reserve. In our framework, the rate of expansion in the supply of money will be elastic with respect to public deficits. Other variables would also go into a full model of the money supply process.

Questions of the interpretation of empirical evidence depend, of course, on the acceptability of the model used for testing. While we have some questions about the models of the money supply process advanced by Barro and Niskanen, this symposium is not the place to initiate an examination of the theory of money supply. It suffices to say here that we find Barro's and Niskanen's results and formulations suggestive, though not definitive. Barro finds a positive relation between deficits and the supply of money until he introduces a variable to account for the impact of the difference between actual and "normal" expenditures upon the supply of money. While Barro interprets this variable as accounting for wartime increases and recessionary falls in spending, it also picks up a period of rising expenditure because of the adaptive lag structure he uses. This gets us right back to the question of the relation among deficits, money, and government spending. Niskanen similarly found a positive relation between deficits and the supply of money. By bringing in a dummy variable for the period since 1966, Niskanen also found the relation between deficits and the supply of money to disappear. But what accounts for the shift in the money supply process that occurred in the mid-1960s? Perhaps the three of us are not in that much disagreement after all. We will need more work on the theory of the supply of money before we can tell.

There are some other questions that can be raised about the causal relationship between budget deficits and the growth of government. In his paper, Donald Gordon identifies a vulnerable aspect of our argument, an aspect that had also been emphasized by Victor Goldberg in his comments on a prepublication draft of the manuscript. Our hypothesis does not "explain" the observed explosion in state and local spending in postwar decades, even after we have made adjustments for central government grants, matching requirements, administrative and judicial mandates, and other federal pressures. Niskanen's evidence supports our reasoning that debt finance will lead to expanded government spending because debt reduces the perceived price of government. This proportion would seem as true for local government as for the federal government. But the money-creating power of the federal government would also seem to give an added impetus to expansion in federal spending. Yet the growth in state and local spending remains a puzzle.

Once again, of course, we must not mistake a particular coefficient for an entire model. Spending increases for many reasons, with debt finance being only one reason. It is always possible that these other factors required to describe a complete model would operate to increase state and local spending more rapidly than federal. In the absence of such a model, the implications of different rates of spending growth for our theory about debt finance must remain open-ended. Perhaps Gordon is correct: perhaps even with strict budget balance and without the Keynesian theory of economic policy, we should have had roughly the spending explosion we have observed. Perhaps history cannot be "explained," even in part, by the influence of the ideas of academic scribblers. If this is the case, we had as well join those of our colleagues who engage in the escapist world of puzzles, theorems, and proofs. But in some final sense, we simply refuse to believe that people, and their ideas, cannot exert some control over events.

VI. The Model of Political Process

Craig Roberts accuses us of political naiveté. He offers an alternative explanation of the factual record by postulating a model of a monolithic government bent on furthering its own interest, which translates directly into maximization of the size of the public sector. Keynesian economics, in Roberts' view, was used merely as the apologetics for the massive power grab that we have witnessed since the close of World War II. His explanation requires no resort to error, illusion, or institutional influence. The actors in his model are coldly rational, and they know quite well what they want and how to get it.

The last part of Donald Gordon's paper finds common ground with Craig Roberts's critique. Gordon suggests the possible contradiction between the position taken in *Budgets and Bureaucrats*,[2] and that represented in *Democracy in Deficit*. In the former, the behavior of a partially independent and uncontrollable bureaucracy in generating the observed acceleration in the growth of government was the focus of attention. The existence of this force need not, however, preclude the complementary element discussed in our book. We make no claim that the Keynesian bias is the only significant explanatory factor. Our purpose was to isolate this factor and to examine its influence critically. There seems to us to be no inconsistency in examining other factors, at other times and places, that may either offset or complement the one that was treated in our book.

We do not deny the apparent correspondence of many aspects of the monopoly-government model and the reality that we observe. But we share with Tobin the view that such a fully closed model leaves no room at all for normatively inspired policy discussion. If all that we can do is describe the behavior of self-seeking agents who act on behalf of the government, what is the point of our activity as economists? Surely, there must be improvement that is possible, and surely there is some role for economists in achieving this. At this level of discussion our position is somewhere between Tobin on the one hand and Roberts on the other. We do not despair of offering normative policy advice, as Roberts's model implies we should. But we do not expect ordinary politicians to have the wisdom of saints, as Tobin's position implies we should. We are neither elitist nor authoritarian, unless these labels should be attached to anyone who honestly tries to evaluate the limits of representative democracy in economic policy management. When these limits are acknowledged (and we suggest that they must be), we take a stand quite explicitly for the introduction of constraining rules, for an explicit *fiscal constitution*, that will keep the political excesses within bounds. It is toward the development and implementation of such rules that our own normative channels for improvement lie. Roberts would, if put to it, have to call the existing situation hopeless. Tobin would have to look for wiser men in politics. We hope for constraining rules based on reasoned consideration of political reality.

We do not suggest that the constraining rules advanced in our book are optimal in any orthodox sense of this term. (We do not quite know what "optimal" means in such contexts, and we are simply at a loss when Gordon starts talking about the "optimal" size of public debt.) We agree with Tobin that much analysis and dialogue is required, but we do insist that normative policy discussion shift to the level of alternative rules as opposed to alternative policy expedients within the existing political process. We do not think that an effective fiscal-monetary constitution would resolve all of the difficulties of our time, nor do we think that its absence caused the Vietnam war. Our claims are much more modest; an effective fiscal-monetary constitution can exert directionally desired influences on political decision-makers, and through a recognition of such influences, can introduce stabilizing elements in the economy.

VII. The Question of Macroeconomic Perspective

Barro and Tobin suggested that we should have made more of a direct contribution to macroeconomics. To do this would have been to adopt a quite different purpose for our analysis than the ones we chose to adopt. Our main interest was simply in treating seriously the straightforward observation that politicians, not economists, make economic policy. The economic impact of the economic policy that emerges from the political process does, of course, depend on the character of the economic order. In considering this impact, we do possess a macroeconomic perspective, and this perspective was revealed at several places in our book.

Indeed, it is recognition of the political implementation of economic policy as filtered through our macroeconomic perspective that allows us to portray the economic consequence of Keynesian policy to be harmful. In our view the economic order is essentially stable, and monetary disturbance operates in nonneutral fashion in the short run.[3] An institutional framework that promoted monetary and fiscal stability would facilitate the coordinating properties of the market economy. The implementation of economic policy within the existing institutional framework, however, acts to generate economic instability. The price signals in the market economy are distorted by policy, so economic discoordination results. When the observed state of economic circumstances is filtered through the Keynesian vision of the economic order, however, economic management to correct the economic discoordination seems to be called for. An economy that is distinctly non-Keynesian in nature can appear to be Keynesian through the implementation of economic policy. Our views on macroeconomics, in other words, enable us to describe the political biases of Keynesian economic policy as something distinctly harmful and responsible for economic malaise.

VIII. Conclusion

Democracy in Deficit was completed in the summer of 1976. Since that time, we have had two additional years of budgetary history. These years have not refuted the book's central hypothesis that the United States has embarked on a regime of permanent deficit financing of significant, and possibly accelerating, scope. We acknowledge in the book, and we reaffirm here, that our purpose was, and is, in part that of constructive dialogue. Only by predicting the consequences of observed processes in advance can these consequences be avoided if they are deemed to be undesirable. We do not need to fall off the cliff in order to convince ourselves that, empirically, the cliff is there. Is it not far better to find out in advance that the cliff is ahead and that we still might prevent disaster if we can reverse direction?

We do not accept the charge that we presented no *analysis*, as such, in the book. We attempt to analyze the workings of political institutions through which macroeconomic policy has been made in the post-Keynesian era. We invite other economists to do the same thing. Our analysis may be incorrect, in the large or in the small. We may not be cynical enough in modeling the behavior of public choosers, as Craig Roberts suggests. Or we may not attribute a sufficient degree of rationality (and political control) to the ultimate taxpayer-voter, as Barro urges. Or perhaps the quantitatively measurable record does not bear our analysis empirically, in some respects, as both Niskanen and Gordon suggest. We are institutionalists in the sense that we think that arrangements or rules do affect outcomes. Ultimately the test of our analysis of politics, and our interpretation of the historical record will stand or fall on empirical grounds. But our concern is that the evidence required to convince recalcitrant professional colleagues may arrive too late to allow the necessary constitutional reforms to be introduced in time to be effective. Quite frankly, we are more interested in opening a dialogue that may generate preventive steps than we are in achieving simon-pure empirical credentials or as being labeled as belonging to this or that camp or school. There is, indeed, a deal of ruin in a nation, as Adam Smith assured us. But defensive dialogue is essential to preserve that which remains vulnerable to those forces that would do the dealing.

Notes

1. James Tobin, "The Burden of Public Debt: A Review Article," *Journal of Finance* 20 (December, 1965): 679.

2. See *Budgets and Bureaucrats: Sources of Government Growth*, ed. T. E. Borcherding (Durham, N.C.: Duke University Press, 1977).

3. See, for instance, Richard E. Wagner, "Economic Manipulation for Political Profit: Macroeconomic Consequences and Constitutional Implications," *Kyklos* 30, no. 3 (1977): 395–410.

23.

Proportional and Progressive Income Taxation with Utility-maximizing Governments

WITH ROGER CONGLETON

I. Introduction

In the *Constitution of Liberty* (1960), F. A. Hayek suggested that proportional taxation of personal incomes is compatible with a social order in which individual liberties are preserved whereas progressive taxation is not.[1] He argued that proportional taxation, in itself, would exert a sufficiently constraining influence on the behavior of government in exploiting its inherent fiscal authority. We may infer from his discussion that Hayek would support a constitutional limit on the taxing power that would allow the levy of proportional income taxation but that would prohibit the imposition of progressive rates.

To our knowledge, the precise effects of such a constraint on the fiscal authority of government have not been fully analyzed. This essay is aimed at partially filling the gap. In highly simplified models, we shall examine the behavior of government under proportionality constraints and we shall compare this behavior with that predicted under progressive taxation. We shall analyze the effects of maximal rate constraints under both proportionality and progression. In the first part of the paper we shall ignore the effects of taxation on incentives to produce taxable income; incentive effects are introduced in the second part of the analysis.

Before we can make the analysis meaningful, some model of governmental decision-making is required, along with some specification of the nontax constraints on fiscal authority. We shall model governmental behavior in very general terms. We assume only that governmental fiscal decisions are made by some subset of the tax-paying citizenry, some less than all-inclusive coalition of the whole polity. The decision-making group may be conceived as a majority coalition representing one of two major political parties, with the total group of taxpayers being divided into members of this majority and members of the minority. Alternatively, we might consider the setting to be one where a ruling clique or committee (in the limit of one person) makes decisions for the polity, in which case the overwhelming majority of all taxpayers fall within the nonruling or potentially exploitable group. We do not need to specify anything about the relative pre-tax income levels of members of the ruling group and the ruled group. The "poor" may or may not be members of the ruling coalition. All that is minimally required for our analytical purposes is that the population of all potential taxpayers be divided into two distinct sets. In the formal analysis of subsequent sections of the paper, we shall use the simplifying two-person setting with one person designated as the "ruler," with the other person treated as the potential exploitee, the "ruled," who has no influence on his own fiscal situation.

It is evident that a constraint or limit on the taxing power or authority of government means little unless this constraint or limit is also accompanied by constraints on the spending power. If a government can implement direct transfers in a discriminatory manner, then members of any ruling coalition can capture for themselves any desired share of the total incomes of the exploited group independently of any structural tax-side constraints that might be constitutionally imposed. In the analysis that follows, we explicitly restrict the spending power of government to the financing of public goods and services, defined in the classic Samuelsonian sense as embodying both complete jointness in consumption and nonexcludability. This requirement may be relaxed to allow for the provision of both impure goods and even for fully divisible goods so long as we retain the assumption that all persons in the community share equally in the benefit flows of whatever goods and services government does, in fact, provide, and, further, that such goods and services are not retradable.

II. Proportionality, No Rate Constraint, No Incentive Effects

Consider a highly simplified two-person (A, B) model with two goods, one private, Y, and one public, G. The public good is available at a constant per unit cost, C, defined in units of the private good. Initial or pre–tax production of the private good (income) are in the amounts, Y_a and Y_b, per period, and through our assumption that incentive efforts are absent, persons will continue to generate private goods or incomes in these amounts per period regardless of the tax-spending decisions that are made, or by whom.

Assume now that the constitution specifies that the same uniform rate of tax, r, must be levied against the private goods incomes of both persons, A and B, and that the proceeds of this proportional tax must be used exclusively to finance the purchase-provision of G.

We shall initially assume that the tax-spending authority is vested exclusively in B, who becomes the "governor" or "ruler." We can now proceed directly to solve B's utility-maximizing problem in the setting postulated. Note that, under the assumptions of the model, A, the "ruled," confronts no choice. B's utility is a function of two arguments, his disposable income (private good) after tax ($Y_b - rY_b$) and public goods, G, as indicated in (1).

(1) $U_b = u_b[(Y_b - rY_b), G]$

It is within B's power to choose the value of G that will maximize U_b, and we assume that B does this by selecting r, the rate of tax that is to be imposed on the incomes of both persons. The budget constraint of the polity is shown in (2):

(2) $rY_a + rY_b = cG$.

Maximizing with respect to r, first-order conditions are satisfied in (3):

(3) $\dfrac{\partial u_b}{\partial(Y_b - rY_b)} \Big/ \dfrac{}{\partial u_b / \partial G} = \dfrac{Y_a + Y_b}{c} \Big/ \dfrac{}{Y_b}$.

This solution is, of course, the familiar tangency requirement for individual equilibrium.

We may depict this solution diagrammatically in Fig. 23-1, where the quantity of the public good, G, is measured on the ordinate and that of the private good, Y, along the abscissa. We set the relative pretax income levels at Y_a and Y_b, with Y_a being double Y_b. The opportunity locus confronted by B is shown as the straight line connecting the point, $(Y_a + Y_b)/c$, at which point all of the private income of the community is used up in purchasing the public good, G, and the point Y_b, at which no G is purchased and B retains his full initial own production of the private good. B's equilibrium is shown at E, where $0g$ units of the public good and $0y_b$ units of the private good are consumed by B.

We have looked directly only at the pre-tax and post-tax positions of B, whom we have assumed to be the decision maker. Note, however, that the pre-tax position of A enters into the determination of B's utility-maximizing position through the intercept and slope of B's opportunity locus. In the model under consideration here, this locus is

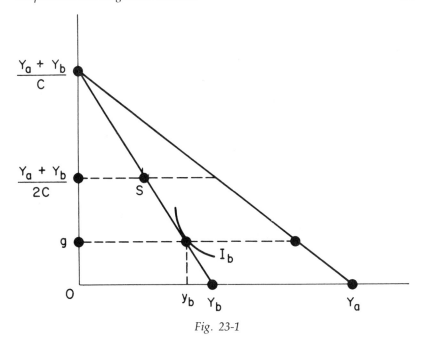

Fig. 23-1

fixed by parametric values for the cost of producing the public good, and for the pre-tax income levels of A and B.

Consider now the position of A, the person who is subject to possible fiscal exploitation because of his powerlessness to influence the tax-spending decision of B. If A should be identical to B, both in preferences and in initial pre-tax incomes, the delegation of decision-making authority to B will not harm A, even in an opportunity-cost sense, because A's most preferred position would be equivalent to B. In such a setting, the political decision rule would not really matter. The opportunity locus of A would, in this case, be coincident with that of B. In order to make the analysis more general, we allow pre-tax incomes of A and B to differ, while continuing to assume identical utility functions. In the construction of Fig. 23-1, the pre-tax income of A, shown as Y_a, is two times that of B, shown as Y_b.

The opportunity locus facing A in Fig. 23-1 is the straight line connecting the same intercept on the ordinate as that for B and the point Y_a on the abscissa. As with the opportunity locus for B, this line is invariant for A once the values of C, Y_a, and Y_b, are set, given the proportionality constraint. A's opportunity set is not affected by the behavior of B in making the community's fiscal decision. If A's income is higher than B's, as drawn in Fig. 23-1, the opportunity locus for A must lie outside that of B throughout the range. Further, as the construction demonstrates, the post-tax private goods consumption of A in relation to the post-tax private goods consumption of B must be equal to the ratio of pre-tax private incomes of the two persons. This is ensured by the fact that both persons must share the same quantity of the public good; hence, regardless of the utility-maximizing choice made by B, both persons must be located along the same horizontal line in Fig. 23-1, with the ratio of private goods remaining in the pre-tax two for one ratio. Consumption cannot be fully equalized as between the two persons so long as any private goods consumption is allowed to take place.

To this point the analysis is fully symmetrical with respect to the identity of the ruler or decision-maker. We have initially assumed that B is the ruler; we may shift the decision-making power to A with similar conclusions. As the construction in Fig. 23-1 indicates, no definitive conclusions may be reached as to whether or not the utility-maximizing proportional tax rate will increase, stay the same, or decrease, as the decision-making power is shifted from B to A. Any one of these directions of change might be possible with the standard convexity properties of utility functions. The direction of change will depend on the combined income and substitution effects which work in opposition to each other under the assumption that G is a normal good, along with Y. If we stay within the assumption that the utility functions for A and B are identical, the location of the utility-maximizing position of A, along A's opportunity locus, will depend on the ratio of the income and "price" elasticities of demand for G. Under proportionality, and because he has a lower initial income, B must face a lower tax-price per unit of the public good than A at all levels. B's tax-price is defined by the slope of his opportunity locus. A shift of decision-making power to A from B would, due to the substitution effect alone, tend to decrease the demand for G. But such a shift also involves moving to a higher income level, and, if G is normal, this will tend to increase the demand for G. If the two effects are just offsetting, there will be no change in the amount of G, and in the proportional tax rate, r, as a result of the switch between persons in fiscal authority. In this case, the proportional tax rate will also guarantee the satisfaction of the normal efficiency conditions for public goods provision; the utility-maximizing position of either person also ensures satisfaction of the Lindahl conditions for public good equilibrium.[2]

III. Proportional Taxation, Maximum Rate Limits, No Incentive Effects

It is relatively easy to extend the analysis to show the effects of maximum rate constraints, while remaining within the proportionality restriction and continuing to assume that there are no disincentives from taxes on behavior of the two persons in generating private goods income, Y. The imposition of a maximum rate constraint effectively truncates the opportunity locus of both the rule and the ruled person, at the level of the constraint, drawn in Fig. 23-1 as 50 percent. Such a constraint may or may not affect the utility-maximizing position of the ruler. If B is the decision-maker, and, prior to the new constraint, equilibrium is located along the segment of the locus below S, there will be no change. If, however, the initial position lies above S, the constraint will become binding, and the effective new rate of tax will be the maximum allowed, with B remaining in a corner solution at S. Note that, in the proportionality setting, there is no difference in effect between a limit imposed on rates of tax and a limit imposed on total tax revenues, or total spending, in relation to income.

IV. Progressive Taxation, No Rate Limits, No Incentive Effects

We may now compare the results under the general proportionality constraint with those that might be predicted to emerge in the absence of such a constraint, while retaining the same model for political decision-making and the same spending-side restrictions. We cannot, however, simply assume the absence of all tax constraints on government. We want to impose the requirement that arbitrary discrimination, related, for example, to political power rather than income, is prohibited and, further, that tax payments be at least proportional to income.

In this model, we should anticipate that the results depend significantly on who is the government. There will be major differences in the utility-maximizing behavior of the "poor" if they are in the politically dominating coalition and the behavior of the "rich" if they are in such a position. This set of differences is not present under the proportionality constraint. An important element of potential political conflict is necessarily introduced by the institution of income tax progression.

As in our earlier treatment, we shall initially assume that B, who earns a pre-tax income only one-half that earned by A, is the ruler. Individual B is free to select the tax structure he prefers, with the residually determined quantity of G. We assume, as before, that there is no utility interdependence.

So long as B is not satiated with the public good at such a limit, we may predict that *all* income above the level of his own earning, above Y_b, will be taxed at the maximum 100 percent rate. Individual B secures without cost that quantity of the public good, G, that is made

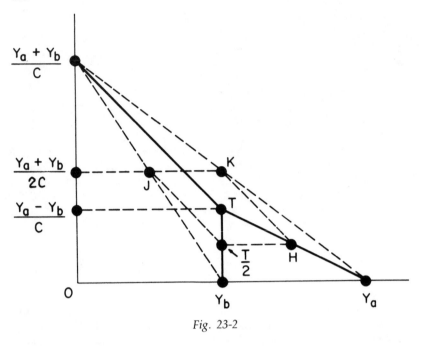

Fig. 23-2

possible by the revenues collected from A over the $Y_a - Y_b$ income range. We depict these results in Fig. 23-2, which is similar in construction to Fig. 23-1. B's position shifts from Y_b to T as a result of the imposition of the maximum tax on the income of A above Y_b. Beyond this limit, the opportunity locus for both B and for A is defined by the line segment connecting T and $(Y_a + Y_b)/C$. Note that, in this unlimited progression model, the final distribution of consumption of *both* the private good and the public good is fully equalized if the equilibrium solution lies on or above T.[3] Hayek's implicit proposition to the effect that tax progression inherently implies post-tax income equalization is validated in this model, even when we restrict governmental fiscal activity to the financing of genuinely public goods and prohibit direct income transfers.

The opportunity locus for B, the person whom we have initially made the ruler, lies everywhere outside that which is available to B under the proportionality constraint, which is shown by the dotted line from Y_b in Fig. 23-2. By contrast, the opportunity locus for A lies everywhere inside that which is available to him under proportionality.

The model is clearly not symmetrical with shift in governorship. If A is the decision-maker instead of B, he would be better off by adopting a rate structure that defines the lowest allowable limit to progression, which is, of course, proportionality. In this case A's opportunity locus remains unchanged from that available to him under the proportionality constraint.

Interesting comparisons emerge only when B is considered to be decisive. Will more or less G be provided under progression than under proportionality? As Fig. 23-2 suggests, no definitive answer is possible merely from the standard convexity properties of preference orderings. If the solution lies above T, the ruler, B, is paying a higher marginal tax price (the slope of his opportunity locus) than that which he confronts under proportionality. But he will also enjoy a higher level of private goods income. Once again we have an income effect and a substitution effect working in opposing directions if we assume that both goods are normal.[4]

V. Progressive Taxation, Maximum Rate Limits, No Incentive Effects

We may now examine the effects of imposing maximum rate limits in a progressive tax setting. In the simple two-person model analyzed, we have shown that in the absence of rate limits, if B is the decision-maker the income of A above that of B will be subjected to a 100 percent marginal rate. The most plausible form of tax limit in such a setting may be one that restricts the allowable marginal rate. Suppose that the maximum marginal rate of tax is set at 50 percent. This limit guarantees that tax revenues collected from A, over the bracket range, $Y_a - Y_b$, will finance public goods provision only up to one-half the amount financed under the fully confiscatory rate. Person B, whom we assume to be the collective decision-maker, finds his own position shifted to $T/2$ in Fig. 23-2. But this position has not brought him into full equality with A, as was the case with unrestricted progression. After paying the maximum marginal rate on the income over the range, $Y_a - Y_b$, and financing $T/2$ in public goods, A finds himself at H.

As in the earlier case, B will confront an opportunity locus with a kink; now located at $T/2$ rather than T. From this point the locus will parallel that of A, drawn from H. At the maximum rate limit, B would find himself at J while A would be at position K. Regardless of B's utility-maximizing choice among his opportunity locus, B's post-tax private goods income will fall short of A's by precisely the maximum marginal rate times the difference in pre-tax incomes. As compared with the full equalization of incomes under no-limit progression, a differential will remain in the restricted-rate model so long as any private goods consumption is allowed. Recall that, under proportionality, except at the limit where all resources are devoted to the public good, the post-fisc ratio of private goods income or consumption remains identical to the pre-fisc ratio. With limited rate progression, by comparison, the post-fisc ratio shifts in favor of the low-income receiver, but the absolute differential remains as determined by the maximum marginal rate.

The construction suggests that the imposition of a maximum limit on marginal rates of tax may be a more effective means of restricting potential fiscal exploitation than comparable attempts to limit total tax revenues on total spending more directly. In the context of Fig. 23-2, suppose that it is desired to restrict total taxation to one-half of total income, that is, to $(Y_a + Y_b)/2$. Further, suppose that this limitation might be imposed by explicit tax rate constraints or by overall constraints on revenues. If, for example, the maximum allowable marginal rate of tax is set at 50 percent, clearly satisfying the overall objective, the opportunity locus faced by B will be that discussed above, with the kink at $T/2$. On the other hand, under the more general total revenue constraints, the opportunity locus for B, the ruler, would be that which kinks at T. As the construction in Fig. 23-2 indicates, the opportunity locus under the general revenue constraints lies wholly outside that defined by the tax-rate constraints. In this sense, the tax-rate constraint becomes more restrictive.

VI. Proportional Taxation, No Rate Constraint, and Incentive Effects

To this point, we have assumed that taxpayers' behavior in generating the tax base, income, is invariant under all possible rates of tax. That is to say, individuals continue to earn the same income, pretax, regardless of the rate of tax that is imposed. The analytical convenience of this assumption is clear; it enables us to construct models in two dimensions, quantities of public and private goods. As we relax this assumption to allow for incentive effects, we necessarily introduce a third "good," nontaxable "leisure" or other desired "outputs" of taxpayers' time than the generation of taxable base, Y.

Let us first examine proportional income taxation with only this one change made in the simple models developed earlier. The person in the two-person community who is subject to potential fiscal exploitation, who is the ruled rather than the ruler, will modify his behavior in producing Y in some generally inverse relationship with the rate of tax that is exogenously imposed on him. As confronted by the ruler, this behavioral change involves a constriction of his opportunity locus. The ruler is, therefore, unambiguously worse off under the behavioral adjustment model than he is in the model in which the potentially exploited taxpayer cannot adjust in response to the tax. Contrariwise, the latter is in an unambiguously improved position. To the

extent that he can "opt out" by shifting some part of his psychic earnings into nontaxable options, he is better off than he should be if he
were somehow to be precluded from making such shifts.

The ruler, or decision-maker, solves his utility-maximizing problem
much as in the simpler model, but he does so in this case by considering both his own opportunities to realize consumption benefits from
the nontaxable activity, L, and the predicted behavioral adjustment of
the potential exploitee under varying rates of tax.

These adjustments may be predicted by examining the optimization
problem of the ruled, A, a problem that does not exist in the simpler
model. The utility function for the person ruled contains arguments
for after-tax, private goods income, $(1 - r)Y_b$, government services
provided, G, and nontaxable income, L_a. His task is to maximize:

(4) $\quad U_a = u_a[(1 - r)Y_a, (r/c)(Y_a + Y_b), (L_a^* - \ell Y_a)]$

The person ruled, A, has, in effect, only a single decision variable, Y_a,
in this specification, since r, and Y_b are determined by the ruler, and
because a choice of Y_a determines the amount of nontaxable income,
"leisure," available, $L_a^* - \ell_a Y_a$, where L_a^* is the maximum amount of
the nontaxable good, L, and where ℓ_a is the rate of transformation between Y_a and L_a. Maximizing with respect to Y_a, the first-order condition is met in (5):

(5) $\quad \dfrac{\partial u_a}{\partial(Y_a - rY_a)}(1 - r) + \dfrac{\partial u_a}{\partial G}\left(\dfrac{r}{c}\right) + \dfrac{\partial u_a}{\partial L_a}(-\ell_a) = 0$

The usual strict convexity assumption thus implies that the amount
of the tax base generated, Y_a, will be functionally related to the tax
rate, r.

Given the adjustment function of the ruled, $Y_a = y_a(r, Y_b)$, the optimization problem faced by the ruler, B, is completely specified. B's utility
is, like that of A, dependent on his consumption of the tax-base good,
$Y_b(1 - r)$, his consumption of government services, $G = r/c(Y_a + Y_b)$,
and his consumption of the nontaxed good or activity, $L_b = L_b^* - \ell_b Y_b$.
His utility function can be represented in (6).

(6) $\quad U_b = u_b\{(1 - r)Y_b, (r/c)[Y_a + y_a(r, Y_b)], (L_b^* - \ell_b Y_b)\}$

In this formulation, the ruler has two decision variables: (1) the rate of
the proportional tax, r, and (2) the amount of the taxable good, Y_b,
that he will generate. The amount of government services, G, and the
level of nontaxable activity, L_b, are determined by these two variables
under his control. Maximizing with respect to r and Y_b, the first-order
conditions are met in the following:

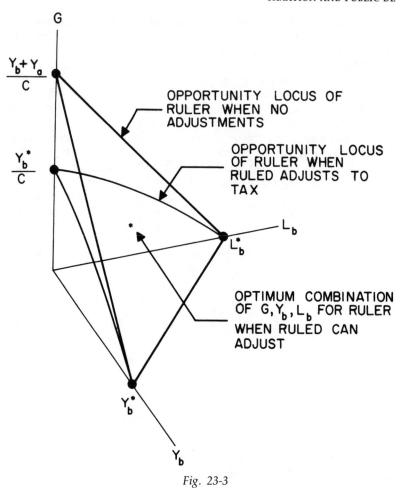

Fig. 23-3

(7) $\quad Y_b \dfrac{\partial u_b}{\partial(Y_b - rY_b)} = \dfrac{1}{c}\,[Y_b + Y_a + r\,\dfrac{\partial y_a}{\partial r}]\,\dfrac{\partial u_b}{\partial G}$

(8) $\quad \dfrac{\partial u_b}{\ell_b \partial L_b} = (1 - r)\,\dfrac{\partial u_b}{\partial(Y_b - ry_b)} + \dfrac{r}{c}\left(1 + \dfrac{\partial y_a}{\partial y_b}\right)\dfrac{\partial u_b}{\partial G}$

The solution is depicted in the three-dimensional Fig. 23-3, for the case where, $y_a(1) = 0$, $\partial y_a / \partial Y_b \le 0$ and $\partial y_a / \partial r < 0$. Note that, regardless of the form of the adjustment function for A, the ruler's opportunity locus will lie below that available when the potential exploitee cannot or does not adjust (depicted in Fig. 23-3 as the triangular surface above the curvilinear one) at every point save those where the tax rate is zero. To the extent that the person ruled, A, adjusts to changing tax rates, the ruler, B, is worse off and the potential exploitee is better off. If the ruler is the less wealthy of the two persons, the utility-equalizing effects of the proportional tax–public goods package are less than those in the absence of adjustment. By shifting his effort away from those activities that generate taxable base, the potential exploitee reduces the utility-equalizing potential for public goods provision. On the other hand, if the ruler should be the wealthier of the two, the utility-equalizing effects of public goods provision may, in fact, be larger with adjustment than in the absence of adjustment. In this case the person ruled may, to some extent, "free ride" on the services provided by government largely at the expense of the ruler.

VIII. Proportional Taxation, Maximum Rate Constraints, and Incentive Effect

The introduction of a maximum rate limit operates in this setting much as in the one without the behavioral adjustments. The details of analysis can be omitted. We should note, however, that the desirability of imposing any maximum rate constraint is lessened in the presence of the potential shift of taxpayers into nontaxable pursuits and away from the generation of taxable base. In this sense, preservation of the availability of nontaxable opportunities that yield utility to the taxpayer can serve as a good substitute for the imposition of rate constraints.[5]

IX. Progressive Taxation, No Rate Constraints, and Incentive Effects

We shift now the setting in which the ruler is allowed to impose progressive rates of tax on incomes, with no constraints as to rates, but now in the presence of behavioral adjustments on the part of those who are outside the ruling coalition. As noted earlier, the solution will be quite different with different rulers or decision-makers. The delegation of power to the high-income earners will tend to produce the proportional tax model already discussed. We can, therefore, limit analysis to the situation where the low-income earner is the ruler or governor.

In this political framework with the no-incentive model, we demonstrated that the ruler would maximize utility by levying a 100 percent rate of tax on all income higher than that which he himself earns. This dramatic result no longer holds when taxpayers have the ability to shift to nontaxable opportunities, and, indeed, in the case discussed above, an optimizing governor will never impose this confiscatory rate on any level of taxable income generated, no matter how high this might be. The utility-maximizing rate schedule over the income range above that received by the ruler, over the range $Y_a - Y_b$, will be that schedule which generates the highest revenue from A, given his predicted adjustment to nontaxable opportunities at alternative rates. As Brennan and Buchanan have shown in related analysis, with linearity assumptions, the rate schedule satisfying this maximum yield criterion will be proportional.[6] This implies that the ruler will levy a uniform rate of tax on all incomes above his own. He will not impose progressive rates for incomes over the higher range. Once the revenue-maximizing rate (or rate schedule) has been levied on incomes in those ranges beyond that received by the decision-maker, the latter finds himself at a kink in his opportunity locus; a specific quantity of public good, G, is available without cost. Whether the decision-maker will remain in this position or whether he will choose to expand the provision of G beyond this point depends, of course, on both the shape of this utility function and the cost of the public good. Beyond this limit, he must pay a tax-price per unit of the public good that is as high as that paid by the potentially exploited taxpayer. The decision-maker in our political framework is assumed not to be able to levy taxes discriminatorily; he cannot impose taxes on the income of A below Y_b, while leaving B's income over this range exempt from levy of tax.

X. Progressive Taxation, Maximum Rate Limits, and Incentive Effects

The presence of nontaxable opportunities tends to limit the rates of tax that any utility-maximizing ruler will impose on taxpayers. In the model considered above, the revenue-maximizing rate of tax (or rate structure) on higher incomes may well be lower than any "reasonable" maximum that might be imposed constitutionally. The consumption-equalizing potential of the progressive rate–public goods fisc, which is clearly present in the no-incentive setting where the ruler is the less wealthy of the two, is reduced to where potential taxpayers can make behavioral adjustments by shifting into nontaxable options, even in the absence of explicit rate limits. To the extent that he can "opt out" in response to the tax, a taxpayer can guarantee to himself the consumption that he privately values, over and above any attempts at consumption equalization via the fiscal process. In terms of utility equalization, location of decision-authority in the wealthy person does not modify this basic result. As noted, the ruler will, in this case, opt for a proportional rate structure. But adjustment must make the ruled "poor" better off and the rich ruler worse off. If the elasticity of substitution between taxable base generation and resort to nontaxable options is relatively low, maximum rate limits may be desired to restrict potential fiscal exploitation. As in the no-incentive model, effective maximum rates will guarantee the maintenance of differentials in the final consumption of private goods as between the potentially exploited high-income recipient and the low-income earner when the latter is the decision-taker. The additional opportunities for resorting to nontaxable options will, in this case, ensure somewhat wider differentials of tax-base consumption than in the no-adjustment case.

XI. Conclusions

In a set of very simple models we have attempted to isolate and to analyze possible differences in the operation of proportional and progressive income tax systems, given specific assumptions about the political decision structure and public spending constraints. Other models could, of course, be developed under widely differing assumptions. In particular, other conclusions would emerge if we relaxed the public spending constraint and allowed for governments to carry out direct income transfers. In recognition of this restriction, our results should be interpreted as carrying implications only within limits. Nonetheless, the results are suggestive in themselves.

Any system of taxation that is more "progressive" than equal-per-head taxes, when combined with spending on genuinely public goods, must equalize final consumption of "goods" in some absolute sense. By definition, persons secure equal quantities of public goods. And if these are financed in any way other than with equal-per-head taxes, some consumption equalization must result.

With proportional taxation, and when taxpayers do not adjust pretax income in response to tax, the ratio of private goods consumption between taxpayers at differing income levels remains the same before and after the tax, regardless of rate. Absolute differentials in private goods consumption (or possibilities for consumption) are, of course, reduced in direct relationship to the rate of the proportional tax.

With progressive taxation, again when taxpayers make no behavioral adjustments, the final consumption of private goods tends to be equalized, both in a relative and in an absolute sense, and in direct relationship to both the quantity of public goods financed and the progressivity of the structure. In the unrestricted utility-maximizing model, rates of tax on all incomes above those earned by the ruler will be fully confiscatory in this model.

If taxpayers make no behavioral adjustments to tax, the presence of constitutional limits on allowable maximum rates, under either proportion or progression, can check the tendency toward consumption equalization. However, such constitutional rate limits may be much less important if taxpayers can be allowed to retain opportunities for shifting into nontaxable utility-generating activities in response to taxes. The existence of such opportunities may well be a more important check to the fiscal powers of government than any formal limits. Hayek's principal concern about progressive taxation need not arise when nontaxable options are significant. The presence of such options does, of course, reduce the *generality* of the tax, whether proportional or progressive. But the admittedly desired features of generality, as an abstract goal, must be matched against the efficacy of nongenerality in limiting the degree of potential fiscal exploitation.

Notes

We are indebted to Geoffrey Brennan and to Yew-Kwang Ng for helpful suggestions. Partial research support for Buchanan's work on this paper was provided by the National Science Foundation.

1. (Chicago: University of Chicago Press, 1960), chapter 20, pp. 306–23.

2. For an early discussion that concentrates strictly on the possible efficiency properties of proportional taxation, see James M. Buchanan, "Fiscal Institutions and Efficiency in Collective Outlay," *American Economic Review* 54 (May, 1964): 227–35.

3. This result is related to that which is shown to emerge under an independent adjustment model by Jeremias and Zardkoohi. They demonstrate that consumption of all goods will be equalized among all persons in a public goods interaction under certain configurations of preferences, even if there is no collective action. See Ronald Jeremias and Asghar Zardkoohi, "Distributional Implications of Independent Adjustments in an Economy with Public Goods," *Economic Inquiry* 14 (June, 1976): 305–308.

4. Geoffrey Brennan has emphasized the shift in marginal tax price under progression as opposed to proportionality in a median voter model. See Geoffrey Brennan, "A Note on Progression and Public Sector Size," *Public Choice* 32 (Winter, 1977): 123–29.

5. In their first paper on tax constitutions, Brennan and Buchanan concentrated their analysis on the potential limits on total revenue that might be ensured by the presence of nontaxable options or opportunities. See Geoffrey Brennan and James Buchanan, "Towards a Tax Constitution for Leviathan," *Journal of Public Economics* 8 (December, 1977): 255–73.

6. Ibid.

24.

Coercive Taxation in Constitutional Contract

I. Introduction

Man does not, and possibly could not, exist in isolation, and most of that which we value depends critically on the presence of civil order, which only collective organization ensures. Man is not the state, but man versus the state is an equally inappropriate metaphor. Man depends on the state. The questions to be explored in this essay involve the implications of this dependence for the legitimacy of coercive taxation in a society that locates sources of value exclusively in its individual members.

How much can the collectivity coercively extract from individuals while satisfying broadly acceptable ethical norms? The libertarians offer a clear answer: *Nothing*. Any tax payment coercively extracted is equivalent to theft and should be labeled as such. This conclusion depends critically on the judgment that individuals have well-defined "natural rights" that are independent of existence in civil society. The contractarian cannot make such a judgment; his response to the question is necessarily more complex.

If Wicksellian contractual criteria are applied directly at the legislative stage of collective decision, and only at this stage, the response is fully consistent with that of the libertarian, but only because taxation becomes voluntary rather than coercive.[1] In the Wicksellian construction, the collectivity, as such, is justified in imposing fiscal charges on the citizenry only if there is general agreement (in the limit, unanimous agreement) on both the purpose of the outlay to be made and the distribution of the tax shares required to finance the outlay. The criterion for legitimacy lies in the process of agreement; it remains silent on both the absolute level of taxation and on the distribution of tax shares.

If the basic contractarian approach is extended to the constitutional stage and applied to the ultimate selection among alternative collective decision-making rules, the Wicksellian test of agreement at the in-period, postconstitutional, or within-rule stage no longer suffices.[2] There is nothing in the basic contractarian construction to suggest that some Wicksellian unanimity or near-unanimity rule would be adopted for each and every fiscal choice confronted by the organized collectivity. It seems possible to derive less-than-unanimity rules for making fiscal choices from conceptually unanimous agreement at the constitutional level of deliberation. Majority voting rules, both for the election of representatives and for decisions within a legislative body, may emerge from a constitutional agreement. In this case, what are the limits to the coercive taxation that legislative majorities may impose?

I shall take as given for my discussion that *some* limits on the taxing power of the collectivity would be laid out in the constitutional contract. Legislative majorities would never be granted fiscal carte blanche; claims made for unrestricted fiscal domain cannot find ultimate legitimization in any contractarian construction. I have presented the general argument for limits elsewhere.[3] My concern in this paper is with ascertaining what these limits might be.

In earlier work written jointly with Geoffrey Brennan, we analyzed the individual's choice of tax limits, but within the restrictions of a model that assumed away the problem that I now address. In our book, *The Power to Tax*,[4] we posed the specific question: Given some postulated preferred outlay for collective purposes, how must the taxing power granted to government be limited so as to ensure that revenues collected remain as close as possible to the levels dictated by the preferred outlay? We showed that the answer to this question requires a modeling both of government's behavior in using the taxing power assigned and the citizens' responsiveness to the imposition of taxes. The different, and more difficult, question I examine in this paper involves the individual's constitutional choice of a desired or preferred level of aggregate collective outlay, a question that must somehow be answered prior to the onset of the Brennan-Buchanan analytical exercise.

My concern is not primarily with those taxes that must be imposed in order to generate revenues sufficient to finance the "protective" or the "productive" state. The first of these adjectives describes the activities of the collectivity that are involved in maintaining the legal umbrella in which individuals interact with one another. These activities include the protection of rights to property, as these rights may be assigned in the basic contract, and the enforcement of contracts made for voluntary exchanges of these rights. The provision of these services to all members of the collectivity involves genuine "publicness."

In addition to these protective or minimal-state activities, however, government may also provide other genuinely public or collective consumption goods and services, described technically as those goods and services that are inherently nonrival in consumption and that are not amenable to efficient means of exclusion. Both types of these goods and services require financing, and taxes must be levied in order to secure the revenues.

Taxes required to finance the two sets of activities must, in one sense, be coercive, since an individual may not voluntarily pay for goods and services that are available to him whether or not he makes payment. There is no difficulty, however, in deriving a constitutional-stage contractarian justification for the imposition of taxes for these activities, along with the minimal coercion that may be necessary. To the extent that the goods and services are genuinely "public," and, therefore, made available on equal-access terms to all persons, there must be some means of assigning tax shares sufficient to finance an efficient level of provision that will meet a conceptual Wicksellian test of agreement in-period. The predicted difficulties of adjusting tax shares so as to secure actual agreement for each good in each period may, however, be such as to justify resort to decision rules that will allow some coercive taxation that fails even the conceptual unanimity test.[5] The restriction of the financing to genuinely public goods would, however, ensure severe upper limits to such taxation. In any case, the problem of deriving a contractarian justification for such taxation becomes minuscule in comparison with the problem that I propose to address in this paper. The specific question I want to address here involves the possible extension of coercive taxation beyond both protective and productive state limits. Can we derive a contractarian-constitutional authorization for the imposition of taxes to finance *purely redistributive transfers?*

In Section II, I describe a highly simplified model that allows the basic question to be examined in a setting that seems most favorable to fiscal transfers. Section III is devoted to a brief treatment of some of the underlying philosophical presuppositions. In Section IV, I look at the results that might emerge from the familiar Rawlsian construction. Section V presents alternative results through geometrical illustrations. In Sections VI, VII, VIII, and IX, the simplified assumptions of the initial model are relaxed, and the implications are analyzed. The whole argument is summarized in Section X.

II. Restrictive Assumptions for an Initial Analysis

I propose to set out the conditions that are the most favorable possible for constitutional-stage agreement on high levels of coercive taxation motivated by the individual's constitutional-stage preference for postconstitutional reductions in income inequalities. Four restrictive assumptions are imposed on the initial model.

1. *All valued product is social rent.*

I assume that, in the absence of collective or governmental activity in the provision of protective-productive state services (minimally, the protection of rights and the enforcement of contracts), no production of value is possible. The life of persons in the Hobbesian jungle is poor, nasty, brutish, and short. As applied to individuals singly and in isolation, this assumption seems plausible enough. But, for this initial model, I shall assume that no production of value is possible in any organized community smaller or less inclusive than the polity's total membership. I also assume that there is only one polity. This set of assumptions ensures that all value produced is "social rent"; without organized collective activity, no product at all is generated.

2. *Full income is measurable independently of observed individual behavior.*

Like Assumption 1, this second assumption is technological in nature rather than behavioral. I assume that, in any postconstitutional period, there exist some means of measuring an individual's capacity to produce or to generate value, here called full income, whether or not the individual is observed to exercise such capacity. Such an independent measurement is required in order to assess the appropriate fiscal charges (either as taxes or transfers).

3. *No excess burden.*

The two remaining assumptions are behavioral rather than technological. I shall assume initially that there is no private-sector behavioral response to either taxation or public spending (including receipt of transfer payments). Persons consume, work, save, and in precisely the same patterns regardless of the level and structure of either the tax or spending side of the fiscal process. There are no incentive effects of the fiscal structure; excess burdens are zero.

4. *No rent-seeking.*

Finally, I shall initially assume that the Brennan-Buchanan reasons for imposing constitutional restrictions on the taxing powers of government are absent. I assume that, in postconstitutional periods, government operates precisely as the preferences of individuals at the constitutional stage might dictate, as reflected in the constitutional-stage agreement. There is no attempt, on the part of political agents, to extend revenue collections beyond those minimally required to meet the collective outlay needs that are predicted to occur. Nor is there any effort, on the part of such agents, to direct the patterns of expenditure away from those constitutionally desired by the citizens and toward those that meet the preferences of the agents. Further, in the case of taxes and transfers (negative taxes) there is no net slippage between collection and disbursement. The tax-transfer process is ideally efficient.

III. To Whom Does Social Rent Belong?

As noted in the introduction, for either the libertarian or the in-period Wicksellian there is no basis for the constitutional authorization of tax financing of pure transfers.[6] The constitutionalist-contractarian may, however, be less negative toward a genuine transfer process. What elements will inform the thinking of a person who is placed behind a veil of ignorance and/or uncertainty in constitutional choice when he or she considers the possible authorization of pure fiscal transfers?

Recall the first extreme assumption introduced. Outside the umbrella of civil order, no person, individually or in coalition with any group less inclusive than the total membership, can generate value. In this sense, therefore, all valued product is imputable to the presence of that order, which is collectively rather than privately supplied. All product is social rent in this setting.

Given the presence of civil order, valued product will be generated through market interaction that will allocate pre-tax shares among persons roughly in accordance with relative productivities.[7] Some withdrawal of product must, of course, take place for the financing of the minimally required protective services and the preferred levels of genuinely collective consumption goods. Assume, for illustrative purposes, that this withdrawal amounts to roughly 10 percent of total product value. Will the person, behind an appropriately defined veil of ignorance and/or uncertainty, choose to restrict the levy of taxation to roughly this 10 percent range, or will there be some reason to authorize the postconstitutional levy of taxes beyond this range in order to finance redistributive transfers?

If the 10 percent level of taxation is all that is constitutionally agreed on and authorized, the remaining 90 percent of valued production in the economy will then be finally allocated among persons in accordance with productivities, as adjusted by some allocation of tax shares for the financing of the protective-productive state services. If, however, the social rent assumption is accepted, this particular set of imputations is only one set from among many that might be chosen, and, as such, it seems to be arbitrary. Behind the veil, would not a person consider that at least some share of this remaining 90 percent of value could appropriately be devoted to the financing of transfers with the purpose of achieving a more desirable final distribution, as evaluated at the constitutional stage? If we put the question differently, how could such a question be answered in the negative?

The model has been deliberately constructed so that the "productivity ethic" offers little or no support to the libertarian. To the extent that this ethic is supportable at all, it can possibly justify the sharing of value in accordance with *external* productivities. It cannot be extended in support of sharing in terms of *internal* productivities in a model that necessarily involves collective organization and provision for civil order. In a functioning market economy (and ignoring the financing of the legal umbrella) that is fully competitive, payments to inputs tend to equal external marginal products rather than internal, and the allocation of rents measured by the differences between these two products is, in a sense, acknowledged to be arbitrary.[8] If we now introduce inclusive collective provision of protective state services as a necessary input to the generation of all value even in an economy with decentralized production, there is an inherent indeterminacy in the imputation of value shares in terms of productivities inclusively defined. The collectivity, as such, can make a claim to a share well beyond that measured by the mere opportunity cost of the inputs it provides, just as can other inputs.[9] Or, if we put the issue in the context of our analysis, individuals, at the constitutional stage of choice of institutional rules, may agree that the social rent is to be shared in accordance with some standard other than that which would dictate collective exaction of the minimal outlays that are required to finance the actual inputs employed in state services. There seems to be no plausible basis for suggesting that all of the social rent over and above this minimum should be institutionally allocated to those who offer the market rather than the collective inputs, especially since, by our assumption, the external productivity of these inputs is nonexistent. Without these inputs, the state can produce no value, but without the services of the state these inputs produce no value.[10]

IV. The Rawlsian Solution

The most familiar attempt to answer the basic question that I have posed, and to do so from a basic contractarian perspective, is that of John Rawls.[11] Using a carefully defined veil-of-ignorance construction, Rawls sets up idealized contractors who are then predicted to agree on two principles of justice that will guide the organization of the society. The two principles are lexicographically ordered; the first is the principle of maximal equal liberty; the second is the maximin or difference principle for the distribution of primary goods.

Economists as well as other critics of Rawls have concentrated attention almost exclusively on the difference principle, and they have failed to recognize that the first principle of maximal equal liberty also has distributional consequences. Both external exit (migration from the polity) and internal exit (secession) must be listed as countable Rawlsian liberties, without which the first principle cannot be satisfied. Including the guarantee of these two liberties in the agreed-on constitutional arrangements ensures that the second Rawlsian principle applies only to social rent, only to that share of value over and beyond the external marginal product of persons or of groups.

In the highly restricted set of assumptions summarized in Section II, all of value that is produced is social rent. Persons possess equal liberties to leave the polity or to secede and form new polities, but, by assumption, they can produce nothing of value in either case. In addition, full incomes can presumably be measured, and persons behave identically regardless of the level of taxes and transfers. In this rarefied setting, the application of the Rawlsian difference principle would equalize the distribution of value among all persons, if we define valued goods as the relevant Rawlsian primary goods. This full equalization result or solution would also emerge from a standard utilitarian stance or from a straightforward equalization norm. The individuals who are genuinely behind the veil of ignorance in this setting would agree to a set of constitutional arrangements that would instruct government, in-period, to implement a tax-transfer scheme that would bring all persons, post-tax and post-transfer, to the same position. Rawls gets differing results only because he does not impose the third restrictive assumption that I have introduced in this essay. His analysis implicitly accepts the three other restrictions.

V. An Emendation of the Rawlsian Solution

I do not want to relax any of the four assumptions at this point. My purpose in this section is to suggest that, even under the highly restrictive assumptions, full equalization would not be predicted to emerge from constitutional-stage agreement among persons who place themselves behind the genuine Rawlsian veil. The Rawlsian exercise, like the utilitarian, omits a critically important element, which, when included in the model, must modify the solution, perhaps substantially. Contractual agreement would be predicted to emerge on arrangements that would embody less than full equalization of incomes among persons, post-tax and post-transfer.

Why would the idealized contractors ever agree to any arrangements that would not produce full equality? They are behind the veil; all product is social rent; full incomes can be assessed for fiscal purposes; there is no excess burden; political agents do not seek rents. The contractors will recognize, however, that any distribution of capacities to produce value along the decentralized production organization must involve some "natural" imputation to separable persons or groups, who can then exert at least nominal claims to the potential values that may be produced. This is to say, individuals will attach putative "rights" to the "natural" assignments.[12] Hence, any *redistri*-

bution of these potential values among persons involves, for one set of persons, a coerced "taking" of valued product that they consider to be "their own" in some nominal sense. There will exist a distinct threshold difference between the predicted loss from a coerced taking of one unit of value by taxation and the predicted gain from the receipt of one unit through transfer. This threshold difference will be anticipated by the idealized contractors, and it must lead to agreement on arrangements that will embody less than full equality in the final distribution of values, even in this model where the extremely restricted assumptions remain in force.[13]

Some utility function geometry.
The general argument sketched above can be more conveniently expressed by resort to simple utility function diagrams. The contractor will predict that the preferences of each person (any person) in any postconstitutional period can be described by a utility function of the standard form. The contractor will not know what his capacity for generating market-related, pretax income will be and hence, what his utility level will be, pre-tax, pre-transfer. But the contractor will predict that, whatever this location, there will be a kink in the function that relates this position to those below and above it that are achievable by the tax-transfer process. There will be a predicted threshold difference between the marginal loss (through tax) of a unit of value and the marginal gain (through receipt of transfer) of a unit of full income.

In Fig. 24-1, the predicted marginal utility of potential market-related, pre-tax, pre-transfer incomes at all levels of income is shown by MU_i. The function is down-sloping throughout the range, and it is drawn as a straight line for simplicity, since the sign of the second derivative of the total utility of full income function is not relevant for my purposes. The reverse image of the function is shown as MU_j. If the relevant institutional choice should be that of some ideal distribution, in the two-person setting shown, the contractor would, of course, choose the position of full equality, shown at Y_E. As noted, however, the choice is not among distributions, since these are determined by elements not within control of the constitutional contractors. The relevant institutional-constitutional choice is among arrangements that will implement some redistribution from the potential market-related, pre-tax, pre-transfer distribution. Behind the veil the contractor cannot identify himself, post-choice; he does not know whether he will be i or j. He can, however, predict that the initial pre-tax distribution will be at Y, with Individual i receiving a full income of OY and Individual j receiving a full income of YZ, with the utility levels shown by the positions on MU_i and MU_j.

The threshold effect is shown by the discontinuities in the tax-transfer curves traced out through the initial position on each basic utility function. For Individual i, the relevant function is that shown

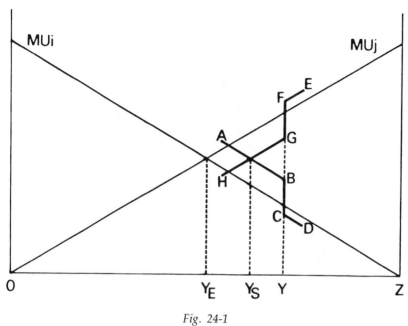

Fig. 24-1

by ABCD, for Individual j that shown by EFGH. The idealized contractor, not knowing whether he will find himself in the position of
i or j, will select a set of redistributive arrangements that will generate
a position at Y_s. Note that, as drawn in Fig. 24-1, this agreed-on position will involve some shift from the potential market-related, pre-tax
position, but that it will fall short of the position of full equality. As
the construction suggests, quite independently of the particular configurations, if the discontinuities in the marginal utility functions are
acknowledged to be present at all, the constitutionally preferred solution must fall short of the equal distribution in the direction of the
market-generated, pre-tax, pre-transfer distribution. If the threshold
differences are severe enough, relative to the inequality in the initial
distribution predicted to emerge, the contractor may choose the uncorrected or market position, despite the fact that the ideal distribution would remain that described by full equality.[14]

VI. Secession, Social Rent, and External Marginal Product

As I have repeatedly emphasized, the results derived in Section V are
those that emerge in the contractarian setting that is deliberately designed to represent the conditions that are most favorable for constitutional-stage agreement on high levels of coercively imposed post-

constitutional taxation for the financing of pure transfers. As we relax
the four highly restrictive assumptions outlined in Section II, idealized contractors can be predicted to agree on fiscal-political arrangements that will generate lower levels of transfer taxation.

I shall relax the four basic assumptions in the order presented. The
first assumption involves the nature of the economy's "joint production function," which was so defined as to ensure that all value produced in the economy, despite decentralized organization of production, could be classified as social rent, because of the necessary
dependence on collectively supplied order. Individuals in isolation
may, plausibly, be modeled as being unable to produce value on their
own and without some legal protection. But groups of persons may
form coalitions that, by seceding from the inclusive membership of
the single polity, may organize for the provision of their own separate
legal-political order, within which value can be produced.[15] To the extent that such prospects exist, or are predicted to exist when persons
behind the veil consider alternative fiscal arrangements, the pre-tax
share of value that can properly be classified as social rent may be dramatically reduced.

The point here can perhaps best be presented with reference to the
existence and measurement of external marginal product of inputs. In
orthodox price theory, the external marginal product of an input unit
is the payment that unit can command in its best alternative use, its
genuine opportunity cost to a potential purchaser-employer. In our
initial restricted model, there is no external marginal product for any
input when the "production function" for the whole economy is considered. No individual could produce value outside of the collectivity,
either singly or in groups. If we now introduce a secession option and
recognize that individuals may, in groups, pull out from the initially
organized collectivity and form their own independent polities for the
provision of civil order, the external marginal products of those persons who might think of themselves as potential members of such seceding coalitions clearly become positive.

A recognition that individuals will strongly feel that they are "morally entitled" to the value status that they might expect to secure in an
alternative political setting will inform all contractors as they consider
fiscal arrangements at the constitutional stage of decision. The prospect that a group of persons who must pay a net tax to finance transfers to others might form a seceding group by pulling away from the
organized collectivity will clearly serve to limit the fiscal coercion that
will emerge from any agreement behind the genuine veil of ignorance. In terms of the discussion in Section V above, the effect will be
that of accentuating the predicted threshold differences between payment of net tax and receipt of transfers.

It is important to emphasize, however, that this modification in the
assumption about social rent will not eliminate from constitutional

consideration all fiscal arrangements that embody coercive taxes for the financing of redistributive transfers. So long as there exists differential advantage in the provision of protective-productive state services to the inclusive membership of the polity, as opposed to the provision of comparable services in potentially seceding units (or indeed in other external polities) there will remain a space over which the choice of postconstitutional tax-transfer institutions may range, a space that will include many alternatives. The prospect for advantageous secession on the part of a net taxpayer group may, in the absence of an actual secession option being exercised, tend only to reduce the agreed-on level of transfer taxes rather than to eliminate such taxation altogether. That is to say, some social rent will remain, and this rent provides a potential source for contractually accepted transfer taxation.

If an exit option does in fact exist, there will be a genuine limit imposed on the level of fiscal transfers for redistributive purposes. At best, in these settings, the net taxpayers can be forced to finance the full costs of protective-productive state services, plus transfers in the amount of the costs of forming a seceding coalition.[16] These essentially prudential considerations will enter the calculus of the idealized contractors as predictions concerning the institutional feasibility space within which choices of fiscal institutions can be made. As such, they are not my primary concern, which is that of placing bounds on contractually preferred levels of coercive taxation within any defined feasibility frontiers.

VII. The Nonmeasurability of Full Incomes

I shall now relax the second of the set of restrictive assumptions in Section II, that which postulated the technological feasibility of measuring the separate capacities of persons to generate value independently of any observed behavior. Without some such assumption, whether or not in extreme form, there would seem to be no basis for any contractarian justification of a redistributive fiscal structure.

This point may be illustrated with reference to Fig. 24-1, the simple two-person example. As drawn, Individual i is expected to be able to achieve a full income level shown by OY; Individual j is expected to be able to achieve a full income shown by YZ. Utility levels are directly related to expected full incomes. Suppose, however, that full incomes, the capacities to produce values, cannot be measured; there is no way to estimate an individual's capacity to produce value independently of his observed behavior. Suppose that actual production of value is all that may be empirically measured.

In this setting, an individual's appropriate fiscal liability (either positive or negative) could not be determined by direct reference to observed income-producing behavior. In Fig. 24-1, OY and YZ, if now defined to measure actual income produced, might well represent behavioral outcomes of choices made by persons with *identical* full incomes. Individual i might, by working more, generate income OY, while Individual j, by loafing, generate income YZ. In this case, a tax-transfer system, based on observed income produced, would be perverse to almost any objectives that might be agreed on by idealized contractors.

If, however, independent measurability of full incomes is simply not technologically possible, must the prospect of some perverse fiscal transfers rule out possible contractarian agreement on all redistributive structures? No answer can be given to this question a priori. The response would depend on contractors' predictions concerning the empirical relationship between individuals' capacities to produce value and their observed behavior in exercising such capacities. If this relationship is strongly positive, that is, if most individuals who are observed to produce relatively low incomes do so because of relatively low capacities to produce, and vice versa for high incomes, a redistributive structure need not seriously undermine legitimate contractarian objectives. Nonetheless, the contractual agreement will be informed by the prospect that any such system will involve some persons who secure transfer payments undeservedly, along with some persons who are taxed undeservedly.

The direction of effect on the basic constitutional choice of redistributive arrangements seems clear. Any relaxation of the second restrictive assumption imposed on the initial model will have the effect of reducing the level of coercive taxation for the financing of transfers that would emerge from any agreement among idealized contractors at the constitutional stage of fiscal choice. The relaxation of the second assumption operates in the same direction as the relaxation of the first. In terms of the geometry of Fig. 24-1, the effect is to widen the relevant threshold between the anticipated utility loss of a dollar of tax, levied on observed income, and the anticipated utility gain of a dollar's transfer, based on observed income. To put this result more generally, to the extent that differentials in observed income levels in the economy are predicted to reflect individual's voluntary choices rather than individually exogenous elements, contractually derived coercive taxation must be lower.

VIII. Excess Burden Introduced

I shall relax the third restrictive assumption imposed in Section II, that which involves an absence of predicted behavioral response of persons as taxpayers and transfer recipients in postconstitutional periods of fiscal operations. It is first necessary to examine the possible absence of behavioral response in a positive economic framework rather than as an assumption imposed on the model for clarity and simplification. Under what conditions is behavioral response unlikely? And, in these conditions, are there direct consequences for the choice among redistributive institutions as evaluated constitutionally?

An individual, facing a coercive tax liability that is measured by some base or source over which he exerts nominal claim, will not modify his behavior if there exist, over the relevant stage of private choices, no nontaxable utility-yielding opportunities. If such opportunities exist, and there is continuous and unconstrained variation between these and taxable opportunities, the individual who attains private equilibrium, pretax, will respond behaviorally. An absence of response would indicate that there are no nontaxable opportunities. A tax that is levied "optimally" on full or potential income would meet this condition, in which case there would be no anticipated utility loss due to excess-burden effects. Institutionally, however, such generality in taxation is not possible with informational requirements alone, and this will be recognized by our idealized contractors. Taxes must be anticipated to generate behavioral responses; persons will react by shifting toward nontaxable opportunities, and this will involve utility losses.

Similar conclusions apply for the transfer side. Here the analogue to nontaxable opportunities for the net taxpayers is eligibility requirements for transfer receipt, which will again involve anticipated utility loss by comparison with that achievable under a conceptually ideal pure transfer scheme. The idealized contractors will take account of the anticipated utility losses summarized under the excess-burden rubric, and constitutional agreement will reflect institutional arrangements that will embody a lower level of taxation (and transfer payments) than would emerge in the no-excess-burden model.[17] Although the institutional arrangements chosen will embody a lower transfer budget than in the no-excess-burden model, there is no means of determining whether or not the final, post-tax, post-transfer position achieved will be characterized by more or less remaining distributional inequality. Since the effect of fiscal incentives is to reduce the level of value produced, overall, a lower level of transfer may generate a distributional position closer to that of equality than constitutional agreement would produce in the absence of response.

IX. Rent-Seeking Introduced

I shall now relax the last of the four restrictive assumptions, that which states that governments in postconstitutional periods act ideally on the implementation of any fiscal institution passed along to them as instructions from the constitutional order. This assumption was imposed strictly for purposes of simplifying the earlier exposition, and such governmental behavior is implausible in any realistic model. The behavior of political agents in seeking to further their own interests, given the constraints within which they are allowed to act, must itself be modeled.[18] Again I shall not advance a specific model here; for my purposes I only suggest the hypothesis that there will be some predicted departure from the norms of political perfection previously assumed. There will be some anticipated wastage or loss of revenues in the fiscal process itself. Some share of tax revenues collected will not be channeled as transfer payments to recipients designated as such in the constitutional instructions. A share of these funds will, instead, be directed toward the provision of benefits (in kind or cash) to those who act as political agents or those whom such agents seek to benefit.

This change in the initial model has the same effect on the results as those that stem from the relaxation of the three other restrictive assumptions. Since the idealized contractor will now recognize that fiscal transfers, no matter how strongly these may be dictated by constitutionally agreed-on criteria of fairness, can never be modeled as dollar-for-dollar replacements of payments for taxes, there will be agreement on a lower level of transfers than would be approved under an ideally operating polity.[19]

We may refer to the simple geometry of the two-person model in Fig. 24-1. The expectation that there will be some slippage between revenues collected in taxes and those that are finally secured by designated transfer recipients will have the effect of increasing the size of the discontinuities in the relevant marginal utility functions.

X. The Whole Argument Summarized

My objective in this paper is the ambitious one of deriving possible limits to the imposition of coercive taxes for the financing of redistributive transfer payments within a general contractarian framework for normative analysis. My intent was not to lay down precise limits, but to outline the directions of effect that might be exerted by several relevant technological and behavioral elements on the possible constitutional delegation of taxing authority to legislatures.

I commenced with a rejection of the libertarian assertion that all taxation is theft, and I extended the Wicksellian unanimity criterion to the level of constitutional choice which allows for the possible activities of an in-period or postconstitutional transfer state. The tax-transfer authority would be limited by constitutional constraints, but this paper does not contain arguments for such general limits, as I have discussed these in earlier writings. My concern in this essay is to analyze the content of such constitutional constraints.

Initially, I set up a model that seemed to be the most favorable possible for the constitutional authorization of fiscal transfers. There are four highly restrictive assumptions. All valued product is social rent in the sense that, without the presence of legal-political order, inclusively defined over the whole membership of the polity, no value is generated at all. Secondly, it is assumed to be technologically feasible to measure individuals' full incomes, in-period, independently of any observed behavior. Thirdly, individuals do not respond at all to taxes and transfers. And, finally, governments operate perfectly in carrying out the dictates of the constitutional agreements.

Even in this highly confined model, the analysis suggested that the full equalization of incomes, which might seem to be dictated by concentration exclusively on the idealized distributive norms, will never be agreed to by the constitutional contractors, who will consider utility losses consequent on any *re*distribution of value among persons. In this rarefied setting, constitutional agreement may be reached, although not necessarily, on arrangements that shift the final allocation of values away from the initial market-related, pre-tax, pre-transfer imputation toward equality, but never on arrangements that will promote full equalization.

The restrictive assumptions were then relaxed in sequence. The first assumption attributed all valued product to social rent, as defined. While this attribution may be plausible with respect to individuals in isolation, who can rarely produce value outside some community-collectivity, the restriction becomes invalid with respect to external exit, even for individuals, and with respect to groups of individuals for internal exit. Groups may be organized for the purpose of seceding from the inclusive political unit, in which case the seceding group would be required to provide its own protective-productive collective services. The analysis suggested that any attenuation of the social rent attribution with respect to either external or internal exit would lead constitutional contractors to reckon on enhanced utility losses when tax exactions exceed properly measured opportunity cost limits. This recognition will reinforce the direction of departure from equality already indicated in the initial pure model.

Relaxation of the second assumption, that which assumes the measurability of full incomes, points in the same direction, that is, toward lower levels of coercive taxation. Practically, incomes that are to be used as the bases for estimating fiscal liabilities must be behaviorally generated, ensuring errors in relating tax and transfer payments to full incomes, the appropriate contractarian base. The idealized contractors will recognize this departure from conceptually ideal measurement and will move toward minimizing errors by placing more weight on pre-tax, pre-transfer imputations.

The third assumption of no excess burden will, when relaxed, shift the results in the same direction as the first two considered. Finally, the relaxation of the assumption concerning the behavior of political agents, when added to the directional effects of the adjustments already noted, may call into question any significant departure from the pre-tax, pre-transfer allocation of shares in value, adjusted for some imputation of payments for the provision of protective and productive state services.

The analysis does not lend itself to laying down hard and fast limits. It does, however, advance the argument beyond that which stops at the criteria for the contractual process itself. That which does emerge from the idealized constitutional contract is, by construction, the "just" solution to the initial question posed. And this ultimate response must be allowed to include a whole set of possible fiscal arrangements. What the analysis of this essay does is to provide additional insights into the calculus of the individual contractor who participates in the constitutional exercise.

Environmental parameters are, of course, critical to any constitutional dialogue, and some directions of effect may be readily predicted. To the extent that persons think of themselves as members of the inclusive political community rather than as individuals in isolation or as members of potentially seceding groups, the range for coercive taxation is expanded. To the extent that genuine publicness in the provision of protective productive services extends over the inclusive membership, the same result holds. To the extent that individuals are homogeneous with respect to utilizing their capacities, the scope for measuring appropriate fiscal liability increases and with it the scope for coercive taxation. The same result follows from homogeneity in response to fiscal arrangements. And, finally, to the extent that agents behave in furtherance of the "public interest," as defined in the constitutional agreement, the threshold between the losses involved in taxation and the utility gains embodied in transfer receipts is reduced. Shifts in these critical parameters in the opposing directions will, of course, generate directionally opposite results.

Notes

I am indebted to my colleague, Viktor Vanberg, and to Geoffrey Brennan, Australian National University, for helpful comments.

1. See Knut Wicksell, *Finanztheoretische Untersuchungen* (Jena: Gustav Fischer, 1896); major portions of this book are published in translation as "A New Principle of Just Taxation," in *Classics in the Theory of Public Finance*, ed. R. A. Musgrave and A. T. Peacock (London: Macmillan and Co., 1958), pp. 72–118.

2. See James M. Buchanan and Gordon Tullock, *The Calculus of Consent* (Ann Arbor: University of Michigan Press, 1962).

3. See my book, *The Limits of Liberty* (Chicago: University of Chicago Press, 1975), esp. p. 73; and my paper, "Taxation in Fiscal Exchange," *Journal of Public Economics* 6 (1976): 17–29.

4. Cambridge: Cambridge University Press, 1980.

5. See Buchanan and Tullock, *Calculus of Consent.*

6. Wicksell explicitly states that the procedural criteria he proposes are for the purpose of promoting justice in taxation, rather than in ultimate distribution of product. He does not prejudge the pre-tax distribution, but he argues that any adjustment in this distribution belongs to the general sphere of law rather than taxation.

To the extent that general agreement emerges on a set of tax-financed transfers in a postconstitutional period, there is, by definition, no genuine transfer of utility involved. Those who agree to be taxed in order to make the transfers to others do so voluntarily, even if collectively rather than privately, and are not, therefore, coerced by the collectivity in the process.

7. Technically, this statement may be interpreted as a presumption about the organization of production in the economy, but it is a presumption that would not be seriously questioned. It amounts to saying that, given the establishment and enforcement of general rules of property and contract, production would be efficiently organized in many separate units (firms), which would exchange both with other units and with persons. The assumption that all valued product is *social* rent, in the sense defined, should not be taken to imply that the whole economy's production is most efficiently organized in a monolithic "team," ensuring that, even with the general rules of property and contract, there would be no means of measuring relative productivities of differing team components. In such a setting, all product would be rent, whether or not we add the word "social" as a qualifier. In the decentralized organization of production and exchange here postulated, payments to inputs need embody no intra- or interfirm or industry rent despite the classification of all valued product as *social* rent. The presumption that decentralized rather than centralized or monolithic organization of production would be efficient, given the general rules of property and contract, is necessary in order for the question addressed in this paper to arise. If the whole economy is best organized as a monolithic "team," there would be no "redistribution" problem, at least in the sense normally discussed.

8. The external marginal product of an input unit is defined as the value that unit could produce in its most highly valued alternative use; this external product value is that which is necessary to ensure that the input remain in the employment specified; this value becomes the opportunity cost of the input to the employing firm. Internal marginal product is, by contrast, the difference in the value of total product in the specified facility attributable to the presence of the input unit in question. This internal product measures the potential opportunity loss that the firm would suffer if the input unit is not employed, but unless the external marginal product is equal to the internal, the internal marginal product is not the necessary opportunity cost of the input unit to the firm. The difference between the internal and external marginal product values becomes genuine rent, and the sharing of such rent between the owner of the input and the employing firm is not determinate in the operation of the competitive market process.

TAXATION AND PUBLIC DEBT

For an example of a practical application of the differences between the internal and external marginal product as bases for input payments, see James M. Buchanan and Robert D. Tollison, "The Homogenization of Heterogeneous Inputs," *American Economic Review* 71 (March, 1981): 28–38.

9. See J. R. Kearl, "Do Entitlements Imply That Taxation Is Theft?" *Philosophy and Public Affairs* 7 (Fall, 1977): 74–81.

10. Care must be taken to clarify the distinction between the nature of the collective input, let us say, *order*, and the ordinary input units that may be employed to produce this collective input, units that may work either in the state or the market sector. There is no basis for suggesting that the ordinary inputs employed in the state sector should secure more than their counterparts in the market sector. But this does not amount to saying that the state, as the collective, may not be authorized, in the constitutional choice process, to collect something over and beyond the necessary market-related payments to its own inputs.

Consider a simple example of a ten-person community. Behind a veil of ignorance, each person knows that no value can be produced without the presence of one police officer, who must be hired by the collectivity as such and who might otherwise produce value in the private sector in the presence of some alternative person as police officer. The collectivity will never be authorized, at the constitutional level, to pay the person hired as police officer more than his opportunity cost. But the collectivity may well be authorized, by agreement at the constitutional stage, to withdraw from the private sector product a total value (taxation) more than the opportunity wage of the single police officer collectively hired.

11. John Rawls, *A Theory of Justice* (Cambridge, Mass.: Harvard University Press, 1971).

12. Consider an example where all product is agricultural and is produced separately by individual families on small plots. The extreme assumptions hold; no value can be produced outside of civil order; full incomes are measurable; excess burdens and rent-seeking are absent. But the person who plants, hoes, and digs the potatoes will come to attach a claim to those potatoes that "he produces," and he will react negatively to any collective "taking" of these for transfer purposes. This negative reaction will be predicted by the contractors who participate in the constitutional dialogue behind the veil of ignorance.

The agricultural example suggests, however, that, as the economy's production processes move beyond those that embody the direct association of the individual or family with observable product, the negative reaction to "takings" by the collectivity will fall in comparison to the reaction under the more primitive structure. As the individual comes to be more and more alienated from the goods and services produced, in the Marxian sense, we should, therefore, predict that idealized contractors, behind the veil, will tend to agree on a higher level of distributive transfers. The linkage between the shift into the industrial society and the rise of the transfer state may, in this way, be conceptually derived from the contractarian calculus. As the economy shifts beyond industrialization toward the service society, the pattern may possibly be reversed.

13. For a general discussion of the difference between the choice of a distribution and the choice from among redistributive institutions, see "Distribu-

tive and Redistributive Norms," chapter 14 in my book *Liberty, Market, and State* (London: Wheatsheaf Books, 1986).

The precise location of the agreed-on solution along the spectrum between some pre-tax, pre-transfer distribution and full equality will be dependent on other institutional choices that are made, notably those that establish the structure of the tax system. To the extent that taxes are imposed directly on bases that are measured on market-related earning, with rates differing among persons, the threshold difference noted will remain important. If, however, the collectivity should be authorized institutionally to extract revenues "off the top," so to speak, prior to any market-related imputation of values among persons, the threshold effect would become less significant. Such a structure would require proportionality in rates, and some gross nonpersonal income base. For my purposes here, I shall neglect these interrelationships.

For a sophisticated discussion of individuals' preferences among tax institutions, although not strictly within a veil-of-ignorance construction, see Charles J. Goetz, "Tax Preferences in a Collective Decision-making Context," Ph.D. dissertation, University of Virginia, 1964 (Ann Arbor, Mich.: University Microfilms, 1965).

14. In terms of the geometry of Fig. 24-1, the initial position will be constitutionally preferred if the vertical displacements (shown as BC on MU_i and FG on MU_j) are sufficiently large to overlap. Note that, as the market position, Y, is shifted toward equal distribution, and/or as the thresholds increase, this result is more likely to occur.

15. I shall concentrate on the possible existence of internal exit through the secession option, within the assumption that there is some initial all-inclusive polity. Much the same analysis can be extended to a setting in which persons or groups have external exit options, that is, where there exist many separate political units, among which migration can take place. The analysis of external exit is more complex because it must involve several units; in addition, this analysis is more familiar because of its discussion under the "Tiebout model" rubric in fiscal theory.

For a preliminary paper that develops further the analysis of internal exit through secession, see James M. Buchanan and Roger L. Faith, "Secession and the Sharing of Surplus: Toward a Theory of Internal Exit," presented at the Public Choice Society Meeting, New Orleans, February, 1985.

16. It is possible to argue that persons behind the veil of ignorance will agree on the principle of maximal equal liberty, the first of the two Rawlsian principles of justice. In this case, it can be further suggested that the liberty of persons to secede and form new polities is a countable Rawlsian liberty, in which instance the community that meets standards of justice must allow such an option to exist. For a discussion of some of the implications of this point, see James M. Buchanan and Loren Lomasky, "The Matrix of Contractarian Justice," *Social Philosophy and Policy* 2 (Autumn, 1984): 12–32.

17. In the setting here postulated, the contractors will also tend to agree on a selection of tax and transfer institutions that will minimize the predicted behavior responses, given a simultaneously determined level of transfer budget. They will do so because the utility losses measured by the excess burdens will themselves be anticipated at the constitutional stage, and efforts will be made to minimize these deadweight losses. Although the model is quite dif-

ferent in purpose from that introduced by Gary Becker, this conclusion emerges from analysis that is in many respects analogous to his. See Gary Becker, "A Theory of Competition among Pressure Groups for Political Influence," *Quarterly Journal of Economics* 98 (August, 1983): 371–400.

18. In our book, *The Power to Tax* (Cambridge: Cambridge University Press, 1980), Geoffrey Brennan and I examined the implications of a single revenue-maximization model for the behavior of governments.

19. The difficulty of implementing any desired tax-transfer policy, as dictated by the objective of justice, through operation of any political institutions is discussed in some detail in chapter 8 of *The Reason of Rules*, by Geoffrey Brennan and James Buchanan (Cambridge: Cambridge University Press, 1985).

25.

Organization Theory
and Fiscal Economics:
Society, State, and Public Debt

WITH VIKTOR VANBERG

I. Introduction

Both the magnitude and the apparent permanence of budgetary deficits have refocused economists' attention on the basic theory of public debt. Although the central issues are different in the debates of the 1980s from those of the late 1950s and early 1960s, a common element in both discussions is the dominance of a macroeconomic methodological perspective. Buchanan's 1958 challenge to the Keynesian macroeconomists, which was only partially successful, applies with equal force to much of the macroeconomic policy discussion of the 1970s and 1980s.

Our purpose in this essay is not to prolong or to extend the debate on the basic economic theory of public debt. We shall not examine the respective macroeconomic consequences of debt versus tax financing, an issue that has occupied much of the received debate. Our purpose is the different one of demonstrating that elementary organization theory can be used to draw attention to relevant dimensions that remained implicit in the arguments that separated Buchanan from his critics.[1] While the thrust of our analysis supports Buchanan's criticism of the macroaggregation embodied in the orthodox view, the arguments used here are quite different from those advanced earlier by Buchanan.[2] The main target of our criticism is not the organic fallacy implied in certain macroaggregationist notions that treat the economy or the community as a unit. Our departure from the orthodox treatment is based, instead, on the latter's failure to distinguish properly between "the state" and "the society" or "the economy," a failure that obscures crucial dimensions of the whole public debt issue. As we shall argue, if the state is properly recognized as an *organization* and distinguished as such from "the society" or "the economy," a reinterpretation of central notions of the public debt debate commends itself, in particular, with respect to such issues as the distinction between "internal" and "external" debt, the relevant effects of public debt, and the debt burden.

II. The State as an Organization

Organizations like clubs, associations, unions, and firms can meaningfully be treated as operating *units* without departing from a methodologically individualistic framework for analysis. Within an organization, persons are typically related in ways that allow for joint decisions and concerted action. This capacity for joint effort reflects the fact that, as a member of the organization, the individual is submitting a part of his resources to the organization's system of control or authority. The essence of organizational membership is subjection to the authority system (however this system may be constructed) as it applies to whatever resources are defined to be within the organization's domain. Within an organization, the resources that are pooled by the individual members are subjected to unitary control. And, as this control is exercised, the organization can meaningfully be treated as a decision-making, acting unit. The unifying principle is that which is embodied in the rules that describe the organization's authority structure.

Individuals are members of particular organizations under specific resource commitments, such commitments varying over types of organizations. In this sense, the difference between, for instance, a golf club, a business firm, and a political party can be specified in terms of the kind and extent of resources committed to the respective organization. The *constitution* of an organization, whether explicit or implicit, states the terms of membership, including a specification of the share of an individual's resources subject to the control of the organization. The constitution also defines the individual's rights of participation in the system of organizational control over the combined resource shares of all members.[3]

"The society" or "the economy" is not an organization. "The society" (or "the economy") is a conceptual construction, a useful name for the totality of socioeconomic relationships among a group of persons, with the group being typically defined by geographical dimensions. The society (or the economy) is not an organizational unit that controls resources somehow pooled by its members. Although the phrase "members of a society" is often used in practice, the sense in which a person can be said to be part of a society (economy) is quite different from what applies to membership in an organization. The society (or the economy) does not exist as a system of authority to which the individual, as member, has submitted some share of his resource endowment.

In contrast, the state *is* an organizational unit in the strict sense defined above. The state is the political organization of persons who live in the society, and it normally holds a monopoly position in its role as a "protective" agency,[4] establishing and enforcing the legal framework within which social interaction takes place. It is an organization through which joint collective actions are taken. As with any organization, individuals are members only with defined shares of their resource endowments, and the legitimate domain of the state extends only to those resources that individuals, as citizens, submit to the state's authority. As with most organizations, the dividing line between resources committed to the control of the organization and those remaining outside the organization's domain may be blurred, and there may be slippages between private and public domains, with accompanying ambiguities. Nevertheless, aside from the limiting case of a perfectly totalitarian structure, for all states, as for all other organizations, a meaningful distinction can still be drawn between those resources that individuals, as citizens, commit to the state's potential control and those resources that they retain for private disposition, individually or in non-state organizations.[5]

In terms of this distinction the dividing line between "the state" and "the society" can be clearly specified: The state comprises all the relations in which individuals engage in their capacity as citizens, and the society comprises all these plus those relations in which individuals engage in their private capacity.

To interpret the state as an organization does not, of course, ignore the unique features that distinguish the state from other organizations. Since the state is the agency through which the "rules of the game" are established and enforced, the state controls to an important extent the institutional environment within which persons act in all private capacities, either individually or organizationally. However, despite the fact that the legal umbrella for the whole society is provided through the auspices of the state, there remains a crucial distinction between what citizens do (or may be required to do) as citizens, as members of the organization "the state," and what persons do in their private capacities, within the constraints of the legal umbrella.

III. Public Debt and Private Claims

There is a straightforward implication of the distinction made above for central issues in public debt theory. Both in the dominant Keynesian macroeconomics of the 1950s and—often more implicitly—in the macropolicy discussion of the 1980s, there is a categorical distinction made between internal and external public debt, with the words *internal* and *external* referring to the distinction between debt held by citizens of the borrowing state as opposed to debt held by foreigners. The inference typically is that public debt obligations held by persons within the economy are, somehow, less burdensome than those held by persons outside the economy, that the former are somehow not net debts, due to the offsetting claims held by persons within the economy.

If we consider an organization such as a golf club or a trade union, it would seem clearly fallacious to suggest that debt incurred by the organization, as such, should be meaningfully balanced against the private savings of those persons who are members. A strict dividing line is drawn between those resources that are subject to the organization's domain (which persons, as members, have submitted to the organization's control) and those resources that are outside this domain, although still owned by the persons who make up the organization's membership. Those resources that remain outside the organization's defined domain are *external* to the organization, no less than resources owned by nonmembers. If, for example, the bonds issued by a country club for the financing of a swimming pool should be purchased by members, the debt so created remains external to the club except in the special case where members were somehow obligated, *in their capacities as members*, to purchase debt obligations. If members are, as a condition of membership so obligated to purchase the club's debt instruments, financing an outlay by "debt" of this kind and financing the same outlay by direct contributions of members would be equivalent in many respects.

If, by contrast, members have no such obligation to purchase the bonds issued by the club, and, instead, purchase these securities (make the loans) on a strictly voluntary basis, the debt financing and the contribution financing alternatives are quite different in effect. If a distinction is made between "internal" and "external" borrowing by the organization, the relevant demarcation line is between loans that might be secured from members *as obligations of membership* and loans that are negotiated with nonmembers or with members in their strictly private capacities. It would be misleading to label as "internal borrowing" funds that are loaned to the organization by members in their private capacities, with "internal" suggesting that the relevant transactions all remain within the collectivity of persons who hold membership in the organization. Such a usage of terms here would ignore the basic fact that only the organization does indeed exist as an accounting unit, the obligations and claims of which can be meaningfully compared. The same cannot be said for the particular group of persons who hold membership in the organization. This group does not exist as a collective unit that inclusively embodies the total resource endowments of the organization's members.

These arguments apply to the organization "the state," notwithstanding the special character of this particular organization. If the government finances outlays by exercising its constitutional authority to impose taxes on citizens or to *require* citizens to purchase bonds as a condition of continuing membership (forced loans), the fiscal operation is clearly "internal," and the two methods of financing would be equivalent in many respects. That is to say, taxation and forced loans are properly classified as internal means of financing for the organization "state."[6]

If, however, government borrows from persons who happen to be citizens but who act only in their private capacities and voluntarily (that is, not as part of their obligations as citizens) purchase the debt instruments, this borrowing would be just as external to the organization, as such, as would be borrowing from persons who are not citizens (from foreigners). Different from the way the internal-external distinction is de facto defined in the public debt debate, the organizational conceptual framework used here suggests that the relevant distinction between internal and external public debt is not that between loans made by citizens on the one hand and loans made by foreigners on the other. The distinction is between those loans that citizens must advance according to the terms of citizenship, that is, forced loans levied upon them by government in the exercise of its duly constituted fiscal authority, and those loans that are made through wholly voluntary purchases of debt instruments, whether by citizens or noncitizens. As stressed above, individuals who, as citizens, are members of the organization "the state" are not identical to individuals as described in terms of *all* their resource endowments, save in those settings where there exists no limits on governmental authority.

In all settings where there are constitutional limits on the exercise of governmental powers over the individual, it becomes misleading, and ultimately inappropriate, to aggregate claims and obligations across "the society" or "the economy" in some national balance-sheet sense of accounting.[7] Balance sheets may be constructed for individuals and for organizations, including the state. The economy, however, is simply not a social unit for which claims and obligations can be meaningfully discussed.

As our discussion suggests, the state, as an organization, is equally obligated and the terms of membership for citizens in the future are equally affected, whether the debt is held by citizens or by foreigners. So long as debt instruments are voluntarily purchased, the source of the loans remains irrelevant for the state's balance sheet; all debt is external. The claims of those who hold the debt instruments, be they persons within the economy or outside, enter into private balance sheets, which are beyond the domain of the political organization.

IV. The Effects of Public Debt: The Burden Issue

A core issue in the long-standing public debt controversy has been the equivalence of, or difference between, taxation and borrowing as means to finance public expenditures, particularly with respect to the question of who bears the burden of the expenditures made. The traditional discussion focused on the macroeconomic consequences of the two financing instruments on savings and capital accumulation in the economy, notably on the realism of the assumptions involved by the Ricardian equivalence theorem or its modern restatement, the Barro neutrality theorem.[8] The organizational theoretical framework used here suggests a different emphasis. Since the state as an organization is the borrowing unit, the effects of using this financing instrument that should be analyzed first are those concerning the current and future members of the organization. For a discussion of these effects, and notably of the effects on future generations of members, a few terminological remarks should be helpful.

If we use the term "corporate action" to define those activities that are attributed to the organized unit as such (to a club, a union, a firm, a state), then the act of borrowing by such a unit may be called "corporate borrowing." Utilizing the analysis of Section III, we can refer to "internal corporate borrowing" when loans are advanced to the organization by its members *in their capacities as members*, and we can refer to "external corporate borrowing" when loans are advanced to the organization by persons who act voluntarily in their private capacities, whether or not they are members of the organization. Drawing an analytical distinction between the membership groups in the organization at the time of and subsequent to the act of corporate borrowing, the term "future members" can be used as a name for the latter group.[9] It is obvious that corporate borrowing implies obligations for future members to amortize and service the debt and, hence, that deficits imply financing current public expenditures by future payments. In this sense corporate borrowing in general and public debt in particular clearly imply that, independently of benefit considerations (alternatively: independently of the character of the expenditure so financed), a burden of *payment* is shifted to future organization members or citizen-taxpayers.

How such a temporal shift of burden is to be judged will depend on the particular circumstances. If, over the relevant period of debt service, the membership group remains the same as at the time the debt was created, the financing arrangement simply involves a postponement of cost within the same group, comparable to a situation where an individual finances current expenditures by borrowing. If, however, the membership group changes within the relevant period of time, this means that, depending on how exactly the composition of the group changes, some or all of the beneficiaries of the debt-financed expenditure are able to shift the burden of payment, in part or even in total, to other persons. In this sense corporate borrowing has a negative impact on the terms of future membership in the respective organization, except in the case where productive investments have been financed that generate sufficient benefits over the relevant period to compensate for the debt burden.[10]

Since corporate borrowing might allow the current beneficiaries of corporate expenditures to shift the costs, at least in part, to other persons, the use of such financing instruments would seem to be a tempting option in an organization's budgetary practice. The extent, however, to which this temptation actually can be effective is obviously dependent on the constraints under which the organization's budgetary decisions are made.

V. Principles of Corporate Borrowing and Opportunity Costs

The potential of an organization to finance corporate outlays by debt is contingent on two sets of conditions. First, there must be some (explicit or implicit) constitutional provisions that allow the organization to borrow and that stipulate the decision-making procedures to be followed when borrowing is considered. Second, there must be present potential creditors who might purchase the debt instruments. The willingness of potential creditors to loan to the organization will depend on the perceived prospect that loans will be repaid and on the opportunity costs of making the funds available. The opportunity costs are basically different to potential creditors as between internal corporate borrowing and external corporate borrowing. For the external creditor, the opportunity costs of loaning to an organization equal the value of the best alternative use of the funds provided, possibly a loan to another organization. For the internal "creditor," the member who is forced to subscribe to the loan as a condition of continuing membership, the choice faced is not among alternative uses of funds, but is, instead, between accepting the compulsory loan in order to remain within the organization and dropping membership and leaving the organization entirely (or facing whatever sanctions are imposed within the organization for failing to meet one's membership obligations). The member can avoid providing the internal loan only by removing himself from the organization where the loan is a requirement of continued membership.

There are structural features of *private* organizations that tend to discourage external borrowing to finance wasteful investments or consumption. Current members, deciding on the organization's financial practices, and/or potential creditors, typically have good reasons to take the impact on future membership conditions into account when deciding on borrowing or providing a loan to finance corporate expenditures. Where membership rights are tradeable (as, for instance, shares of stock in a corporation), anticipation of negative effects on future terms of membership, which can be expected to decrease the value (price) of membership rights, will limit current members' inclination to use corporate borrowing as an instrument to finance unproductive expenditures. Where membership rights are not tradeable, but where, for other reasons, current members are interested in keeping the terms of membership sufficiently attractive to draw new members and to retain present members, a similar argument applies. In both cases current members face a trade-off between potential gains from debt financing and potential losses, either in terms of a decreasing value of tradeable membership rights or in terms of disadvantages resulting from the organization's inability to attract new and/or to keep old members in periods subsequent to the debt creation.

Independent of the organization's current members' inclination or reluctance to finance unproductive expenditures by borrowing, potential creditors—whether members of the organization or nonmembers—have their own reasons to pay attention to the consequences the debt-financed expenditures will have on the future attractiveness of the terms of membership. The probability that the loan they provide will be properly repaid depends on the existence of members who comply with the organization's debt obligations over the relevant repayment period. As current expenditures and the way they are financed make future terms of membership less attractive, the risk increases of there being no members in the future willing to fulfill the organization's obligations (notice that bankruptcy is one way for "future members" to evade the organization's debt obligations), and potential creditors will be proportionally less inclined to provide a loan to the organization. Consequently, in private organizations we can identify mechanisms that on one side tend to provide current members a motive to curb their temptation to finance unproductive outlays by debt, and, on the other side, set external limits to their capability to engage in such a financial practice.

VI. Public Debt and the State as an Organization

In the case of private organizations, the freedom of entry (or refusal of entry) and exit essentially limits the potential exploitation of future members (members in periods subsequent to the debt creation) through the debt financing of wasteful outlay. Individuals may simply refuse to join and, thus, to take on the debt obligations of financially shaky organizations, or, if they are members of such an organization, they may exercise their option to leave the membership group. As a general rule, the easier it is for persons to refuse entry and to exit from an organization once entered, the better the interests of future members are protected.

It is precisely the weakness of this self-enforcing feedback mechanism that characterizes the state, considered as an organization. Membership rights in a state are typically not transferable[11] and they are typically not acquired by explicit decision. Potential entrants who are born into citizenship do not have the option of refusing entry into the organization, as such, and by the time they are old enough to make a deliberate decision to stay or leave, the costs of exit will be high, compared to the typical exit costs for private organizations. The principal reason for the comparatively high exit costs is, of course, that *citizenship* and *residency* are typically coupled, that one cannot, as a rule, quit one's membership in a state without moving one's residence outside the state's geographical boundaries.[12] Because of these high exit costs, however, decisions to leave or to stay will be relatively unresponsive to changes in the attractiveness of the terms of membership, and, accordingly, the temptation of any group of current members to shift costs temporally is enhanced. By financing outlay with debt, with the proceeds used to produce current-period benefits, the current-period membership group can effectively pass on the net costs of the combined fiscal operation.[13]

The obverse of the same point involves the possible behavior of creditors in their expressed willingness to lend to the organization. When they consider loans to a private organization, they must reckon on the future impact of current budgetary practice on the attractiveness of membership and/or the transfer prices of shares in the organization. When the same creditors consider loans to the state, as an organization, the same concerns are not present. The high exit costs along with the compulsory entry of future members offer assurance that there will be a set of persons who will necessarily be members of the organization. The risk of default will still be present, as it would with private organizations, but the relative weakness of the entry-exit option for citizens remains an important differentiating characteristic of the state, one that will surely influence the behavior of potential creditors.

A somewhat different, if closely related, aspect of the creditor's attitude toward state debt is grounded in the recognition that the future members cannot isolate themselves wholly from charges incurred by past members. Public debt allows past members of the state to leave enforceable claims against income of future members, which may exceed, in total, the value of the assets transmitted to those persons as members of the state.[14] In contrast, negatively valued bequests are not legally possible for families, and they are ruled out practically for voluntary private organizations. Potential creditors of the state need not, therefore, be concerned with the temporal "productivity" of the debt-financed outlay, so long as the limits of the state's taxing authority have not been reached.

VII. Exit, Voice, and the Democratic State

The interests of persons who will be members of the state are not protected from potential fiscal exploitation to the same extent that they would be in organizations characterized by voluntary entry and exit. This fact alone does not, of course, imply that such exploitation must occur. What remains to be examined is the potential effect of the voice option, which in A. O. Hirschmann's classic book is mentioned as the second principal means for individuals to control an organization's performance.[15] The dynamics of the internal decision-making process remain to be analyzed. The rules that define procedures through which organizational decisions are reached make up a part of the constitution of any organization.

Implicitly, in references to such procedures earlier in our discussion, we have presumed that membership implies potential participation; that is, we have presumed that the organizations are, in some sense, ultimately "democratic." Such a structure embodies the constitutionally defined rights of members to exercise the decision-making authority of the organization, either directly through some voting procedures or indirectly through a delegation of authority to a designated agent or group of agents. This basic presumption of democratic decision-making need not apply, generally, to all states, as organizations. Since, however, our primary concern is with Western countries, we shall restrict attention to those states that do embody democratic processes in the sense indicated. We want to examine the extent to which democratic decision processes act to reflect the interests of persons who will be members of the community in periods after that in which fiscal decisions are made.

For any organization, the membership group at the time of debt creation and the membership group in subsequent periods are typically different, due to the exit of old members and/or the entry of new ones. But there is always an intersection of these two membership sets. To the extent that there is a mix of old and new members, and to the extent that their time horizons *as members* vary, some being more concerned than others about the impact of current organizational decisions on future terms of membership, the interest of future generations of members should have some voice in current organizational decision-making. For the state this means that the temporal shift of debt burden is restricted to the extent that current members themselves anticipate they will be affected themselves in subsequent periods and also to the extent that they take into account the interests of their own heirs.

However, as with the entry-exit dimension of membership, there are also special characteristics of the state, as an organization, that are relevant for the "voice" dimension. One such feature is the discrepancy between the set of *voters*, participants in decision procedures for the organization, and the set of *members*. In private organizations that embody democratic rules, the right to vote (to participate) is typically acquired on entry into membership. Hence, the set of voters is typically coincident with the set of members. With the state, however, persons typically become citizens, or members, by birth, while voting rights are attained only on maturity. Those who are franchised make up only a subset of those defined as members.

The implication of this discrepancy for the public debt issue is straightforward. It is precisely those members who should exhibit the most long-range or farsighted interests who are the disenfranchised. The decision process is biased toward the temporally characterized interests of those members who participate. These interests will necessarily exhibit somewhat shorter time horizons than those that would emerge if all members could be treated as full participants. The effect here is accentuated by the necessary shortening of the time horizons for all members (and voting participants) as they approach or pass retirement age.

As indicated earlier, the interests of persons who are currently not franchised but who will become members of the state will be, to some extent, incorporated within the interests of those who do participate in current-period decisions. Persons are not indifferent to the interest of their children, grandchildren, nieces, nephews, and even the children of strangers. These interests in future citizens will, of course, mitigate the willingness of present members, as voters, to transfer the cost of public outlays forward in time. There seems to be no reason, however, to expect that such caring for future members would totally offset the effects of the nonrepresentation of future interests in the overall political process.

Reform aimed at ensuring more direct representation of future interests runs afoul of other problems. Reduction in the voting age immediately raises questions of competency, and the weighting of adult votes to take account of minor dependents violates basic norms of political equality. Analogous to the legal representation of a minor by a guardian, a "political guardian"—presumably one parent, who could vote on behalf of a "political minor"—is a conceivable arrangement, but there are obvious difficulties. There seems to be no escaping the conclusion that, whereas for private organizations the typical interests of current members and/or potential creditors can be expected sufficiently to constrain the use of borrowing, the dynamics of interests cannot be expected to do the same for the state. Explicit constitutional constraints may be needed as a safeguard against the temporally biased interest of the franchised members.

Such constitutional constraints could, of course, take several forms. A simple prohibition on deficit financing or some requirement that supermajorities in legislatures are necessary to authorize such financing may prove workable. (Most versions of the proposed balanced-budget amendment to the United States Constitution involve the requirement that three-fifths of both houses of Congress approve any departure from projected matching of revenues and outlays.) A rule limiting government's debt instruments to forced loans only may be a much more effective constraint. Alternatively, required administrative differentiation between consumption and capital outlay in the state's budget, with debt financing restricted to the latter, might seem to offer prospects for improvement, despite observed failure of such procedures in several European countries.

VIII. The Limited State and the Theory of Macroeconomic Policy

We have deliberately eschewed entering the lists on either side of the various arguments among economists on the macroeconomics of public debt and deficits, especially in the economists' own terms. Our purpose has been restricted to the demonstration that some of the elementary principles of organization theory can point toward a clarification of some of the apparent ambiguities that remain in the economists' arguments. While our chosen area of inquiry has been that of public debt, there are evident implications of the analysis for wider and more inclusive issues in the theory of macroeconomic policy.

Our central proposition is that the "state" should be defined as an organization with *limited* claims on the resource endowments of its members, and that this organization, as such, be distinguished categorically from "the society" or "the economy." This proposition may be of more relevance for normative than for positive analysis, but its normative thrust applies at the level of fundamental political philosophy rather than at alternative methodological presuppositions for macroeconomic theory. And we submit that the definition of the state as being subjected to some limits on its potential command of resources is a normative model that finds widespread acceptance among social scientists and philosophers in Western societies. As our discussion may suggest, however, much of the theory of macroeconomic policy may be based, albeit unconsciously, on quite a different normative model of the state, one that even its practitioners would never explicitly adopt.

Notes

1. J. M. Buchanan, *Public Principles of Public Debt* (Homewood, Ill.: Richard D. Irwin, 1958); J. Ferguson, ed., *Public Debt and Future Generations* (Chapel Hill: University of North Carolina Press, 1964); J. M. Buchanan and R. Wagner, *Democracy in Deficit: The Political Legacy of Lord Keynes* (New York: Academic Press, 1977).

2. A main target of Buchanan's criticism of what he called "the new orthodoxy" is a macroeconomic perspective that, by focusing on "the aggregate totals which make up the national balance sheet" (Buchanan, *Public Principles of Public Debt*, p. 41), implicitly adopts an organic conception of the nation or community, a conception that is inherently inconsistent with the individualistic economic tradition (p. 36). Buchanan's emphasis is on the fallacy of aggregation that is committed by treating "the economy" ("the society," "the community") as the unit for which the relevant trade-off between costs and benefits of public debt are to be assessed.

3. J. S. Coleman, *Power and the Structure of Society* (New York: Norton, 1974), p. 38ff; V. Vanberg, *Markt und Organisation* (Tübingen: Siebeck [Mohr], 1982); V. Vanberg, "Organizations as Corporate Actors," Working Paper, Center for Study of Public Choice, George Mason University, 1984.

4. J. M. Buchanan, *The Limits of Liberty: Between Anarchy and Leviathan* (Chicago: University of Chicago Press, 1975).

5. The constitutionally defined demarcation between an individual's resources that are committed to an organization and those that remain outside the organization's domain is an issue different from the distinction between full versus limited liability. A business firm, for instance, has in its domain those resources that, according to the firm's constitution, the owner-members have committed to the firm's authority system. Whether limited or full liability, the firm's authority to dispose over its owner-members' resources is restricted to the resources constitutionally committed and does not extend to any other resources owned by its members as persons. The question of whether the owner-members are fully liable for external claims held against the firm does not affect the definition of the firm's legitimate domain as an organization.

In this context, it seems to conform to common understanding, as well as to international legal practice, to view the state as a "limited liability" organization. The state's members, the citizens, are not held personally responsible for the state's debts. A creditor could not shift a legal claim against, say, Argentina to an Argentinian citizen as a private person.

6. Conceptually, three different types of such forced loans can be distinguished: first, *nontransferable* loans, generating claims tied to the original purchaser; second, *transferable* loans, generating claims that can be transferred (e.g., by bequest) to other members of the organization, but not to nonmembers; and third, *tradeable* loans, generating claims that can be sold or transferred to anybody, including nonmembers. The differences between these types of forced loans may be of interest in some context, but they will be ignored here, in order not to complicate our analysis.

7. To argue, as Abba P. Lerner (see Buchanan, *Public Principles of Public Debt*, p. 12) did, that "for national debt which is owed by the nation to citi-

zens of the same nation . . . [there] is no external creditor. . . . We owe it to ourselves . . ." is to blur the fundamental distinction between the organized unit "state" and "the society" or "the economy." If by "nation" Lerner meant *the state*, and by "we," all the citizens in their capacity as members of the state, then for what is called "national debt" there is an "external creditor," namely, citizens in their *private capacity*, i.e., with those of their resources that remain outside the state's domain, and the statement "We owe it to ourselves" is simply misleading. The imputed collectivity "we" ("the society," "the economy") simply does not exist as a "unit of account." Only in the limiting case of a perfectly totalitarian system would the proposition "We owe it to ourselves" make sense.

8. Compare Ricardo (*The Works and Correspondence of David Ricardo*, ed. P. Sraffa with M. Dobb [London: Cambridge University Press, 1951–55], 1: 244–46, 4:149–200) and Barro (R. J. Barro, "Are Government Bonds Net Wealth?" *Journal of Political Economy* 82 [1974]: 1095). For a discussion with further references to the literature, see R. G. Holcombe, J. D. Jackson, and A. Zardkoohi, "The National Debt Controversy," *Kyklos* 34 (1981): 186. For a careful distinction between the equivalence theorem and the neutrality theorem, see J. M. Buchanan and J. Roback, "The Incidence and Effects of Public Debt in the Absence of Fiscal Illusion," Working Paper, Center for Study of Public Choice, George Mason University, 1985.

9. The "future members" in an organization, according to this definition, may include current members to the extent that they remain within the organization after the debt has been incurred, as well as new members who join the organization after the creation of the debt.

10. In this sense, and except for the situation specified, public debt imposes a cost on future generations, a cost that cannot be eliminated. If the future generations should choose, either explicitly or implicitly (by inflation), to repudiate the debt, the effect is only to shift the ultimate distribution of incidence, not to eliminate it.

Note that the intertemporal shifting of a net burden to members of the organization in their capacities as members depends only on the productivity of the debt-financing outlay relative to the state's borrowing rate. Possible adjustments in saving by members, in their private capacities, aimed at offsetting the personal impact of future payments does nothing to affect the debt-created obligation for future payments by members in their organizational roles.

11. A. Alchian, "Some Economics of Property Rights," in Alchian, *Economic Forces at Work* (Indianapolis: Liberty Press, 1977), p. 137ff.

12. In principle, citizenship and residency are, of course, separable, a fact which may have interesting implications. As a *nonresident-citizen*, a person may be able to escape certain membership obligations (notably, for instance, payment of taxes) without giving up citizenship. On the other hand, a *resident-alien* may be burdened with what are typical membership obligations (again, notably, tax payment), and he may be able to escape these burdens only by relocating his residence.

13. States will, of course, differ with respect to the exit costs faced by citizens. Local units of government are less able than more centralized units to exploit either current-period or future-period taxpayers (see G. Brennan and

J. M. Buchanan, *The Power to Tax: Analytical Foundations of the Fiscal Constitution* [Cambridge: Cambridge University Press, 1980]).

14. Buchanan and Roback, "The Incidence and Effects of Public Debt."

15. Albert O. Hirschmann, *Exit, Voice, and Loyalty* (Cambridge, Mass.: Harvard University Press, 1970).

26.
Private Ownership and Common Usage

One of the most famous illustrative examples in the literature of economic theory is that of the good, narrow road and the rough, but wide, road. This example was introduced by Professor Pigou in his *Wealth and Welfare* and in the first edition of *The Economics of Welfare* in an attempt to lend support to his general proposition that overall economic efficiency could be increased by a transfer of resources away from increasing cost industries.[1] The validity of this argument was questioned by Professor Frank Knight in his now-famous article, "Fallacies in the Interpretation of Social Cost,"[2] in which he used the specific road example to show that in a regime of private ownership, prices tend normally to be so adjusted as to ensure the necessary conditions for optimum resource use. The road illustration was also employed by many of the other participants in the great debate involving resource allocation among industries of differing cost characteristics.[3]

In this paper I shall be concerned with the specific analysis of the road example rather than with its generalization. This concentration will require a more complete examination of the various institutional structures which might provide a framework for the example. From this approach several interesting and complex points arise which tend to be overlooked when the purpose is that of using the road case merely to illustrate more important general principles. While the results of the analysis will not affect the consensus which has been reached by economists on the broader issues, they will modify accepted conclusions concerning utilization of facilities when common usage is present. When technological external diseconomies exist, changes in the resource ownership pattern as a means of producing efficient resource usage will be shown to be of more limited efficacy than has been generally supposed. Although the analysis applies particularly to the field of highway policy, especially when direct toll charges are imposed on users, it may readily be extended to other problems such as the common oil pool, the common fishing ground, and the common hunting preserve.

I

I shall first restate the example briefly. There are two roads, one of which is broad and poorly constructed and can handle traffic of any volume without generating congestion. The other road is narrow, and, therefore, limited in its traffic capacity, but it is smooth and fast. Original construction costs are neglected. Commercial vehicles are the only users of the roads.

Pigou showed that if there were no tolls placed on the usage of the superior road, too many vehicles would tend to travel on it. Toll charges placed on the usage of the good road would be in the social interest. On this point there was, and is, no dispute. Knight objected, however, to the extension of the Pigou argument to the general case, and he specifically stated that under a regime of private ownership the correct tolls would tend to be established without governmental interference.

Professor Knight was led to this conclusion by reasoning from the application of labor to superior and marginal land, correctly showing that under private ownership the market will tend to equalize marginal, not average, products of labor on the two types of land. He did not find it necessary to distinguish the various possible institutional arrangements through which this allocation could be achieved. It will be useful if such a distinction is made here.

The first, and most immediately suggested, arrangement is that in which the landowner hires the labor. As the owner of a unit of superior land hires additional units of labor, he is conscious of the decrement in average product, or, in other words, the marginal adjustment is internal to his decision. Labor will be allocated in such a way that its marginal product is equated on the two types of land. It is noted that this result will be forthcoming under *any* ownership pattern of the superior land provided only that the final product is competitively priced. There could exist completely centralized (single) ownership of the superior land if the total production on this land is small relative to total production in the economy.

A second institutional arrangement in which the necessary conditions for optimum resource allocation are present is one in which labor hires the land. Individual workers hire the use of discrete units of superior land. Each worker estimates the demand for land units on the basis of the familiar law of variable proportions—land to fixed labor in this case. Competition among workers will tend to equalize returns to labor on the superior and marginal land as before. But, in order to ensure that the full amount of the superior land be utilized, the ownership pattern of this land must be such that the superior land units are competitively priced. If the total amount of superior land is fixed and not reproducible, completely centralized ownership may result in competitive pricing, that is, the monopolistic and competitive solutions may be equivalent.[4] This is a special case, however, and in order that competitive pricing be guaranteed, the landownership pattern must be effectively decentralized. If the restriction of fixity is removed, and superior land is reproducible, land prices must be at marginal cost levels. Effectively decentralized ownership will always be required to produce the proper resource allocation in this situation.

If a third type of institutional arrangement is now introduced, the problem of describing the process through which the market achieved the efficient resource adjustment becomes more difficult. Assume that individual workers hire the land, but not in discrete units as before. Instead, they are now allowed to purchase rights to contribute to and to share equally in the total product. Workers do not hire land in separable physical units; the amount of land per worker is reduced as more shares are purchased. In buying these shares the individual will not be able to take into account the decline in the average product of others that is brought about by his own action. Interdependence among individual productivities is present, or, in more precise terms, technological external diseconomies. Workers will tend to equalize individually estimated marginal products on superior and marginal land, but this will not produce equality between social marginal products of labor on the two opportunities. If this interdependence among individual productivities is to be taken into account, it must be done through an institutional ownership pattern which will price superior land shares in such a way that the correct usage is promoted.

II

The problem having been introduced in terms of the more familiar land-labor example, the road case may be reconsidered. The analogy between the two is analytically but not institutionally complete. The essential difference is that whereas in the land-labor example real-world institutional arrangements are normally of the first or second types, in the road case the standard pattern is the third type. This difference explains why this third type of adjustment has never been carefully considered when the purpose was that of illustrating general principles. This provides the basis for Knight's statement that the illustration is "clearer if we think of the owner of the road hiring the trucks instead of their hiring the use of the road."[5] By this assumption, the road example is made equivalent to the normal or first land-labor case, and the market selects the desired resource adjustment through a reasonably simple allocation process. The owner of the superior road can take into account the decrease in the average product of "each" truck caused by the addition of one truck, and, therefore, he can equalize the marginal products of trucking resources on the superior and the inferior road. Immediately following the above cited statement, however, Professor Knight continues, "the effect is the same either way; it is still the same if some third party hires the use of both." In order to understand under what conditions the effect is the same, certain specific institutional assumptions will have to be closely examined.

A second institutional arrangement that will produce the required equalization of marginal products can be indicated. If there is a single large trucking firm choosing between the superior and the wide road, the services of both being free, this equalization will be effected. It is assumed that the market for the final product—freight services—remains competitive even in this case of the single large trucking firm. The conclusion that the necessary conditions for optimum resource allocation are present when road services are free holds so long as we retain the assumption of fixity and permanence in the two plants. If we consider the road plants as subject to depreciation, competitive pricing of the road services is required in order to ensure that the centralized trucking firm will allocate trucking resources properly.

An institutional arrangement which would clearly not produce the desired results is one in which a single large trucking firm, large enough to make the required adjustment internally, is faced with a single owner of the superior opportunity. In this case too many resources will be devoted to the wide (free) road since any positive price placed on superior road services will cause the large trucking firm to restrict usage below the point where the marginal product of trucking resources on the wide (free) road is equated with the marginal product on the superior road. This conclusion remains true whether the market for the final product, freight services, is competitive or monopolistic.

III

The three arrangements mentioned are not, however, as interesting or as realistic as others that will be discussed here in somewhat more detail. The most interesting is provided in the case of centralized ownership of the superior road and the common usage of the road by a fully competitive trucking industry. This case should also offer more constructive suggestions concerning the proper pricing policy for highways than any of the others. Assume trucking to be a fully competitive industry, composed of a large number of firms. The superior road is owned by a single profit-maximizing firm, public or private. The road is assumed indestructible, allowing the whole question of maintenance costs to be neglected; this simplification will not affect the analysis. The trucking firm hires the use of the road, not the whole road, nor even divisible shares of road surface per unit of time, but rather rights to use the road during a particular time period along with an undetermined number of other truckers. To the individual trucking firm there are clearly external diseconomies of superior road use. The marginal product of road service (described as the right to use the road) which will enter into the firm's decision is greater than the aggregate marginal product of that road service. The individual firm's own action in purchasing a share of the highway reduces the productivity of shares to all other truckers.

There is general agreement among economists that the market does not produce the efficient allocation of economic resources when technological external diseconomies are present. The diseconomies involved in road use are obviously technological rather than pecuniary. As more trucks use the superior road, the average productivity of all trucks falls solely due to the physical effect of congestion. The production functions of the trucking firms are changed.[6]

The important question, and it is one which transcends the particular application to the road problem, concerns the fundamental reason why the existence of technological external diseconomies arising out of common usage prevents the market mechanism from producing the necessary conditions for the optimum allocation of resources. Is it because individual utilities or productivities are interdependent? Or is it because some resources which are commonly used are not centrally owned? Or do these two reduce to the same thing? If the absence of centralized ownership is emphasized, all that appears to be required to produce overall efficiency is some modification in the ownership of the relevant resource, along with the profit-maximizing pricing of the resource services. Monopoly pricing which maximizes rent on the superior opportunity would seem to be the socially desirable arrangement.[7] The commonality of usage may still remain. On the other hand, if the failure of the market mechanism is held to stem from the interdependence among individual decisions, the required efficiency may be produced only by a centralization of the decision-making, or, in other words, a removal of the commonality of use. In the first case, centralized ownership of the commonly used resource is the only institutional change suggested. In the second case, centralized ownership of the resource and centralized decision-making concerning its use is recommended.

The argument that centralized ownership alone will produce the required usage may be examined first. Its validity depends on the proof that the owner of the commonly used resource, the good road, will be led by the profit motive to fix a price which will, in fact, cause individual users of the facility to produce the efficient utilization. It must be emphasized that the actual resource adjustment must result from the actions of the individual competitive trucking firms, not from any direct action on the part of the owner of the good road.

The demand for the services of the good road must originate with the individual trucking firms. As discussed in the second land-labor illustration above, there would be no serious problem of deriving a demand function if the individual trucking firms could purchase highway services in discrete and homogeneous units. The demand function for the individual firm would be derived by the application of successive units of highway services (square feet of road space per unit time) to the fixed amount of non-highway factors.[8] The law of variable proportions would be fully operative. If we leave congestion out of the picture, this is essentially the situation. There will be a down-sloping demand curve for highway inputs for each trucking firm. The aggregate demand curve for superior road services could then be derived by the normal summation of individual demand curves.

Now congestion must be introduced. The productivity of "rights" to highway usage received by the individual firms will depend on the usage of the road by other firms. This additional factor will enter into the individual firm's purchase decisions. Individual demand functions will be shifted by expectations of traffic volume.

This may be illustrated geometrically in Figs. 26-1 and 26-2. Fig. 26-1 depicts the demand curve of the individual firm for the inputs described as rights to use the good road during a particular period of time. D_1 represents the firm's demand curve when no congestion is expected.[9] D_2 and D_3 represent lower levels of demand (marginal value product) based on expectations of traffic volume sufficient to generate congestion.

Fig. 26-2 is drawn with the factors reversed. The road is now considered the fixed factor, and the curve AP is the average product of trucking resources as they are applied to the superior road. It should be noted that the factors are reversed for the aggregate of firms, not for the individual trucking firm. This is an important step since the definition of the appropriate dimension appears to have been the source of much of the confusion surrounding this road problem. (See note 6 for Kahn's denial of external diseconomies.) The declining average productivity is not due to the action of any one firm but rather to the action of all firms. If the base line is taken to represent the average (marginal) productivity of trucking resources on the free road, the proper investment of trucking resources on the good road is shown at 00', where marginal productivity on the two opportunities is equated.

Fig. 26-2 is related to Fig. 26-1 only in that the location of the demand curve for "rights" to superior road use is a function of expected traffic volume or the amount of aggregate trucking resources applied to the fixed road. The downward shift of the individual demand curves is due to the declining average productivity of trucking resources. If the individual trucking firm expects no congestion, that is, if it expects total usage to be less than ON, D_1 is the relevant demand curve. On the other hand, if it anticipates total traffic of 00', the demand will

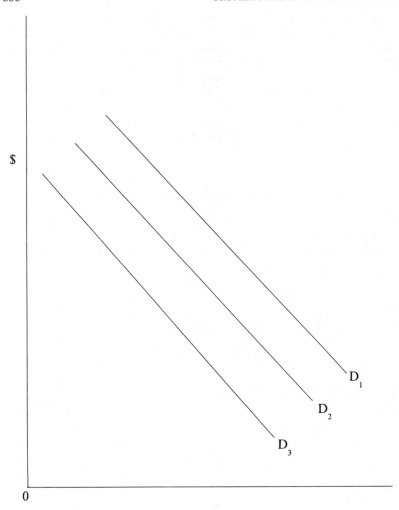

Fig. 26-1 Demand for road inputs

be D_2. The individual firm has no power of determining the operational point along AP.

The market demand curve for "rights" to use the good road during a particular time period is not derived by a simple summation of individual demand curves except when congestion is absent. Once congestion appears, the individual demands become interdependent. The road owner must take into account not only the declining individ-

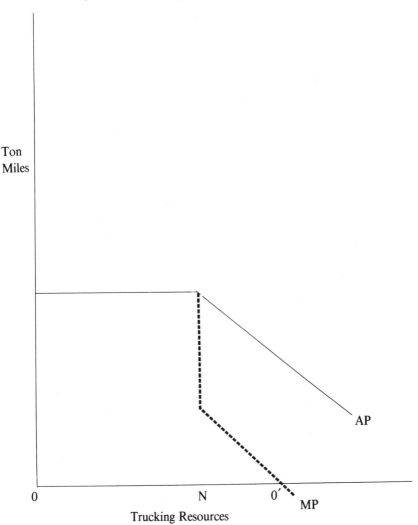

Ton
Miles

0   N   0′   MP

AP

Trucking Resources

Fig. 26-2 Productivity of trucking resources

ual demand curves but also the declining average productivity of trucking as total traffic increases. The interdependence among productivities requires that each firm estimate as correctly as possible the action of all other firms and base its own action upon this estimate. Mutually correct prediction of this sort by all firms is, of course, impossible. After a traffic pattern has been established, however, reasonably accurate prediction of total volume may be possible, and the road owner may be able to determine a profit-maximizing price within limits of uncertainty somewhat broader than the usual monopolist.

In either the congestion or the no-congestion case, it seems clear that the pricing policy of the single owner of the good road will result in road usage, in terms of "rights" per time period, which is not identical with that represented by 00' in Figure 26-2. The total number of toll tickets sold will produce a traffic volume on the good road smaller than that which would be necessary to equalize the marginal productivities of trucking resources on the two opportunities. The profit-maximizing pricing policy of the road owner will generate an overly restricted usage of the superior facility.

This result may be easily demonstrated in the no-congestion situation. If congestion is not present on either road, no trucks should use the poor road, and the good road should be operated as if it were a free good. But the single ownership arrangement will cause a price to be placed on its services. If the individual firm's demand curve for the services of this road is down-sloping, the existence of any positive price will tend to restrict road usage to some degree.

The result is similar, although somewhat more complicated, in the presence of congestion. The single road owner will be able to take into account the declining average productivity of trucking as traffic volume increases. The marginal adjustment will be internal to his pricing decision. Insofar as this factor alone is reflected in the price chosen, the correct usage will tend to be promoted by the single owner's action. But the owner will also take into account the down-sloping demand curves of the individual trucking firms. Insofar as he incorporates these data into his pricing decision, the usage of the road will tend to be below that which is socially efficient.

Only if the individual firm's demand curve for superior road use should be horizontal will the institutional arrangement in which the single owner sells road inputs to a fully competitive trucking industry tend to produce the efficient allocation of traffic between the good and the free road. In this situation, the aggregate or market demand curve would tend to reflect only the declining average productivity resulting from increased traffic volume. Monopoly pricing on the superior road, subject to the special uncertainties created by the interdependence among individual decisions, would tend to promote socially desirable results under these conditions. This type of individual firm demand curve appears to have been implicitly assumed in some of the arguments which suggest that centralized ownership alone will produce the desired results. But this construction appears to have little in its support. With a fixed amount of non-road factors, e.g., trucks and terminals, a trucking firm will pay a greater price for the first few rights to travel on the road during a given time period than for the n-th right. Beyond its normal capacity of operations, additional trips would require double shifts, undermaintenance of equipment, and so on. In other words, rights to road use are no different from any other type of input. The law of variable proportions must be operative, at least after the initial range.

It must be concluded that single ownership of the superior opportunity along with monopoly pricing of road services will not produce the allocation of resources which is dictated by efficiency criteria. The monopoly control arises in the sale of superior road services only. Throughout the analysis we are assuming that the market for the final product, freight services, remains fully competitive.

IV

The case in which the ownership of the superior opportunity is assumed to be decentralized will now be examined. In the restricted road example, this ownership pattern is not possible, but it is interesting to determine the results as if it were. Therefore, assume that the overall superior road is broken up into a number of smaller superior roads, the number being sufficiently large so that no single road can influence significantly the total traffic. If these good roads are physically separated, congestion will arise independently on each road. A declining demand curve will face each of the superior road firms; this will arise, not because the firm is sufficiently large to influence the total supply of road services, but because of the declining average productivity of trucking resources as they are applied to the individual road. In terms of the earlier figures, the down-sloping functions for road services facing the road owner will arise from factors which are the basis of Figure 26-2 alone. Insofar as each of these road firms estimates the declining average productivity of trucking resources accurately, and in so far as the various trucking firms correctly predict the amount of traffic volume on each road, the profit-maximizing pricing of the superior road services will tend to promote the correct allocation of total trucking resources among the several superior roads and between the superior roads and the free road.

This appears to be the institutional arrangement that is implicit in Professor Knight's argument. Although the arrangement is impossible in the specific road example, since there is only one good road, it indicates that there does exist an institutional pattern in the common usage case which provides the necessary conditions for optimum resource use. But several interesting features are to be noted. The area of common usage, and thus interdependence, is reduced to the size of the individual small superior road. And monopoly pricing, not competitive pricing, is the basis for the individual road firm's policy. There is an interesting combination here of competitive and monopoly elements. Competition in the market for final product is assumed throughout. Competition among individual trucking firms is also present. And there are a sufficient number of road firms to allow competitive conditions to be present. But each road firm must be a price maker. It follows a monopoly pricing policy in that it equates marginal revenue, which is less than price, with marginal cost. The firm's only control over price must arise from congestion or from the existence of the external diseconomies in road use; the monopoly arising from the control over the total supply of "rights" to superior road usage which was present in the centralized ownership case must be absent. Rent on each of the several superior roads will tend to be maximized by this arrangement, but it is to be emphasized that total rent on the superior opportunity as a whole will *not* be maximized. Mr. Kahn is therefore correct when he indicates that competitive ownership of the superior opportunity is required, and that monopoly ownership will lead to an overly restricted usage.[10] Both Knight and Gordon are wrong when they state that aggregate rent must be maximized on the superior opportunity.[11] The single owner could, by taking into account monopoly elements arising through his control over "rights" to road use which are independent of congestion, exact from users of the facility a higher total rent than could the aggregate of the numerous owners in the alternative case.

V

The remaining institutional arrangement which must be examined is the one in which both competitive ownership and competitive pricing of the superior opportunity is present. Assume that there are a sufficient number of superior roads to ensure that no one appreciably affects the total traffic, but also assume that these roads are interconnected in such a way that congestion arises on the whole road system and not on a single road. Congestion is a function of total superior road usage, not the usage of any single superior road. This may be imagined as the case where the numerous superior roads cross each other at frequent intervals and congestion appears at the intersections. Although far-fetched in this particular application, this arrangement is not without relevance in the real world. In fact, this is the arrangement most closely analogous to the stock examples of external diseconomies, for instance, the smoking chimneys. Each road owner will be faced with a horizontal demand curve for road services since he has no control over the total supply of superior road "rights" to be put on the market; each road owner will be a price taker since congestion is not a function of traffic on his individual road at all. Price will be established at marginal cost, which is zero in this example. An explanation of the zero price may be in order. If there were a fixed total supply of "rights" to superior road usage, there would tend to be a positive price established. This would be similar to our land-labor example where laborers hire discrete units of land from competitive landowners. The price would then be set at the market-clearing level, or, in geometrical terms, where the aggregate demand curve cuts the vertical supply curve. But in the highway problem, there is no fixed total supply of rights to use the road. Road services do not "run out" regardless of the number of users. Since additional users of a single road would impose no cost on the individual road owner, competition among such owners will tend to bid the toll charges down to zero. Over-usage of the superior opportunity will result from this sort of *competition*, which may have been assumed implicitly in Pigou's original contention. There would, of course, be costs imposed on society by the addition of users to the total superior opportunity. But since these costs arise solely from congestion they will not be borne by road owners but by other users, and, therefore, they cannot influence road supply and, through supply, price.

VI

The several possible ownership and pricing arrangements have been traced through in order to determine which of these patterns would produce the required necessary conditions for optimum resource allocation. It was found that single ownership of the superior opportunity along with monopoly pricing of the resource services would result in a socially undesirable restriction on the usage of the good road whether or not congestion is present. Too many trucks would be forced into using the free road. It was shown that competitive ownership and competitive pricing of road services would result in overutilization of the good opportunity relative to the poor one when congestion is present. This ownership and pricing pattern produces efficient results only when congestion, that is, external diseconomies, is absent. Only in the intermediate pattern, in which competitive ownership prevails but monopoly pricing principles are followed, are the results consistent with efficiency criteria when interdependence among user decisions is present. Only in this case will the superior road owner, when making his pricing decisions, take into account solely the decline in the average product of trucking resources which is due to congestion.

These arrangements have been examined as if they were all possible. If the analysis is limited to the original specific example of the one good road and the one free road, no private ownership pattern for the road alone will produce the necessary conditions for efficient resource use. The efficient usage may be achieved in any one of the three following ways. First, trucking operations may be centralized and all roads made free, provided that alternative transportation media are sufficiently good substitutes to keep the market for freight services fully competitive. Second, a single superior road owner may be forced to operate as well as own the road, hiring the use of trucking resources, treating them as inputs, and marketing the final product (freight services) himself in a fully competitive market. Third, the government may own the roads and price the road services at the level of marginal social cost. In application to the real world problem of highway operation, this third alternative provides the only meaningful criterion for operational efficiency.[12]

The questions raised earlier may now be answered. The statement that individual utilities or productivities are interdependent is equivalent to saying that some resource which is commonly used is not centrally owned. But from this it does not follow that a change in ownership alone is always sufficient to produce the necessary conditions for attaining a Paretian utility frontier. The difficulty in securing the efficient resource utilization by changes in ownership alone stems from the institutional facts of life. In many cases, it is impossible to secure the centralization of ownership required to make the external diseconomies of usage internal to a single owner without *at the same time* providing the single owner with a degree of monopoly control over the total supply of resource services. Insofar as technological external diseconomies arise from an expansion in usage of a whole resource category or even a substantial part of this, it is clear that ownership changes alone will not be sufficient. Only in those cases where the extent of the commonality of usage is limited to a relatively small proportion of the total resource supply (not final product supply) can ownership arrangements be exclusively relied upon to produce desirable results.

Although this paper has been limited to an analysis of the road case under each of the several possible institutional arrangements, the conclusions reached may be readily extended to all problems where commonality of usage creates interdependence among user decisions. Familiar examples are the common oil pool, the common fishing ground, and the common hunting preserve. The analysis indicates that the centralization of ownership of the common oil pool, for example, may cause an overly restricted usage of the pool even if the market for oil remains fully competitive. If the pool possesses any advantages that make it unique as a superior resource, the single owner may sell drilling "rights" to competitive purchasers, and, by so doing, he can secure a greater rent than he could if he does all the drilling himself. Only if the individual common pool is one among many like pools will the proper rate of pumping be promoted by single pool ownership. Assuming, as has been the case throughout the analysis, that the market for the final product remains fully competitive, both the ownership and the operation of the superior facility must be centralized if the efficient utilization of resources is to be produced without direct governmental interference.

Notes

I am indebted to Marshall Colberg, Malcolm Hoag, Richard Leftwich, Roland McKean, and Jerome Milliman for helpful suggestions at various stages of this paper.

1. A. C. Pigou, *Wealth and Welfare* (London: Macmillan and Co., 1912), p. 163; *The Economics of Welfare*, 1st ed. (London: Macmillan and Co., 1920), p. 194.

2. *Quarterly Journal of Economics* 38 (1924): 582–606. Reprinted in *The Ethics of Competition* (London: Allen and Unwin, 1935), pp. 217–36. Subsequent reference will be to the latter.

3. A useful summary of the general discussion may be found in Howard S. Ellis and William Fellner, "External Economies and Diseconomies," *American Economic Review* 33 (1943): 493–511. Reprinted in *Readings in Price Theory* (Chicago: Richard D. Irwin, 1952), pp. 242–63.

4. In simple geometrical terms, this would be the case if the vertical supply curve should cut a straight-line demand curve to the left of its midpoint.

5. "Fallacies in the Interpretation of Social Cost," p. 221.

6. Road usage provides a specific, and not unimportant, example of the fourth type of interdependence mentioned by Scitovsky, the only one which he characterizes as "external economies and diseconomies." The production function of the individual trucking firm depends not only on the factors utilized by the firm but also on the output of other firms. This fits Meade's precise definition of external diseconomies. (See Tibor Scitovsky, "Two Concepts of External Economies," *Journal of Political Economy* 62 [1954]: 144–45; J. E. Meade, "External Economies and Diseconomies in a Competitive Situation," *Economic Journal* 62 [1954]: 67.)

The road case has been used by many economists to illustrate the existence of external diseconomies. See, for example, Jacob Viner, "Cost Curves and Supply Curves," *Zeitschrift für Nationalökonomie* 3 (1931): 221.

R. F. Kahn was able to deny the existence of external diseconomies in the specific road case by a peculiar chain of reasoning. Having defined marginal private productivity as a change in a firm's output resulting from a change in the input of one factor, the firm's expenditure on and the total amount of the other factors remaining unchanged, and marginal social productivity as the change in the total output of the community under the same conditions, he makes the following statement: "In considering the application of all other factors, considered as one composite factor, to the factor 'road,' our definition of marginal social productivity—and by implication of external diseconomies, which are said to exist when marginal social productivity falls short of marginal private productivity—requires that the amount of road space utilized by the firm which increases its output shall remain constant. It follows that the amount of road space available to all other firms also remains constant. Their output is consequently unaltered; and marginal social productivity does not differ from marginal private productivity." Quite clearly, however, any change in output must be measured in vehicle or ton-miles per time unit and must change the amount of road space utilized by the firm under consideration as well as change the amount available to other firms. Mr. Kahn was apparently trapped by his own definition into assuming an impossible situation (R. F. Kahn, "Some Notes on Ideal Output," *Economic Journal* 40 [1935]: 18).

7. This is explicitly stated by H. Scott Gordon in his analysis of the common fishing grounds problem. His treatment is similar to that of Professor Knight, and the fishing grounds problem is similar, in most respects, to the road problem. See H. Scott Gordon, "The Economic Theory of a Common-Property Resource: The Fishery," *Journal of Political Economy* 62 (1954): 124–42.

8. All non-highway inputs cannot, of course, remain fixed. Certain inputs (e.g., fuel, driving time) must co-vary with highway inputs.

9. Similar down-sloping demand curves, at a lower level, could be derived for the services of the free road, but these are not necessary to the argument.

10. Kahn, "Some Notes on Ideal Output," pp. 17–18.

11. Knight, "Fallacies in the Interpretation of Social Cost," p. 224; Gordon, "Economic Theory of a Common-Property Resource," p. 129.

12. See my "The Pricing of Highway Service," *National Tax Journal* 5 (1952): 97–106, for a discussion of this criterion.

27.
Notes on Irrelevant Externalities, Enforcement Costs, and the Atrophy of Property Rights

In an earlier paper, a Pareto-irrelevant externality was defined to exist in a two-person context when there is no way that an activity which enters as an argument in each person's utility function can be modified so as to improve the position of one party without worsening the position of the other party.[1] In other words, there are no potential gains-from-trade that remain to be secured, even though the well-being of one party may be affected by the activity which is under the control of the other. Pareto-irrelevance implies that the value of the "internal economy" enjoyed by the acting party equals or exceeds the value of the loss that his action imposes externally on the affected party.[2] My purpose in these notes is to apply this concept of Pareto-irrelevant externalities to explain one basis for modifications in property rights, modifications which amount to atrophy in the basic structure.

I

By way of introducing the more interesting and more complex issues, I shall first apply the notion of irrelevant externality to the now-famous Coase theorem.[3] This states that, in the absence of transaction costs and income effects, the assignment of property rights or claims does not affect resource allocation. As normally interpreted, this theorem proves the invariance of the allocative solution under alternative directions of exchange or trade between the parties to an interaction. In the context of Coase's familiar example, the final resource allocation is the same whether the ranchers hold rights that allow their cattle to roam at will over the surrounding croplands or whether the wheat farmers hold rights which allow them to exclude the straying cattle or to exact payment for damages from ranchers. In the first case, trade takes the form of compensations or "bribes" paid by the farmers *to* the ranchers, if indeed trade takes place at all. In the second case, trade involves the payment of "charges" to the farmers *by* the ranchers in exchange for straying privileges, if trade takes place at all. The differing initial assignment of rights will produce differing initial positions from which internalization through trade might commence; the differing positions attained under strictly unilateral behavior bracket the efficient allocative outcome that will tend to be established through trading.[4]

Consider now an example in which an externality may be Pareto-irrelevant under one set of rights and Pareto-relevant under the other. One assignment may generate trade; the other may not do so. If the rancher holds rights that allow his cattle to roam freely over the croplands, there may be no acceptable trade or exchange that the farmer who is damaged can offer once the rancher attains his position of independent-adjustment equilibrium. Suppose, for example, that in this position, the marginal value of free straying to the rancher is seventy dollars per steer, while the marginal damage or loss imposed on the farmer is only sixty dollars per steer. No internalization through trade can take place in this setting. But consider the alternative assignment of rights. Suppose that the farmer holds exclusion rights in the croplands and that these rights may be enforced *without cost*. In this situation, the private-adjustment equilibrium will be characterized by Pareto-relevant externalities. To remove these, and to attain the position that he reached unilaterally under the alternative assignment, the rancher must purchase straying rights from the farmer. The Coase theorem, as such, is not modified. The initial position unilaterally selected by the rancher is Pareto-efficient under one set of rights; by definition, no internalization through trade or otherwise is required for Pareto-irrelevant externality. Under the other set of rights, trade is necessary to shift from an initial inefficient position produced by unilateral or independent adjustment to the efficient allocative outcome that would be attained without trade under the alternative assignment.

II

The analysis may be extended while remaining within the context of the rancher-farmer example. I want to concentrate on only one of the two assignments discussed above, that in which the farmer holds rights of exclusion in the croplands. As suggested, if these rights are enforceable at no cost, the farmer can prevent all damage from the rancher's straying cattle, either by requiring his prior agreement upon compensation or by collecting the full value of damages incurred, as such claims are ideally adjudicated by a third party or agency.[5] In either case, the arrangement will embody an income transfer from the rancher to the farmer.

If, however, the exclusion rights nominally held by the farmer are enforceable only at some positive cost to him, some damage or loss may be tolerated without reaction. These costs can be measured in bother, time, or monetary outlay. Everyday routines are interrupted by seeking legal relief; relationships with others in the social group may be made less pleasant; laywers can only be hired for money; time delays involved in legal proceedings may be significant. When this is recognized, the farmer may find that any attempt to enjoin or prevent external damage from the rancher's cattle or to make claims for damages after it is done may cost more than the damage itself. In the numerical illustration, the value of the loss is $60 per period per steer. We may assume that the loss function is linear; each steer destroys $60 worth of potentially marketable wheat regardless of the number that stray. By contrast with this plausibly realistic linearity in the damage or loss function, the farmer is likely to encounter severe lumpiness in his enforcement cost function. The costs of enforcing his nominal property rights to the croplands are likely to depend only indirectly if at all on the size of the damages incurred, at least over some initial ranges of damage. For purposes of illustration here, assume that the farmer anticipates a fixed outlay of $360 to be required to ensure full enforcement of his property rights. For this sum, he knows that he can collect full damages from the rancher.[6] In this situation, so long as the rancher keeps the number of straying cattle below six, the farmer maximizes his profit by accepting the external loss without reaction. The situation becomes equivalent to that which is observed when the rancher rather than the farmer holds the nominal rights in the croplands. The effect is as if the external diseconomy is Pareto-irrelevant. The enforcement cost threshold of the farmer allows the rancher to behave as if the assignment of rights is the reverse of those which are nominally in existence. The property rights that may be inferred from external observation are, in this setting, sharply different from those which are nominally defined and which may, upon a sufficient outlay, be legally enforced.

The quantity limits must be recognized as critical in generating this no-reaction outcome. If the private, profit-maximizing adjustment of the rancher, subject to the internal constraints that he confronts, should dictate that he allow *more than six* steers to wander onto the cropland, the farmer will find it advantageous to enforce his nominal exclusion rights. The rancher will be required to pay damages for losses to the farmer, and possibly a share of the enforcement costs in addition. Whether or not the rancher's private, profit-maximizing behavior, considered separately from the interaction with the farmer, results in less than or more than six straying cattle will depend on cost-revenue arguments that are internal to his own decision calculus. The point to be emphasized here is that, under some conditions, this behavior may violate nominally accepted property-rights assignments without setting off enforcement reaction from the affected party or parties.

If the rancher should recognize the decision-making setting that the farmer confronts, his own behavior may, of course, be modified in a strategic sense. He may find it profitable to restrict his action so as to keep within the predicted allowable limits of counteraction. In our illustration, suppose that the pure profit-maximizing behavior of the rancher, treated as exogenous to the interaction with the farmer, should involve eight steers who damage croplands. In other words, this number would be allowed to stray if the rancher held full rights to the croplands. If the farmer holds exclusion rights, and if his costs of enforcement are known to be lumpy and in the amount of $360, the rancher will try to keep damage below this level to forestall claims for damages. If all eight steers stray, and action is taken, the rancher will be required to pay a minimum of $480 to the farmer (eight times $60). In the conditions of the Coase theorem, he would, if necessary, pay this total and continue to allow all eight animals to damage crops.

Let us suppose, however, that the rancher knows the payoff structure facing the farmer. He finds that, by reducing his herd to five, he may forestall a certain outlay of $480 and perhaps more. If the benefits per animal are constant at $70 each, as we have postulated, the rancher loses only $210 by reducing the herd from eight to five. It will, therefore, be in his interest to reduce the size of the herd. Whether for such strategic reasons or whether private behavior involves such restriction naturally, if the quantity limits dictated by the enforcement-cost threshold of the farmer are not overrun, the result is that the nominal assignment of rights is eroded or undermined. The behavioral pattern that is observed departs from that pattern which would be observed under strict adherence to the rights that are nominally assigned to the parties and which, ultimately, would be legally enforced.

III

The possible divergence between nominal property rights and actual or effective rights, as observed in behavior patterns, takes on added significance when we shift to a dynamic setting. It is possible to analyze the effects of enforcement or nonenforcement behavior in one period on the decision calculus of each party to an interaction in subsequent periods.

We have assumed specifically that, in Period 1, the assignment of rights is acknowledged by all parties; these rights are enforceable with certainty once the damaged party makes the required investment in enforcement. The costs of making this investment represent the only barrier to enforcement. This offers a starting point for a sequential modeling of rights enforcement. In periods subsequent to this base period, t_1, I shall assume that the delineation of property rights that will ultimately be enforced by the courts depends on two elements rather than on one. There is the initial acknowledged assignment of nominal rights, the certain basis for the enforcement in Period 1. In addition, the ultimate enforcement in later periods will depend on the observed pattern of rights reflected in behavior during earlier periods of time.

In Period 1, we know that the probability of effective enforcement of nominally defined property assignments is one, upon the initiation of legal action by the damaged or potentially damaged party. That is,

(1) $\quad P(E)t_1 = \dfrac{N}{N} = 1,$

where P(E) refers to the probability, (E) to the enforcement of nominal rights in the period indicated by the subscript, and N defines an index of the nominal rights assignment. In Period 2, however, we get

(2) $\quad P(E)t_2 = \dfrac{(N - O_{t_1})}{N} < 1,$

where O defines an index for the divergence between the observed patterns of rights and nominally assigned rights in the subscripted time period. Hence, we see that, if the farmer in our illustration takes action in Period 1 to enforce fully his nominal rights, the situation in Period 2 becomes equivalent to that which he faced in Period 1. If, however, he rationally refrains from taking enforcement action, because of the quantity threshold limits and the lumpiness in enforcement costs, the probability of securing nominal rights enforcement in Period 2 is less than unity. The benefits expected from legal action in Period 2 must be discounted by this reduced probability factor in any rational comparison with costs. That is, for enforcement to become rational in Period 2, (3) below must be satisfied:

(3) $\quad P(E)t_2 \displaystyle\int_{s=0}^{s=s^*} D > C.$

The total damage or loss, represented by the integral over the interval determined by the externally imposed quantity limits, discounted by the appropriate probability factor must be less than the expected total cost of initiating legal action. To this point, we have assumed that this cost is independent of the quantity of damage incurred. For generality, however, the condition represented in (3) could be rewritten as:

$$(4) \quad P(E)t_r \int_{s=O}^{s=s^*} D > F(D),$$

where the subscript, tr, refers to any time period subsequent to the base, and where total cost, C, is written as a function of the damage or loss, f(D).

The effects are clear. The quantity threshold in Period 2 is widened over that of Period 1 if the probability of successful enforcement falls below one. Having rationally acquiesced in the external intrusion into his nominal property rights in Period 1, the farmer in our illustration finds that his enforcement task is even more difficult in Period 2.

It is relatively easy to extend the analysis by incorporating additional periods of adjustment. Consider period, t_m, where we might have,

$$(5) \quad P(E)_{t_m} = \frac{N - \sum_{t=1}^{t=m-1} 0}{N}$$

This could be rewritten so that more weight could be given to periods close in time to t_m.

$$(6) \quad P(E)_{t_m} = \frac{N - \sum_{t=1}^{m-1} w_t 0}{N}$$

where w_t allows for differential weights for specific time period observations.

This formulation allows us to define a situation where nominal property rights have completely atrophied. This is a situation where the holder of such nominal rights will not find it rational to enforce these regardless of the quantity of damage that is actually or potentially inflicted on him externally. This condition is defined to be present when (7) below is satisfied:

$$(7) \quad P(E)_{t_r} \int_{s=O}^{s=\infty} D < f(D), \text{ where } C = f(D).$$

This states that regardless of the number of units of external damage, straying steers in the Coase illustration, the costs of effectively enforcing nominal rights remain greater than the expected benefits.

IV

Objection may be raised to the analysis sketched on the grounds that it fails to allow for a recognition of the intertemporal relationships in the decision calculus of the potentially damaged party. That is to say, the model assumes implicitly that decisions about enforcement or non-enforcement are made in each time period on a cost-benefit comparison relevant for that period in isolation. It may be argued that a more comprehensive definition of rationality would include the intertemporal interdependence. As the model indicates, the benefit-cost ratio from investment in enforcement in future periods is increased by positive action in the present. Rational behavior should be based on a recognition of this; it would seem that enforcement efforts would be strengthened.

This should, however, be considered with some caution. Suppose that in Period 1, the anticipated external damage is less than expected enforcement cost. That is,

$$(8) \quad \int_{s=0}^{s=s^*} D < C.$$

In the rancher-farmer illustration, only five steers are observed to stray onto the croplands. For this period alone, enforcement response on the part of the farmer is not economically rational. Let us assume, however, that he fully recognizes the interdependence between what he does in Period 1 and his choice situation in subsequent periods. On the basis of this recognition, let us suppose that legal action toward enforcing Period 1 rights is instituted.

As Period 2 arrives, the potentially damaged party is once again confronted with an *ab initio* setting. If the estimates of enforcement cost and potential damages again indicate that (8) is satisfied, the farmer faces precisely the same calculus he did in Period 1. In this manner, we could demonstrate that, if intertemporal interdependence effects dictated protective legal action in Period 1 despite present-period irrationality, the same would hold for Period 2 and for each subsequent period. Hence, the potentially damaged party would be acting against his single-period interest in each period over an infinite sequence.

The conclusion is inescapable that incorporation of this effect will do nothing toward removing the possible threshold-induced atrophy in property rights. So long as the condition defined in (8) holds in some initial period, the rational course of action for the potentially damaged party remains one of nonenforcement.

V

If the nominal assignment of rights is to be strictly enforced in a world where enforcement must involve cost, the damage threshold of the externally affected party must be reduced. This can be accomplished either by (1) increasing the benefits of enforcement, or by (2) reducing the costs of enforcement. We may discuss these alternatives in turn.

In the expressions of Section IV, the benefits from enforcement action are measured in recoverable losses. Implicitly, we have assumed that the affected party, by taking legal action, can forestall damages, or if *ex post*, can collect in full for losses suffered, but that he cannot collect from the acting party *more* than these losses, accurately estimated. The benefits from undertaking successful legal action to the affected party could be increased only if he could, somehow, collect more than the explicit damage that he suffers from the external diseconomy in itself. This excess-of-damage prospect is not, of course, completely foreign to existing legal systems (e.g., triple damage suits under American antitrust statutes).

Consider the illustration at hand. If the farmer is allowed to collect, say, double damages from the rancher, or $120 per steer on the croplands, he will be motivated to initiate legal action if he observes, say, five animals, whereas he would not do so if only direct damages can be collected. In this new situation, he would stand to collect $600 for an outlay of $360, for a net gain of $240. Let us suppose, however, that the offending rancher recognizes the double indemnity aspects of the external diseconomy, as well as the payoff structure faced by the farmer. If he simply adjusts his behavior so as to keep within a newly defined and more restrictive threshold, the same analysis applies. If, for example, only two steers are allowed to stray now, even double assessment of damages will not provoke the farmer's rational response in defense of his property. In order to ensure that the damaged party will act as if enforcement costs are zero, the potentially recoverable claims from the acting party must equal actual losses *plus* the full costs of enforcement. For initial quantity ranges this might well involve some multiple of the estimated losses imposed. To an extent, the charging of all legal fees and court costs to the party that is found liable for damages accomplishes the purpose here. But this device, even if it is fully utilized, fails to ensure adequate enforcement if the potentially or actually damaged party suffers nonpecuniary costs in the form of personal discomfort, inconvenience, and time. To my knowledge, direct compensation is rarely allowed for these very real costs of property-rights enforcement. To the extent that they are not, however, some erosion and ultimate atrophy of nominal or assigned rights must be predicted to occur.

In the illustration, the familiar rancher-farmer interaction, we could of course assume that the potentially damaged farmer might conceivably collect from the rancher claims sufficient to cover all estimated losses plus all enforcement costs, including subjective costs. A different and more difficult problem emerges, however, when we impose financial constraints on the rancher's ability to pay claims in excess of the gains that his action secures if uninhibited. Suppose that the rancher simply cannot pay more than $70 per steer. In this case, there is no way that the farmer can be assured a collection of $360 plus $60 per quantity unit, the offer schedule that we have demonstrated to be required to ensure that he will effectively enforce his nominally assigned rights. Consider a situation where the struggling rancher earns a bare subsistence income unless he allows his cattle to roam on the croplands. If he is not prosecuted, he earns $70 per animal above subsistence but no more. In such case, the farmer can, at most, collect this total and in the process reduce the rancher to subsistence income.[7]

If the affected party cannot, for any reason, be allowed to expect collection of claims sufficient to offset all costs, including those that are purely subjective, an alternative approach might involve explicit reduction in such costs. It is clear that, if the affected party can in fact enforce his property rights at or near zero costs, the argument for excess-of-damage claims disappears. The processes of enforcing assigned rights that have been or may be externally violated involve genuine costs, both in resources and in personal utility. Consider only the resources cost, reflected in necessary monetary outlays on legal proceedings, lawyers, courts, clerks, etc. For our purposes, let us assume that these are supplied at competitive rates. If the costs of enforcement measured by such necessary outlays are to be reduced for the externally affected party to an interaction, they must be increased for someone in the community. The implication is that these costs, or at least a portion thereof, might be shifted to the general public, to the taxpayers as a legitimate expense of government.

In vague statements, several public finance scholars may have referred to law enforcement as a "public good." And there seems little question but that some general structure of law fulfills many of the necessary technical characteristics for a "public good." But the analysis here forces us to be more specific with respect to the community's role in financing the enforcement costs that are incurred in defending nominally assigned property rights. As the analysis demonstrates, a shift in such costs away from the party whose nominal rights are threatened will tend to increase his willingness to initiate enforcement action. Is this, in itself, sufficient justification for governmental assumption of these costs? To make out a positive argument here, we must be able to show what will happen when enforcement response is taken promptly and effectively. To this point, we have not gone beyond an implicit assumption that effective enforcement of nominal rights is a desirable attribute of social order. But why? The answer seems to be that only with effective enforcement can the efficient allocative outcome be achieved and, at the same time, the socially unnecessary costs of litigation minimized.

We may return to the rancher-farmer illustration. If, either by allowing claims sufficient to cover all litigation costs plus estimated damages, or by reducing costs of litigation for the farmer, effective enforcement of nominal rights is ensured, and promptly, uncertainty is reduced. The basis is laid for genuine contractual negotiations between the interacting parties, and agreements can be anticipated that will fully internalize the potential externality. If the farmer's exclusion rights to the croplands are enforced, and are known to be enforced, the rancher will find it advantageous, and regardless of his income-asset position, to negotiate from the assigned status quo. Mutual gains from trade can be exploited; all parties can be placed in improved positions and without erosion and atrophy of property rights, and without unnecessary resource outlay on lawyers and litigation.[8] The presence of major efficiency gains suggest that the productivity of public investment in absorbing these costs may be large indeed, even if the standard "public goods" rubric does not seem fully appropriate.

If the taxpayers, generally, are to be charged with the costs of enforcing property rights, there remains the issue "which taxpayers"? How are the tax costs for such outlays to be distributed? In this sense, there may be both equity and efficiency arguments for relating such taxes directly to measured values of nominal asset ownership.[9] That is to say, the costs of enforcement still might properly be borne by the owners of property threatened by external intrusion. The institutional arrangements dictated by the analysis involve a possible shift of these costs from the specifically damaged or potentially damaged party in an interaction to the community of potentially damaged owners of property. The important element is to break the direct linkage between the incurring of personal cost and the initiation of enforcement action. Even though the affected party may, indirectly, bear most of the resources cost of enforcement, he may be motivated to act as if these costs are low.

Conclusions

This essay should be interpreted as a set of provisional notes rather than definitive conclusions. My concern is to open up discussion of the economic calculus that may be involved in the enforcement of nominally assigned property rights. There are many elements of this calculus that are not developed fully here, and notably the "public goods" aspects. As indicated, the paper concentrates on the calculus of the nominal owner in protecting and enforcing rights. The calculus of the other party is equally significant for any comprehensive analysis, that is, the party or parties who choose deliberately to violate nominally existing property rights.

Notes

1. James M. Buchanan and W. C. Stubblebine, "Externality," *Economica* 29 (1962): 371–84.
2. Note that both external economies and external diseconomies can be brought within this context by considering the failure to extend an activity that exerts economies as an external diseconomy.
3. See R. H. Coase, "The Problem of Social Cost," *Journal of Law and Economics* 3 (1960): 1–44.
4. One of the controversies stimulated by the Coase theorem was the alleged symmetry between "bribes" and "charges." The result of this discussion seems to have been that the symmetry depends critically on the proper definition of the starting point.
On the general effect of institutional structure on allocative outcomes, see my "The Institutional Structure of Externality," published in *Public Choice* 14 (Spring, 1973): 69–82, and presented as chapter 28 in this volume.
5. It is important to distinguish rights to exclude from rights to claim for damages. In the first, agreement of the potentially affected party must be secured before action is taken; in the second, the affected party may not forestall action but may claim damages if and after the action is taken. For a discussion of this distinction between "property rules" and "liability rules," see Guido Calabresi and A. D. Melamed, "Property Rules, Liability Rules, and Inalienability: One View of the Cathedral," *Harvard Law Review* 85 (April, 1972): 1089.
6. This must be the estimated outlay over and above that part of total enforcement costs that might be imposed on the rancher in any legal proceedings.
7. Note that, in our whole analysis, concentration is placed on the decision calculus of the affected party. This is appropriate when we are concerned with positive action toward enforcement of assigned property rights. We have explicitly left out of account the decision calculus of the acting party who must, in one sense, violate either legal or ethical norms or both in imposing or threatening to impose the external diseconomy on the other party. To the extent that the reward-punishment structure can be manipulated so as to

reduce external intrusion into established or assigned rights, the danger of erosion and atrophy stemming from a failure to react by the affected party is, of course, reduced.

8. I have advanced roughly these arguments in quite a different context. See my "Politics, Property, and Law," *Journal of Law and Economics* 15 (October, 1972): 439–52. Gordon Tullock has elaborated in some detail on the social gains that might be secured from institutional rearrangements that minimize or eliminate the resource costs that are invested in pure conflict resolution, widely defined. See his *The Social Dilemma* (mimeographed; Blacksburg, Va.: Center for Study of Public Choice, 1974).

9. For the efficiency argument, see Earl Thompson, "Taxation of Wealth and the Wealthy," UCLA Working Paper, March, 1972.

28.

The Institutional Structure
of Externality

I. Introduction

An emerging consensus on the theory of externality embodies a clear
conceptual distinction between small-number and large-number interactions. When the parties to a potential externality relationship are
few, market-like voluntary contractual arrangements are predicted to
emerge.[1] Although bargaining difficulties are acknowledged, the contractual outcomes are predicted to satisfy broad efficiency norms.
When the parties are many, prohibitive transactions costs are predicted to prevent the emergence of tolerably efficient voluntary agreements, and some resort to collective or governmental choice processes
may be indicated when the externality exerts significant effects.

Subsidiary discussion has taken place within each of these major
categories. Those who have concentrated on voluntary contractual internalization in the small-number cases have been fascinated, perhaps
unduly, by the properties of the now-called "Coase theorem." This
theorem states that, in the absence of transactions costs *and* income
effects, the allocative results are invariant under changes in property
rights. Regardless of the initial assignment of rights in a potential externality interaction, the efficient allocative solution will be attained
under the restrictive assumptions of the theorem. On the other hand,
those economists who have sought to carry forward the neoclassical
Pigovian policy prescriptions, and this includes most of those who
have worked specifically on practical problems of environmental quality, have evoked the transactions costs rubric as a protective device
that allows them to ignore the developments in the theory of small-
number externalities. Their attention has turned to the specific formulation of corrective schemes which might ideally be introduced by
collective or governmental agencies.[2]

My purpose in this essay is to demonstrate that the two-part classification of potential externality relationships into small-number and large-number cases obscures several considerations that are directly relevant to institutional rearrangements. Transaction costs are present in all potential exchanges, but these costs can vary greatly between one set of circumstances and another. In many of the large-number cases, a "publicness" aspect of an interaction is present, but in many others, this aspect is absent. The differences in transactions costs in these two subcategories can be significant. Concentration on two-party models in the small-number cases necessarily causes the "publicness" or joint-consumption aspects to be overlooked, but there seems to have been an implicit assumption that these aspects are always characteristic of large-number externalities.

It is widely recognized that all joint-consumption relationships are themselves externalities. In the strict sense, therefore, the failure of contractual arrangements to emerge may depend critically on the presence of *two* potential externality relationships rather than one. There may be an externality between the "producer" of an effect and the "consumer," but there may also be an externality *among* separate "consumers." The second of these may occur without the first, in which case we have the standard collective goods paradigm. Or the second of these may accompany the first, in which case we have the collective or public goods paradigm plus an additional externality relationship, that between the group of joint consumers, considered as one party, and the producer or generator of the effects in question. Voluntary action will not produce fully efficient results in either of these two cases. By contrast, the externality relationship between producer and consumer of an effect may be present without the presence of any collective goods externality. In this case, voluntary contractual internalization may occur regardless of the number of consumers.

II. Extending the Taxonomy

We need a somewhat more complete taxonomy of externalities. I propose to supplement the existing array only in terms of numbers affected by an interaction and by the presence or absence of joint-consumption efficiency or "publicness." When this extension is made, we can show that the assignment of property rights may be critical in determining the efficiency of alternative institutional arrangements in some cases while not at all relevant in others.

I shall illustrate the analysis exclusively in terms of the example that was introduced by Coase and which has been much discussed since his paper was published. This involves the cattle raiser(s) or rancher(s) on the one hand and the owner(s) of growing crops [farmer(s)] on the other. The cattle are liable to stray, and in so doing they trample the

	Cattle Raisers Have Legal Rights to Allow Animals to Stray		Cattle Raisers Have NO Rights in Croplands
One cattle raiser, one farmer	I.	Bilateral bargaining toward efficient allocation.	II. Bilateral bargaining toward efficient allocation.
One cattle raiser, many farmers	III.	Inefficient results due to "publicness" interaction among farmers.	IV. Inefficient results due to holdout power of each farmer.
Many cattle raisers, one farmer	V.	Efficient results with minor bargaining costs under competition. Possible inefficiencies under monopsony.	VI. Efficient results with minor bargaining costs under competition. Possible inefficiencies under monopoly.
Many cattle raisers, many farmers	VII.	Inefficient results due to "publicness" interaction among farmers.	VIII. Inefficient results due to holdout power of each farmer.

Fig. 28-1

wheat, hence destroying a part of the crop. There is no direct interaction among the separate cattle who might stray; the presence of one steer on the cropland does not affect the costs or benefits from other straying animals. The cattle that stray are as likely to trample one part of the total wheat crop as any other, regardless of particular location.

In this familiar setting, we can examine the possibilities for attaining allocative efficiency under alternative institutional arrangements. We allow the numbers on each side of the potential externality to vary along with the property-right arrangements. We can exhaust the range of possibilities in a four-by-two matrix illustration. The alternative ownership arrangements in terms of numbers is arrayed along the rows of Fig. 28-1, while the two possible property-right arrangements are arrayed in the columns.

The approach taken by most economists has been to lump Cells I and II together in the small-number set (for which the Coase theorem is widely acknowledged to be correct within its restricted assumptions *and* to possess genuine predictive power) and all other Cells (III through VIII) into the large-number set, where transaction costs are alleged to prevent the attainment of efficiency through contractual arrangements. Several things become apparent from the matrix presentation. Note that efficiency may be attained by voluntary agreements in the settings described by Cells V and VI, despite the fact that there are many persons involved in the total externality relationship. Note, further, that the location of liability *does* influence the prospects for attaining efficiency in some situations. As we shall demonstrate, in all large-number interactions, the location of liability affects the ease with which bargaining among participants may move toward efficient final results.

The separate cells may be examined in turn. There is little need to treat the analysis of Cells I and II in detail, since these have been exhaustively covered in relationship to the Coase theorem. As the figure indicates, efficiency in allocation will tend to be produced if we disregard the possible difficulties that are inherent in bilateral bargaining negotiations. If we include bargaining costs as a part of transaction costs, we can then accept the version of the theorem that states the invariance of solution under the separate assignments of rights along with the efficient characteristics of this solution.

The situation depicted in Cell III is that which is often assumed to be descriptively relevant for many environmental quality issues such as air and water pollution. Attention here tends to be concentrated on the "antisocial" behavior of a person or firm which exerts external costs (diseconomies) on many other persons or firms. The classic illustration is, of course, the factory whose smoke fouls the laundries of the neighborhood housewives. As we have noted above, there are two externality relationships present in this setting. In the context of our cattle raiser–farmer example, the straying cattle impose external diseconomies on each farmer. But, as among the several farmers, there is a joint-consumption external economy, at least in a potential sense. If a single farmer succeeds in negotiating with the rancher for a reduction in the number of straying cattle, *all* farmers secure equal benefits. The familiar "free rider" dilemma emerges among the many farmers. The single farmer, acting privately and independently, may not be motivated to purchase the total reduction in cattle straying that is sufficient to satisfy efficiency norms. All farmers might be better off, along with the rancher, under some collective-cooperative agreement which would allow the farmers, as a group, to negotiate bilaterally with the rancher. Once such an organizational step is taken, the institutional setting becomes analogous to that depicted in Cells I and II. And if the straying cattle do, in fact, generate Pareto-relevant external diseconomies, some reduction in their numbers can be predicted to emerge from the bilateral bargaining that would ensue. A priori it is impossible to determine whether or not an initially apparent external diseconomy is or is not Pareto-relevant. In the absence of some collective bargaining unit which represents the farmers, we can say that the observed results will tend either to be (1) fully efficient, or (2) inefficient in the direction of too many straying cattle and too little wheat. This setting makes clear that the barrier to the achievement of efficiency through voluntary contractual arrangements lies in the "publicness" or joint-consumption interaction among the many farmers who are affected by the diseconomy.

Under the producer-consumer numbers of Row 2, a shift in the assignment of property rights *can* significantly alter the path toward tolerably efficient outcomes, provided that the initial situation is inefficient. Look now at the situation depicted in Cell IV, where there are many farmers and the single rancher, as before, but where the rancher no longer has a property right to allow his animals to stray over the croplands. Full ownership rights in the latter are now held by the farmers, separately and independently, and the rancher must purchase the permission of *all* farmers before allowing his cattle to roam. In this case, the publicness or joint-consumption interaction among the several farmers may generate allocative results that are just the opposite to those attained under Cell III. Since, by our assumptions, the rancher cannot specify in advance just whose crops will be damaged, and since the parcels of cropland are not separately fenced even though they are separately owned, he must secure the agreement of *all* members of the group before he can turn loose his cattle. This requirement places each and every farmer in a unique bargaining position that allows him to block or to veto any prospective agreement with the rancher, even one which has been accepted by all of his fellow farmers. The situation here is fully equivalent to the operation of a unanimity rule for collective decision-making. This rule fails because it allows each person to be put in the strategic position of bargaining against all other persons in the group. Since it can be predicted that, in a many-person group, there will be at least one person who will exploit this strategic position, the "producer" of the external effect—in our example, the rancher—will not normally be able to secure the agreement that efficient results might require, almost regardless of the relative values that are placed on the alternatives. Even should the value which the rancher places on cattle straying substantially exceed the cost imposed on all farmers, as a combined group, the agreement required for attaining efficient results may prove impossible to reach. In this setting, by contrast to that depicted in Cell III, therefore, we can say that the observed results in the absence of agreement will tend either to be (1) fully efficient, or (2) inefficient in the direction of too few straying cattle on the croplands.

This possible tendency toward an underproduction of the externality-generating good or service is the central flaw in the proposals to resolve environmental quality problems by the creation and assignment of new "amenity rights" to citizens. This term, along with the proposals, may be associated with the work of E. J. Mishan.[3] If, for example, each householder should be assigned a property right to "pure air" and "noise-free sound wave," defined in such a way as to require his agreement before any "pollution" occurs, we should predict with a high degree of certainty that an inefficiently low level of polluting activity would take place.

The submodel depicted in Cell IV calls attention to the necessity of distinguishing carefully between the clear assignment of property rights to do things, to carry out specific acts, and the assignment of liability for damages once they are done. A right of a farmer to prevent cattle from invading his croplands can be voluntarily relinquished only through some explicit agreement with the rancher, under the circumstances we have discussed above. This right of the farmer may be *violated* without his prior permission having been secured, and the rancher made liable for the damages done. This is an inherently different setting, however, because third-party adjudication of damage claims must be introduced. The modification of property rights to allow violation of rights with damages subsequently assessed would convert the setting into one analogous to the exercise of eminent domain by governmental units. The strategic bargaining or hold-out position of the individual farmer in our example would be eliminated by this procedure, but only at the expense of substantially extending the necessarily arbitrary power of third parties in an adjudication role. In this respect, there is a Cell III analogue to the liability-for-damage interposition of Cell IV. If third-party adjudication is introduced, efficiency might be secured under the arrangements of Cell III by allowing some external agent to assign to farmers individual shares in the costs of securing the agreements required from the rancher.

Many Producers, One Consumer.

The settings described in Row 3, Cells V and VI, have not been widely discussed, but the understanding of these models may be important for certain directions of policy reforms. In our example, there are now many "producers" or "generators" of the external diseconomy, many cattle raisers, but there is only one "consumer," one decision-maker who is subjected to the external costs. Also, because of the carefully specified assumptions in our illustration, there is no joint consumption or joint consumption efficiency in the interaction among the separate ranchers.

Consider, first, the setting depicted in Cell V, where the cattle raisers have an initial legal right to allow their animals to roam over the cropland, which is under single ownership. Since there is no "publicness" present, that is, since the external costs are exclusively concentrated on the single decision-maker, this farmer can negotiate separate agreements with cattle raisers if indeed such agreements are profitable to him. He can trade separately with each rancher, and aside from bargaining difficulties, we might predict that efficient outcomes would be forthcoming. If both the cattle industry and the farming industry are broadly competitive, in the sense that the prices of final products are established in a larger market than the interaction under consideration here, the position of the farmer as the single buyer, as a monopsonist, need not affect the generalized prediction that an efficient result will be produced voluntarily. He could not, in this situation, squeeze a monopsony rent by paying less to a rancher than the latter could earn in an alternative location for cattle raising.

In a more general model, the effects of the single purchaser's monopsony position should be taken into account. If the price of reducing the external diseconomy increases as more units are purchased by the monopsonist, and if he cannot discriminate among separate sellers in price, he will tend to purchase a lower reduction in external diseconomies than overall efficiency considerations warrant. We can conclude that the contractual bargaining result that would emerge will be either (1) reasonably efficient, or (2) inefficient in the direction of a remaining excessive generation of external diseconomies. If no bargaining is observed to take place, we can, of course, conclude that the initial situation is efficient.

The situation depicted in Cell VI involves a reversal of property rights. Here the single farmer holds full title to the croplands, and the ranchers have no rights to allow their animals to roam. If no bargaining is observed to take place, we can again conclude that the initial position is roughly efficient. If, however, bargaining is observed, we should examine the implications of this effort for allocative outcomes. The results are the obverse of those traced out for Cell V. If competition prevails in both industries, the single-seller or monopolistic position of the farmer cannot affect the price at which he may sell straying rights to ranchers. However, in the more general case, this monopoly position might allow him to exploit the several buyers. If he cannot discriminate among these buyers in price, but if he can exploit his monopoly power, we should expect that he would sell fewer straying rights than that number which strict efficiency conditions would dictate. We can conclude that the observed results of the bargaining process would either (1) be efficient, or (2) involve the production of a less than optimal amount of external diseconomies.

In Row 3, as in Row 2, there is a substantive difference in allocative results generated by the shift in property-right arrangements as between the two sides of the interaction. In both Rows the direction of effect is the same; the assignment of rights to the acting party or "producer" of the external effect biases the outcomes in favor of an excessive supply of the diseconomy, whereas the reversal of this assignment biases the results toward an undersupply of the diseconomy. In this row, however, the inefficiencies stem from the potential monopsony and monopoly position of the single "consumer" in the two cases. In Row 2, by contrast, the inefficiencies that might arise are due to the "publicness" interaction among the separate "consumers." This major difference can be turned to advantage in the institutional reforms that might be suggested.

Many Producers, Many Consumers.

Before discussing specific reform proposals, we should consider the institutional settings depicted in Row 4 of Fig. 28-1. In our example, there are now many ranchers and many farmers. In Cell VII the ranchers initially hold property rights which allow their cattle access to croplands owned by many farmers; in Cell VIII the farmers hold the rights of exclusion. The results are predictable from our analysis of the simpler cases. The complex interactions may be factored down into a set of Cell III and Cell IV models, in each of which many separate farmers confront a single rancher or "producer" of the external diseconomy. This factoring down is possible because of our initial assumption that there is no direct interdependence among the ranchers themselves. The straying of one rancher's cattle neither raises nor lowers the costs to other ranchers. With this restriction, the predictions made for Cell III and Cell IV settings become directly applicable in Cells VII and VIII. When the ranchers hold property rights in the range, inefficient results may be generated that take on equilibrium characteristics due to the "publicness" interaction among the separate "consumers" of the externality, the farmers in this example. This "publicness" is incorporated with respect to the straying of each rancher's cattle onto the croplands. For a single farmer, therefore, there is little or no incentive to enter negotiations with a single rancher for the purpose of reducing the damage to crops. Nor will a single farmer be able to accomplish much by entering into a bargaining coalition with only one or a few of his fellow farmers. A bargaining coalition of a size sufficiently large to ensure gains to potential members (and nonmembers) may not be formed. Insofar as inefficiency persists, therefore, it will be in the direction of relatively excessive damage to the crops. There is likely to be too much of the external diseconomy.

When the property rights are reversed, the potential allocative error changes direction, as in the Cell IV comparison with Cell III. When the individual farmers are authorized to exclude cattle from the unfenced croplands which include their own holdings, no single rancher will be able to purchase all of the permissions that would be necessary to allow his cattle to roam freely, almost regardless of the relative benefits and costs to the parties involved. The reason is that each farmer is here placed in a position which allows him to block or to veto an agreement with any rancher. Hence, insofar as allocative inefficiency exists in this setting, the direction is surely that of preserving the croplands relatively free of straying cattle. There is likely to be too little of the external diseconomy.

III. Institutional Elements in Reform

The matrix presentation of Fig. 28-1, along with subsequent discussion, allows generalized predictions to be made concerning the effects of institutional structure on allocative outcomes. To the extent that this structure itself is subject to collective modification and control, the analysis should suggest ways toward reform. In this respect, attention must be centered on the situations described in Cells III, IV, VII, and VIII. If the institutional setting depicted in these cells can be shifted so as to approximate the setting of Cell V or VI, the necessity for detailed correction of allocative inefficiencies may be eliminated. Such a shift will, in all cases, involve the internalization or elimination of the "publicness" aspect of the interaction. In our example, there must be some shift from a "many farmers" to a "one farmer" model. The number of ranchers, or "producers" of the external diseconomy is irrelevant to the problem.

This indicates that some sort of collectivity or coalition should be formed among the many separate "consumers" of the external diseconomy, so long as the effects are nonexcludable among them. Once this step is taken, a single agent can act for the coalition, for the group, and as this single agent confronts the one or the many separate "producers," tolerably efficient outcomes may be expected to emerge from the bilateral bargaining process.

This conclusion is simple enough, and it has, of course, long been recognized. It has not often been incorporated directly in specific proposals for reform. For the most part, reform proposals embody some collectively enforced modifications in the conditions of choice confronting the individual "producers" of the external effect. Corrective devices involve the levy of taxes directly on the participants, with the levels of these taxes being determined from some measure of the extent of spillover damage exerted. By comparison with this, the institutional reform suggested here eschews any attempt to determine optimal solution values, a step which is essential if the corrective taxes are to be efficiently levied. The institutional changes require only that a single bargaining agent be authorized to act on behalf of the "consumers" with no directions as to the specific outcomes which may be forthcoming in his negotiations with the separate "producers."

Several advantages stem from this institutional approach. In the first place, attention is focused on the limits to the size of the effective coalition represented by the bargaining agent. The size of the coalition is determined by the limit of the "publicness" interaction. Nothing but inefficiency can result from the appointment of an agent which acts for a coalition of "consumers" that are not related through a genuine publicness interaction. In our example, if each farmer fences his croplands, and hence can privately exclude cattle, there is no problem of an agent to act for all farmers. We are in a Coase setting from the outset, and no coalition need be formed at all.

This elementary point has important implications for many of the problems of pollution control. There is, for example, surely no argument for *federally* imposed general standards of water purity. The

"consumers" of the external diseconomy of water pollution are partners in a "publicness" interaction that is limited to the separate water-
sheds. It is for these separate groups of "consumers" that separate
bargaining agents might be appointed.

The approach also draws attention to a second important, if also
elementary, principle. The bargaining agent for the "consumers" of
the external effect should be divorced from any and all pretense that
its objective is to act in the "public interest." The interests of those
who are externally affected by the diseconomy are not the interests of
the whole public. This remains true even if all members of the community, as "consumers" or affected parties, should be included in the
coalition. The essentially opposing interests of those who exert or impose the external diseconomy cannot be properly represented in the
coalition.

Once empowered to act for those persons who bear the external diseconomy, the agent may bargain for either *more* or *less* of the
externality-generating activity. A common fallacy is that of assuming that the genuine interest of consuming parties is always that of
reducing the level of spillover damage that they suffer. This direction
of change is, of course, desirable if there are no offsetting compensations. But if the value of extending the external diseconomy to the
"producer" exceeds the damage value to the combined group of "consumers," the latter's interests lie in agreeing to such an extension
rather than in preventing it. The power of the collective agency representing or acting for the group of "consumers" in either direction
depends, of course, on some initial definition of property rights. If a
Cell III setting is descriptive, the direction of change will tend to be
that which involves the purchase of agreements to limit the degree of
spillover damage. By comparison, in a Cell IV situation, the direction
of reform may be the opposite.

In a generalized institutional reform, how should property rights
be defined? It may be plausibly argued that the status quo provides a
basis for explicit definition in those areas of emerging interaction.
"Producers" and "consumers" might be granted rights to carry out
activities in the same form and to the same limits as observed on a
specific and unannounced date in some current period. This definition of rights along with the agency representing the sharers of the
"publicness" interaction, acts to create an institutional structure from
which changes would tend to be directionally efficient. If initial levels
of the activity should be inefficiently high, the collectivity which acts
for "consumers" could purchase agreements for reductions. For all
increases, by contrast, the "producers" would be required to compensate the agency appropriately. In all cases, the final results will depend on the process of bilateral bargaining between the agency and
the producer of the diseconomy.

The institutional changes discussed here do not, however, resolve the more difficult issues concerning individualized shares in the potential costs and benefits that might emerge from agreements reached between the "consumers" agent and the producers of the external effect. How can the agent, acting on behalf of its members, properly assess aggregate costs and/or benefits from a particular agreement until and unless it is provided with some means of imputing shares to its members? Ideally, the evaluations of members must be used as the basis for such measurements. Some attempt might be made, at a practical level, to estimate these evaluations for adding-up purposes, but there remains the problem of *financing* and *disposition*. If the agent is to secure an agreement to limit the extent of spillover damage, financial outlays must be made. To secure funds, the agency would require taxing powers, and this will necessarily allow some determination of tax shares. Essentially the same problem arises when the agency's decision is to sell rights for extensions in the externality-generating activity. Funds will be collected, and these funds will have to be distributed to members of the "consumer" coalition in some fashion.

A Scheme for Tax and Dividend Shares.

How could the agency secure accurate evaluation data from those whose interests it is supposed to represent, data which might be used both for entering into exchange agreements with the "producers" of the diseconomies and for the imposition of tax shares on the one hand and for the disposition of dividends on the other? The problem of voluntary revelation of individual evaluations seems to arise in all public goods interactions—the "free-rider" dilemma. Individuals will find it advantageous to conceal their true preferences if they presume that others in the group will provide sufficient funds to secure the public good. Consider how this applies to the present example. Individual "consumers" of the external diseconomy are presumably asked to state their evaluations of the "public good" that is represented by some limitation on the external diseconomy. These evaluations are, in turn, to be used as the basis for tax shares to be collected in the process of financing potential agreements with "producers." In this unidirectional setting, the single person will have an incentive to understate his preferences: he will grossly undervalue the limitation on the diseconomy. As a result, the aggregation of individual evaluations will not reflect the true "social" value of the public good that is in question. Consider, however, the adjustment process in the other direction. Suppose that the agency also asks the separate consumers what values they place on the extension of the diseconomy, values which will be used both to measure the extent of the costs that a potential "producer" must cover in any agreement, and the disposition of the dividends of funds collected. In this case, the free-rider dilemma works in the opposing direction. Individuals will now have a strong incentive to overstate their true evaluations. In so doing they hope to secure a relatively large share of the dividends that potential "producers" might provide. The results are likely to be inefficient in that no exchanges will be made due to the aggregate overevaluations of the costs of extending the diseconomy.

The solution to the problem is suggested in the juxtaposition of the two effects discussed. If individuals are asked to reveal their evaluations of changes in the level of the diseconomy, with this evaluation required to hold for changes in both directions, the free-rider dilemma works in offsetting ways. For possible limitations on the activity, for which they will be subjected to tax, individuals will have a strong incentive to understate their true preferences. For extensions in the activity on the other hand, from which they will receive dividends, individuals will have a strong incentive to overstate their true evaluations. If they are now required to reveal their evaluations for determinable discrete changes in the level of the activity that generates the external effect, with the direction of change to be determined by the negotiations between the agent and the "producers," we should expect some rough approximation of an efficient outcome.[4]

Suppose that all persons should understate their evaluations on changes in the diseconomy, reflecting that the tax-side aspect of the free-rider dominates the potential dividends side. In this case, the agency will be required to confront potential purchasers of rights to extend the activity with a relatively low aggregate evaluation. There would, in this case, be a strong prospect for an extension of the diseconomy. Individuals would find that their free-rider strategy has backfired on them; they would be subjected to further spillover damages for which they would secure inadequate compensation. On the other hand, suppose that all persons should overstate their evaluation on the diseconomy, reflecting that the potential dividend side of the problem dominates the tax payments side in their behavior. In this case, the agency will confront potential purchasers and sellers of changes in activity levels with a relatively high aggregate evaluation. These "producers" will find it advantageous to sell rights that they hold, hence, reducing the level of the diseconomy. Individuals will find that the spillover damage exerted by the diseconomy is reduced; but they will be subjected to accompanying tax shares that exceed their own true evaluations of the gains which are secured. In either of these two cases, the attempt on the part of individuals to behave strategically will be counterproductive. To the extent that this is recognized, persons will find it advantageous to submit evaluations which are based on their own best estimates of the true value of the diseconomy over the discrete changes that are defined as prospects.[5]

IV. Conclusions

The detailed operation of the institutional agent cannot be discussed in this essay. The set of institutional reforms sketched out will serve to ensure that some proximate solution to the serious problems of environmental quality are attained. Major constitutional problems have been neglected. By what criteria is society to judge whether or not the environment as observed is sufficiently nonoptimal as to require the sometimes dramatic institutional reformation which the reform proposals may embody? When is a watershed or river basin so polluted as to require the establishment of an agent for all users of the river along with a precise delineation of pollution rights? Such steps are costly in themselves, and attempts at reforms could be justified only beyond some limits of inefficiency. These broader and more basic constitutional issues are too seldom mentioned in the familiar discussions of environmental quality.

This essay has been explicitly limited. The institutional structure of potential externality relationships was first examined. The analysis revealed that the presence of a "publicness" interaction among "consumers" or bearers of a potential external diseconomy is critical for the predicted failure of voluntary contractual arrangements. Once this point is accepted, the way is opened for the institutional reforms that are required. These involve the replacement of the many-person reactions on the "consumer" side by some agent or collectivity that is empowered to act on behalf of all "consumers." This institutional agent is then placed in a position to negotiate directly with those individuals or firms who might find it privately profitable to generate the external effect. The agent may, on behalf of its constituent members, agree to sell or to purchase rights to carry on the activity, with the delineation of initial levels of activity being determined in accordance with some selected status quo position. Agency determination of the evaluation of its members on the "public goods–public bads" involved in such limitations or extensions can be made on the basis of a specific scheme which exploits the two-sided prospects for directional change.

Notes

Work on this paper began as a direct result of a discussion with Professor J. G. Head of Dalhousie University in October, 1970. It was presented in preliminary form in a seminar at the University of Chicago in February, 1971. The paper was revised in early 1972.

1. Economists' recognition of this tendency toward contractual internaliza-

tion of potential externality in the small-number cases stems from the basic paper by R. H. Coase, "The Problem of Social Cost," *Journal of Law and Economics* 3 (October, 1960): 1–44.

2. For a representative example of a paper in this general area, see William J. Baumol, "On Taxation and Correction of Externalities," *American Economic Review* 62 (June, 1972): 307–22.

3. See, for example, E. J. Mishan, *The Costs of Economic Growth* (New York: Praeger, 1967).

4. In a seminar presentation of this scheme, Professor Lester Telser of the University of Chicago objected strenuously to the implicit assumption that consumer evaluation schedules are linear over relevant decision ranges. To the extent that significant nonlinearity is characteristic, the valuation placed on increases in activity levels above the status quo may diverge from that placed on decreases in activity levels below this point. In this situation, when forced to state a single valuation on a proposed change in activity level, while remaining uncertain as to direction, the consumer may find himself in a position of lower utility after change, in either direction. This difficulty suggests that, should the scheme be implemented, proposals for change should be made in terms of small, discrete steps rather than large ones.

5. Although independently developed, the scheme presented here is related variously to several other arrangements which have been invented, and elaborated upon in considerably more detail, to accomplish the same objective. Among those that have been brought to my attention are: Edward H. Clarke, "Multipart Pricing of Public Goods," *Public Choice* 11 (Fall, 1971): 17–34; T. Nicolaus Tideman, "The Efficient Provision of Public Goods" (unpublished manuscript, 1970); E. Malinvaud, "A Planning Approach to the Public Good Problem," *Swedish Journal of Economics* 73 (March, 1971): 93–112; Peter Bohm, "An Approach to the Problem of Estimating Demands for Public Goods," *Swedish Journal of Economics* 73 (March, 1971): 55–66.

I should emphasize that my purpose here is not to advance a particular scheme of arrangement, and I am not interested in examining the operating characteristics in detail. My purpose is, instead, that of isolating the *institutional* setting that seems to be suggested for any approach to efficient outcomes.

29.

The Coase Theorem
and the Theory of the State

Things were really quite simple in the post–Pigovian world of micro-economic policy, a world characterized by possible divergencies between private and social marginal cost (or product). The classically nefarious factory might be observed to spew its smoke on the neighboring housewife's laundry, and in so doing impose costs that were not reckoned in its presumed strict profit-maximizing calculus. The remedy seemed straightforward. The "government" should impose a corrective tax on the factory owner, related directly to the smoke-generating output (or, if required, a particular input) and measured by the marginal external or spillover cost. Through this device the firm would be forced to make its decision on the basis of a "socially correct" comparison of costs and revenues. Its profit-maximizing objective should then lead it to results that would be "socially optimal."

Things have not seemed nearly so simple since R. H. Coase presented his analysis of social cost.[1] Coase's central insight lay in his recognition that there are two sides to any potential economic interdependence, two parties to any potential exchange, and that this ensures at least some pressure toward fully voluntary and freely negotiated agreements. Moreover, such agreements tend to ensure the attainment of efficiency without the necessity of governmental intervention beyond the initial definition of rights and the enforcement of contracts. Applied to the example in hand, if the damage to the housewife's laundry exceeds in value the benefits that the firm derives from allowing its stacks to smoke, a range of mutual gain exists, and utility and profit-maximizing behavior on the part of the two parties involved will result in at least some reduction in the observed level of smoke damage, a reduction that can be taken to be efficient in terms of total product value. No governmental remedy may be called for at all, and indeed Coase argued that attempted correction by government might create inefficiency. Such intervention might forestall or distort the negotiations between the affected parties. As a further aspect of his analysis, Coase advanced the theorem on allocational neutrality that now bears his name. This states that under idealized conditions, when transaction costs are absent and where income-effect feedbacks are not relevant, the allocational results of voluntarily negotiated agreements will be invariant over differing assignments of property rights among the parties to the interaction.

Much of the discussion since 1960 has involved the limitations of this theorem in the presence of positive transaction costs. In this setting, differing assignments of rights may affect allocative outcomes. Furthermore, the transaction costs barrier to voluntarily negotiated agreements that can be classified as tolerably efficient may be all but prohibitive in some situations, notably those that may require simultaneous agreement among many parties. The generalized transaction-costs rubric may be used to array alternative institutional structures, with the implied objective being that of minimizing these costs.

My purpose in this essay is not to elaborate these extensions and/or limitations of the Coase analysis, many of which have become familiar even if an exhaustive taxonomy of cases has not been completed. My purpose is almost the opposite. I want to extend the Coase analysis, within his assumptions of zero transaction costs and insignificant income-effect feedbacks, to differing institutional settings than those that have normally been implicitly assumed in the discussions of the neutrality theorem. This approach leads to the question: Why did Coase suggest that the Pigovian prescriptions might produce inefficient results? Or, to put this somewhat differently, why does the theorem of allocational neutrality stop short at certain ill-defined institutional limits? Why can it not be extended to encompass all possible institutional variations, variations that may be broadly interpreted as differences in the assignments of property rights? What is there in the implied Pigovian institutional framework that might inhibit the voluntary negotiations among parties, always assuming zero transaction costs? If the neutrality theorem holds, why should the political economist be overly concerned about institutional reform, as such?

There is a paradox of sorts here between the theorem of allocational neutrality, interpreted in its most general sense, and Coase's basic policy position. One implication of the theorem, so interpreted, would be that the thrust of classical political economy may have been misdirected. Adam Smith's central message points toward institutional reform and reconstruction as two means of guaranteeing overall efficiency in resource usage, and, as noted, we can always interpret institutions as embodying specific property rights. Governmental authorities were to be stripped of their traditionally established rights to interfere in the workings of the market economy; or, stated conversely, individual traders were to be granted rights to negotiate on their own terms. The central theorem of classical economies might be summarized as the demonstration of the differences in allocational results under divergent institutional structures. I do not think that Coase would disagree with my statements here, and I think that he shares with me an admiration for Adam Smith and that Coase, too, places Smith's emphasis on institutional-structural reform above the modern policy emphasis on detailed and particularistic manipulation of observed results.

The apparent paradox may be resolved when we take account of the theory of the state or of government that is, perhaps surprisingly, shared by Adam Smith, Pigou, and Coase. My argument proceeds in several steps. First, it is necessary to distinguish carefully between property rights and liability rules. Secondly, I shall demonstrate that governmental or collective action, if conceived in the Wicksellian framework or model, does not modify the applicability of the neutrality theorem. Thirdly, I shall show that government, conceived in a non-Wicksellian model, need not modify the applicability of the theorem, but that, in such case, property rights are explicitly changed with the introduction of governmental action. Finally, I shall suggest that the theory of government decision-making implicit in both classical and neoclassical economics, and carried over in Coase's analysis, offers the source of the seemingly paradoxical limits on the neutrality theorem.

I. Property Rules and Liability Rules

In his basic paper, Coase did not carefully make a distinction between the assignment of rights to particular individuals and the rules determining the liability of particular individuals for damage that their behavior might impose on others. His example, the now-familiar one of the interaction between the rancher and the farmer, was discussed in terms of alternative rules for bearing liability for damages. Either the rancher, whose cattle strayed onto the neighboring croplands, was liable for damages that the farmer might suffer, or he was not liable. If both cattle and grain were marketed competitively, the neutrality theorem showed that the same allocative outcome would be generated, regardless of which set of liability rules should be in existence. In the former case, the rancher, knowing in advance that he would be liable for damages caused by his straying animals, would include these payments as an anticipated cost in making his size-of-herd decisions. In the latter case, the farmer, knowing that he can collect no damages from the rancher (and that he must respect the property rights of the rancher to cattle), will find it advantageous to initiate payments to the latter in exchange for agreements limiting the size of herd, if indeed the value of crop damage at the margin exceeds the value of the additional grazing to the rancher.

Coase overlooked the fact that the institutional structure was significantly different in the two cases. In the second case, the shift toward an efficient outcome takes place through an ordinary market or exchange process, in which none other than the two parties need get involved. In the first case, however, as presented by Coase, there must be third-party interference by a "judge" to assess charges for damage that has been done. In the context of his discussions, this institutional difference does not matter, since the third-party can, presumably, measure and assess damages with complete accuracy. The difference is nonetheless important in the more general setting. Consistency should have dictated that the first case be presented, not as one where the rancher was liable *ex post* for damages caused by his straying animals, but as one where the farmer held enforceable property rights in his croplands, rights that were inviolate except on his own agreement. In this framework, the rancher would have had to negotiate an agreement with the farmer in advance of any actual straying of cattle. This converts the institutional setting on this side into one that is parallel to the converse case. No third party, no judge, is required to intervene and to assess damages *ex post*.

We may define this setting as one in which property rules are established and enforced, as opposed to liability rules.[2] This setting calls direct attention to the motivation that both parties have to exploit the potentially realizable surplus by moving from the initial inefficient position. This setting also allows for an extension of the neutrality-efficiency theorem beyond those strictly objectifiable circumstances suggested to be present in the Coase example. If the precise degree of damage caused by external imposition is ambiguous, the third party must necessarily exercise his own best judgment in making a settlement. By contrast, if property rules are defined, with the necessity of prior agreement on the part of the potentially damaged party, the latter's own subjective assessment of potential damage becomes controlling in determining the range over which final outcomes may settle. This assessment is, of course, a better measure of actual value lost than the estimate made by any third party.

II. Wicksellian Unanimity

For my purposes in this essay, the specification that parties to an interaction are defined by property rather than liability rules facilitates relating the Coase theorem on allocational neutrality to the underlying conception or theory of government or of the state. In the simplest possible model, we may conceive of a polity that is limited in membership to the parties directly involved in the potential interaction. The interacting group can be made coincident in membership with the political unit. On this basis, we can interpret the "trades" among the parties as being analogous to collective or governmental decisions reached under the operation of a Wicksellian rule of unanimity.[3] Consider either the earlier factory-housewife example, or Coase's familiar rancher-farmer one. In either illustration, we can think of the two-party group as comprising the all-inclusive membership in the political community, in which case agreement between the two parties on any matter is equivalent to unanimous accord. Resort to third-party adjudication is impossible for the simple reason that no third party exists.

From this context, it becomes easier to conceive "the State" merely as the instrumental means or device through which individuals attempt to carry out activities aimed at securing jointly desired objectives. This is, of course, the traditional framework for all theories of social-contract origins of government. In this setting, all activities of the public sector are explained in exchange terms, even if it is recognized that the exchange process is significantly more complex than that which makes up the central subject matter of orthodox economic theory. There is at least no conceptual or logical necessity to think of "the State" as an entity that exists separate from and apart from citizens.

If we remain within the strict contractarian conception of collective action, where all decisions require unanimous consent by all members of the political community, and if we retain the assumption that transaction costs are absent, the Coase theorem on allocational neutrality may be applied beyond those limits within which it has normally been discussed. In this model, collective or governmental decision-making remains equivalent to freely negotiated voluntary exchange. Hence, there is little or no cause for concern about "governmental intervention" as such, because any action that might properly be classified as "governmental" would not emerge unless all parties agree on the contractual terms.

Differences in the assignment of rights might, as in the standard simple exchange cases, generate differences in distributional outcomes, but the contractual process would lead to allocational results that are both efficient and invariant. Consider a classic example, which introduces what we may appropriately call collective or public goods: David Hume's villagers, whose utility would be increased by drainage of a meadow. The neutrality theorem, applied to this example, demonstrates that an efficient and unchanged allocational result will emerge from freely negotiated contract whether the postulated initial position should be one in which individuals own separate plots of land through which the swampy stream flows or whether the whole meadow is defined as communal property, accessible to all parties. With an effective unanimity rule, and with zero transaction costs, the complex exchange that is required for efficiency would be worked out under any initial structure of individual rights. The sharing of the gross gains-from-trade among separate persons would, of course, be influenced by the particular property assignment in being. If the sharing of such gains modifies individual demands for the common good, at the margin, that is, if income effects are present, differing assignments can produce slight differences in allocational results, but, under the assumptions here, those results produced will continue to be efficient.

III. Simple Majority Voting

When the unanimity requirement for collective decisions is abandoned, governmental action no longer represents a complex equivalent of a voluntary exchange process.[4] If decisions that are to be binding over the inclusive group can be made by a subset of this group, there is no guarantee that a particular individual holds against the imposition of net harm or damage. Once his own contractual agreement to the terms of governmental or collective action is dropped as a requirement, an individual can no longer be certain that he will share in the gross gains that governmental action will, presumably, generate. From this it seems to follow that collective action, motivated by improvement in the positions of members of a decisive coalition smaller than the totality of community membership, need not produce results that are efficient, even with zero transaction costs.[5] Any nonunanimity voting rule, for example, that of simple majority voting, would seem to produce results that may be, in the net, inefficient.

The neutrality theorem is, however, more powerful than might be suggested by cursory attention to this example. Efficient outcomes will tend to emerge from the contractual process, even under less-than-unanimity voting rules for collective action, if the modified structure of property rights consequent on the departure from unanimity is acknowledged, and if individuals are allowed freely to negotiate trades in these rights. Economists have not fully incorporated the property-rights structure of less-than-unanimity voting rules into their orthodoxy, and they tend to stop short of the extension of the neutrality theorem herein suggested.

Consider a situation in which individuals hold well-defined rights, which are acknowledged by all parties, and which are known to be enforceable without costs. If no collective action is undertaken, individuals trade such rights among themselves in simple exchanges, ensuring mutual gain. If collective action is undertaken, but only on the agreement of all parties, mutual gain (or, at the limit, absence of loss) is ensured. If this requirement is dropped, and individuals may be subjected to damage or harm through collective action, the value of their initial holdings is necessarily changed, again on the assumption of zero transaction costs. Individuals no longer hold claims that are inviolate against imposed reductions in value. A new and ambiguous set of rights is brought into being by the authorization of governmental action taken without the approval of all parties. Any potentially decisive decision-making coalition, a simple majority of voters in our example here, possesses rights to the nominal holdings of the minority. These rights are, in this instance, ambiguous because they emerge only upon the identification of the majority coalition that is to be decisive with respect to the issue under consideration for collective action. Once identified, however, members of the effective majority hold potentially marketable rights. These may be exchanged, directly or indirectly, and the contractual process will again ensure that the efficient allocative outcome will be achieved, and that this will be invariant, given the appropriate assumptions about transaction costs and income effects.

We may illustrate this in a highly simplified three-person example. Consider a community that includes three men: A, B, and C. Collective decisions are to be made by simple majority voting. Initial holdings of units of an all-purpose and numberable consumption good are, let us say, 100 for A, 60 for B, and 30 for C. In this environment, let us suppose that a governmental project is proposed, one that promises to yield benefits of 30 units, distributed equally among the three persons. The gross costs of this project are, however, 40 units; clearly, the proposal is inefficient. Despite this, if B and C can succeed in organizing themselves into a majority coalition, and if they can impose the full tax costs of the proposal on A, they can make net gains. In this case, the results would appear as follows:

Person	Benefits	Costs	Net
A	10	40	−30
B	10	0	10
C	10	0	10

Once B and C are identified as the decisive members of the coalition, however, individual A can negotiate trades, or side payments, that will be mutually beneficial to all parties, and which will keep this inefficient outcome from being achieved. Individual A can, for example, offer either B or C a net gain of 15 units to join a different majority coalition that will disapprove the project. Or, if both B and C hold firm, they can exact from A a payment of 10 units for their agreement to withold the project. The side payments, which must be allowed to take place under our assumption of zero transaction costs, will ensure that all inefficient projects are forestalled, and, similarly, that all efficient projects will be carried out.[6]

The values to individuals of the "property rights in franchise" embodied in a majority-voting regime depend critically on the constitutional limits within which majorities are allowed to take collective political action. These values will also depend on the technological possibilities for potential coalition gains within the given set of constitutional constraints defined. Detailed exploration of these interesting and mostly unresolved issues would not be suitable in this essay. For the present purposes, the points to be recognized are, first, that any departure from unanimity in collective decision processes modifies the structure of rights from that which is defined exclusively by private-sector claims and obligations, and, second, that even with this modified set of rights, the theorem on allocational neutrality remains valid within the required, and highly restricted, assumptions concerning transaction costs and income effects.[7]

IV. Administrative Authority

In traditional economic policy discussions, the arguments for and/or against governmental intervention in the private sector rarely take place under explicitly defined models for collective decision-making. For the most part, those who propose "corrections" to the outcomes of voluntary exchange processes, like those who oppose them, are content to treat governmental decisions as exogenous to the valuations of the persons in the economy itself. If, however, these arguments are interpreted consistently within any collective decision-making framework, the structure that can most readily be inferred is neither that of unanimity nor simple majority voting. The model of government that accords most closely with economic policy discussions is one in which authority to take collective action is vested in an administrator, a bureaucrat, an expert, who chooses for the community, presumably on the basis of his own version of the "public interest," or, in technical economist's jargon, some "social welfare function."

It is useful, therefore, to extend our analysis of the theorem on allocational neutrality to this administrative-decision model of public choice. Probably because the model is essentially implicit rather than explicitly postulated, little or no attention has been paid to the alternative means through which the single decision-maker for the collectivity may be selected. Nor need this concern us here. Strictly speaking, the conclusions developed below follow whether the decision-maker be divinely ordained, democratically elected, arbitrarily appointed, selected in competitive examination, or hereditarily determined.[8] I want to examine a model in which a single person has been empowered to make decisions for a whole community. This defines a specific structure of rights, an assignment, and the problem is to determine the allocative results that will emerge in comparison with those predicted under alternative structures. The first point to be noted is the same as that made with respect to simple majority voting. The delegation of decision-making power to the single person modifies the set of rights in existence, even prior to the onset of any imposed governmental action. The designated chooser for the community holds potentially valued claims that were nonexistent before he is constitutionally authorized to act.

Consider again Hume's drainage of the village meadow. Instead of operating through a rule of unanimity, we now assume that the village has empowered a single person to act on behalf of all persons in the group and, furthermore, it is acknowledged that his decisions will be enforced. Formally, it does not matter whether the decision-maker is chosen from within or from outside the group. For expositional simplicity, however, we shall assume that he is selected from outside the village. We now assume that a drainage project, lumpy in nature, will yield to villagers symmetrically distributed benefits valued at one thousand units of the *numéraire* commodity. The project will cost a total of eight hundred units, and the taxing institution requires symmetrical sharing. The project is clearly Pareto-efficient, and, as indicated earlier, under an operating rule of unanimity, the project will be undertaken, given our zero transaction costs assumption, and including all free-rider behavior under the transaction costs rubric. The question becomes: Would this project necessarily be selected by the single decision-maker, the alternative structure of property rights under consideration?

It is illegitimate to assume that the single administrator knows the preferences of the citizens, or, even should these be estimated with accuracy, that he would necessarily embody individual values dollar-for-dollar in his own choice calculus. The administrator or bureaucrat will select the project if the costs that he bears are less than the benefits that he personally secures. But these costs and benefits are not, and cannot possibly be, those of the community of citizens. Apparently, there is nothing in this model to ensure correspondence between the bureaucrat's choices and those results that are to be classified as efficient by orthodox economists' criteria. This suggests that the theorem of allocational neutrality breaks down.

If, however, we move beyond this naive model of administrative behavior, the applicability of the neutrality theorem may be restored. By acting in accordance with his own subjective evaluation, the bureaucrat may be failing to maximize the value of the property right that has been assigned to him constitutionally. To show this, let us assume that, naively, the decision-taker decides against the project noted. In this decision, he deprives the citizenry of benefits valued at one thousand units and, at the same time, avoids the imposition of tax costs of eight hundred units on the community. In a setting with zero transaction costs, where large numbers can readily reach contractual agreements, the citizenry, as an inclusive group of taxpayer-beneficiaries, would be willing to offer side payments up to a total of two hundred units to secure a change from negative to positive action on the project.[9] If the decision-maker, the administrator or bureaucrat, uses these side payments, either indicatively or actually, to determine his final choice, the drainage project will be carried out. The theorem of allocational neutrality is apparently validated in this more sophisticated model for bureaucratic behavior. So long as the decision-maker acts to maximize the potential rent on the property right delegated to him, the right to make the final decision for the whole community, the allocative result will be identical to that forthcoming under alternative rights structures, with, of course, the transaction-costs, income-effect assumptions postulated. As in all property-assignment shifts, the distributional results may be quite different under differing assignments. If the bureaucrat maximizes the potential rent on his right to choose for the group, and, furthermore, if he collects this in the form of a personal side payment, there is an income transfer from members of the original group to the "outsider" selected as decision-taker.[10]

Objection may be raised to rent-maximizing as the appropriate norm for bureaucratic behavior, even if we neglect ethical considerations (these will be introduced in Section V). To postulate that the designated decision-maker maximizes the potential side payments that he can receive from taxpayer-beneficiaries as a group implies that the decision-maker himself is indifferent to the alternatives, that he places no personal evaluation on the differences among these opportunities available to him. If, in fact, the bureaucrat or administrator is external to the affected group of persons in the community, this assumption may seem plausibly realistic. If, however, he is chosen from within the community itself, his own evaluation must be taken into account. Whether the decision-maker is selected from within or without the original group of members, his own evaluation can be, and must be, included in any correct assessment of costs and benefits.

We may return to the numerical illustration introduced above. Suppose that the gross benefits of the proposed drainage project, to all persons other than the decision-taker, amount to one thousand units of a *numéraire* good (we may call these "dollars"), and that the gross costs, to all persons other than the decision-taker, amount to eight hundred. Suppose, however, that the decision-maker, himself, places a monetary value of, say, four hundred dollars on the "natural beauty" of the swampy and undrained meadow. Even should he be required to pay no part of the tax costs of the project, this four hundred units of value necessarily becomes a component in the total opportunity cost of the drainage scheme. Under these conditions, the bureaucrat will refuse the proffered side payment of two hundred units. The project will not be undertaken.

Does this result suggest that the theorem of allocational neutrality breaks down? The question of whether the decision-taker is selected from within or outside the initial membership of the group becomes critical at this point. If the selection is internal, the project is inefficient under the conditions suggested, and it will not be undertaken under any rights assignment. This is because the person's negative evaluation would be an input in any internal contractual negotiations that might produce an allocative outcome. In this case, the neutrality theorem remains valid. Suppose, however, that the bureaucrat is not in the initial group of members. In this case, his own personal evaluation of the project alternatives will not enter and will not affect allocative outcomes when the assignment of rights is limited to initial members. This decision-maker's evaluation will, however, enter as a determinant when he is assigned the rights to choose for the group. The neutrality theorem would not be valid under these conditions unless the decision-maker is, in fact, wholly indifferent with respect to the alternatives.

This result should not be at all surprising. The theorem on allocational neutrality, even under its restricted set of required assumptions, should hardly be expected to extend to rights assignments that embody differing memberships in the group. For fixed memberships, the theorem remains fully valid. Even when the decision-maker is selected from outside, the theorem suggests that any change in rights assignments, once the additional member is included, among this new membership will produce identical allocational results.

V. The Theory of the State

It is possible to interpret both the policy implications of Coase's theorem on allocational neutrality and Pigovian corrective policy prescriptions in terms of the underlying conceptions, models, or theories of government. As the analysis above has suggested, under certain conceptions of governmental process, neither Coase nor the Pigovians should have been greatly concerned about institutional change as a means of generating allocative efficiency. If distributional considerations are neglected, and if decision-makers for the community are chosen from within the group, the structure of rights will modify allocative outcomes only because of differentials in levels of transactions costs, provided that the decision-takers are motivated by economic self-interest. The policy thrust of Coase's discussion is, however, to the effect that governmental or collective intrusion into the negotiation processes of the market economy tends to retard rather than to advance movement toward allocative efficiency. Conversely, the policy thrust of the whole Pigovian tradition is that governmental or collective intrusion into the market economy tends to be corrective of distortions and leads toward rather than away from those results that might satisfy agreed-on efficiency criteria.

The Pigovian model of the state may be examined first. The decision-taker, the person or group empowered to impose the corrective taxes and subsidies, is presumed to act in accordance with rules laid down for him by the welfare economist. His task is that of measuring social costs and social benefits from alternative courses of action, a task that he is presumed able to carry out effectively. On the basis of such measurements, the decision-taker is to follow the rules laid down, quite independently of the personal opportunity costs that he may face in refusing side payment offers. The Pigovian policy-maker must be an economic eunuch. The idealized allocative results are, of course, identical with those that would emerge under a regime where the decision-maker is wholly "corrupt" in the sense of strict maximization of the potential side payments or rents on his rights to make decisions. If he is expected to behave as a rent-maximizer, however, there would be no need for elaborated and detailed instruction in the form of rules or norms, as derived from the theorems of welfare economics. Within this Pigovian conception, the decision-maker for the group does not and/or should not maximize the rental value of the rights of decision that he is granted. This may be treated either as a positive prediction about bureaucratic behavior or as a normative proposition for bureaucratic behavior.

In the Coase conception,[11] an interpretation that is similar in certain respects seems to follow. If, in fact, governmental decision-makers act as strict rent-maximizers, the neutrality theorem suggests that there should be little or no concern about allocative results, per se. The evidence of such concern must, therefore, indicate some denial of the rent-maximizing behavioral hypothesis. Again, this may be taken as positive prediction or normative statement. The governmental decision-maker, the bureaucrat, empowered to act on behalf of the group, either does not maximize rents on the rights that he commands or he should not do so on moral-ethical grounds. In either case, the Coase concern for allocational efficiency returns since the negotiating pressure toward optimality is removed once the decision-making power is shifted from the market to the public sector.

It is perhaps surprising to find common elements in the basic conceptions of political process held by the proponents of essentially opposing policy positions. But in both the Pigovian framework and in that imputed here to Coase, the governmental decision-maker, either singly or as a member of a choosing group, is and/or should be "incorruptible." In this respect, the two conceptions of governmental process seem identical, despite the sharp differences in information possibilities attributed to the governmental authority in the two models.

In the Pigovian tradition, the bureaucrat is both informed and incorruptible; in the Coase framework, he is ignorant and incorruptible.

Agreement on this "incorruptibility" characteristic of governmental decision-makers, and indeed the introduction of the term "corruptible" in this familiar usage, suggests that there exist widely shared ethical presuppositions concerning the inalienability of the delegated rights to make collective choices. That is to say, some shift away from the unanimity rule for collective decisions may be accepted as necessary, with the accompanying acknowledgment that new and previously nonexistent "rights of decision" are brought into being, rights that have economic value that is potentially capturable by the subset of the citizenry empowered to make decisions on behalf of all. Such rights may, however, be considered to be inalienable; that is, the holder is not entitled to sell them or to exploit his possession of them through collection of personal rewards, either directly or indirectly.[12] It would be inappropriate in this essay to examine in detail the validity of such ethical presuppositions, although this opens up many interesting and highly controversial topics for analysis.[13]

The existence of such presuppositions can scarcely be denied. The pejorative content of such terms as "vote-trading," "logrolling," "political favoritism," "spoils system," and "pork barrel legislation"—these attest to the pervasiveness of negative attitudes toward even minor attempts on the part of possessors of political decision-making rights to increase rental returns. If these attitudes are sufficiently widespread, prohibitions against bureaucratic and political rent-maximization may extend beyond the mere promulgation of ethical norms for behavior. The rewards and punishments that are consciously built into the governmental structure may be specifically aimed at making such rent-maximization unprofitable for any person empowered to make decisions on behalf of the whole group. The designated bureaucrat who is assigned authority over one specific aspect of public policy may not be morally or ethically inhibited from accepting side payments. But he may face harsh legal penalties should he accede to monetary temptations. To the extent that these constitutionally determined constraints ensure that the economic self-interests of governmental decision-makers dictate behavior unresponsive to proffered side payments (direct or indirect) it may be argued, almost tautologically, that any outcomes chosen for the community by the "incorruptibles" must be, by definition, classified as "efficient." This would produce the paradoxical conclusion that the conditions for efficiency depend critically on the institutional structure and that, even with unchanged personal evaluations, solutions which are deemed efficient under one set of institutions may be inefficient under another.

The avoidance of this paradox becomes possible if we are content to define as allocationally efficient only that set of possible outcomes that could emerge from the contractual negotiation process among persons in the community, on the assumption that no rights are inalienable. In this case, the introduction of inalienability in the rights of governmental decision-takers clearly makes the theorem of allocational neutrality invalid. Under the highly restricted assumptions of zero transaction costs, any activity will be efficiently organized in the absence of governmental intervention, and without income-effect feedbacks, the allocational outcome will be invariant over differing assignments of private and alienable rights. Under such conditions as these, it is the inalienability of rights that the shift to the public sector introduces which removes the guarantee that outcomes will be efficient, not the shift to governmental decision-making per se. If we avoid the apparent paradox in this manner, however, the implication is left that the constitutional shift of activities to the public sector is an almost necessary source of inefficiency. When other considerations are accounted for, however, this implication need not follow. When transaction costs are recognized, and especially when distributional implications are considered, efficiency "in the large" may dictate the governmental organization of activities along with the inalienability of the rights delegated necessarily to bureaucratic decision-makers. There is no final escape from the requirements that each particular institutional change proposed must be examined on its own merits, on some case-by-case procedure, with the interdependence among separate organizational decisions firmly in mind.

Notes

I am indebted to my colleagues Winston Bush, Dennis Mueller, and Gordon Tullock for helpful suggestions.

1. R. H. Coase, "The Problem of Social Cost," *Journal of Law and Economics* 3 (1960): 1–44.

2. This terminology is adopted from the discussion by Calabresi and Melamed, whose paper clarifies the distinction between these two. As they state, a property rule "is the form of entitlement which gives rise to the least amount of state intervention." See Guido Calabresi and D. Melamed, "Property Rules, Liability Rules, and Inalienability: One View of the Cathedral," *Harvard Law Review* 85 (1972): 1089–1146; see also Harold Demsetz, "Some Aspects of Property Rights," *Journal of Law and Economics* 9 (1966): 64–65.

In another paper, I have also called attention to the distinction between these two institutional arrangements, noting in particular the necessary resort to third-party action under liability rules. See Buchanan, "The Institutional Structure of Externality," *Public Choice* 14 (Spring, 1973): 69–82, and chapter 28, this volume.

3. Collective decision-making under a rule of unanimity is associated with the name of Knut Wicksell in modern public finance theory analysis because

he proposed institutional reforms that embodied unanimity in the reaching of tax and expenditure decisions. See K. Wicksell, *Finanztheoretische Untersuchungen* (Jena: Gustav Fischer, 1896). The central portion of this work appears in English translation as "A New Principle of Just Taxation," in *Classics in the Theory of Public Finance*, ed. R. Musgrave and A. Peacock (London: Macmillan and Co., 1959), pp. 72–118.

4. It is possible to use the analogue to voluntary exchange at the level of constitutional, as opposed to day-to-day choice. That is to say, we might analyze the selection of a political constitution, the rules for the reaching of collective decisions, under a postulated unanimity rule. It is then possible to derive a logical basis for nonunanimity rules from unanimous agreement at the constitutional level. This is the approach taken in J. Buchanan and G. Tullock, *The Calculus of Consent* (Ann Arbor: University of Michigan Press, 1962).

5. With zero transaction costs, any departure from unanimity voting rules for collective action would hardly be acceptable at the constitutional level. But this modification is introduced here for purposes of developing the exposition of the argument, not for descriptive relevance.

6. It is often erroneously argued that individuals with superior economic power, A in our example, can exercise more influence in the formation of dominant coalitions than individuals with inferior economic power, C in our example. If, however, C fully recognizes the exploitation potential available in the situation described, he can offer B precisely the same terms as those offered by A. In the basic arithmetic here, there is no more likelihood that the net gains from not undertaking the project, ten units, will be shared by A rather than by B or C. In effect, the Von Neumann-Morgenstern solution set of imputations to the simple majority game becomes:

$$(5,5,0) \quad (5,0,5) \quad (0,5,5)$$

For an elaboration of this analysis, see Buchanan and Tullock, *Calculus of Consent*, chapters 11 and 12.

7. In another paper, I have developed somewhat more fully some of the possible implications of the modified rights structure that majority voting rules embody. See Buchanan, "The Political Economy of the Welfare State," Center for the Study of Public Choice Research Paper No. 808231-1-8, June, 1972. This paper was prepared for the Conference on Capitalism and Freedom, in honor of Milton Friedman, in Charlottesville, Virginia, October, 1972, and published in the volume of conference proceedings.

8. The method of selection may affect the motivation of the decision-maker and, in this way, modify the likelihood that the behavioral hypotheses implicit in the orthodox conceptions will be corroborated.

9. In the numerical example, the potentially capturable rent seems to be two hundred units because of the assumptions that both benefits and costs of the drainage project are shared symmetrically among all of the villagers. If these assumptions are relaxed, the decision-maker can collect a larger sum in rent. His potential gains, will, in all cases, be the sum of the *larger* of the *positive* or the *negative* differences between benefits and costs, the sum being taken over all members of the community.

10. This modifies the standard economist's treatment of the distinction between allocational and distributional results. The latter may, for certain purposes, be neglected if the zero-sum aspects are confined to a stable group of

"members." If, however, a new rights assignment, such as that discussed, generates distributional transfers outside the original group, the effects, for this group, are negative-sum. Applied to the realistic setting in which transaction costs are present, this suggests that a community may, under certain conditions, find it advantageous to put up with allocative inefficiency rather than to secure its removal at the expense of distributional transfers to delegated decision-takers.

11. For an explicit statement of the Coase-Chicago position, see Demsetz, "The Exchange and Enforcement of Property Rights," *Journal of Law and Economics* 7 (1964): 21–22.

12. In "Property Rules, Liability Rules, and Inalienability," Calabresi and Melamed discuss the inalienability of rights at some length, and particularly, they draw attention to several examples where inalienability is accepted. See *supra* note 2.

The precise location of "inalienability" in the situation discussed may be questioned. In delegating decision-making authority to an agent, citizens may not be considered to be transferring the economic value inherent in the "right to choose." In this framework, it is the rights of the citizenry that are "inalienable" in some fundamental sense, and the agent could scarcely transfer a "right" that he does not possess. In my discussion, I have equated the empirically observed delegation of decision-making authority with an effective transfer of a valuable "right" that is then supposed to be "inalienable."

13. The ethical bases for such widely shared attitudes may be challenged when the economic analysis is carefully developed. In the case of marketing rights to make decisions for the community, the relative undesirability of the distributional results provide a sufficient reason for inalienability. Conceptually, the decision-maker can capture *all* of the potential surplus from constitutionally authorized action. In this limit, those who presumably make the constitutional delegation of authority, the citizenry, find themselves with zero net gains from collective action. So long as the delegation of decision rights along with the inalienability is predicted to generate positive net gains, the citizenry's economic position is enhanced. The possible inefficiency in the standard allocative sense is more than offset by the distributional gains.

30.
Entrepreneurship and the Internalization of Externalities

WITH ROGER L. FAITH

I. Introduction

In an idealized setting for the operation of markets, it becomes artificial and redundant to interpret the production-trade process itself as involving the internalization of potentially relevant externalities. Nonetheless, it may be useful to think of the ordinary operation of the market in these terms when we want to move beyond the economists' idealized construction to settings where "externalities," defined in the orthodox sense, may exist. In such settings, trade becomes only one among several institutional arrangements for "internalizing externalities." In this essay, we suggest that for the particular types of economic interaction consequent upon the inauguration of entrepreneurial ventures the internalization embodied in a well-functioning legal structure may be superior to either trade or overt political arrangements. Our purpose is to compare alternative means of "internalizing" potential externalities in terms of the effects on the activity of entrepreneurs, and, through such activity, on the pace of economic development.

Consider the two-party example made familiar by R. H. Coase in his now-classic paper on social cost.[1] At an elementary level of analysis, the interaction between the cattle rancher and the wheat farmer is not different from that between any two ordinary traders; indeed, this point was the fundamental one in Coase's argument. To the extent that the "externality" is Pareto-relevant, exchange will tend to take place, hence "internalizing" the effect and guaranteeing an efficient outcome.[2] Although much of his discussion was posed in terms of "liability for damages," the implicit model for Coase's analysis is one that assumes all property rights to be well defined and enforced and, hence, tradeable.[3] In Calabresi-Melamed terms, the basic Coasian analysis presumes that entitlements are protected by a *property rule*, ensuring that, absent transaction costs, the operation of the market will effectively internalize a potential externality.[4] We propose initially to compare and contrast the operation of a property rule with that of a *liability rule*,[5] both assumed to be operative in a regime that does not involve explicitly collectivized efforts at "internalization."[6]

Our concern is not with the comparative allocative results of alternative assignments of entitlements or rights, the question that is central for most of the Coase theorem analysis. Instead, we concentrate on alternative results under the differing institutional arrangements through which a specific assignment of rights is protected or enforced. In this respect the first part of our analysis is an extension of the Calabresi-Melamed discussion rather than that of Coase. Nor are we directly concerned with the static efficiency properties of the two arrangements, which was central to the analysis of Frech and, to a large extent, that of Polinsky. In the more inclusive sense, we are interested in the "dynamic efficiency" properties of the alternatives examined.

We are also concerned primarily with lumpy projects or ventures rather than with marginal extensions of already-existing activities. We concentrate attention on the anticipated gains and anticipated damages consequent to the commencement of a new entrepreneurial venture. While some predictions as to the "rate of production" within the project, once started, must inform any estimates of gains or losses to the venture as a whole, the internal margin of adjustment (which has been the central focus of attention in almost all the analysis of externalities) is not of direct relevance for our purposes. The appropriate margin for our analysis is that between commencing and not commencing an entrepreneurial venture.

Comparisons that have been made of the effects of the property rule and the liability rule have concentrated on the differences in the strategic setting faced by the participants under the alternative means of protecting nominal entitlements. Under a property rule, where the permission of the party who may be potentially damaged must be purchased *in advance*, the bargaining position of the damaged party is much stronger than it is under liability-rule protection, where the potentially damaged party can file enforceable claims *ex post*, claims that will be settled by some third-party adjudicator. This differential in bargaining strength under the two rules will be present even if all parties, those inside as well as those outside the interaction, predict the same level of damages consequent on the inauguration of the entrepreneurial venture.

Our emphasis in this essay, however, is not directly on such *strategic* effects on behavior and on the predicted influences on such effects on results. Our emphasis is on the *subjective* aspects, and in particular on possible predictable differences between potentially estimated and realized damages.[7] We shall argue that these aspects alone generate a predictable difference between the effects of the property rule and the liability rule under certain restricted conditions.[8] The effects that we stress here tend to reinforce and perhaps to overwhelm in importance those that may be traceable to the effects stemming from strategic influences on behavior in the two idealized legal settings.

Our comparison of legal arrangements will provide the basis for an analysis and examination of collective alternatives. As the institutional "internalization of externalities" shifts from that situation best described by the operation of law to one that is described by general collectivization of decisions on development, we can predict a dampening of entrepreneurial innovation, a closing off of opportunities for the implementation of optimistic expectations, a stifling of hope in the sense of continuing or accelerated growth based on technological advance.

II. The Costs and Benefits of Alternative Stylized Legal Arrangements for the Internalization of Externalities

We propose now to examine in more detail the costs and benefits that might be associated with the two stylized legal arrangements. We defer until Section III discussion of the actual operation of legal institutions. In Section IV we introduce explicit collectivization of the internalization process.

Return to the Coase example and assume that the wheat grower, himself a former entrepreneur, holds an entitlement to his crops that is protected by a strict property rule. No one can damage this entitlement without first securing the farmer's permission. Or, if someone indicated such an intent, the farmer could seek, and expect to be granted, an injunction that would effectively prohibit the enjoined activity. Suppose, now, that a new entrepreneur, a rancher, proposes to graze cattle on lands adjacent to the wheat, but that there is the prospect for straying and destroying crops. There is no reason for assuming that the two parties place the same anticipated value on the genuinely uncertain prospects for crop damage. Let us assume that the rancher estimates anticipated damages optimistically at a low value, while the farmer estimates damages pessimistically, at a high value. The relatively more optimistic rancher thinks that his operation will be profitable within broad ranges of his damage estimates, but not if he is required to make payments at the level of damages estimated by the farmer. Under the strict property rule the rancher will be required to purchase grazing rights *before* any cattle are pastured. In the situation indicated, no bargains can be struck. No cattle will be grazed on the lands adjacent to the growing wheat.

If the wheat grower should estimate damages at a lower value than the entrepreneur-rancher, the strict property rule would not inhibit the commencement of the grazing operation since the permission of the farmer could be purchased at anticipated "bargain prices." In general, however, we should expect that entrepreneurs tend toward optimism, both with respect to the internal profit potential emergent on the productive activity and to the value of possible spillover damage. In any case, the strict property rule will prevent some projects from being undertaken.

Let us now assume that the wheat grower's entitlement in his crops is protected by a strict liability rule rather than a property rule. In this case, the rancher will put cattle on the lands if he thinks the operation profitable, even when he reckons on making damage payments. The farmer cannot prevent such entrepreneurial action. Under the liability rule, if the rancher's expectations prove correct, "development" will take place and will be validated *ex post*. The total product of the economy will be higher under the liability than under the property rule. On the other hand, if the entrepreneurial estimates are overly optimistic, the new venture will be unable to cover costs, and product value in the economy may be lower under the liability rule than the property rule. The costs of error, however, are borne by the entrepreneur, not by those who might suffer damages. In the net, the differential effects on total product value under the two rules cannot be predicted. But the differential effects on the development of new projects are clear; *more* projects will be carried forward under the liability rule than under the property rule.

We should stress that our comparison of the two legal arrangements is restricted to the effects on entrepreneurial decisions to begin new projects. We assume that "entrepreneurial vision" is limited to the profit potential in particular activities. This assumption allows us to rule out the merger option that would realize potential gains-from-trade emergent upon any difference in subjective estimates of spillover damage. In our example, if the rancher-entrepreneur estimates damages to be less than those estimated by the wheat grower, and if direct purchases of permissions to allow cattle to graze do not seem profitable under a property rule, the rancher might be able to buy out the wheat-growing operation with the prospect of managing the combined or merged activities.[9] This result requires, however, the presumption that the entrepreneurial talents of the rancher extend to farming as well. The assumption of entrepreneurial specialization is designed to rule out such merger options.[10]

For purposes of discussion here, we want also to rule out the prospects for contingency contracts which might serve partially to exploit the mutual gains to be had as a result of the differing evaluations placed on the uncertainty involved in the interdependence of the two activities. The rancher could offer the farmer a contract that commits him to pay full damages, as measured by a third party, *plus* some premium. The farmer may accept if he considers third-party adjudication reasonably accurate. In this way, some of the slow-down effects of a property rule may be mitigated, although the direction of effect remains. In the presence of transaction costs, the working out of such contingency contracts may prove difficult. Quite apart from transaction costs of the ordinary sort, the bankruptcy potential may inhibit the implementation of contingency contracts in situations where the value of the interdependence looms large relative to the value of the direct production.[11]

Calabresi and Melamed suggest that a liability rule may be more desirable in certain situations because of the holdout power that a strict property rule grants to the holders of existing entitlements. As noted above, our argument reinforces the Calabresi-Melamed support of liability rules by our introduction of the predicted difference in subjective estimates of damage, a difference that becomes important precisely in those situations where entrepreneurs tend to be relatively more optimistic about the profitability of new resource combinations than holders of existing property rights. In a stationary economy, where by definition entrepreneurial activity does not exist, there could be little argument for a liability rule in preference to a property rule in the protection of entitlements.[12] The value of a well-defined property right to the use of a resource unit, the productivity of which is known, will be higher if this right is protected by a strict property rule. Since this applies to all units of resources, total value will be higher in an economy with a universalized property rule than it will be in an economy that allows a liability rule for the protection of any or all entitlements.

The case for a liability rule arises only when the dynamic properties of the economic process are recognized. Whereas the value of existing resources will tend to be higher under a generalized regime of property rules, the rate of increase in this value through time will tend to be larger than a regime that offers only liability-rule protection of established entitlements against new and untried intrusions that may be minimal requisites for any development at all.

The economy could scarcely be characterized by growth and development while nominal entitlements are all protected by strict property rules. Such legal arrangements would tend to ensure that little change from the status quo is possible. The potential for the profitability and productivity of new resource combinations can first be imagined only in the minds of entrepreneurs. Others in the economy cannot share such visions.[13] Further, any activation of such entrepreneurial projects must necessarily involve uncertainty about their total effects. And there seem to be no grounds for assuming that such effects can be contained (internalized) within the strictly defined entitlements under the responsibility or accountability of the entrepreneurs. Spillover effects, or externalities, will almost necessarily accompany any development or change from the status quo.

To the extent that the entrepreneurs anticipate such effects, and are liable for possible damages under a liability rule, they can proceed without generating net "social damage," measured in some *ex post* sense. They suffer the consequences of their action. If their vision errs on the side of overoptimism, they pay the full costs, save in the case where bankruptcy proceedings allow them to escape.

III. Law and Externalities

The law has necessarily evolved in the dynamic economy of the real world. It is not, therefore, surprising that the law does not precisely mirror the stylized distinctions that would emerge from economic analysis. But the degree to which legal arrangements have operated to further the "dynamic efficiency" of the economy seems worthy of notice. Within broad limits, the common law has tended to treat negative externalities by what is essentially a liability rule rather than a property rule.[14] Interpretations of the law of nuisances seem to have incorporated the recognition that restrictiveness akin to a strict property rule would stifle technological development. Entrepreneurs have not generally been required to purchase "rights to generate spillover damages" prior to the undertaking of new ventures. And especially when the promised gains more than overbalance the spillover damages imposed, courts have been reluctant to go beyond the requirement that damages be paid. The tendency seems to have been to grant injunctive relief only in settings where the damages are large relative to the gain.[15]

The restrictive limit of the liability rule that seems to be operative in law is perhaps more interesting for economists.[16] The protective umbrella of the liability rule has been extended more or less in accordance with the economists' efficiency criterion. Liability for damages tends to be restricted to "physical" damage, broadly defined, and this liability has not been normally extended to cover damages transmitted through market prices for inputs and outputs. In this respect, the legal boundaries for actionable claims seem to follow, to a very rough first approximation, that between "technological" and "pecuniary" ("price" or "exchange") externalities, the distinction which has been the traditional criterion used in theoretical welfare economics for suggesting corrective measures.[17] Although the analytical treatment of the precise differentiation between technological and pecuniary (or price) externalities remains unsatisfactory,[18] the thrust of the orthodox economic argument for generalized policy neglect of the latter is located in the notion that market forces operate to ensure that potential gains exceed potential losses. It should be evident that a comprehensive property rule for the protection of nominal entitlements could not possibly make the distinction between the two types of spillover damages. There will, of course, be pecuniary gains to offset purely pecuniary losses, but those third parties who have prospective opportunities to secure the gains could have no standing in the legal interaction between the directly acting party and the parties threatened with damages. But, even within liability-rule protection, what remains interesting and somewhat surprising to us is the fact that the law, which has evolved in terms of individual rights, should have drawn the liability-for-damages line at roughly the technological-pecuniary limits, obviously independently of any "macro" or "systemwide" consideration of total effects. Pecuniary externalities imposed on an individual or firm via exogenous changes in demand prices or supply prices engender "suffering" and "damage" that are indistinguishable in a personal sense from those damages that do become legitimate bases for claims against perpetrators. What is the origin of the limits of the law in its failure to protect such "rights"? We can, given our dynamic efficiency perspective here, be pleasantly surprised that the law, as it has evolved, has not incorporated even liability-rule protection for pecuniary or market-transmitted externalities. In a legal order that attempted to embody such cumbersome definitions of "rights" eligible for protection, the scope and range for entrepreneurial activity would be exceedingly narrow, and in the presence of such an order, we might have remained in the "dark ages" of economic development.

IV. The Collective Institutionalization of Property Rules

The comparison of alternative legal arrangements in the two preceding sections is not presented as an exhaustive analysis for what seems surely to be a subject worth more extensive explorations, both by economists and by legal scholars. Despite its length here, it is intended only to serve as a lead-in to our discussion of explicitly collective or governmental instruments of internalization.

Let us suppose that some proximate equivalent of a liability rule has historically existed with respect to the hazy areas where spillover damages may occur, where well-defined rights, defendable by something akin to a property rule, cannot have come into being prior to the emergence of the relevant interdependencies. In this situation, persons and groups who think that they may be potentially damaged, either physically or financially, by development projects may seek and succeed to secure the overt collectivization of the internalization process, effectively bypassing the ordinary operations of the law. Political economists have emphasized the significance of shifts between the market and the collective sector, but little attention seems to have been given to the accompanying shift from law to politics as means of resolving conflicts. Basic institutional change of the sort here discussed seems descriptive of the movement toward collectivized regulatory controls in the 1960s and 1970s, controls over many aspects of the environment, whether of the workplace, the quality and range of products, or the more general "atmosphere" for living. Well-defined property rights could never exist in such things as occupational or product safety, quality of air and water, and "silence." An awakened emphasis on observed deterioration in the environment, defined generally, led to the establishment of direct control agencies rather than to the more efficacious extension and application of traditional legal remedies.[19] Essentially the results embody the collectivized analogue to a very strict property rule with the effects on entrepreneurial development prospects that are predicted by our analysis.

Direct control institutions make no clear distinction between technological and pecuniary externalities.[20] By contrast and as noted earlier, the law has always been discriminatory in this respect. Legal protection of "entitlements" has never been extended to include capital values, as such. The franchisee of the local McDonald's could hardly expect the law of nuisance to protect his capital value against the potential loss from the opening nearby of a Burger King. But if the internalization of externalities comes to be institutionalized in an explicitly political manner, there is no distinction to be drawn between sources of potential damages. The private costs consequent on a shift in the "market environment" (a shift in demand price or supply price) are indistinguishable from those costs consequent on a shift in the "physical environment." The motivation for an attempted response by potentially affected individuals or firms is equivalent in the two cases. The firm is threatened with capital loss in either case and it will seek to influence political outcomes.

Consider a familiar setting. Assume initially that there is no zoning ordinance in a municipality. Entrepreneurs may develop parcels of land as they see fit under what amounts to an operative liability rule. Physical damages to properties that may result from the development become the basis for legitimate claims. Assume now, however, that owners of properties in the municipality seek to maintain the capitalized market values of their rights by the enactment of a zoning regulation. They collectively appoint a zoning administrator, whose approval is to be required, *in advance*, before the development of any project that involves any departure from known patterns of activity.

Suppose that, subsequent to this institutional change, an entrepreneur sees prospects for a development that will possibly exert some spillover or external damages on adjacent owners. These potential damages may take two forms: (1) those that affect production functions or the utility functions of persons or firms in the neighborhood, and (2) those that affect the demand prices or the supply prices of outputs or inputs for neighborhood producers and/or consumers but which do not affect production or utility functions directly. As noted earlier, in the absence of politicization, the law of nuisance might be anticipated to operate so as to ensure the payment of claims for the first of these types of damage. Assume that the entrepreneur, the developer, fully reckons on the first sort of spillover damages and considers these to be a part of the cost of his project, as estimated subjectively prior to onset of development itself. He then seeks the approval of the zoning administrator, who, we now assume, acts strictly as agent for the set of potentially damaged parties. In this role, the zoning administrator will make no distinction at all between the two types of anticipated external damage.

The role of the administrator might be expanded somewhat by allowing him to act as agent for all parties other than the entrepreneur-developer—those who are to be potentially damaged and those who are to be potential spillover beneficiaries. If the latter are included, their prospective gains will offset market-transmitted losses in the administrator's decision calculus. He will be sensitive only to the spillover damages that are not offset by spillover benefits. There seems, however, to be a categorical difference between the interests of potentially damaged parties and the interests of potentially benefited parties. The former are threatened with losses in existing capital values, whether these be generated through prices or through nonpecuniary channels. The latter are prospective recipients of now nonexisting increments to capital values; as such these parties seem highly unlikely to exert an influence on political agents that is comparable to that exerted by those who are potentially damaged.

In any plausible setting where the agent does not take the interests of the entrepreneur into account, it seems clear that the results are *even more* inhibitory toward positive development than would be the operation of a strict property rule in the absence of politicization. Under the latter, the developer could, at some price, "purchase" rights to impose the anticipated damages, even if this price would have to reflect the subjective estimates of both pecuniary and nonpecuniary damages to the owners of existing entitlements. Inefficiencies would tend to emerge under the property rule protection because of the inclusion of market-transmitted effects and also because of differences in subjective estimates. In the case where the approval of an administrative official, acting as agent for the potentially damaged parties, is required in advance, however, inefficiencies are even greater. The entrepreneur is not allowed to purchase, *at any price*, "rights" to impose possibly anticipated damages, provided we assume there is no overt corruption or bribery. Regardless of the potential profitability of a project, as envisaged by the entrepreneur, there is no way that a part of this expected profitability can be readily transferred as a "purchase price" for rights to impose external damages to those who may be affected. There is no scope for contractual or bargained "agreement" in the standard sense. Under normal institutional arrangements, the zoning administrator cannot act strictly as a bargaining agent for the potentially damaged parties. He cannot merely act as a conduit between the entrepreneur and his "clients," at least directly. Under these conditions, the zoning administrator will tend to prohibit the development of any project that will impose even minimal anticipated spillover effects, whether nonpecuniary or pecuniary, and even when it is understood by everyone that claims for physical damages may be actionable in the courts.

We may modify this severely restricted result if we assume that the zoning administrator acts as agent "for the whole community," including the entrepreneur, and not simply as agent for other parties. The plausibility of such a genuine "public interest" administrator may be questioned, but it will be useful to examine the logical implications of such a model. If the administrator assigns equal weights to dollars of costs and benefits, by whomever these might be borne or received, he will try to estimate whether a proposed project is or is not beneficial in net terms. He will tend to be somewhat more pessimistic than the entrepreneur who proposes to develop the project, by the simple fact that the latter is the entrepreneur and not the administrator. But the difference may not be large, and the effects on the rate of development in the community, by comparison with a liability rule without zoning may be relatively limited. The direction of effect will, however, remain as before. In effect, the "public interest" agent becomes the institutional equivalent of a modified "property rule," with the assignment of all entitlements other than those of the entrepreneur to himself for purposes of decision. If he estimates that net benefits of a project exceed net costs, this calculus produces results fully analogous to the "purchase" of rights under a property rule, the only difference being the difference in decision-makers and, of course, in the incentive structure. Such a "public interest" calculus will offset the positive expected values for entrepreneurial profits and specialized resource rents against the negative expected values for pecuniary rents on existing entitlements and anticipated physical damages. If the net sign is positive, the project will be approved.

The differentially restrictive effects of political internalization of potential externalities would tend to be eliminated only in the setting where the political agent or administrator acts for the potential entrepreneurs rather than for the potentially damaged parties or for the "public." In such a "capture" setting, where the zoning administrator acts for developers, the advance approval requirement becomes perfunctory, and the liability rule effectively operates.

V. From Single Party to Multi-party Decision-making

The differential restrictiveness of the prior approval requirement may be increased or decreased when the decision-making authority for the collectivity is lodged, not in a single person, but in a committee or board operating under a specified decision rule. Consider a five-person board empowered to act by simple majority voting rules. A coalition of three members of the board must be secured before the approval of any proposed development project is forthcoming.

There are at least two effects that warrant note here. In the consideration of any project, a majority-rule requirement places decisive power in the hands of that board or committee member who is *median* along an "optimism-pessimism" scale. We can presume that the entrepreneur who proposes a new development project will be more optimistic about its prospects than any zoning-board member. But board members may themselves be arrayed in some optimism-pessimism dimension, at least by project.[21] To the extent that the median member acts in the "public interest," as defined above, the majority-rule result will tend to be equivalent to that produced by a strict property rule, with such a median member acting as if he might have been the owner of the entitlements, although without, of course, any direct financial incentive to consider alternatives carefully. The median member of such a board or committee may be more or less optimistic than any single administrator.

In the composition of a board or committee, however, there is surely less plausibility in a "public interest" model for individual behavior than in the single-person model. We should normally expect members of such boards to consider themselves to be representative of particular constituencies, ranging from the entrepreneurs themselves on the one hand to the holders and protectors of existing entitlements on the other. In such settings as those for a board or committee of zoning appeals, a "capture" theory of bureaucracy or regulatory agency would suggest that potential developers or entrepreneurs might have concentrated interests in and be successful in securing effective control. On the other hand, in settings where the potential impact is diversified so as to affect many industries, as with environmental control boards, the bias in representation may well be toward constituencies that seek primarily to inhibit change.

To the extent that more than a simple majority of a board or committee is required for advance or prior approval of projects, whether such an inclusive rule be formal or informal, the shift of decision power toward the relatively pessimistic end of the scale is enhanced. In the limit, if unanimous agreement is stipulated, the power of determining the pace of development rests with the most pessimistic member.

VI. Unanimity, Majority, and Individual Action

Our analysis suggests that any overt politicization of the internalization of externalities tends to reduce, perhaps dramatically, the scope and range for entrepreneurial activity generally, with the growth-inhibiting effects becoming most severe when something akin to a unanimity rule is allowed to operate, either for the whole set of persons in a community, or for the subset of representatives chosen to act on behalf of defined constituencies which, in turn, encompass the whole community. In effect, a unanimity rule allows the status quo values of all existing entitlements to be preserved against any unpredictable possible intrusions from the spillover effects of new and untried ventures, with no distinction between physical (technological) and financial (pecuniary) effects.[22]

Such a characteristic of a unanimity rule has been stressed, in the general setting of political theory, in the critiques developed by Douglas Rae, James Fishkin, and others.[23] Quite apart from the acknowledged costs of attaining unanimous agreement, which may make a unanimity rule "inefficient" in the sense that it would rarely, if ever, be chosen constitutionally,[24] Rae and Fishkin criticize the rule even as an idealized benchmark for political decision-making. They argue that while a unanimity rule may effectively prevent the collectivity from undertaking action that will damage individual interests, from "sins of commission," the rule will also prevent the collectivity from taking action that might prove, in the net, beneficial, due to the recalcitrance of some stubborn pessimists, who will effectively hold decisive power. Note that this argument is *not* equivalent to that based on the possibly prohibitive decision costs (transaction costs) of securing unanimous agreement. Even in the total absence of such costs, the pessimist's preferences tend to be satisfied.

This essay is clearly not the appropriate vehicle for an examination of the Rae-Fishkin argument in the context of normative political theory. We would suggest only that the whole analysis, both normative and positive, of "political externalities" must be categorically separated from the more narrowly circumscribed "economic externalities" which are, of course, always restricted within the confines of a legal order. Our concern here is with the limited set of issues that involve potential "economic" externalities and alternative processes of internalization. As we have already noted, essentially the same argument, even if somewhat less emphatically, can be made against the use of majority-rule decision-making. The dividing line for our analysis is that between overtly political attempts at internalization (whether through an administrative bureaucracy, through boards or committees that act on majority rule, or through effective unanimity rules) and the internalization of emergent externalities that will be predicted to take place through the law of liability. We have suggested that any politicization tends to generate results akin to a severely restrictive property rule.

We should note that these conclusions follow regardless of the control mechanisms that may be used. Economists, generally, tend to support corrective taxes and subsidies as opposed to more direct schemes for controlling externalities, especially in large-number settings. The argument is based on the notion that, with appropriately set rates, private decision-makers can adjust optimally to measures of "true" social costs and benefits. However, the whole argument about alternative control devices presumes that the potential spillover or external costs or benefits of economic activities are fully predictable in advance. There is no recognition of the elementary fact that new ventures will necessarily be unpredictable, both with respect to their internal profitability and to their spillover effects. Any political setting of corrective rates of tax would tend to embody the predictions of the politician-bureaucrat-administrator who would necessarily tend to be relatively more pessimistic than the entrepreneur who alone has the vision and imagination for the new resource combination that a project represents. The same conclusions will, of course, apply to more direct control measures such as the setting of standards or limits. Further, and perhaps more significantly, the whole of the economists' argument must presume that the political decision concerning the distinction between "correctable" and "noncorrectable" spillover effects has been made, or will be made, correctly.

The thrust of our argument suggests that individual entrepreneurial action, rather than political action carried forward by administrative agency, by majority voting, or by unanimity, should be unimpeded except by the *ex post* adjustments that are required in tort law, where those who generate physical damages to others stand liable. When the potentially damaged parties are numerous, cost thresholds may prevent the individualized origination of claims. Recognition of this prospect justifies some institutional arrangements for class-action suits.

Numerous economists seem to have overlooked the elementary fact that many Pareto-relevant externalities are internalized by the operation of the law itself. With respect to negative externalities, our argument becomes what might be called the "legal" supplement to Coase's "economic" one. Although he surely did not neglect the operation of the law itself, Coase has been largely interpreted by economists as suggesting that, given freedom of contract and absent prohibitive transaction costs, the market or exchange process will effectively internalize potential externalities that are Pareto-relevant. We suggest here that for those areas where rights remain ill-defined or where, for any reason, contractual processes break down or do not come into being, if litigation is not prohibitively costly, the law itself provides for *ex post* internalization, at least for negative externalities.

As Staaf and Wares point out, the law of torts does not extend to cover positive externalities or external economies. Here the legal institution for internalization is limited to the law of contract. For our purposes, however, the legal asymmetry is not significant since it is the processes of internalizing negative externalities that assume dominant importance in our "dynamic efficiency" framework. Entrepreneurial activity, the primary source of economic growth and development, seems to be much more likely to be adversely affected by legal and/or political protections against possible external diseconomies than it is to be thwarted by the failure of entrepreneurs to collect payments for the possible spillover benefits that their activities confer on others.

Our argument should not be interpreted as suggesting that "texas-style" entrepreneurs be unloosed and allowed free rein to invade or otherwise intrude upon any and all entitlements, subject only to the enforcement of a liability rule. Entrepreneurial activity is instrumental to economic development or growth, but such growth is, of course, only one among several objectives for viable social order. "Security of person and property" is surely of equal importance, and for whole classes of entitlements, this objective can only be achieved with an enforceable property rule or its equivalent. Our argument suggests only that on the legal-economic interfaces created by technological advance, where new and necessarily uncertain "invasions," "spillovers," or "harmful effects" may take place, liability-rule protection offers a legal climate within which economic growth can proceed, whereas property-rule protection of all claimed entitlements will surely retard such growth. In particular, the opportunity costs of the attempted extension of "rights" under the protection of the politicized equivalent of a property rule should be recognized.

Notes

We are especially indebted to our colleague, Robert Staaf, whose combined law and economics expertise has, we are sure, kept us from some egregious blunders. But he cannot be held responsible for those that may remain.

1. R. H. Coase, "The Problem of Social Cost," *Journal of Law and Economics* 3 (1960).

2. For the basic definition of Pareto-relevant externality, see James M. Buchanan and William Craig Stubblebine, "Externality," *Economica* 29 n.s. (1960): 371.

3. Compare H. E. Frech III, "The Extended Coase Theorem and Long-Run Equilibrium," *Economic Inquiry* 17 (1979): 254. See also James M. Buchanan, "The Coase Theorem and the Theory of the State," *Natural Resources Journal* 13 (1973): 579.

4. "An entitlement is protected by a property rule to the extent that someone who wishes to remove the entitlement from its holder must buy it from

him in a voluntary transaction in which the value of the entitlement is agreed upon by the seller." Guido Calabresi and A. Douglas Melamed, "Property Rules, Liability Rules, and Inalienability: One View of the Cathedral," *Harvard Law Review* 85 (1972): 1089, 1092.

5. "Whenever someone may destroy the initial entitlement if he is willing to pay an objectively determined value for it, an entitlement is protected by a liability rule" (ibid.).

For a similar distinction that does not introduce the terms, property rule or liability rule, see James M. Buchanan, "The Institutional Structure of Externality," *Public Choice* 14 (1973): 69.

6. A. Mitchell Polinsky has comparatively analyzed the property rule, the liability rule, and tax-subsidy schemes. His emphasis is on static efficiency properties, degree of protection for entitlements, and the consequences of information, none of which is central to our analysis here. See his "Controlling Externalities and Protecting Entitlements: Property Right, Liability Rule, and Tax-Subsidy Approaches, *Journal of Legal Studies* 8 (1979): 1; and Polinsky, "On the Choice between Property Rules and Liability Rules," National Bureau of Economic Research Working Paper No. 286, October, 1978.

7. Staaf and Wares emphasize the subjectivity of costs and benefits in externality relationships as a means of distinguishing tort law and contracts as alternative guarantors of efficiency in allocative results. They do not, however, extend their discussion to the dynamic effects that we examine here. See R. Staaf and W. Wares, "Individual Choice, Social Choice, and Common Law Efficiency" (unpublished paper, University of Miami, Florida, December, 1979).

8. In a totally different context, we have demonstrated that differences in subjective estimates of the working properties of alternative institutions can exert predictable effects on joint decisions. See James M. Buchanan and Roger Faith, "Subjective Elements in Rawlsian Contractual Agreement on Distributional Rules," *Economic Inquiry* 18 (1980): 23.

9. As Frech notes, much of the Coase theorem discussion has proceeded on the assumption that the merger option is ruled out by transaction-cost differentials. Polinsky, for example, tends to ignore the merger option.

10. Failure to recognize the mutuality of advantage from merger, under the restrictive assumptions of the Coase theorem analysis, led Greenwood and Ingene to argue that the basic Coasian proposition on resource allocation is incorrect under differing attitudes toward uncertainty. See Peter Greenwood and Charles Ingene, "Uncertain Externalities, Liability Rules, and Resource Allocation," *American Economic Review* 68 (1978): 300.

11. We should also note that, given the property rights assignment assumed in our example (the farmer has full rights in his crops), there is no scope for insurance contracts of the ordinary sort to emerge. Since the farmer's crops are fully protected by the strict property rule, he will never need to pay for insurance against potential damage from straying cattle. Such an insurance contract between the farmer and rancher will emerge only if the farmer, who anticipates more damages than the rancher, is protected by *neither* a property nor a liability rule.

12. This conclusion requires the presumption that the "bundle of allowable activities: to be protected by either alternative is defined in some plausibly efficient manner. If a generalized property rule is applied to a definition or

assignment of rights that is overly restrictive, liability-rule protection might be desired, even in a stationary setting.

13. Our conception of the entrepreneur will be recognized as similar to the views of Schumpeter and Kirzner, which, although differing in detail, can be generically related. See J. A. Schumpeter, "Theory of Economic Development" (*Redvera Opie* trans. 1934); and Israel M. Kirzner, *Competition and Entrepreneurship* (Chicago: University of Chicago Press, 1973).

14. The law of nuisance and of negligence has not, in some situations, been extended to the limits that an economic interpretation of a liability rule, defined in Calabresi-Melamed terms, would require. Persons whose entitlements suffer physical damage, inclusively defined, may not be able to file enforceable claims if the acting party can demonstrate "reasonableness" in any of several dimensions. Courts may "balance hardships" rather than seek to protect nominally defined entitlements. A possible logical basis for some departure from applying a strict liability rule in the law of nuisance may be found in the inherent or "natural" fuzziness or ambiguity of entitlements in precisely those situations where negative externalities (nuisances) seem most likely to arise.

15. See, in particular, the opinion of the majority of the New York Court of Appeals in *Boomer* v. *Atlantic Cement Co.*, 26 N.Y.2d 219 (1970).

16. The liability rule is, of course, subject to abuse through overextension by legal zealots. Artificially contrived and orchestrated extensions of damage claims beyond those traditionally legitimized, along with increasingly costly litigation, might convert a liability rule into an instrument that would match a property rule in its restrictiveness on potential entrepreneurship.

17. The precise relationship between the treatment of externalities in the law and in normative economic analysis has not, to our knowledge, been examined. This seems to be a project of some interest.

18. There is surprisingly little explicit discussion or analysis of this distinction in the economics literature, perhaps due to the inherent difficulties. For what remains one of the best treatments, see Roland N. McKean, *Efficiency in Government through Systems Analysis* (New York: Wiley, 1958).

19. It is interesting to speculate on why the traditional legal remedies were deemed to be failing and, if such judgments were correct, on what adjustments and extension in law might have been required for correction.

20. The relationship between exchange or "price" externalities and political attempts aimed at protecting values of existing entitlements was discussed by Kenneth Goldin, "Price Externalities Influence Public Policy," *Public Choice* 23 (1975): 1. Goldin did not, however, relate his analysis to the legal setting in the absence of political action.

21. If members of a collective decision-making group, a committee or board, can be characterized generally in terms of their relative optimism or pessimism over a whole set of sequence of decisions, predictions may be made about the set of outcomes under simple majority voting, independently of knowledge about particular preferences. Interestingly, this setting offers several analogues to the more familiar voting theory problems that arise when the choice options extend beyond the yes-no alternatives. See Roger L. Faith and James M. Buchanan, "Toward a Theory of Yes-No Voting," chapter 6, this volume.

22. Striking empirical support of our hypothesis is provided by the relative

absence of fenced grazing lands on the Navajo Indian reservation. Although fencing costs are borne by the government, few fences are built because of the requirement that the unanimous consent of all neighboring herders must be secured prior to such action, along with the consent of all others who might be affected. See Gary D. Libecap and Ronald N. Johnson, "Legislating Commons: The Navajo Tribal Council and the Navajo Range," *Economic Inquiry* 18 (1980): 69.

23. See Douglas Rae, "The Limits of Consensual Decision," *American Political Science Review* 69 (1975): 1270; James S. Fishkin, *Tyranny and Legitimacy: A Critique of Political Theories* (Baltimore: Johns Hopkins University Press, 1979), esp. pp. 67–72.

24. Compare James M. Buchanan and Gordon Tullock, *The Calculus of Consent* (Ann Arbor: University of Michigan Press, 1962).

31.

Market Failure and Political Failure

I. Introduction

On several occasions, I have summarized the theoretical welfare economics of the mid-century decades as "theories of market failure" and the public choice economics of the post–middle decades as counterpart "theories of political failure." This statement captures the central thrusts of the two research programs, but, nonetheless, the statement is confusing because it suggests that both positive analyses of institutional operation and criteria for operational failure are comparable over the two applications.

The criterion for success, and hence, failure, applied to the operation of a market order by the practitioners of theoretical welfare economics is widely recognized to be efficiency in the utilization of economic resources. But both the meaning and the normative appropriateness of the efficiency criterion can be questioned. If "efficiency" is attained only through the working of the market process, how can it be set up as an independent criterion with which to evaluate the workings of the process itself? Even if this basic question is somehow finessed, arguments must be advanced in defense of the efficiency norm.

In extension to politics and political process, can something akin to allocative efficiency be invoked at all? Or is a totally different success criterion appropriate here? If so, how is it to be defined? And, once defined, how can the two potential institutional "failures" be assessed on some comparable bases until and unless the evaluative norms are themselves reduced to a common scalar?

The essay is organized as follows. In Section II, I briefly examine some of the basic issues that arise in assessing market or political failure. The heart of the essay is contained in Section III in which an attempt is made to assess the prospects for political correctives for a single particular example of market failure, utilizing the standard efficiency criterion. Section IV is very short, but it introduces a discussion of changes in the basic structure of rules, in the constitution, that seem to be suggested if any prospect for attaining the efficiency gains promised upon diagnosis of either market or political failure is to be realized. Section V is also brief; it introduces the alternative of setting up some distributional ideal to evaluate the performance of market and political structures. The discussion in both Sections IV and V is severely restricted in this essay, since adequate treatment of either of these two areas of inquiry would require full-length treatment quite apart from the main thrust of the argument here.

II. Ideal Points and Feasibility Sets

Even if we remain within the confines of political economy, when we examine either market or political failure (or success) we must confront issues that have been centerpieces of philosophical argument for many centuries. Can an ideal be defined independently from that which can be observed? And if this question is answered affirmatively, can an ideal state that lies admittedly beyond the limits of the set of feasibility attainable states serve as a standard of evaluation for an observed state?

These questions may be examined with specific reference to the identification of market failures stemming from theoretical welfare economics. Consider efficiency in the utilization of an economy's resources—can idealized efficiency be defined in other than conceptually formal terms? We can, of course, state specifically the necessary conditions that must be met in order to satisfy the ideal. Resources are placed in their most highly valued uses when units of each homogeneous resource yield identically valued returns in all uses to which they are put. Values are equalized on all margins of adjustment; marginal rates of substitution in final use are equalized with marginal rates of transformation in production.

But what is homogeneity among units of any resource? Do we define homogeneity by an observed equalization of market prices? If we do, how can any observed differences in prices be employed as a criterion for an absence of allocative efficiency? Until and unless the economist presupposes independent knowledge about preference functions and production functions, he cannot define idealized efficiency. And, if this epistemological limit to analysis is acknowledged, how can any market be judged to fail? Quite apart from this epistemological barrier to the very definition of efficiency, there remains the necessary dependence of the value-maximizing allocation of resources on the premarket distribution of endowments among persons. Acceptance of efficiency as a norm for success or failure carries with it implied normative support for (or at least acquiescence in) the initial ditribution of endowments, or else it requires that corrective steps embody distributional objectives over and beyond those defined by the efficiency norm itself.

For purposes of discussion here, I shall assume, with the theoretical welfare economists, that the required information about preference and production functions may be presupposed, and that the premarket distribution of endowments be accepted as the basis from which value-enhancing changes are to be evaluated. Idealized efficiency can then be defined independently of any observation of market adjustment processes, and it would seem proper that this norm be used as a success indicator. Even within these limits, however, is it appropriate to use this idealized efficiency norm as a means of evaluating that which is observed? If the norm is so employed, market "failure" may be readily identified. Almost all observed market arrangements generate results that fall short of achieving the ideal. The reasons are familiar. Such an assessment of failure does not, however, carry any implication for ultimate institutional or policy change until and unless a pattern of results from an alternative set of arrangements demonstrated to be feasible can be shown to exist. If the attainment of the idealized efficiency norm is shown to require technological-institutional and/or behavioral characteristics that cannot be incorporated within the feasibility set, how much help is provided by resort to the norm as a criterion of success or failure?

III. Political Correctives for Market Failure: The Case of External Diseconomies

The theoretical welfare economists of mid-century did not raise this question because they assumed, implicitly, that the political alternative to the unimpeded operation of the market itself operated ideally. That is to say, it was simply presumed that "failures" in market arrangements could be ideally corrected by politically directed adjustments in the rules guiding market participants.

The prospect that any feasible political corrective for market failure might also fail when compared with the ideal standard of efficiency was not examined. Some positive theory of the workings of observed political process is required before this essential step in a comparative institutional analysis can be taken. The theory of public choice has, in a sense, made such an analysis possible. It remains nonetheless surprising that public choice economists have not concentrated more attention on the identification and analyses of political failures for purposes of making more specific comparisons with familiar market failure propositions.[1]

I propose to introduce a single highly stylized, simplified, and familiar model of market failure. There exists a small, but fully competitive industry that produces a final good, X, which trades at price, p_x, in full equilibrium. No resources are specific to this industry, and there are no rents received by owners of resource inputs, even short-run quasi-rents. Consumers secure some rents from the availability of this product on the market at the competitive price. The production of X, however, generates spillover or causes external damages for many persons. The producing firms do not take these external diseconomies into account in their decisions. Hence, relative to the idealized efficiency norm, there are too many resources devoted to the production of X. In traditional Pigovian language, marginal private costs faced by the firms are less than marginal "social costs."

The question then is: Will politicization of this external diseconomy ensure correction? For purposes of simplicity in exposition, I shall initially assume that the control instrument is a per unit tax or subsidy on the industry's output. The constitution is altered to allow such a tax or subsidy to be imposed by the workings of a political decision rule.

I shall assume that all persons in the economy and polity have full information as to the incidence and effects of the tax, and, also, that all persons vote or otherwise act politically to further their own measured economic interest. In the market failure setting postulated, under these restricted assumptions, politicization of the externality will ensure that the efficiency norm is satisfied only under an extremely narrow set of circumstances. If *all* persons in the polity are damaged by the external diseconomy, and are also *equally* damaged; if *all* persons are also consumer-buyers of the industry's product, and also purchase *equal* quantities; if the revenues from the tax are shared *equally* among *all* persons, and without pass-through loss, then politicization will ensure full correction for the market failure, regardless of the political decision rule. In this setting, it will be in each and every person's interest to impose the idealized Pigovian tax. Market price will rise precisely by the amount of the tax; production will fall; some resources will shift to other uses. Revenues from the tax will be shared equally by all persons. Each person will gain an amount measured by the size of the familiar welfare triangle.[2]

Once we move beyond the world-of-equals restrictions on the model, politicization will *not* operate to correct for the efficiency loss imposed by the nonpoliticized operation of the market. Distributional effects must enter the calculus of individuals, and their interests must include these effects as well as the potential gains and losses in efficiency, as usually measured. And *distributional* effects necessarily introduce potential conflicts of interests among persons. Hence, the predicted results of the operation of any political decision rule will depend both on the rule itself and on the relative sizes of those persons in the sets that secure distributional gains and losses under the imposition of a tax on the industry's product, along with the disposition of revenues.

The political economist might be prompted to inquire into prospects for working out some structure of compensations such that, even in the setting that violates the highly restricted equality assumptions, general agreement might be reached on the idealized solution dictated by the efficiency norm. Suppose that all relevant members of the polity can be classified into three sets: (1) buyers of the industry's product, (2) sufferers of the external damage generated by production, (3) persons totally unaffected by the industry, neither buyers nor sufferers of damage.

We know that, if the external diseconomy is Pareto-relevant, the members of (2) should be able to compensate fully the members of (1) for the losses incurred in the price change consequent on the reduction of industry output.[3] Note, however, that this compensation will require payment over and above the return of all revenues collected under the efficiency-inducing unit tax rate to members of (1). Such a return of revenues will still leave purchasers with net losses measured by the familiar welfare triangle. The restriction to the single control instrument must be dropped if general agreement on the Pareto-superior shift to the idealized efficiency solution is to be attained.

Further, and more important, note that even if political implementation is limited to the "exchange" between members of (2) and (1), and if some payments above and beyond return of tax revenues are arranged, the structure of compensations (return of revenues plus subsidies) must include individualized adjustments among persons in (1) to allow for variations in the quantities of the good purchased and in the elasticities of demand over the relevant range of price change. These purchase-related differentials in transfer payments would be required to ensure that income effects be neutral for all members of (1), quite apart from the arbitrary assumption that there is no substitution effect of the transfer payments, despite the required direct relationship between the sizes of the payments and the individual rates of purchase. If substitution effects are extended to purchase-related transfers, so that all members of (1) fully reckon that any excess outlay generated by the higher price will be returned as a transfer, then the whole attempt to "correct" behavior via the imposition of the unit tax will fail from the outset.

In order to ensure that the levy of the tax modifies behavior, as well as for more general political reasons, the revenues from the tax would likely be returned to persons on some broad-based sharing scheme, even if the transfers could be limited to members of a single class, such as members of (1). But, once any such departure from the idealized scheme is introduced, however, distributional interests of persons are introduced that might be directionally counter to any efficiency-inducing "exchange" through the political process.

Even such partial political intervention as represented by the return of revenues generally to members of (1) would seem, however, to be highly improbable. Persons in (3), those who are totally unaffected by the external diseconomy, would almost necessarily be included in the political choice process, directly or indirectly, and they will have interests that are exclusively distributional. Suppose that the political economist proposes the levy of an efficiency-inducing unit tax on the industry's output, with revenues returned to buyers of the product, with the differentiation as required, along with some supplemental payments to cover the losses measured by the welfare triangles. In other words, assume that the "exchange" between members of (1) and (2) meets all of the requirements for agreement, and that the political implementation of this "exchange" promises to generate the idealized efficiency solution. But persons in (3) may not acquiesce in the observed payment of cash transfers to members of (1). Persons in (3) will insist on sharing in the funds made available from the apparently newly discovered revenue source. To the extent that members of (3) are brought into the revenue-sharing group, members of (1) will oppose the whole scheme, again on strictly distributional grounds. No longer would they be fully income-compensated for the change in price of the good consequent on the change in industry output. And members of (2), those who suffer the external diseconomy, can scarcely be expected to "bribe" all members of (3) sufficiently to ensure the viability of the efficiency-inducing rate of tax. Politically, the efficiency-inducing tax seems a nonstarter.

We can extend the analysis and try to make some very general predictions about politicization of the externality in the example. We retain the three-set classification of persons, and we now introduce the assumption that the political choice process works as if it were a simple majority voting rule. For purposes of simplicity in exposition, assume initially that the three sets are of equal size, and that a person holds membership in only one set. We can array the policy options or alternatives as follows:

(1) T_o —leave competitive result alone; levy zero rate of tax.
(2) T_e —impose efficiency-inducing rate of tax; return all revenues to members of (1), buyers of product, in individualized shares appropriately adjusted.
(3) T_m —impose revenue-maximizing rate of tax; distribute revenues equally among all members of politically dominant coalition.
(4) T_p —impose prohibitive rate of tax.

We can now examine the ordinal ranking of these alternatives by the members of the three sets. There are two possible arrays, depending on the relationship of T_e and T_m. In the first array below, I assume that the efficiency-inducing rate of tax falls below the revenue-maximizing rate of tax; in the second array, this relationship is reversed. The rankings are as follows:

Set (1)	Set (2)	Set (3)
Buyers	Sufferers	Unaffected
	(I: $T_e < T_m$)	
T_o	T_p	T_m
T_e	T_m	T_e
T_m	T_e	T_o, T_p
T_p	T_o	
	(II: $T_e > T_m$)	
T_o	T_p	T_m
T_m	T_e	T_e
T_e	T_m	T_o, T_p
T_p	T_o	

It is evident from examination of these arrays that, under the assumption that the sets are equi-sized, T_m is the stable majority choice. The preferences are single-peaked. There is a two-group majority coalition favoring T_m over either of the other alternatives.

This result is relatively insensitive to changes in the distribution of revenues from the tax that is levied and to the amount of pass-through wastage in the fiscal process. The ranking for members of (3) will remain as indicated if there is any positive net transfer to them. And note that members of this set are the median preference holders; the interests of those persons in sets (1) and (2) are strictly opposed in either of the two rankings. Members of (1), the buyers, will have the ordinal rankings indicated if there is any drainage of revenues from their hands, and, in addition, if they do not secure the required supplementary payments over the simple return of all revenues. Sufferers (2) will always prefer the prohibitive tax, except in those cases where they might, as major sharers in revenues, prefer the revenue-maximizing tax.

The T_m result is also relatively insensitive to changes in the relative sizes of the three groups. So long as neither (1) nor (2) is sufficiently large, on its own, to enforce a majority choice, the members of (3) are in control, even if their size is small. If either (1) or (2) is sufficiently large to impose a majority choice, then T_o or T_p will emerge. Note that in no case will T_e emerge from the operation of the voting rule. The efficiency-inducing rate of tax is dominated by one of the other three alternatives, under any and all variations in the relative sizes of the three sets.

If the efficiency-inducing rate of tax falls below the revenue-maximizing rate (I in the arrays above), then politicization of the externality will generate an allocative result that involves final industry output below that which is Pareto efficient. Whereas the uncorrected market result involves industry overproduction, the politicized result involves underproduction relative to the standard efficiency norm. If the efficiency-inducing rate of tax lies above the revenue-maximizing rate (II in the arrays above), politicization will involve industry output that remains above that which the efficiency criterion would indicate to be ideal but below the output in the uncorrected market. In this case, politicization is at least directionally corrective.

The failure of politicization to correct for the externality seems clear in the single example examined in detail here. But does the divergence between the predicted political solutions and those that might satisfy the efficiency criterion depend on the "institutional structure of externality"?[4] The existence of *any* surplus, whether producers' or consumers', that results from the market generation of an activity that exerts large-number externalities, negative or positive, will ensure that distributional aspects enter directly in any political control process. Participants in the political decision process seek to maximize their own utilities, given the instruments available to them. They may only be secondarily interested in their shares in the efficiency gains that idealized market correction might promise.[5] Models other than the single one analyzed in some detail above might, of course, be introduced to demonstrate the generality of the results.

But the overall conclusion remains the negative one, that politicization of market failures will be highly unlikely to secure the objective of moving the economy toward satisfaction of the idealized efficiency norm so long as the political process itself embodies the expressions of differential interests by citizens.

IV. Can the Potential Efficiency Gains Be Captured?

As the discussion has indicated, there will remain unexploited efficiency gains in the operation of the market and/or the political process. In both cases, we can imagine or dream of idealized allocative changes that could prove advantageous to all parties in the economy or polity. And, as the simple analytics of the Pareto classification show, there must exist means of moving from what is to an optimal solution in such a way that no person is harmed by the change. But the accomplishment of any such change may require a complex and sophisticated structure of highly personalized tax and subsidy schedules, compensations, side payments, and transition rules that are beyond the capacity of either market or political structures as we know them. It may not be institutionally feasible to capture more than some fraction of the efficiency losses that market and political failures seem to impose upon us.

The very existence of such gains should ensure, however, that there will remain a role for the political economist who might be able to advance proposals that will embody mutuality of gain.[6] If he reckons on the predicted operating properties of both ordinary markets and ordinary politics, the political economist will presumably be led to consider reform at the level of basic institutional-constitutional rules, where the distributional aspects can be mitigated if not totally eliminated from consideration. Why should anyone, as a potential participant in political process, be interested in abstract efficiency? As the analysis has suggested, the participant will, in particular cases, place primary emphasis on distributive shares. If, however, general rules are considered, rules that are to be applied to a large number of separate cases of potential political control, the participant does have an interest in an efficient structure. Since he cannot know how, distributionally, he will be affected on any one from the whole set of issues that may emerge for political decision, the individual will be led from consideration of his own interest to promote efficiency in the predicted working properties of the inclusive institutional structure.[7]

If the inclusively defined set of institutional constraints is treated as exogenous, and hence not subject to change, there is a sense in which any observed allocation is efficient. To the extent that participants maximize their utilities, given the constraints within which they act, there remain no efficiency gains to be exploited. Reference to potential efficiency gains must, therefore, imply a belief that some constraints are subject to change.[8]

V. The Efficiency Norm and Distributive Standards

To this point, the discussion has been exclusively contained within an acceptance of the efficiency norm as the basis for evaluating institutional performance. The epistemological claims of the theoretical welfare economists have been presupposed, even though these claims appear to me to be open to serious challenge at a more sophisticated level of philosophical inquiry. For most neoclassical economists trained in the post–welfare economics era, there is nothing unusual or unacceptable in using the efficiency norm for evaluating the performance of the market process. These same economists might, however, question the use of the same norm to evaluate politics. Why should politics be expected to generate efficiency in resource use? As noted, however, unless the same scalar is employed, how can relative "failure" or "success" be judged at all?

Some distributional norm or standard is perhaps the most likely alternative to efficiency. By comparison here, however, there seems to be little or no agreement in a precise definition of a distributive ideal. If such an ideal could be defined, then the operation of the market might be compared with that of political process. Once again, both processes would surely be judged to fail to achieve the norm.

In application to the achievement of any distributive norm, however, care must be taken to define the distributive potential of the two separate institutions. The market operates and, in so doing, it generates a particular distribution of the surplus that emerges from social cooperation in the usage of the premarket resource endowments held under legally defined ownership of separate persons. The market cannot, and does not, act directly on the distribution of the endowments of persons. By contrast and comparison, politics may make little or no distinction between the distribution of the surplus emergent from social cooperation and the distribution of initial endowments among persons. There is no constraint on the operation of ordinary politics that is at all akin to that imposed by the legal structure on the operation of the market. When, therefore, the market is compared unfavorably with politics from the criterion of some distributive ideal, the relatively open-ended potential for political redistribution is seldom noted.

Even when such comparisons are made properly, however, the discussion is often concentrated on the prospects of idealized attainment of the distributive ideal rather than on any realistic analysis of the distributional changes that might be implemented in the workings of democratic politics. As is the case with efficiency, persons are not likely to express interests in abstract distributional ideals for the society in general when they participate in political decisions. They are likely, instead, to seek to further their own well-defined interests. Whether or not political process will, indeed, be able to "improve" on market-determined distributive results remains an open issue that social scientists have been surprisingly reluctant to analyze seriously.[9] Until and unless politics, as it works, and not as it might ideally be imagined to work, can be demonstrated to generate better distributive results than the market, "better" in terms of some reasonably acceptable standard, advisors should be reluctant to encourage distributional politics.

This essay does not deliver the assessment of analytical developments in the context of the experience of the quarter century, the assessment that was assigned to me as a topic. The analysis has been aimed at raising more questions than it attempts to answer, and the paper's message is perhaps best interpreted as a sketch for a research program that seems hardly to have been commenced. By inference, the argument might be taken as a criticism of the naiveté of both the market-failure welfare economists and the market-works–politics-fails stance of many modern public choice and new neoclassical economists. By comparison with idealized standards, both markets and politics fail. Recognition of this simple point is a mark of "scientific" progress. Such recognition directs attention to comparative institutional analysis and to the structure of the set of constraints within which either market or political behavior takes place. The domain of "constitutional economics" beckons; let us get on with it.

Notes

I am indebted to my colleagues Robert Tollison, Gordon Tullock, and, especially, Viktor Vanberg for helpful comments on an earlier draft.

1. I raised the issue in an early paper, but there my primary concern was with the presence of externalities in the political decision process generally and not with attempted political correctives for specific market failures. See my "Politics, Policy, and the Pigovian Margins," *Economica* 29 (February, 1962): 17–28.

In a second early paper, Gordon Tullock and I analyzed comparative market and political failure under reciprocal external economies. The analysis was, however, largely concentrated on a world-of-equals model, and we did not examine the politics of distribution that accompany attempts to correct for market failures. See James M. Buchanan and Gordon Tullock, "Public and Private Interaction under Reciprocal Externality," in *The Public Economy of Urban Communities*, ed. Julius Margolis (Washington, D.C.: Resources for the Future, 1965), pp. 52–73.

2. The result depends on the presumption that the unit tax will modify behavior in purchasing the good, but that the return of tax revenues in the form of transfers will *not* influence behavior, despite the direct relationship between the size of an individual's transfer payment and rate of purchase. In other words, only the tax exerts a substitution effect.

3. Through our simplifying assumption about the absence of producers' rents, the incidence of the tax falls exclusively on buyers.

4. In an early paper entitled, "The Institutional Structure of Externality," I examined several models in terms of the sources for market failure in each case. I did not, however, follow up and examine the same models for possible implications under political control. See, "The Institutional Structure of Externality," *Public Choice* 14 (Spring, 1973): 69–82, and published as chapter 28, this volume.

5. For a general recognition of this point, see Marilyn Flowers and Patricia Danzon, "Separation of the Redistributive and Allocative Functions of Government: A Public Choice Perspective," *Journal of Public Economics* 24 (August, 1984): 373–80.

6. In a very early paper, I defined the role for the political economist to be that of seeking out possible proposals for change that would command consent. See my "Positive Economics, Welfare Economics, and Political Economy," *Journal of Law and Economics* 2 (October, 1959): 124–38.

7. The logical foundations of this bridge between efficiency and individual self-interest were presented in James M. Buchanan and Gordon Tullock, *The Calculus of Consent* (Ann Arbor: University of Michigan Press, 1962).

8. For further discussion, see my "Rights, Efficiency, and Exchange: The Irrelevance of Transaction Costs," in *Ansprüche, Eigentums- und Verfügungsrechte* (Berlin: Duncker und Humblot, 1984), pp. 9–24. Reprinted in my *Liberty, Market, and State: Political Economy in the 1980s* (Brighton, England: Wheatsheaf Books, 1985; New York: New York University Press, 1985), pp. 92–107.

9. For a preliminary attempt to analyze transfer or redistributive political process in positive terms, see chapter 8 in Geoffrey Brennan and James Buchanan, *The Reason of Rules* (Cambridge: Cambridge University Press, 1985). Further work on this topic is in the planning stages. For a related argument that concludes that the market process may be the only distributional system that avoids conflict, see Dan Usher, *The Economic Prerequisites to Democracy* (Oxford: Basil Blackwell, 1981).

Index